IMPROVING ORGANIZATIONAL PERFORMANCE

The Cube One Framework

Richard E. Kopelman

Routledge
Taylor & Francis Group

NEW YORK AND LONDON

First published 2020
by Routledge
52 Vanderbilt Avenue, New York, NY 10017

and by Routledge
2 Park Square, Milton Park, Abingdon, Oxon OX14 4RN

Routledge is an imprint of the Taylor & Francis Group, an informa business

Library of Congress Cataloging-in-Publication Data
Names: Kopelman, Richard E., author.
Title: Improving organizational performance: the cube one framework /
Richard E. Kopelman.
Description: 1 Edition. | New York: Routledge, 2020. | Includes
bibliographical references and index.
Identifiers: LCCN 2019042344 (print) | LCCN 2019042345 (ebook) |
ISBN 9781138951747 (hardback) | ISBN 9781138951754 (paperback) |
ISBN 9781315668048 (ebook)
Subjects: LCSH: Organizational effectiveness. | Organizational behavior. |
Management.
Classification: LCC HD58.9 .K67 2020 (print) | LCC HD58.9 (ebook) |
DDC 658.4/09–dc23
LC record available at https://lccn.loc.gov/2019042344
LC ebook record available at https://lccn.loc.gov/2019042345

ISBN: 978-1-138-95174-7 (hbk)
ISBN: 978-1-138-95175-4 (pbk)
ISBN: 978-1-315-66804-8 (ebk)

Typeset in Bembo
by Deanta Global Publishing Services, Chennai, India

IMPROVING ORGANIZATIONAL PERFORMANCE

This book presents the Cube One framework, which provides a basis for understanding, diagnosing, and improving organizational performance. It is based on the premise that successful organizations enact practices that satisfy three key constituents: the enterprise itself, customers, and employees. This book offers a uniquely empirical approach by examining enterprise-, customer-, and employee-directed practices. Validity evidence is provided by survey research, studies of financial metrics, and the analysis of cases involving well-known organizations (such as Google, Four Seasons, and Mayo Clinic). The Cube One framework is equally applicable to organizations in the for-profit, nonprofit, and government sectors. After reading this book, students and scholars, as well as organizational practitioners in the fields of organizational behavior and management, will find a practical approach to improving organizational performance.

Richard E. Kopelman is Professor of Management at the Zicklin School of Business, Baruch College, USA. His research focuses on improving work motivation, productivity, and organizational performance. He has published in several key journals, including the *Academy of Management Journal*, *Decision Sciences*, *Organizational Behavior and Human Performance*, and the *Journal of Applied Psychology*.

CONTENTS

PREFACE

The backstory on this book begins in the 1970s. As a young professor, my research and writing primarily focused on work motivation and reward systems. I began branching out to examine the effects of other human resource practices on productivity, including employee selection and goal setting. Around 1980, U.S. companies were losing market share to Japanese competitors, in several industries—and productivity became a national concern. This prompted several books on Japanese-style management; and management consultants Thomas Peters and Robert Waterman set out to find some examples of highly successful companies in their classic 1982 book, *In Search of Excellence*.

In 1980, a friend of mine who reported to the CEO of a Fortune 30 company described a fascinating opportunity. Within weeks I was commissioned to prepare a report on productivity-enhancing practices: specifically, which techniques worked and which did not. From time to time my friend advised me that the CEO was getting impatient to see my report. In 1983, I announced that I was ready to submit my 245-page report on the effectiveness of different productivity-enhancing techniques. The CEO, unfortunately, was no longer interested in productivity.

So, I expanded my report, and in 1986 McGraw-Hill published it as a textbook, *Managing Productivity in Organizations*. I had authored several articles on productivity and was honored to serve on the editorial review board of the *National Productivity Review*. During the ensuing decade I undertook a number of projects, mostly related to measurement. Over the years I have collaborated in developing the first measure of work/family conflict; updated the venerable *Study of Values*; developed the Job Search Behavior Index; and developed and validated a measure of McGregor's Theory X and Theory Y cosmologies.

Twelve years after the publication of my text on productivity, I authored an article published in the *National Productivity Review* entitled "Managing for Productivity: One-Third of the Job." It had slowly occurred to me that in addition to managing for productivity, successful organizations, logically, also had to satisfy customers and employees. So, I went back to the drawing board.

In 2004, I presented data at an American Psychological Association meeting pertinent to the validity of a three-dimensional model of the determinants of organizational performance. The three dimensions consisted of enterprise-, customer-, and employee-directed practices. By 2010, the three-dimensional model morphed into the Cube One framework described herein. For the past decade my colleagues and I have conducted research that has taken the form of case analyses, survey research studies, and research on the stock market capitalizations of publicly traded companies.

I much appreciate—and owe great debt to—the dedication, competence, and creativity of my coauthors who contributed importantly to the Cube One research endeavor. In chronological order, David Prottas, Liz Letzler, Andy Chiou, Louis Lipani, Zhu Zhu, Phoebe Massimino, and Meg Joseph collaborated with me in writing research papers and articles. Data from Singapore and Brazil were obtained by Prabu Naidu and Alcides Campos Neto, respectively. Louis Monier provided firsthand insights about management at AltaVista.

As the research started to cohere, I decided to present the collective results in the form of a book. Toward this end, a number of faculty colleagues contributed by providing comments on early drafts of chapters and offering helpful suggestions. I appreciate the constructive comments and suggestions of Stephan Dilchert, Allen Kraut, and Jeff Greenhaus, who toiled through early versions of chapters. Will Millhiser, Adita Jain, Emre Veral, Ajay Das, Peter Pepper, Naomi Gardberg, Donald Vredenburgh, Ely Weitz, and Anna Marie Valerio also provided helpful assistance. I am particularly grateful for the extensive statistical guidance provided by my Baruch colleague, Ann Brandwein. Louise Klusek, from the Baruch College Library, was exceptionally helpful in tracking down articles, and with the myriad details necessary for accurate citations.

I also appreciate the professional editorial contributions of Joseph Dobrian, who strove mightily to rid my writing of infelicities of expression. With his guidance I have started to reduce the occurrence of split infinitives; and I now occasionally adopt the active voice.

At Routledge I have been fortunate to have had the enthusiastic support of two teams of action editors. I first benefited from the work of Sharon Golam and Alston Slatton. My present Routledge action editorial team is Meredith Norwich and Mary Del Plato.

I have been fortunate over the years to have the assistance of several dedicated research assistants. In chronological order, they are Priya (Priyadharshini) Janarthanan, Angela Salerno, Michelle (Binghui) Wang, Shu Yang, Georgia Dina Konstantopoulos, Rita (Hongzhu) Niu, Miti Sheth, and most recently, and extensively, Marina Nepomuceno. I also appreciate the analytic research assistance provided by Afzaal Mohammed, Nadia Zahingir, William Yip, David Falk, and Zeljko "Zel" Sockovic.

The assistance of Jay Fialkov, Fred Haber, Van Morrill, and Victoria Mraz eased the daunting process of obtaining permissions. For their help I am most grateful.

Notwithstanding the help of many people, I alone take responsibility for any inaccuracies—although I'd like to cast all blame elsewhere. That would be Management 101 according to the Dilbert column—but not a viable option, alas.

PART I

1

THE CUBE ONE FRAMEWORK

That management matters has been well documented in academic and practitioner literature. For example, Rumelt found that organization-level differences have at least six times the effect on profitability as industry has,[1] and Hansen and Wernerfelt found that management practices had twice the effect on profit than economic factors such as competition or firm size had.[2] More anecdotally, Professor Kim Clark offered the following observation when he was interviewed by *Business Week* upon his elevation to Dean of the Harvard Business School.

As an economics professor he would study companies in a given industry (such as cement) and he had an "unlikely epiphany" when he found that time and again a few companies were consistently far more profitable than their competitors, despite having similar capital structures and technology. Clark stated, "It was one of those life-changing events that nothing that I had studied in economics prepared me for." His conclusion: it had to be better management.[3]

If management matters, what, specifically, do successful companies do? What are the key determinants of organizational performance, and what exactly should managers do to bring it about? Tsoukas and Chia noted, in their *Organization Science* article, "organizations do not simply work; *they are made to work*" (emphasis in original).[4] How, specifically, do successful managers get their organizations to work? What are the key determinants of organizational performance? What should managers do to achieve success?

Cummings and colleagues have cautioned that,

> organizational theories can serve as a definitive blueprint for action only if they are elegant enough to have been adequately tested, are supported by the cumulative weight of research evidence, and are powerful enough to

account for much of the variance in organizational behavior. These criteria are not met by current organizational theories.[5]

The Cube One framework responds to this challenge. The framework is capable of empirical evaluation. It has been tested and supported via three types of analyses: survey research, case studies, and longitudinal research on management ratings and relative market capitalizations. It has achieved a high level of explained variance. It is applicable to organizations in all three sectors (for-profit, nonprofit, and government) and it is useful for diagnostic and intervention purposes. So, what is the Cube One framework about?

Multiple Stakeholders

Successful organizations are need-satisfying places. Successful organizations must, according to the Cube One framework, simultaneously satisfy the goals of three primary stakeholders: *customers* who provide revenues; *employees* who produce products and provide services; and *providers of funding* (such as shareholders and lenders in the private sector; donors, grantors, taxpayers in governmental and nonprofit sectors) who seek returns on their investments/outlays. Customer-, employee-, and enterprise-directed practices form the three dimensions of the Cube One framework.

By enacting and monitoring the three sets of practices, organizations can *move* within the Cube One framework, thereby improving their performance. Chapters 2 to 4 provide examples of the efficacy of each set of practices. Chapter 5 describes five survey research studies, and Chapter 6 examines the performance of companies using market capitalization data. Chapters 7 to 10 provide in-depth cases that examine practices across time and/or between companies. The last two chapters indicate how data pertinent to enacted practices can be used for diagnostic and implementation purposes. In light of diagnostic data, changes in practices can be enacted that will lead organizations to achieve higher levels of organizational performance.

The three sets of practices correspond to a multiple stakeholder perspective approach, which is, of course, not new. But to date multiple stakeholder research and writing has typically been simply theoretical.[6] More recently, case studies of successful companies have been used as vehicles to support the multiple stakeholder perspective.[7]

For instance, Mackey and Sisoda have argued for the existence of five inner circle (major) stakeholders whose interests need to be recognized and addressed, plus six outer circle stakeholders that indirectly affect the organization through their impact on the inner circle stakeholders. The evidence supporting this framework rests primarily on an in-depth analysis of the case of Whole Foods Market. Their approach, which they call "conscious capitalism," has been generally well received, but the evidentiary basis for this framework is weak at best.[8] To date, there have been no systematic studies that directly measure the concepts invoked (including the degree to which various stakeholders are satisfied), and thereby explain the relative performance of companies within industries.[9]

Another influential multiple stakeholder perspective, the service–profit-chain, has been advanced by Heskett and colleagues. They suggest that employee satisfaction drives customer satisfaction which, in turn, impacts profitability. Their evidence consists of in-depth case studies which describe practices at some successful companies that are consistent with the posited model.[10]

Finally, it might be noted that the popular Balanced Scorecard technique represents a partial multiple stakeholder approach. One of the four strategic dimensions relates to customers, and the other three relate to enterprise-directed matters: financial results, internal processes, and learning and growth. Notwithstanding the publication of numerous books and articles, the authors have only cited case studies of successes. The analysis is also custom-made for each client organization.[11] When examined empirically in the academic literature, mixed results have been reported.[12]

Multiple Disciplines

Although some authors have advanced a multiple stakeholder perspective of management, most books on organizational performance have been guided by the particular field of study or discipline of the investigator(s). Abundant evidence speaks to the effectiveness of specific techniques, such as lean six sigma and supply chain management, in improving productivity and providing a superior return to providers of resources. These works are within the province of operations management.[13] Writers and researchers in marketing and quality management have demonstrated the utility of customer-centric practices, and customer surveys, especially those asking the "ultimate question" as pertinent to heightened brand loyalty.[14] Likewise, scholars in human resource management, organizational behavior, and organizational psychology have examined techniques to raise employee work motivation; to make work more engaging and workplaces "stickier" so as to reduce voluntary turnover.[15]

Therefore, research and writing pertinent to the goals of the three key sets of stakeholders (providers of funding, customers, and employees) relate to differing fields of inquiry and academic disciplines. However, research and writing on organizational performance has typically been conducted through the lens of a single discipline; the researcher's academic field of study and expertise.

In contrast, the Cube One framework is multidisciplinary, examining practices pertinent to various fields of study including operations management, industrial engineering, service quality management, marketing, organizational behavior, industrial and organizational psychology, human resource management, and financial management. The first premise (or axiom) associated with the Cube One framework is that a full explanation of organization performance requires a multidisciplinary perspective.

Policies versus Practices

The second premise undergirding the Cube One framework is that what really matters are the practices actually enacted—not espoused values, vision statements, or even written policies and procedures. To be sure, corporate strategies, cultures, and climates provide a framework for the practices enacted, but it is the practices *per se* that are crucial.[16] To reiterate the comment of Tsoukas and Chia, "Organizations do not simply work; they are *made to* work." Hence, it is the practices enacted by organizations that *make them work*.[17]

To illustrate the difference between policies and actual enacted practices, consider the following two examples:

1. High-level executives commonly claim that their organizations have adopted "family friendly" work-life practices. However, these policies often are unavailable, or only available with penalties. Illustrative of this is the departmental supervisor who announced, "My employees can have flextime so long as they're here from 9 to 5."[18]
2. A large department store chain (a Fortune 100 company)—famous for its pay-for-performance philosophy—provided store managers with detailed performance appraisal instruments, merit pay guidelines, and pay increase grids. But, examination of actual pay-performance practices in nearly 400 stores indicated that in only one-third of the stores was there a sizable positive association between pay and the rated performance of department managers. In about 40% of the stores there was a weak positive association, and in one-quarter of the stores the association was actually negative, meaning that higher-rated managers received *lower* pay increases. Had all stores been as profitable as those in the first group—the one-third with a sizable association between pay and rated performance—the company would have earned $30 million annually in additional profits, the equivalent of $105 million in 2015 dollars.[19]

The Cube One Framework

The Cube One framework focuses on three sets of practices: those that are enterprise-, employee-, and customer-directed. These practices are locatable in three-dimensional space, so that an organization can be scored as High, Middle, or Low on each dimension. Organizations that enact high levels of customer-, employee-, and enterprise-directed practices (High, High, High) are classified in Cube One; organizations that are low with regard to enacting these three sets of practices (Low, Low, Low) are classified in Cube 27. Figure 1.1 provides a schematic representation of the Cube One framework.

To provide a preview as to the validity of this three-dimensional taxonomy, the rated performance of organizations in Cube One has been found to be 14 standard errors (or 14 Sigma) higher than the performance of organizations in

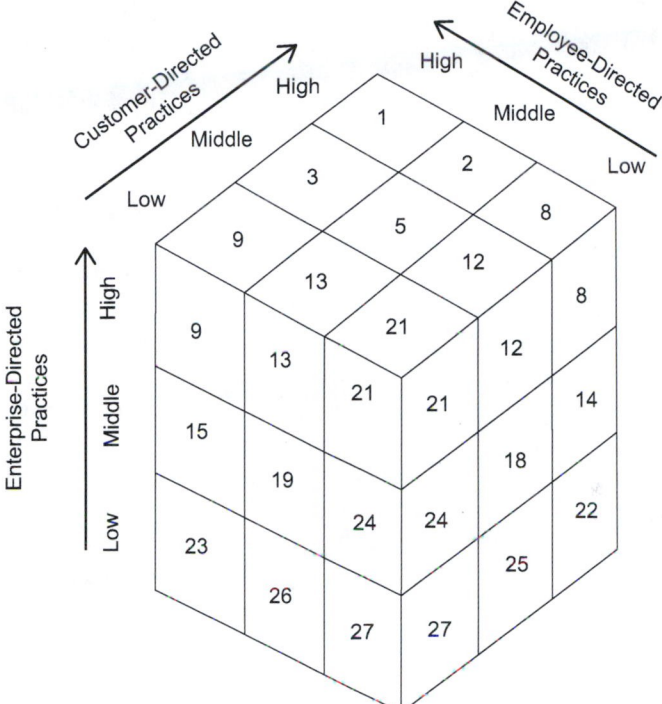

FIGURE 1.1 Schematic Representation of the Cube One Framework

Cube 27. To put the magnitude of this difference into a more familiar context, the famous Six Sigma threshold applied to quality management, corresponds to 3.4 occurrences per million observations (a probability of 0.000034). Therefore, a difference of 14 Sigma in organizational performance means that a whole lot of extra zeros need to be added to the probability that the difference in organizational performance can be attributed purely to chance.

Enterprise-directed practices include techniques that raise productivity via increased employee motivation (such as through goal setting and incentives) and that raise employee ability (via training and systematic selection). A much fuller description of enterprise-directed practices is provided in Chapter 2.

Chapter 3 describes several employee-directed practices, including: reducing hierarchical status differences; providing enhanced employment security; and practices that reduce work-family conflicts.

Chapter 4 focuses on customer-directed practices, such as: the use of surveys to assess customer satisfaction and loyalty; a continuing focus on improving product/service quality; and the use of customer preference data to enhance the customer experience—bringing delight, not just satisfaction.

Having described the conceptualization of a three-dimensional taxonomy of organizational practices, it remains to be explained more fully why organizations in Cube One should be the most successful and, why "getting to Cube One" is of importance. Each set (or dimension) of practices leads to a particular intermediate outcome that might be viewed as a capability. Organizations that enact high levels of customer-directed practices achieve the capability of attracting, satisfying, and retaining a relatively high proportion of customers. Enactment of a high level of employee-directed practices enables an organization to attract and retain valued employees. And enacting a high level of enterprise-directed practices tends to attract and retain funding. Capabilities can be viewed as assets of an organization and can be increased or depleted over time.[20] Capabilities mediate (or intervene) between the three sets of enacted practices and organizational performance. The causal mechanisms tying enacted practices to organizational performance are depicted schematically in Figure 1.2.

Note the interdependencies posited between the capabilities. This corresponds to the widespread recognition, for example, that employee satisfaction/loyalty leads to customer satisfaction/loyalty, and vice versa. The Service–Profit-Chain model explicitly recognizes the linkage between employee satisfaction and customer satisfaction.[21] Especially in a service setting, employees cannot reasonably be expected to treat customers better than they themselves (employees) feel they

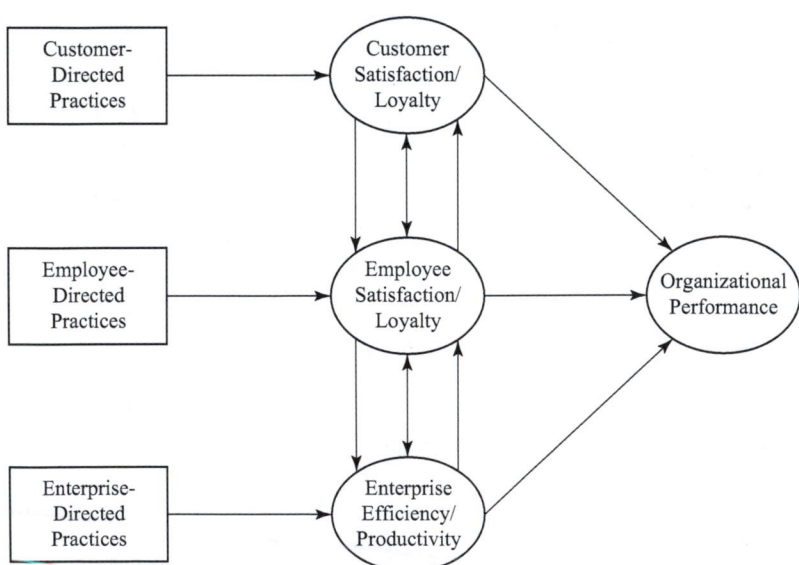

FIGURE 1.2 Schematic of the Causal Newtwork

are being treated. Rosenbluth and Peters have emphasized this point in their book, *The Customer Comes Second*, as has Nayar in *Employees First, Customers, Second*.[22] Rigorous research studies pertinent to the validity of this claim have been conducted, and the results have consistently supported it.[23]

The Importance of Data

The Cube One framework provides the conceptual basis for a more holistic and comprehensive examination of the primary determinants of organizational performance than has frequently been articulated. However, little or no systematic empirical research exists pertinent to many theories of organizational performance. The criticality of empirical research as a basis for evidentiary support constitutes the third assumption underlying the Cube One framework.

Measurement is central to the Cube One framework. Data are needed to measure the extent to which an organization enacts the three sets of practices; to classify companies within the 27-cube taxonomy; to measure capabilities; to make diagnostic interpretations; to assess organizational performance and changes in performance; and, thereby, to evaluate the effects of actions taken.

Consider the comments of Sir William Petty, in 1676, on the importance of empiricism and measurement to advances in human affairs:

> Instead of using only comparative and superlative words, and intellectual arguments ... I have long aimed ... to express myself in terms of number, weight, or measure [and] to use only arguments of sense, and to consider only such causes as have visible foundations in nature; leaving those that depend upon ... opinions ... and passions ... to the consideration of others.[24]

About 200 years later, Lord Kelvin (née Sir William Thompson) made a similar assertion in 1876:

> When you can measure something about which you are speaking and express it in numbers, you know something about it; but when you cannot express it in numbers, your knowledge is of a meagre and unsatisfactory kind; it may be the beginning of knowledge, but you have scarcely in your thoughts, advanced to the stage of science, whatever the matter may be.[25]

So instead of saying "this object seems really quite warm," Kelvin developed a measurement metric, the Kelvin scale, (which can be converted to Celsius by a simple subtraction). So, per the Cube One framework, it is hoped that organizations will start to measure the frequency with which enterprise-, employee-, and customer-directed practices are enacted.

Yet a high degree of skepticism is in order regarding the rapidity with which organizations will commence implementing the measurement of practices. As Benjamin Franklin wrote (in 1786):

> You will observe with concern how long a useful truth may be known and exist, before it is generally received and practiced on.[26]

Illustrative of this phenomenon is the discovery of the consistently reliable Spacing Effect by Herman Ebbinghaus in 1885.[27] He found that the spaced presentation of information produces 25 to 50% greater retention compared to the immediate or batched repetition of information. Yet this phenomenon remains largely ignored to this day in higher education.[28]

Measurements are necessary to:

- assess the extent to which practices are enacted;
- ascertain levels of intermediate criteria, such as capabilities, as well as levels of organizational performance;
- provide diagnostic information;
- serve as a gauge of success in improvement efforts;
- provide validity evidence which supports the basic theory.

In this regard (and pertinent to Cummings' comments regarding the limited utility of theories of organizational performance), the Cube One framework can be compared to 11 theories advanced in successful books on organizational performance in terms of the above-mentioned criteria. Table 1.1 provides a summary of these characteristics for the 11 focal theories (and associated management books) and for *The Cube One Framework*. Additional information pertinent to the theoretical underpinning of each book/theory is provided—whether it is primarily based on logical deductions or derived from inductively observed patterns.

Whether a theory is primarily based on logical deductions or inductive observations is important for a simple reason. If a theory is developed based on empirically observed patterns, there is no way for it to be disproved with the same data used for its development. The theory has already been made to "fit the facts."[40] Hence, inductively based theories must subsequently be replicated (and validated) with independent data. New inductions may emerge, and this constitutes the cycle of science.

An important issue is how organizational performance is assessed. In several works listed in Table 1.1, performance was assessed in a binary fashion. Some organizations were classified in the Visionary or Great category based on reputation or growth in stock market capitalization; others were placed in the Comparison or Good group, again based on reputation or growth in stock market valuation. This two-fold classification is hardly applicable to most companies that want to assess their own organizational performance.

TABLE 1.1 Prominent Books/Theories on Organizational Performance

Book	Theory	Research Design: Inductive/ Deductive	Organizational Performance Measurement: Continuous vs. Binary	Independent Variables— Systematic Measurement?	Validity Evidence	Utility for Diagnosis
BTL[29]	Core ideologies enacted	Inductive	Binary classification: VCs versus CCs	Case examples/no systematic measurement	Stock market valuations	Unclear
ISOE[30]	7S Framework + 8 Practices	Inductive	Prior financial performance: binary no comparisons	Case examples/no systematic measurement	Stock market valuations	Unclear
TUA[31]	K*I*P*R	Primarily inductive	Unclear	Case examples/no systematic measurement	Unclear	Possibly feasible
5th D[32]	5 disciplines	Inductive	Not provided	Some disguised case examples	Unclear	Unclear
VM[33]	New mgt. practices and 4 competing values	Inductive and deductive	Binary classification: VCs versus OGs	Lots of company examples	Unclear	Possibly feasible
RTC[34]	Recommended implementing steps	Inductive	Unclear	Unclear	Vivid case studies with data	Unclear
GTG[35]	8 ideas	Inductive	Binary classification: great vs good	Case examples/no systematic measurement	Stock market valuations	Unclear
MFM[36]	3 pyramids: employee, customer, and investor	Primarily deductive	Unclear	Case examples/no systematic measurement	Case studies	Unclear

(Continued)

TABLE 1.1 Continued

Book	Theory	Research Design: Inductive/ Deductive	Organizational Performance Measurement: Continuous vs. Binary	Independent Variables— Systematic Measurement?	Validity Evidence	Utility for Diagnosis
TOQ[37]	7 variables: including employee satisfaction, customer satisfaction, and profits	Deductive	Organizations selected based on extensive literature review	Case examples (potential systematic measures listed in Appendix B	Case studies	Could be excellent—but no data are reported
GBC[38]	5 ideas (e.g., 20-mile marches; firing bullets not cannonballs)	Inductive	Binary classification: great vs. good	Case examples	Stock market valuations	Unclear
TPWY[39]	Have goals plan, follow-through	Primarily deductive	Unclear	Lots of vignettes	Vignettes	Unclear
TCOF	3 sets of practices	Primarily deductive and inductive	Employee ratings, USN and WR ratings, and market valuations	Systematic surveys; most admired company rankings; and case studies	Ratings of performance; relative market valuations; other metrics such as USN and WR ratings	Practices and capabilities scores versus norms; also within-company changes over time

Notes: BTL = *Built to Last*; ISOE = *In Search of Excellence*; TUA = *The Ultimate Advantage*; 5th D = *The Fifth Discipline*; VM = *Vanguard Management*; RTC = *Reengineering the Corporation*; GTG = *Good to Great*; MFM = *Peak: How Great Companies Get Their Mojo from Maslow*; TOQ = *The Ownership Quotient*; GBC = *Great by Choice*; TPWY = *Taking People With You*; TCOF = *The Cube One Framework*.

Another important issue is the way in which the key managerial (or causal) variables—the factors that determine organizational performance—are measured. Without specific guidance as to how to measure the purportedly key practices, it would be difficult for a user to ascertain if the recommended practices are being applied at high or low levels, and if enacted levels have increased or decreased over time. Absent this measurement, it is unclear how the reader can apply the theory in practice. Most of the books in Table 1.1 describe the recommended practices in terms of case studies but provide no systematic measurement tools. *The Ownership Quotient* (TOQ) provides (in appendix B) a 50-item questionnaire that could be used to systematically assess the recommended practices. However, the authors of TOQ did not use the instrument in their own published work. Similarly, in their earlier book, *The Service Profit Chain*, they provided a 44-item instrument that evidently was not used in the book's research.[41]

In addition to measuring the factors that should drive organizational performance, and the level of organizational performance, itself, it is important to consider the validity evidence upon which a theory rests. If the focal companies are selected based on reputation or stock market valuations, finding increased disparities over time in market capitalizations (e.g., between Visionary and Comparison companies or Great and Good ones), is suggestive, but not definitive evidence that observed patterns of practices are causal. Furthermore, stock market valuations, although an attractive, objective metric, are not an applicable performance criterion for the vast majority of U.S. companies (which are small, privately owned enterprises); and market capitalizations are irrelevant to organizations in two of the three sectors; nonprofit organizations and government agencies. The Cube One framework is demonstrably pertinent to organizations in all sectors.

An amusing example of a truly irrelevant approach to validation was provided years ago in the 1991 movie *City Slickers*. Ira and Barry (who portray characters based on Ben and Jerry of the famous ice cream company) are part of a wilderness expedition. Ira announces to the group that Barry "can pick out the exact right flavor of ice cream to follow any meal. Go ahead, challenge him."

Barry menacingly glares and says, "Come on push me!" So, Mitch (played by Billy Crystal) describes a meal: sea bass, sautéed, with potatoes au gratin, and asparagus. Barry furrows his brow, squints, and with sweat appearing on his forehead ultimately responds, "Rum raisin ... phew." At which point Mitch asks, "How do you know he's right?" Ira states:"Fourteen hundred retail outlets across the country, that's how we know" (followed by Ira and Barry doing a high five "Whoof").[42]

Sources of Data

A fourth premise (or axiom) upon which the Cube One framework rests is that accurate information regarding the enactment of enterprise-, employee- ,and customer-directed practices should come not only from interviews with top managers (or their recollections as published in books), or even from company handbooks/manuals—what might be called the "formal organization." Information should also come from the "informal organization"; employees and customers who know first-hand the practices actually enacted, as distinct from espoused. Top managers might know what is supposed to take place in their organization but they do not always know what is really going on.

The formal organization refers to intended areas of responsibility, reporting relationships, operational methods, and procedures (per job descriptions, organization charts, etc.). The informal organization describes the way things really happen.[43] Along these lines, some theorists distinguish between espoused theories (which may provide satisfaction by their mere contemplation or verbalization) but may differ from the theories in use: policies and practices that managers actually implement.[44]

Whenever possible, it's best to ascertain the views of employees with regard to enactment of specific practices. As shown in the causal model in Figure 1.2, employee views are central to measuring the capability of employee satisfaction and loyalty. Such information can be obtained from questionnaire surveys, and also from various Internet sites that aggregate such perspectives (e.g., Glassdoor.com.) Employee input is also relevant to assessing the enactment of enterprise-directed practices, and to a lesser degree toward assessing enterprise capability. Intended customer-directed practices should be identified by management, and ideally be measured by customers. Customer data can be obtained from traditional sources such as the American Consumer Satisfaction Index (ACSI), along with the Foresee Experience Index (FXI), the Centers for Medicare and Medicaid Services (CMS) surveys (for hospital data) and several Internet sites, such as TripAdviser.com, and Reseller.com. With regard to customer surveys, Reichheld and colleagues have demonstrated the impressive utility of the "Ultimate Question"—how likely is a customer to recommend the company to a friend or colleague—when it comes to profitability.[45]

No Silver Bullets

No comprehensive list of best practices or techniques exists, that will provide a perpetually enduring measurement as to how organizations should best address the interests of the enterprise, employees, and customers. New techniques emerge continually. In the 1970s the rage was T-groups (group-based, human relations training). In the 1980s techniques like quality circles, skip-level reviews, and 360-degree performance assessments gained currency. In the 1990s, lean manufacturing and supply chain management, along with Six Sigma quality metrics, were the *techniques du jour*. Since 2000, companies have used "big data" (see Chapter 4) to map generic profiles of customer preferences, along with sophisticated Internet experimentation. Advocates of new techniques can sometimes create enough excitement that new management and/or marketing fads emerge, each purporting to be the new "silver bullet."[46,47]

Thus, the fifth assumption that undergirds the Cube One framework is that practices are somewhat substitutable, or as the phenomenon is called in academic circles, there is "equifinality" with respect to practices.

Chapter 5 delineates 30 practices that were used in connection with a large survey research project. For diagnostic purposes, mean scores and measures of variability for each of the 30 items are provided in Tables 11.1, 11.2, and 11.3—along with normative data for organizational performance in Table 11.4. However, these scales are not perfect (or timeless) measures of the three sets of practices that comprise the Cube One framework.

Practices Are Not Inherently Antithetical

Some organizational theories begin with the premise that the interests of stakeholders represent a zero-sum game. Thus, it is assumed that organizations must make inescapable trade-offs. O'Toole, in *Vanguard Management*, for example, sees a continuum between efficiency on one end of the horizontal spectrum and employee quality of work life at the opposite end.[48] Quinn, in his competing values framework, described in *Beyond Rational Management*, posits that managers must choose between achieving increased productivity through change or through maintaining stability.[49] A recent meta-analysis (a study of studies that quantitatively summarizes research results) concluded that Quinn's purportedly opposite quadrants "are not competing or paradoxical. Instead they coexist and work together …[and] Instead 'competing values' may be more complementary than contradictory."[50]

Therefore, a sixth assumption of the Cube One framework is that the interests of the key stakeholders are not inherently antithetical. This assumption parallels the perspective advanced by Collins and Porras in *Built to Last*, which emphasizes the need to avoid the "tyranny of the OR." They dispute the necessity of choosing between change OR stability; low cost OR high quality, etc. In their view, visionary companies are able to embrace the "genius of the AND" so instead of choosing between A OR B they figure out ways to achieve A AND B.[51]

Per the Cube One framework, practices designed to satisfy one key stakeholder need not be detrimental to the interests of the other key stakeholders. This view is not just a matter of faith. It has been consistently supported empirically. In this regard, the Cube One framework is similar to popular multidimensional models of organizational performance such as the Triple Bottom Line—for which research has shown that social responsibility, environmental performance, and economic success go hand in hand.[52]

In the current book, survey research (described in detail in Chapter 5) provides data from two large U.S. samples and from three other countries that support the premise that enterprise-, customer-, and employee-directed practices are sizably associated with organizational performance. The survey data also show a high level of consistency between the extent to which an organization enacts each of the three sets of practices. We conclude that well-run organizations are concerned about all three stakeholders and implement high levels of associated practices.

Whereas survey research studies focus on a relatively small (parsimonious) set of variables, case studies can "flesh out" detailed practices and identify the positive spill-over effects (positive interdependencies) that arise when some practices are enacted.

The seventh axiom or assumption associated with the Cube One framework is that practices can be classified in terms of which stakeholder is the primary intended beneficiary. But the effects of practices are not always entirely unidirectional. Take the case of Continental Airlines (described in Chapter 8), which was indisputably the worst major airline in the U.S. before the arrival of CEO Gordon Bethune in 1994. As Bethune put it in *From Worst to First* "We weren't just the worst big airline. *We lapped the field.*"[53]

To improve customer satisfaction, Continental decided to focus on improving on-time arrivals (a source of anger and frustration among passengers). In January 1995, the company decided to provide a modest ($65) bonus payment to all employees if Continental made it to the top four in on-time arrivals in a given month. Within a month (by February 1995) on-time arrivals improved from tenth out of ten to fourth best in the industry, and averaged second-best for the entire year. Not surprisingly, employee satisfaction also improved (from not having to deal with furious passengers and getting a check in the mail); and the amount paid to employees was less than half what Continental had been spending to reimburse customers for missed connections and layovers. This directly benefited the company.

Consider the case of Nordstrom (described in detail in Chapter 9.) Nordstrom rewards outstanding customer service with a generous commission plan that far exceeds salespeople's salary if specific targets are met. So, salespeople do not just show the pair of shoes desired by the customer. They bring out six other pairs of shoes with varying styles and colors—and will show photos of additional shoes available in other branches. Customers appreciate the extraordinary service; salespeople earn nearly twice the hourly wage paid in other department stores; and the company is exceptionally profitable.

The arrows in Figure 1.2 schematically show interactions between the effects of practices on capabilities. Positive interactions explain the tendency to find positive correlations across companies between aggregate scores on enterprise-, customer-, and employee-directed practices, and associated capabilities. Yet, it is recognized that at times some practices can have antithetical effects on other capabilities.

In general, productivity can be improved by achieving increased outputs using the same resources, or by maintaining the same level of outputs using fewer resources. In a healthcare setting, decreasing resources—an approach that might be characterized as "cost savings productivity"—may lead to increased patient wait times, and be accompanied by reduced patient satisfaction and increased employee stress. However, increased outputs resulting from process improvements—what might be labeled "client-focused productivity"—has the potential to enhance both efficiency and patient satisfaction.

Examples of increased efficiency accompanied by high patient satisfaction and high profit margins are dramatic at Mayo Clinic, where the comprehensive new appointment scheduling system enables patients to move through tests and consultations efficiently. "First, patients benefit from the seamless service that is created. Second, the institution benefits because the productivity of physicians, labs, and procedural areas is optimized as well."[54] (We present the Mayo Clinic case and examine multisource data in Chapter 10.)

Organization of the Book

Part I of this book focuses on the conceptual basis of the Cube One framework, which incorporates the following assumptions (axioms). The Cube One framework:

(1) Employs a multiple stakeholder perspective which necessitates incorporating a multidisciplinary approach;
(2) Emphasizes enacted practices, rather than espoused policies;
(3) Examines empirical evidence from multiple types of studies, recognizing that measurement is crucial for diagnostic, implementation, and validation purposes;
(4) Assumes that data should be provided from multiple sources, especially with regard to enterprise- and employee- directed practices and resulting capabilities;
(5) Adopts the notion of substitutability (i.e., there is no single set of "silver bullets" that will universally and eternally be the best practices to employ);
(6) Does not assume that the interests of the three key stakeholders are inherently antithetical;
(7) Believes that practices can be classified in terms of the primary intended stakeholder (or beneficiary).

Chapters 2–4 present the rationales for the interests of each of the three key stakeholders and provide examples of practices that have been demonstrably effective in promoting their interests along with organizational performance. We recommend that organizations develop surveys pertinent to each set of practices. Chapters 2–4 suggest practices that might be identified, enacted, and tracked.

Part II focuses on research that has systematically examined the validity of the Cube One framework. Chapter 5 describes the findings of five surveys: two large U.S. samples as well as data from Singapore, Brazil, and South Korea. Evidence shows a systematic association between the 27 cubes and levels of organizational performance.

Chapter 6 looks at data pertinent to *Fortune* magazine's list of America's Most Admired Companies. Information on enterprise-, employee-, and customer-directed practices comes from about 1,000 knowledgeable raters. We use these ratings, per the Cube One framework, to predict performance relative to other companies in the same industry. On an industry-by-industry basis, we examine the ratings of practices in connection with relative market capitalization. By examining longitudinal data over two- and four-year intervals, we can make inferences about causality. Do good management/marketing practices lead to higher market capitalization or does market capitalization (and profitability) lead to good management/marketing practices? As is evident from the schematic in Exhibit 2, the fundamental premise of the Cube One framework is that the former relationship is more accurate—that is, practices lead to organizational performance, more so than vice versa.

Part III focuses on four in-depth case studies. Chapter 7 looks at practices at Google and AltaVista, two companies that pioneered in the Internet search engine space. Although AltaVista initially achieved a moderate degree of success and earned a following of avid adopters, Google made all the right moves per the Cube One framework.

Chapter 8 describes the astounding turnaround at Continental Airlines. Based on the changes implemented by Gordon Bethune, Continental Airlines literally went *From Worst to First*. The top management team made virtually all the right moves, per the Cube One framework. But they did not invoke a generalizable conceptual framework. Rather they formulated a "Go Forward" plan which consisted of such idiosyncratic components as "Fly to Win." Thus, it would be difficult to generalize Continental's success to companies that, for example, make pillows, or import jade jewelry. The Cube One Framework, in contrast, is more universally applicable across organizations and industries.

Chapter 9 looks at three exceptionally successful customer-centric companies: Zappos.com, Four Seasons, and Nordstrom. We examine primary data on employee and customer satisfaction along with financial results. All three customer-centric companies enacted many practices that were employee- and enterprise-directed; customer centricity was but one-third of the job.

Chapter 10 focuses on hospital performance, with a particular emphasis on Mayo Clinic and resolution of the question "Is Mayo Clinic's reputation deserved?" We examine data on the three sets of practices that comprise the Cube One framework, each obtained from a separate, independent source. Employee satisfaction data come from a popular Internet website (Glasdoor.com); patient satisfaction data from the annual survey conducted by the Centers for Medicare and Medicaid Services (CMS); hospital efficiency data from another public database. Per the Cube One framework, we examined data pertinent to the three key stakeholders in concert with a modified (more comprehensive and more objective) version of the hospital performance ratings provided by *US News & World Report*. An exceptionally high level of hospital performance is accounted for (or explained) by the data. Regarding the Mayo Clinic's reputation, we conclude that its high rating is justified and Mayo's success is "fleshed out" with case materials including some inspiring and poignant vignettes.[55]

Part IV consists of two chapters. Chapter 11, entitled, "Toward an Organizational Diagnosis," examines ten approaches to organizational diagnosis. We compare nine prominent diagnostic models to the Cube One framework in terms of multiple criteria, such as whether the levels of practices enacted are systematically measured, and whether there exist established norms. It is concluded that the Cube One framework is the only diagnostic approach that provides a means to systematically measure pertinent practices, to track changes in practices, and to target areas for improvement and intervention.[56] In a different context it has been suggested that almost every major innovation has been preceded by an advance in measurement. This emphasis is part of what the Cube One framework seeks to contribute.[57]

Chapter 12, "Toward Organizational Action," offers an approach to implementing change that incorporates the Cube One framework as the basis for improving organizational performance. We review several approaches toward implementing changes, including the Normative Model of Planned Change originally developed by Dalton,[58] Lewin's insights as reflected in the Psychological Force Field,[59] and the powerfully energizing approach advocated by Kotter in his *A Sense of Urgency*.[60] We also discuss the counterintuitive protocol associated with Appreciative Inquiry.[61] That is, people feel more receptive to change when it is framed in terms of recapturing prior excellence, instead of trying to identify the causes of present problems (and by implication, the culprits).

Beyond the necessity of organizational buy-in, the mechanics of implementation require formulating an action plan likely to successfully improve organizational performance. The universe of potential practices is, of course, quite large.[62] However, the 30 practices listed in Chapters 2–4 are a good place to start. The development of a sound approach to organizational improvement does not mean employees will be receptive to the proposed change. Some may try to sabotage a change effort, possibly using subtle methods that lead to organizational oblivion. Chapter 12 contains ten possible objections that may be used to short-circuit a change effort—and recommends responses to these objections.

This book concludes with a call for action. Ultimately, the use of the Cube One framework rests on the measurement of practices and performance. The tracking of practices and performance may entail some degree of apprehension. But a bold approach will set organizations on the path to Cube One, thereby making them more need-satisfying places for all key stakeholders: customers, employees, and investors.

Notes

1 Rumelt, R. (1991). "How much does industry matter?" *Strategic Management Journal*, 12(3), 167–185.
2 Hansen, G. S., and Wernerfelt, B. (1989). "Determinants of firm performance: The relative importance of economic and organizational factors." *Strategic Management Journal*, 10, 399–411.
3 Byrne, J. A. (May 19, 1996). "Harvard b-school's professor fixit." *Businessweek*, p. 90.
4 Tsoukas, H., and Chia, R. (2002). "On organizational becoming: Rethinking organizational change." *Organization Science*, 13(5), 567–582. The quote comes from page 577, italics in original.
5 Cummings, T. G., Mohrman, S. A., Mohrman, A. M., and Ledford, G. E., Jr. (1985). "Organization design for the future: A collaborative research approach." In E. E. Lawler III, A. M. Mohrman, S. A. Mohrman, and G. E. Ledford Jr., eds. *Doing research that is useful for theory and practice*, San Francisco: Jossey-Bass Publishers. Quotation reproduced with permission of Wiley. Copyright © 1985 by Jossey-Bass Inc. Publishers.
6 Freeman, R. E. (1984). *Strategic management: A stakeholder approach*. Boston: Pitman. This book is the seminal work on the multiple stakeholder perspective. Subsequently, a largely theoretical sequel was written by Freeman, R. E., Harrison, J. S., and Wicks, A. C. (2007). *Managing for stakeholders: Survival, reputation and success*. New Haven: Yale University Press.
7 Siroda, R. S., Wolfe, S. B., and Sheth, J. N. (2007). *Firms of endearment*. Upper Saddle River: Wharton School Publishing provides examples of world-class companies (such as Trader Joe's, Whole Foods, and Southwest Airlines) that reflect management principles involving the perspectives of customers, employees, and investors.
8 Mackey, J., and Sisoda, R. (2013). *Conscious capitalism*. Boston: Harvard Business Review Press. There has been qualified enthusiasm regarding conscious capitalism in academic circles, see O'Toole, J., and Vogel, D. (2011). "Two and a half cheers for Conscious Capitalism." *California Management Review*, 51(3), 60–76. The authors attribute the missing half cheer to two primary concerns about conscious capitalism: Is it sustainable in the face of global competitive pressures which may result in outsourcing manufacturing to organizations in developing countries, possibly leading to employee layoffs? Is the approach generalizable to the vast majority of businesses? "The fact is, most American businesses are small, marginally profitable operations." (p. 71) and "lack sufficient funds to behave generously to their employees and other stakeholders even if they would like to" (p. 73).
9 Pertinent to the lack of systematic research using standardized measures, C. Wong questions the validity and generalizability of conscious capitalism research, given that it is based on a selective, small sample of "role-model" firms. See Wong, C. (2013). "On the scientific status of the conscious capitalism theory." *California Management Review*, 55(3), 97–106.
10 Heskett, J. L, Sasser, W. E., Jr., and Schlesinger, L. A. (1997). *The service profit chain*. New York: The Free Press. Heskett, J. L., Sasser, W. E., and Wheeler, J. (2008). *The ownership quotient*. Boston: Harvard Business Press. Practices, based on secondary sources, are examined at 12 companies and are invoked to support the service–profit chain. The linkage research of Wiley and Campbell examined primary source data on customer-related and management practices (but for only a single organization): Wiley, J. W., and Campbell, B. H. (2006). "Using linkage research to drive high performance: A case study in organization development." In A. I. Kraut ed., *Getting action from organizational surveys: New concepts, technologies, and applications*. San Francisco: Jossey-Bass.
11 Kaplan, R. S., and Norton, D. P. (1996). *The balanced scorecard*. Boston: Harvard Business School Press. More recently, Kaplan, R. S., and Norton, D. P. (2006) have authored *Alignment*. Boston: Harvard Business School Press. An important observation regarding the Balanced Scorecard methodology is that each implementation is custom-made for

the focal organization. It is also complex, entailing a ten-step, 16-week implementation program, with the four dimensions weighted differently according to the user. Kaplan and Norton (1996) describe differing structural configurations—for examples see *Skandia* (p. 212), and *Echo Engineering* (p. 255).

12 Regarding the efficacy of the Balanced Scorecard methodology, a survey of users found that fewer than 20% realized measurable performance improvements—see Williams, K. (2004), "What constitutes a successful balanced scorecard?" *Strategic Review*, 86(5), 19–20. In an even harsher commentary, one author stated that the perception that the Balanced Scorecard, in and of itself, will lead to organizational alignment is a "fairy tale."—see Buytendjik, F.A. (2007). "Challenging conventional wisdom related to defining business metrics: A behavioral approach." *Measuring Business Excellence*, 11(1), 20–26. However, positive results were found in a small sample of Australian companies studied by Iselin, E., and Sands, J. (2008). "The effects of the balanced scorecard on performance: The impact of the alignment of the strategic goals and performance reporting." *Journal of General Management*, 33(4), 71–85. Another observation regarding the Balanced Scorecard methodology is that each implementation is custom made for each for the specific organization and strategy to be implemented. Not only is it complex, entailing a ten-step, 16-week implementation program, the four dimensions relate to each other differently according to the user. Kaplan and Norton (1996) describe differing structural configurations—for examples see *Skandia* (p. 212), and *Echo Engineering* (p. 255).

13 Among the most influential books written from an operations management perspective are: Liker, J. K (2004). *The Toyota way*. New York: McGraw-Hill; Pande, P. S., Neuman, R. P., and Cavanagh, R. R. (2000). *The six sigma way: How GE, Motorola, and other top companies are honing their performance*. New York: McGraw-Hill; George, M. L. (2003). *Lean six sigma for service*. New York: McGraw-Hill; and the handy and comprehensive book by George, M. L., Rowlands, D., Price, M., and Maxey, J. (2005). *The lean six sigma pocket handbook: A quick reference guide to nearly 100 tools for improving process quality, speed and complexity*. New York: McGraw-Hill.

14 Two classic texts are Zeithaml, V.A., Parasuraman, A., and Berry, L. L. (1990). *Delivering quality service*. New York: The Free Press; and Schneider, B. and Bowen, D. E. (1995). *Winning the service game*. Boston: Harvard Business School Press. More recent customer-focused offerings include Keiningham, T., and Vavra, T. (2001). *The customer delight principle: Exceeding customers' expectations for bottom-line success*. New York: McGraw-Hill; Roman, E. (2011). *Voice-of-the-customer marketing: A revolutionary five-step process to create customers who care, spend, and stay*. New York: McGraw-Hill; and the third book by Reichheld, F. (2011). *The ultimate question 2.0: How net promoter companies thrive in a customer-driven world*. Boston: Harvard Business Review Press.

15 Among the classic books based on organizational behavior are Lawler, E. E. III. (1992). *The ultimate advantage: Creating the high-involvement organization*. San Francisco: Jossey-Bass; and also Pfeffer, J. (1998). *The human equation: Building profits by putting people first*. Boston: Harvard Business School Press. Less academically grounded but fascinating human resource-related books include Conley, C. (2007) *Peak: How great companies get their mojo from Maslow*. San Francisco: Jossey-Bass; Novak, D. (2012). *Taking people with you: The only way to make BIG things happen*. New York: Portfolio/Penguin; and Baker, W. E., and O'Malley, M. O. (2008). *Leading with kindness: How good people consistently get superior results*. New York: AMACOM.

16 Pertinent to the importance of enacted practices is the following comment by Collins and Porras in *Built to Last*, (placed within a small rectangle for emphasis) "the single most important point to take away from this book is the crucial importance of creating tangible mechanisms" (p. 89). And on p. 135 they write that "The visionary companies translate their ideologies into *tangible* mechanisms aligned to send a consistent set of reinforcing signals" (emphasis in original).

17 Tsoukas, H. and Chia, R. (2002). "On organizational becoming: Rethinking organizational change." *Organization Science*, 13(5), 577, italics in original.

18 Hamilton, W. (1989). "Helping out with the kids." *D & B Reports*, 37(2), 19. Illustrative of the career-jeopardizing nature of some work-family initiatives is the work by Thompson, C. A. (2008). "Barriers to the implementation and usage of work-family policies." In S. A. Y. Poelmans, and P. Caligini, eds. *Harmonizing work, family, and personal life: From policy to practice*. New York: Cambridge University Press. (pp. 209–234).

19 Kopelman, R. E., Rovenpor, J. L., and Cayer, M. (1991). "Merit pay and organizational performance: Is there an effect on the bottom line?" *National Productivity Review*, 10, 299–307.

20 Letzler, E. A., and Kopelman, R. E. (2006). "Organizations: An integrated model." *Proceedings*, 60th Annual Meeting of the Academy of Management. Also, Letzler, E. A., and Kopelman, R. E. (2008). "An integrated model of organization performance." *Advances in Management*, 1(4), 7–15. It should be noted that the causal input-output model in Figure 1.2 was originally developed by Elizabeth Letzler, including conceptualization of the capability construct.

21 Heskett, J. L, Sasser, W. E., and Schlesinger, L. A. (1997). *The service profit chain*. New York: The Free Press. Heskett et al., op. cit.

22 Rosenbluth, H. F., and Peters, D. M. (2002). *The customer comes second*. New York: HarperCollins. Nayar, V. (2010). *Employees first, customers second*. Boston: Harvard Business Press. The same idea is expressed by Sharp, I. (2009). *Four seasons: The story of a business philosophy*. Toronto: Viking Canada.

23 Susskind, A. M., Kacmar, K. M., and Borchgrevink, C. P. (2003). "'Customer service providers' attitudes relating to customer and customer satisfaction in the customer-server exchange." *Journal of Applied Psychology*, 88, 179–187. Also pertinent are the articles by Bowen, D., Gilliland, S. W., and Folger, R. (1999) "How being fair with employees spills over to customers." *Organizational Dynamics*, 27(3), 7–23; also, Sutton, D. H. (2006). "Do the best companies to work for provide better customer service?" *Managerial and Decision Economics*, 27, 667–683; and in addition, Liao, H., and Chuang, A. (2007). "Transforming service employees and climate: A multilevel, multisource examination of transformational leadership in building long-term service relationships." *Journal of applied Psychology*, 92, 1006–1019. Evidence that customer satisfaction and employee engagement were related to financial success was published by Schneider, B., Macey, W. A., Barbera, K. M., and Martin N. (2009). "Driving customer satisfaction and financial success through employee engagement." *People & Strategy*, 32(2), 22–27. There is also evidence that customer-employee interactions are a two-edged sword, so to speak. See Walker, D. D. van Jaarsveld, D. D., and Skarlicki, D. P. (2013). "Exploring the effects of individual customer incivility encounters in employee incivility: The moderating roles of entity (in)civility and negative affectivity." *Journal of Applied Psychology*, 99, 151–161.

24 Sir William Petty, Political Arithmetick. These words were written in 1676 and published posthumously in 1690. The e-text was prepared by Rod Hay and posted at the Archive for the History of Economic Thought, McMaster University, Canada, April 1, 1998. Retrieved at http://www.marxists.org/reference/subject/economics/petty/

25 Lecture on "Electrical Units of Measurement" (May 3, 1883), published in Popular Lectures I, p. 73, as quoted in *The Life of Lord Kelvin* (1910) by Silvanus Phillips. Retrieved at http://en.wikiquote.org/wiki/William_Thomson

26 This quote concluded a letter written on July 31, 1786, on the hazards associated with drinking water from corroded lead pipes, a matter long known to be dangerous. See http://franklinpapers.org/franklin

27 Ebbinghaus, H. (1885). *Über das Gedchtnis. Untersuchungen zur experimentellen Psychologie*. Leipzig: Duncker & Humblot; the English edition is Ebbinghaus, H. (1913). *Memory. A contribution to experimental psychology*. New York: Teachers College, Columbia University (Reprinted Bristol: Thoemmes Press, 1999). Christopher Green, York University, Toronto, Ontario provided this information: http://psychclassics.yorku.ca/Ebbinghaus/wozniak.htm

28 In one study, participants using spaced (or distributed) practice outperformed participants using massed (or batched) practice more than 90% of the time. See Cepeda, N. J., Pashler, H., Vul, E., Wixted, J., and Rohrer, D. (2006). "Distributed practice in verbal recall tasks: A review and quantitative synthesis." *Psychological Bulletin*, 132, 354–380. Although there are numerous explanations as to why the spacing effect is so infrequently employed, and also why it usually works, perhaps the most compelling explanation for the latter is boredom. See Dempster, F. N. (1988). "The spacing effect: A case study in the failure to apply the results of psychological research." *American Psychologist*, 43, 627–734. After you tell someone something, and then you repeat the point for emphasis, perhaps in a slightly different manner, the listener thinks: "Boring! You just told me this." And then the "listener" tunes out; hence the information is neither reinforced nor better remembered. That the Spacing Effect is largely ignored in higher education is evidenced by the all too common observation of a faculty member saying "Last week we covered A and B. This week we're going to cover C and D." Most students have little remembrance of A or B and may be unprepared to learn C and D if they build on A and B.

29 Collins, J. C., and Porras, J. I. (1994). *Built to last: Successful habits of visionary companies.* New York: HarperBusiness/HarperCollins.

30 Peters, T. J., and Waterman, Robert H., Jr. (1982). *In search of excellence: Lessons from America's best-run companies.* New York: Harper & Row.

31 Lawler, E. E III. (1992). *The ultimate advantage: Creating the high-involvement organization.* San Francisco: Jossey-Bass.

32 Senge, P. M. (1990). *The fifth discipline: The art & practice of the learning organization.* New York: Doubleday.

33 O'Toole, J. (1985). *Vanguard management: Redesigning the corporate future.* Garden City: Doubleday.

34 Hammer, M., Champy, J. (1993). *Reengineering the corporation: A manifesto for business revolution.* New York: HarperCollins.

35 Collins, J. (2001). *Good to great: Why some companies make the leap … and others don't.* New York: HarperCollins.

36 Conley, C. (2007). *Peak: How great companies get their mojo from Maslow.* San Francisco: Jossey-Bass.

37 Heskett, J. L., Sasser W. E., and Wheeler, J. (2008). *The ownership quotient: Putting the service profit chain to work for unbeatable competitive advantage.* Boston: Harvard Business Press.

38 Collins, J., and Hansen, M. T. (2011). *Great by choice: Uncertainty, chaos, and luck—why some companies thrive despite them all.* New York: HarperBusiness/HarperCollins.

39 Novak, D. (2012). *Taking people with you: The only way to make BIG things happen.* New York: Portfolio/Penguin.

40 Statisticians refer to the phenomenon of fitting the theory to existing data as leaving no data (or degrees of freedom) to test the theory, all the existing variance having been "used up." Michael Shermer speaks directly to this issue in his article "How the survivor bias distorts reality," (August 19, 2014) in *Scientific American*. Regarding the 2001 book *Good to Great* (which sold 3,000,000 copies), Shermer cites the comments of economist Gary Smith: "Collins culled 11 companies out of 1,435 whose stock beat the market average over a 40-year time span" and then searched for shared characteristics that might have accounted for their success. Smith states that, "It is not fair or meaningful to predict which companies will do well after looking at which companies did well! Those are not predictions, just history." In fact, Smith notes, from 2001 through 2012 the stock of six of Collins's 11 "great" companies did worse than the overall stock market, meaning that this system of post hoc analysis is fundamentally flawed. Retrieved at https://www.researchgate.net/literature.PublicationsWithoutF ulltextOverview.html?cp=re125_x_p2&ch=reg&loginT=UjSdLnQR9fqD5inaXP CGOHGelq5FJW9UaSF0j8rQ9jZ9yw80Vrpmhw%2A%2A&pli=1

41   The provision of instrumentation in *The Ownership Quotient* and *The Service Profit Chain* can at least facilitate a future test of the basic model. A book that included the instrumentation used to develop and test the model advanced was authored years ago by Rensis Likert (1967). *The human organization: Its management and value.* New York: McGraw-Hill. Likert's book is relatively unique in that it both presented a theory (Systems 1 to 4) and provided a way to use it for diagnostic and implementation purposes.

42   Here is the link to *City Slickers* http://www.youtube.com/watch?v=4pbVxyL-O eM&sns=em

43   The distinction between the formal and informal organization has been central to organizational behavior for the past 75 years. As Roethlisberger, F. J., and Dickson, W. J. (1929/1939), noted in *Management and the worker.* Cambridge: Harvard University Press: "The formal organization includes all the explicitly stated systems of control introduced by the company" (p. 558), and the informal organization exists at all levels of the organization as a necessary condition for collaboration (p. 562). Similarly, as Nobel Laureate Herbert Simon (1945/1957) noted in *Administrative behavior.* New York: The Free Press. "The term 'informal organization' refers to interpersonal relations in the organization that affect decisions within it but either are omitted from the formal scheme or are not consistent with that scheme." p. 148.

44   Argyris, C., and Schon, D., A. (1974). *Theory in practice: Increasing professional effectiveness.* New York: Wiley & Sons. Somewhat analogously, Douglas McGregor (1960) in *The human side of enterprise.* New York: McGraw-Hill, posited that some managers hold a Theory X orientation (seeing workers as lazy, untrustworthy, and lacking in capacity to contribute meaningful ideas). According to McGregor other managers hold a Theory Y orientation, seeing employees as naturally energetic, responsible, and capable of contributing to the organization. Because of the attractiveness of the Theory Y worldview, in practice the vast majority of managers see themselves as much closer to Theory Y than Theory X in their assumptions. Yet, examination of actual work *behaviors* (as distinct from *assumptions*) mitigates the social desirability bias, and the bias of inaccurate positive self-assessments. See Kopelman, R. E., Prottas, D. J., and Falk, D. W. (2010). "Construct validation of a Theory X/Y behavior scale." *Leadership & Organization Development Journal*, 31, 120–135.

45   See Reichheld, F. F. *The loyalty effect: The hidden force behind growth, profits, and lasting value.* Boston: Harvard Business School Press; also, Reichheld, F. F. *The ultimate question.* Boston: Harvard Business School Press. In his most recent book, Reichheld, F. (2011). *The ultimate questions 2.0: How NET PROMOTER companies thrive in a customer-driven world.* Boston: Harvard Business Review Press, Reichheld shows how the Newt Promoter Score 2, and 3 [Evidently, the Net Promoter Score (based on whether customers are promoters, passives, or detractors) is an even more powerful metric than the ultimate question when it comes to profitability.]

46   The continuing succession of fads has been documented numerous times over the past 50 years. In his speech as outgoing president of the American Psychological Association Marvin Dunnette delivered his classic indictment. See Dunnette, M. D. "Fashions, fads and folderol in psychology." (1966). *American Psychologist*, 21, 343–352. Thirty years later a similar caution was issued to the field of management. Abrahamson, E. (1966). "Management fashion." *Academy of Management Review*, 21, 254–285. Likewise, Hymowitz, C. (May 15, 2006) has cautioned that "Executives must stop jumping from fad to fad and learn to manage," *Wall Street Journal*, p. B1.

47   Notwithstanding these cautionary commentaries, many lists of best practices can serve as benchmarking tools and as potential resources for managers regarding management techniques. In chronological order consider the following: Ernst and Young and the American Quality Foundation's (1992), *Best practices report.* New York: American Quality Foundation; Cleveland: Ernst & Young. Langdon, D. G., Whiteside, K. S., and

McKenna, M. M. eds. (1999). *Intervention resource guide: 50 performance improvement tools*. San Francisco: Jossey-Bass/Pfeiffer. Rigby, D. (2001). "Management tools and techniques: A survey." *California Management Review*, 43(2), 139–160. Mercer Human Resource Consulting. (2002). *Effective performance management practices*. New York: Mercer Human Resources Consulting. Relying in part on *post facto* results, including the durability of a technique's influence, Danny Miller and colleagues attempt to distinguish fads from classics. See, Miller, D., Hartwick, J., and Le Breton-Miller, I. (2004). "How to detect a management fad—and distinguish it from a classic." *Business Horizons*, 47(4), 7–16.

48 O'Toole, J. (1985). *Vanguard management: Redesigning the corporate future*. Garden City: Doubleday.

49 Quinn, R. E. (1988). *Beyond rational management*. San Francisco: Jossey-Bass.

50 Hartnell, C.A., Ou, A.Y., and Kinicki, A. (2011). "Organizational culture and organizational effectiveness: A meta-analytic investigation of the competing values framework's theoretical suppositions." *Journal of Applied Psychology*, 96, 677–694. Quotations are from page 687.

51 Collins, J. C., and Porras, J. I. (1994). *Built to last: Successful habits of visionary companies*. New York: HarperBusiness/HarperCollins.

52 It should be noted that Orlitzky, M., Schmidt, F. L., and Rynes, S. T. coauthored a meta-analysis that has been cited nearly 3,000 times. "Corporate social and financial performance: A meta-analysis." *Organization Studies*, 2003, 24(3), 403–441. Bethune, G. (1998). *From worst to first: Behind the scenes of Continental's remarkable comeback*. New York: Wiley. Quote is on page 4, italics in original.

53 Bethune, G. (1998). *From worst to first: Behind the scenes of Continental's remarkable comeback*. New York: Wiley. Quote is on page 4, italics in original.

54 Berry, L. L., and Seltman, K. D. (2008). *Management lessons from Mayo Clinic: Inside one of the world's most admired service organizations*. New York: McGraw-Hill. Quotation is from page 84.

55 Berry, L. L. and Seltman, K. D. (2008).

56 Gratzer, D. (February 14, 2011). "Our health is worsening at a time when medicine has never been better." Retrieved at http://www.kevinmd.com/blog/2011/02/health-wo rsening-time-medicine.html

57 As Doug Lemov, the managing director of Uncommon Schools has put it, "Almost every major historical innovation has been preceded by an advance in measurement, and I believe we are living on the cusp of a golden age of educational measurement." (Maybe the same claim can be made for improving the performance of organizations in general. At least that is a goal of the Cube One framework, albeit it might be seen as a BHAG—a Big Hairy Audacious Goal.) The reference for the article about Lemov is as follows: "A toolkit for teachers." (June 2013). *HBS Alumni Bulletin*, 89(2), p. 31.

58 Kopelman, R. E. (1986). "The implementation of planned change in organizational settings," (chapter 13) in *Managing productivity in organizations*. New York: McGraw-Hill, pp. 271–288.

59 Lewin K. (1943). "Defining the field at a given time." *Psychological Review*, 50, 292–310. Republished in *Resolving social conflicts & field theory in social science*. Washington, D.C.: American Psychological Association, 1997.

60 Kotter, J. P. (2008). *A sense of urgency*. Boston: Harvard Business Press.

61 Cooperrider, D. L., and Whitney, D. (2005). *Appreciative inquiry: A positive revolution in change*. San Francisco: Berrett-Koehler.

62 Nelson, B. (1994). *1001 ways to reward employees*. New York: Workman.

2

ENTERPRISE-DIRECTED PRACTICES

As noted previously, the Cube One framework combines research and writing from multiple disciplines, including human resource management, organizational behavior, industrial/organizational (I/O) psychology, operations management, quality management, marketing, and to some extent even finance and economics. The basic premise is that all organizations—for-profit, nonprofit, or governmental—must accomplish the aims of three key participants: the providers of capital (investors, lenders, donors, research grantors, taxpayers); external customers who ultimately purchase the goods or services provided; and internal customers (primarily employees, but also contractors, vendors, and suppliers), who provide the means to convert inputs to outputs.

As noted in Chapter 1, there is no ideal set of "best practices," and even successful organizations do not always implement the same practices.[1] What matters is conscientious implementation of high levels of demonstrably effective enterprise-, employee-, and customer-directed practices. Given the assumption of substitutability (or using a more fancy term, equifinality) the primary objective is for organizations in all sectors actually to enact (not just espouse) pertinent practices. The next three chapters provide examples of demonstrably effective practices pertinent to the three key dimensions of the Cube One framework. In instances where the quality of implementation or the quality of effectiveness evidence is questionable, we provide comments in the text or endnotes.

Productive organizations will, by definition, have a lower cost of goods/ services sold which, in turn, will be reflected in lower prices and/or superior products and services for the same price. Improved productivity permits an organization to invest in research and development; to raise the pay level of its employees; and to attract capital more easily via debt or, in the for-profit sector, additional equity. An infinite variety of practices have been employed by organizations to improve productivity. We describe the most prominent and demonstrably effective ones here.

Productivity-enhancing practices that focus on people generally seek to improve employee motivation and/or skills. Technology and various exogenous (external) factors, such as regulations, also affect productivity. Productivity is just one facet (although a crucial one) of enterprise-directed practices. Organizations also must pay attention to product/service quality, and costs. New technologies can improve profitability, and if transformative—what Christiansen calls "disruptive technology/innovation"—they can affect entire industries.[2] Likewise, operational practices can influence costs such as those associated with inventory, various forms of waste, and, in broad terms, the "make or buy" decision. To provide a roadmap of this chapter, we first review enterprise-directed practices that increase productivity through people; then cost-reducing practices via technology and operations management. Finally, we discuss how to identify and mitigate some external factors through financial management.

Productivity Improvement through People

Enterprise-directed practices that promote high levels of employee work motivation and job performance include systematic workforce planning; employee recruitment and selection; training; goal setting; feedback; performance appraisal; performance management; delegation of authority; decentralization; participative management; and appropriate performance-contingent rewards—based on individual or group performance metrics, or both. These practices are often collectively labeled High Performance Work Practices.[3] The domain of practices that can increase productivity is almost boundless. Furthermore, practices can be examined at various levels of granularity. As noted in Chapter 1, Nelson has identified more than 1,000 ways to reward employees.[4]

About a decade ago, Drucker noted that productive efficiency is every bit as essential in the nonprofit as in the for-profit sector.[5] Today good intentions do not "cut it" with the boards of nonprofit organizations. Increasingly, their managements are being held accountable for achieving measurable results, within limits imposed by budgets. Likewise, donors and grantors have become ever more vigilant as to how their funds are used. A recent innovative example is the nonprofit venture *GiveDirectly*, founded by then-graduate students in economics at Harvard University and the Massachusetts Institute of Technology. Their charity directly provides cash payments to people in need, facilitates transparency to donors, and makes available research on effectiveness. It is now commonplace for charitable organizations to provide annual reports documenting their achievements, and such reports are essential in competing for donations. Even religious organizations need to compete for membership dues (which likely reflects the spiritual satisfaction and solace members attain.) Entities such as charitynavigator.org review performance and transparency of nonprofit organizations and charities, and in doing so provide an essential service to donors who are "comparison shopping."

High Performance Work Practices

About two decades ago, researchers concluded that it is more useful to examine human resource practices in sets (or "bundles") than to examine them separately. They found that predictions of organizational performance are stronger when based on multiple rather than single practices.[6] This finding is clearly consistent with the basic premise of the Cube One framework: that successful organizations enact high levels of three *sets* of practices, those being enterprise-, employee, and customer-directed.

Fast-forward to 2012. Researchers have identified three major dimensions of HR practices: (1) skill/ability-enhancing practices (sometimes abbreviated as A); (2) motivation-enhancing practices (abbreviated as M); and (3) opportunity-enhancing practices, (abbreviated as O).[7] Subsequently, a multi-cultural meta-analysis (a study that statistically pools the results of many independent studies) identified the same three dimensions of HR practices and collectively conceptualized them as High Performance Work Systems (HPWS). The results and conclusions drawn from them are thus based on more than 35,000 companies in 29 countries.[8]

In total, 14 practices comprise the three dimensions of HPWS, the practices being grouped into categories A, M, and O. From the perspective of the Cube One framework, nine of the 14 practices can clearly be classified as enterprise-directed insofar as they should improve work motivation and job performance. The other five initiatives could more aptly be identified as employee-directed practices, as they relate to the intermediate outcomes of employee satisfaction, retention, and loyalty. The nine clearly enterprise-directed practices follow.

1. Selection

In his article, "The Seven Practices of Successful Organizations," Jeffrey Pfeffer notes the utility of having a large hiring pool.[9] He cites for example how Southwest Airlines, arguably the most highly regarded airline in the industry's history, received in one year 125,000 applications for the 4,000 positions filled. Similarly, Singapore Airlines, an organization that differentiates itself based on service, had a selection rate of 2%. Selection rates at Procter & Gamble, a leader in the consumer goods industry, are about 1% for the one million individuals who apply each year. In 2015, Google received more than two million applications for the 50,000 positions it filled, a selection rate of about 2%. As Laszlo Bock, Google's former senior vice president of people operations noted, it is easier to get admitted to Harvard than be hired by Google.[10]

Beyond having a large applicant pool, organizations must identify the requisite knowledge, skills, abilities, and other characteristics (i.e., KSAO) associated with successful performance in a specific job. (This information is typically obtained from a job analysis.) Based on information about essential job requirements, a behavior-based, structured (and standardized) interview, with scoring norms and trained interviewers, will yield more valid and fair predictions of job performance than the traditional unstructured "shoot the bull" interview.[11] Further, any and all tests must be validated professionally with normative data and validity evidence. For legal purposes, any systematic selection procedure (e.g., required job experience; interviews; background, reference, criminal history checks) are considered "tests." Therefore, it is crucial that tests be validated and administered by individuals knowledgeable about legal regulations and requirements.[12] (As an aside, it might be noted, that in order to facilitate the development of valid interview questions, Google has developed an internal tool called qDroid.)

A structured interview, in which the same job-related questions are posed to all candidates, essentially resembles an oral test and this approach has been found to be highly valid in predicting job performance.[13] Even higher levels of predictive validity are found in situational interviews: a type of structured interview where candidates face a dilemma that entails mutually exclusive choices.[14] For example, consider the following scenario, which would be posed to all applicants.

> You are the assistant manager of a bowling alley. It is 7:35 pm on a Tuesday, and two strangers approach your desk seeking to bowl. The lanes are almost completely empty; but they will be entirely filled by 8pm, because Tuesday is league night. Your boss has repeatedly emphasized that you should maximize revenues to the fullest extent possible. What do you do?"[15]

The scoring protocol for the situational interview above would include assessments of judgment, capability to act independently, and problem solving ability, as reflected in a concern for long-term profitability. Ideally, the assistant manager should explain the problem, provide an apology, and offer each potential customer two free tickets to bowl any time other than a Tuesday evening.

Similar to the structured interview, and a lot easier to develop, is a behavior-based interview. After performing the requisite job analysis, candidates might be asked to describe occasions when they demonstrated the requisite skills/competencies. Examples of such a line of questioning are: "Tell me about an occasion when you were especially resourceful given limited funds"; "Tell me how you developed creative solutions to challenging work-related problems"; "Tell me how you dealt successfully with difficult colleagues."

Many companies have concluded that technical skills are relatively easy to impart via training, but dispositional characteristics are not. As the vice president of performance and development at the Cheesecake Factory put it "We can teach people how to set the tableware, but we have realized that we can't teach them to smile and be upbeat."[16]

In their classic empirical examination of the relationship between staffing practices and organizational-level measures of performance, Terpstra and Rozell found solid support for the use of biographic inventories. Such inventories collect information about candidates' past experiences that relate to future job performance. Nowadays this practice is typically conducted via an Internet application form.[17] Along these lines, at Context Media, in addition to multiple interviews and a role-playing exercise, the company looks for candidates who have organized volunteer groups for their school, community, or house of worship. This kind of initiative "shows the ability to operate within traditionally flat organizations."[18]

Enterprise Rent-A-Car, the largest car rental company in the U.S., seeks college graduates who have good sales skills and a commitment to excellent service. Dennis Ross, Enterprise's chief operating officer, (wryly) notes, "We hire from the half of the college class that makes the upper half possible. We want athletes, fraternity types: 'people people.'"[19]

Using a multilevel analysis of 102 technology firms in an eastern province of China, it was found that selective hiring, when coupled with other high-commitment strategic human resource practices, was associated with greater individual creativity. Results were strengthened when there was high team cohesion and high team task complexity.[20]

At Method, a leading manufacturer of biodegradable household cleaning products, the selection process begins with a phone-screen or Skype interview, followed by two rounds of in-person interviews. The first interview is with prospective teammates; the second with employees in different departments. The interview typically begins with the question "Why Method?" and the last question is "What have you learned?" The object is to find out whether candidates only focus on selling themselves, or are listening and learning. The selection process includes a challenging homework assignment, which only 60% of applicants pass. One goal of the assignment is to encourage managers to hire people who are smarter than they are. The president of the company, Eric Ryan, also acknowledges the importance of chemistry: "We try to hire people we'd be happy sitting next to on a plane during a cross-country flight."[21]

A number of organizations have retained professional recruiting firms that claim to specialize in "topgrading" organizations; i.e., loading their clients' workforces with "A" players. Fifteen to 20 recruiting firms conduct rigorous interviews, perform meticulous reference checks, and employ validated tests to identify "top players." One prominent firm, Smart & Associates, Inc., claims to have brought the "topgrading" concept to such *Fortune* 1,000 companies as General Electric, Barclays, and Lincoln Financial. The senior vice president of HR at Lincoln Financial commented: "[By "topgrading"], you spend far less money on blowout hires that don't make the grade. It makes a huge difference."[22] Along these lines, a Right Associates survey of 444 North American firms found that the financial cost of an unsuccessful hire is about two and a half times the annual salary of the position.[23]

Notwithstanding the fact that Google receives about 50,000 job inquiries a week, Google spends about twice as much as the average company on the recruitment process. As Bock observed, except when recruiting on college campuses, the best and brightest potential employees are individuals who are not looking for a job. Rather, these are top performers who are amply rewarded where they presently work; enjoy their careers; and appreciate the recognition they have received. Hence, Google continuously scans the Internet and attempts to identify and hire "passive job seekers." Google recruiters start networking through phone calls, emails, doing whatever it takes to hire stars. In one instance, Google knew of a team of brilliant engineers in Denmark. The team wanted to remain where they lived, so Google swooped in and opened an office in Aarhus, Denmark.[24]

The recruitment process covers not only selection and staffing. It also entails introducing the newly hired employees to the organization, i.e., onboarding. On day one of the traditional onboarding process, new employees complete lots of paperwork, then sit passively through dull presentations about the organization's history, core values, culture, strategy, and structure. Instead, at Wipro Ltd. in New Delhi, India, some of the 605 newly hired call center employees went through an orientation process in which individuals were asked to speak publicly about the time in their lives that they found most personally satisfying—a time when they felt "born to act." Six months later, the new recruits who experienced the employee-centered orientation had a 32% lower quit rate than those who sat through the company-focused onboarding process.[25]

Although the article describing the Wipro experiment did not provide an in-depth explanation for the success of the employee-centered orientation, the experiment can be interpreted as a vivid demonstration of Appreciative Inquiry (AI). AI is often used in the context of creating positive organizational change. Instead of focusing on what the organization has been doing wrong—the typical diagnostic, problem-fixing approach, which yields defensiveness and resistance—AI attempts to identify and reproduce examples of prior successes. The process often yields positive energy, increased engagement, and enthusiasm toward change.[26]

Information technology is starting to play an increasingly vital role in the process of employee selection. Professional recruiting firms see transformation as emerging from the "four horsemen" of 21st century recruiting: big data, the Cloud, mobile devices, and social media. One company, CEB TowerGroup, claims to have a new product that tracks market dynamics in 1,200+ cities in more than 100 countries—creating a data set of more than 100 million knowledge workers. In 2014 alone, the data set contained assessments of 1.3 million employees, and on a cumulative basis, its CloudSuite platform purportedly has information on 25% of the entire U.S. workforce. Tarak Raman, vice president of the firm's Human Capital Group, cites the case of a sportswear retailer that saved thousands of hours, and its "new hires generated about 16 percent more in dollar sales per hour" compared to employees hired the old way. Although Raman recognizes that hiring managers know how to match skills with job descriptions, the granularity of his database can show "the behavioral DNA of candidates." There are differences, for instance between the behavioral profiles of top-performing department store employees in women's shoes versus top performers in men's suits.[27]

Companies differ in terms of organizational culture, and also, therefore, the types of individuals they would like to attract and select into their workforces. Different cultures are suitable and effective for organizations in different industries or different stages of business maturity. Notwithstanding cultural differences, organizations should observe the basic principles of applicant assessment in employee selection. They must use reliable assessment tools grounded in the requisite knowledge, skills, and other characteristics that accurately predict job performance, and treat candidates respectfully and fairly during the selection processes.

2. Training

An essential component of virtually all High Performance Work Systems is extensive training.[28] Data reported by Pfeffer indicate that among auto factories located in the U.S., workers in U.S.-owned companies received on average 42 hours of training during the first six months of employment, and 31 hours annually after one year. In contrast, Japanese-owned plants located in the U.S. provided 225 and 52 hours of training, respectively. With respect to European plants in Europe the hours of training were 178 and 52. One reason why Japanese plants provide substantially more training is because they rely on flexible production. The conduct of cross-training is also pertinent to operations management.[29]

The evaluation of training effectiveness in organizational settings is challenging because in practice, *ceteris paribus* (i.e., "all other things being equal") does not apply. Hence, isolating the effects of one factor (such as training) is difficult. However, data can be suggestive, at least. An analysis of data collected by Deloitte and reported in their "Corporate Learning Factbook 2014" showed that "high-impact learning organizations experienced three times greater profit growth than their competitors over the prior four years ... and also have higher levels of engagement and retention."[30] A meta-analysis by Arthur and colleagues documents the effectiveness of various training programs.

In 2012, Jiang, Lepak, and Baer introduced a causal model that viewed skill-enhancing HR practices as increasing human capital which enhance organizational and financial outcomes. The three skill-enhancing HR practices they examined were comprehensive recruitment, rigorous selection, and extensive training. As hypothesized, skill-related practices related more to human capital than to employee motivation, and were superior to motivation or opportunity-enhancing practices as a predictor of financial outcomes. Framed in terms of the metric of standard deviations, a one standard deviation (SD) increase in employee skills was associated with a 0.13 SD increase in financial performance.[31] Such statistics become much more persuasive when framed in terms of return on investment (ROI) calculations. The question here is, "How much is a 0.13 SD increase in performance worth?" For most companies the answer is, "A lot!"

In their meta-analysis of the effects of three factors—incentives, feedback, and social recognition—on organizational performance, Stajkovic and Luthans found that incentives enhance motivation, however motivation is a necessary but insufficient condition for effective organizational performance. Effective performance requires the development of employees' competencies through training that increases knowledge of the task, improves skill levels, and helps develop better task performance strategies.[32] Moreover, it has long been posited, and to some extent demonstrated, that there is a multiplicative interaction between motivation and ability with respect to job performance. After all, even an employee with exceptionally high motivation will not be productive without the skills essential to the tasks at hand. Hence, training is important for enhancing performance as well as the development of human capital.[33]

Numerous case studies describe highly successful companies that devote sizable resources to training. In the Container Store, for example, all new employees receive 263 hours of training their first year, much of it on the job.[34]

The grocery chain, Wegmans, is famous for extensive training. Consider the following vignette describing an informal "experiment" conducted by the authors of an article about Wegmans:

> If you want to find out why Wegmans rules among supermarkets, try this. We tested this at the Wegmans in Fairfax, Va. by asking for a Tomme de Savoie, a savory, semi-hard cheese made in the part of France that surrounds the southwestern corner of Switzerland. For the record, Wegmans carries 700 kinds of cheese but not Tomme de Savoie. And here's the cool part. The saleswoman not only knew instantly that the Tomme was not among Wegmans' 700 offerings, but she knew why. It's made with raw cow's milk and therefore can't be sold in the United States. This degree of knowledge is one of the secrets of Wegmans' success.[35]

Wegmans sends out about a million copies of its quarterly magazine, *Menu*, the contents of which are reinforced in the stores by knowledgeable cooking coaches and sales staff in various departments. Every week every store conducts a session on how to make the meal of the week, and store staff are trained in the preparation of different foods. As CEO Danny Wegman put it, offering a low-priced, high-quality artichoke is of no value to customers if they do not know how to cook it. According to Mr. Wegman, the quality of service has reached a new level. "I hear that when folks are in a bad mood, they go to Wegmans to cheer up."[36]

Another trend in the provision of training is for companies to collaborate with universities in the development and delivery of customized courses. After an extensive search, Ingersoll-Rand partnered with Indiana University's Kelley School of Business in developing a customized three-year "blended" MBA program. According to Rita Smith, Dean of Ingersoll-Rand University, the retention rate among the first 70 enrolled students was 100%.[37]

Far larger in scope, is the collaboration between Home Depot and three online universities through which, in 2006, Home Depot offered credit-bearing customized courses to its 380,000 employees. Employees can take up to 12 credit-bearing courses that yield up to 41 college credits in subjects including horticulture, interior design, and sales.[38]

3. Goal Setting

More than 1,000 academic studies, primarily lab and field experiments, have found that goal setting consistently improves *individual* performance.[39] One review found a success rate of about 95%, with a median increase in job performance of 16%.[40] There have been far fewer studies pertinent to the effects of goal setting (alone) on *organizational* performance.

A 2015 article in *The Economist*, entitled the "quantified serf," quotes Kris Duggan, a founder of BetterWorks, as stating that the "traditional once-a-year setting of employee goals and performance review is totally out of date." Rather, Duggan asserts that goals need to be set more frequently, their progress measured more often, and they should be transparent on a company-wide basis.[41] Consistent with this perspective, a study by Deloitte found that companies which set goals quarterly were nearly four times as likely to be in the top quartile of companies.[42]

In one of the first studies of the relationship between the use of individual-level goal setting and organizational performance, Terpstra and Rozell found a significant (but modest) relationship. The impact in terms of increased profits, on average, amounted to slightly less than $1 million, annually.[43]

In 2011, Kleingeld and colleagues conducted a meta-analysis on the effects of group-level goals on group performance. Specific and difficult group goals yielded a substantially higher level of group performance compared to groups with nonspecific goals. Surprisingly, task interdependence, task complexity, and employee participation in the goal setting process were unrelated to the effects of group goal setting. The authors concluded that individual goals can also raise group performance, so long as individual performance was not antithetical or competitive to group performance.[44]

Although the positive results associated with goal setting are impressive, an even stronger form of goal setting has been developed, called implementation intentions. Just as a specific goal ("I will grade twenty term papers this weekend" is more effective than a vague wish, ("I'd like to visit Scotland one of these years") implementation intentions are even more powerful than specific goals.[45] An implementation intention specifies exactly when, where, and how a goal-accomplishing activity will occur ("I will grade 15 term papers at my desk on

Saturday from 11am to 2pm, and five papers between 5pm and 6pm.") Hence, it is harder to "duck" completing an implementation intention. Implementation intentions are particularly effective when it comes to health promoting and disease-preventing endeavors. Because activities such as regular exercise or a change in diet have immediate costs and only long-term benefits, goal attainment is more likely to be achieved if stated in terms of implementation intentions (e.g., I will attend a spin class at my gym every Monday and Thursday.)

The majority of studies on group goal setting have been conducted in lab settings often with students, it is likely, nonetheless, that group goal setting will be effective in for-profit, nonprofit, and government settings. Of course, the goals assigned should be specific and relevant to the organization's mission.

As noted in a *Harvard Business Review* article, charities also need a bottom line (or a fundamental, mission-related objective) to guide their activities. Pertinent to the necessity of mission-related goals is the case of a U.S. charity that wanted to assist in improving education in Peru. A young field worker signed onto the project and dedicated two years of exceptionally hard work building more than 200 new classrooms in remote areas at a very low cost per unit. Unfortunately, unbeknownst to the volunteer, the charitable organization's specific mission was to increase grade school literacy and attendance at existing schools. Subsequently, the young volunteer was "devastated" when he found out that his "tremendous effort" was largely for naught.[46] As the management guru Don Campbell noted: "If you don't know where you are going, you'll probably end up somewhere else."

Atul Gawande, a physician who has written about the power of a checklist, provides a dramatic example of the utility of goal setting. In 2007, approximately 80,000 patients in the U.S. developed infections associated with the insertion of a line (i.e., a tube) in their bodies, leading to approximately 25,000 deaths. Consequently, Dr. Peter Pronovost developed a five-item checklist comprised of steps commonly known to physicians and accepted as standard practice—yet some of the steps were too often skipped. Initially, Dr. Pronovost himself, was somewhat skeptical as to the impact of his checklist. The results, however, were so startling that use of the checklist for inserting lines was implemented throughout the state of Michigan. The undertaking was called the Keystone Initiative. In 2006 the results were published in the eminent *New England Journal of Medicine*. In the Keystone Initiative's first 18 months, hospitals saved an estimated $175 million in costs and more than 1,500 lives. As noted by Gawande, these results were sustained for almost four years, and in his words these remarkable results were "all because of a stupid little checklist."[47]

4. Feedback

In broad terms, feedback refers to information about behavior or performance, which can be provided at various levels: individual, work-unit, department, or organization. It should be noted that there is great variety in the specificity and factual basis of the feedback provided. If an individual is given vague feedback such as "you need to sharpen your sense of responsibility" or "you should increase your initiative at work," the recipient will likely have no idea what to do differently, even after much head-scratching. Feedback of this kind not only fails to motivate better performance; it can be frustrating to the recipient, and possibly detrimental to performance.

In contrast, some forms of feedback can be objective, if based on specific, observable, factual information. Objective feedback is virtually incontrovertible, more readily accepted, and has been found to be highly motivational and instructional: cueing needed improvements and/or the adoption of different tactics.[48]

One reason why the management technique of goal setting discussed above is so effective is that it is usually accompanied by the provision of knowledge of results in terms of the metric of the goal, i.e., it typically entails the provision of objective feedback. Locke and Latham emphasized the importance of feedback in their first book, *Goal Setting: A Motivational Technique that Works!* In their words (p. 65): "In sum, *feedback is necessary if goal setting is to work*" (emphasis in the original).[49] In their follow-up book, Locke and Latham incorporated evidence based on additional goal setting studies. They reported that in 17 out of 18 studies, the combination of goal setting and feedback was superior to goal setting alone.[50]

In a comprehensive survey of 72 studies that used objective feedback, data were examined for 30 laboratory and 42 field interventions. Results indicated that the median performance improvement in laboratory studies was 11.6%; in field studies, 15.2%. The more sizable effects in field studies might reflect the nature of the setting. The average laboratory experiment lasted for 70 minutes; in contrast, the median duration of the field interventions was 29 weeks. Additionally, more significant consequences are usually associated with performance on one's job (which is often one's livelihood), than is the case in a laboratory experiemt.[51]

Examples of field experiments that employed objective feedback include the provision of monthly feedback to telephone reservationists at Aer Lingus. The reservationists had been instructed to use the caller's name frequently, and never to interrupt. Upon receiving the monthly objective feedback, the reservationists were astonished to discover how infrequently they used the caller's name, and how frequently they interrupted the caller.[52]

At a cafeteria staffed by student employees, there had been a problem of "shrinkage" (i.e., theft) in four food items: potato chips, milk, ice cream, and sandwiches. The use of objective feedback resulted in a composite reduction in shrinkage of 94%. Interestingly, when feedback was first provided for potato chips, shrinkage of potato chips immediately dropped by 100% (to zero), but for the other three food groups, shrinkage actually increased. This pattern continued when objective feedback was provided successively for the other three groups, indicating that the effects of objective feedback tend to pinpoint specific, focal behaviors.[53]

Along these lines, the director of safety at a large package delivery organization used publicly posted data to provide objective performance feedback for each of three shifts of the company's 24-hour workday. Data were provided over a 43-week period regarding (1) the number of vehicular accidents and (2) days since a lost time injury for employees in one borough. Because the intervention occurred in a metropolitan area with multiple boroughs, accidents and injuries in two other boroughs served as a basis for comparison (as they had very similar weather conditions). The net result was a reduction in both accidents and injuries in the borough where objective feedback was provided.[54]

The provision of real-time storewide feedback is a distinctive feature of the management process at the Container Store. The workday begins with the staff conducting a huddle where the store manager announces the sales goal for the day. During the workday, staff can see minute-by-minute status reports for all stores in their area, and if they are not keeping up, the manager will coach them. Almost 12% of revenues go to salaries, and store employees earn an average of $48,000 a year, about twice the typical retail salary.[55] (Similarly, sales associates at Nordstrom can see their own hourly sales results as well as those of their colleagues, the data being posted in the staff rest area. Nordstrom salespeople earn nearly twice the national average. A more in-depth description of practices at Nordstrom appears in Chapter 9.)

The meta-analysis by Stajkovic and Luthans of 72 studies with a total population of more than 13,000 participants examined the effects of three potential motivators on task performance. The three motivators were money, feedback, and social recognition. The study defined the focal dependent variable, task performance, in terms of measurable, task-specific, performance-related behaviors. Defining task performance in terms of a quantitative metric enabled the provision of objective feedback. Results, stated in terms of the percentage of improvement in task performance, were as follows: money (23%), social recognition (17%) and feedback (10%). When all three potential motivators were applied simultaneously, the result was sizable: an improvement of 45%.[56]

Interestingly, the Stajkovic and Luthans meta-analysis found that when only the two factors of money and social recognition were examined—excluding feedback—the positive impact of money was reduced by 90%, and the positive impact of social recognition was reduced by 76%. Evidently, the effects of providing money and social recognition yielded a "mismatch cost" due to combining personal and interpersonal rewards. However, the addition of feedback to money and social recognition multiplied the combined effect by 26.8 times: from an increase of about 2% to 45%.[57]

Even if not always objective—i.e., factual and virtually incontrovertible—feedback can help improve organizational performance. In her blog, Karen Caruso notes that she has heard managers at all levels say that providing feedback is unnecessary and takes up too much time. "*We are adults; we all know when we are doing a good job. We don't need to be told by someone else.*" (Emphasis is in original.) Yet she asserts that if people do not receive positive feedback they will use their imagination to fill in the missing information. As a result, their opinions of their own performance may be negative and inaccurate. An employee may be thinking, "I must not be doing that great a job, or my boss would have said something." According to Caruso, this is true for employees at all organizational levels.[58]

Feedback interventions can be classified as either positive or negative, with the latter intended to motivate employees to improve and fill performance gaps.[59] Critical or negative feedback must be handled with great care. A recent pair of laboratory studies found that destructive criticism—negative feedback that is inconsiderate in style and content—produced a variety of adverse effects. Harsh and inconsiderate feedback led most recipients to perceive the feedback provider as intending to harm. The recipients experienced a lack of trust, and were often angry. Only individuals with high trait competitiveness responded to harsh criticism by intending to work harder—but despite their constructive intentions, their performance was lower than individuals with low trait competitiveness.[60] The bottom line is clear: delivering one hour of nonstop insults, and calling people "Buster," is not a good idea.

Recipients of performance appraisal feedback more readily accept objective or behavior-based information, compared to subjective ratings. The former is inherently more factual and often indisputable, whereas recipients may view the latter as biased.[61] Objective or behavior-based feedback is vastly more acceptable to recipients than peer-comparison ranking data. An early study of employees at GE found that 98% rated themselves above average in job performance, a phenomenon analogous to the "Lake Wobegon effect".[62] Therefore, it is reasonable to assume that in any organization the vast majority of employees (perhaps 90%) think they are at least average in job performance.

A more rigorous study conducted of faculty at the University of Nebraska found that 68% of faculty members rated themselves in the top 25% in teaching.[63] When peer-comparison performance feedback data indicate that an employee is below average in job performance, approximately 90% of the recipients of this feedback will view this information as incorrect. Recipients will express disagreement, and experience frustration, anger, and other negative emotions.

Yet, when it comes to performance data, half of all performers must, by definition, be below average. Consider the apocryphal tale of the dean who wanted to spur his faculty to achieving greater heights and urged them to get more students into the top half of their classes. The faculty strove mightily, but their efforts were fruitless.

5. Incentives

The concept of incentive compensation has received multiple labels. At the individual (employee) level, practices are often described using terms such as pay-for-performance, merit pay, pay differentiation, contingent pay, and where there are measurable units of work, behavior-based or piece rate pay. At the group, division, or organizational level, incentives have taken the form of profit sharing, group bonuses—and, where there are countable outputs, gainsharing.

According to the *Handbook of Human Performance Technology*, three major benefits result from incentive pay: recruitment of talented individuals, retention of these individuals, and an overall increase in productivity.[64] Yet few HR topics are more controversial than incentive pay. Three primary objections have been voiced. First, some writers believe that individual incentives will necessarily harm cooperation and teamwork.[65] Recent research described below, though, indicates that the opposite is more accurate.

Second, some have suggested that although incentives may enhance extrinsic motivation, intrinsic motivation may decrease—yielding a possible overall reduction in work motivation.[66] A recent meta-analysis that studied pertinent research over a 40-year period, though, found that extrinsic rewards were not antithetical to intrinsic motivation. The authors of the meta-analysis actually acknowledged that they had set out to confirm the contention that extrinsic rewards diminished intrinsic motivation. However, they (perforce) concluded: "Counter to the claims otherwise, our research demonstrates the joint impact of incentives and intrinsic motivation is critical to performance."[67]

Third, some writers seem philosophically opposed to paying for performance—seeing such a practice as demeaning and akin to bribery.[68] However, if high performers receive the same pay and pay increases as low performers, how will organizations attract and retain talented people—especially when other organizations recognize and reward individual performance? Many employees will conclude that equal pay is not equitable.

It is useful to separate incentive plans into two categories: those based on countable outputs or behaviors, which are relatively objective indicators of performance; and plans that rely largely on subjective ratings of performance. The latter plans are often referred to as merit pay, or pay for performance. Both objective and subjective criteria can be recognized and rewarded at individual, group, and organizational levels. The evidentiary support for the use of output- or behavior-based incentives is reviewed first, followed by evidence pertinent to the use of judgment-based reward plans. Both reviews address, to some extent, the three primary criticisms of incentives mentioned above.

In their text, *The Management of Compensation*, Nash and Carroll cite the results of five early surveys encompassing more than 4,700 individual and group incentive plans. The average increase in productivity after switching from time-based pay to output-based pay plans ranged from 29 to 63%, the median increase being 34.5%.[69]

A review by Ed Locke and colleagues of four methods of improving productivity found that individual incentive plans increased output by 30%, and group incentive plans typically increased output by 18%.[70] A survey of various types of people-based interventions reported the results of eight studies that examined the effects of financial incentives. Results were positive in all cases with the median performance increase being 32.1%.[71]

Summarizing the extensive research on the use of incentives, John Miner, the author of comprehensive texts on management and organizational behavior, writes that whatever the literature one reads, "the evidence for the motivating effects of … contingent rewards is quite overwhelming."[72] Perhaps this explains why psychologists speak of the Law of Effect, rather than the Theory or Hypothesis of Effect.

Using a before and after analysis, economist Edward Lazear studied what happened at Safelite Glass Corporation, a large auto glass company, when it switched from hourly wages to piece-rate pay. Examining data from about 3,000 workers over a 19-month period, the results were "dramatic and completely in line with economic theory." Productivity increased by 44%.[73]

A field study published in 2006 compared financial and non-financial incentives on business-unit performance over nine months among fast-food franchise stores. Employees in three of the 21 stores received increases in pay based on samples of observed work behaviors. These observations resulted in pay increases that averaged $33, $55, and $71 per employee per month after the first three, six, and nine months respectively. Employees in six stores were provided graphed objective feedback, plus behavior-based praise and weekly memos emphasizing progress. Twelve of the 21 stores served as the control (or more strictly, the comparison) condition, in that no intervention was conducted. Gross profits were unchanged in the control stores (at around $63,000 a month) and rose in the incentive and feedback plus praise groups to $84,000 and $83,000. In both conditions, the improvements amounted to about 30% within nine months. Top management was reportedly so impressed that they planned to incorporate financial incentives coupled with feedback and praise in all 21 stores.[74]

In a study of nonprofit rural electricity cooperatives, 11 different High Performance Work Practices were separately examined, allowing comparison of the effects of each practice. Incentive-based compensation (including merit pay, group variable pay, gainsharing, and bonuses) tied for first with internal advancement opportunities (e.g., promotion opportunities, mentoring, and coaching,) as the most effective HPWP in terms of distribution center productivity.[75]

In one early field study, a large paper company switched from a performance-based to a time-based system. The result: a dramatic and significant reduction in productivity. Similarly, a piece-rate system was discontinued in favor of an hourly wage, and the result was failure. Performance went down and turnover went up. Two years later, thanks to a plant-wide incentive system, productivity went up 45%, and turnover dropped to a lower level than before the piece rate system was dropped.[76]

With respect to tying pay to measured outputs, successful companies have a long history of measuring and rewarding a combination of individual and organizational results. Nucor, the largest U.S. steel company, was profitable for 130 consecutive quarters (as of 2005) having an employee turnover rate of 0%. The company consistently awarded bonuses of 80 to 150% of base pay to hourly workers.[77] Likewise, Lincoln Electric has thrived on a combination of piecework pay in concert with the employee's merit rating and company profits. For decades, performance-based increases have averaged more than 90% of base wages.[78]

Over the years, several studies have examined the effects of tying rated job performance (as distinct from measured outputs) to organizationally mediated rewards (salary increases, bonuses, promotions.) In a study of three engineering organizations, the one with the highest correlation between rated performance and pay increases had a substantially more motivated workforce than the company with the lowest pay-performance correlation.[79]

Another study examined the correlation between rated individual job performance and pay increase across ten branches of a metropolitan New York City bank. The pay-performance correlations varied widely across branches (from 0.09 to 0.66) even though all branches were supposed to use the same performance appraisal and pay increase protocols. As predicted, the branches with the higher pay-performance correlations had higher average individual performance ratings.[80]

A third study looked at pay-performance correlations among 5,100 department managers at 398 branches of a prominent department store chain. Although the company's famous founder had attempted to instill a strong culture of merit pay, sizable differences existed across stores in within-store pay-performance correlations. This variation occurred despite standardized rater training, a uniform performance rating system, and a grid that linked rated performance to pay increase. Surprisingly, in one-third of the stores the correlation was negative, meaning that lower-rated department managers/supervisors received larger pay increases than higher-rated managers. What makes this study powerful is the availability of profitability data for each of the 398 stores. As expected, the higher the pay-performance correlation, the more profitable the store. Had all stores been as profitable as the 50% with at least moderately high pay-performance correlation, the company would have earned $30 million more in profits annually (about $105 million in 2015 dollars).[81]

A meta-analysis by Jiang and colleagues published in 2012 examined 14 HRM practices across more than 31,000 organizations. The five practices associated with motivation (including incentive pay) had the strongest impact on organizational financial performance. An increase of one standard deviation in the motivational HRM practices was associated with a 0.18 standard deviation in financial outcomes. Unfortunately, this study did not permit parsing the effects of incentives by themselves.[82]

A 2014 meta-analysis by Rabl and colleagues examined the effects of high-performance-work systems on business performance in 29 countries. The study, which comprised more than 35,000 firms, found that HPWS were positively associated with business performance in every country—despite predictions that national culture would delimit the strength of the association between HPWS and profitability. Specifically, it was hypothesized that results would be more positive in cultures that were lower on power distance (a higher tolerance for unequal power distribution) and lower on collectivism (having an emphasis on group over individual interests). However, contrary to standard national culture-based logic, it was found that HPWS actually were *more positively* associated with business performance when the fit between HPWS and national culture was *lowest*. In short, pay for performance is, at minimum, no less effective in cultures with a collectivist national culture.[83] A plausible explanation for this seeming anomaly is that in cultures that do not emphasize individual recognition and rewards, there exists more opportunity for improvement, due to the "spare capacity" that is not utilized.[84]

One of the issues that concerns critics of incentive pay is that the creation of pay differentials may undermine teamwork. As the authors of a recent empirical study write, "pay dispersion in interdependent work settings is virtually universally argued to be detrimental to performance."[85] The researchers reasoned that due to differences in individuals' productivity and contributions, there is both dispersion explainable pay (DEP) as well as performance-unrelated (and dispersion unexplained) variability in pay (DUP). The researchers found that in interdependent work "where individual contributions are identifiable, inequity perceptions are more likely *without* pay dispersion, [i.e., with pay equality]." (Emphasis in the original, p. 591.) Three types of evidence supported the finding that DEP yields advantages in attracting and retaining of high performers and this subsequently facilitates team performance.[86] In brief, equal payments are not always seen as equitable. The researchers explicitly dispute (and refute) Pfeffer's assumption that pay differences will lead to jealousy, disruption, and impair interdependent work. Analogously, it is unlikely that the teammates of Michael Jordan resented the pay differential he received.

Along these lines, it has been questioned whether it is a good idea to tie rewards to creativity. A meta-analysis yielded a subtle distinction. It is constructive to tie rewards to creative behaviors, but not to creative accomplishments. The former encourages people to try out new ideas and has a positive effect on creativity, while tying rewards to creative accomplishment has essentially a zero effect on creativity.[87]

Although pay-for-performance plans are widely adopted in businesses, their use in professional organizations has been minimal. One exception is the Rochester Individual Practice Association, a large network of more than 3,500 physicians that contracts work with health plans. There, the Blue Choice Health Maintenance Organization adopted a pay-for-performance plan in 2002. The data consisted of the performance of 337 primary care physicians during three prior years (1999–2001) and during the three-year intervention period (2002–2004). Physician performance improved significantly during the three years of the pay-for-performance intervention.[88]

Another issue that has raised some concern is whether performance-contingent extrinsic rewards (e.g., pay increase) will undermine performance quality. A meta-analysis of the effects of extrinsic rewards on both performance quantity and quality found that financial rewards significantly enhanced performance quantity, but not performance quality. The effects on quantity were substantially stronger in field studies with employed adults, when compared to laboratory experiments (average correlations being 0.48 and 0.24, respectively). The authors explicitly noted that contrary to Deci and Kohn's claims that financial rewards jeopardize job performance, financial rewards have a positive effect on performance quantity.[89]

A study of more than 750 North American companies, conducted by the consulting firm Towers Perrin, concluded that the high-performing companies excel at the "tough stuff"—which they defined as implementing differential rewards for top performers and investing time in performance management. Towers Perrin concluded that companies in the top quartile in terms of total shareholder return were "getting the pay thing right." They provided a consistent and meaningful level of pay differentiation to their top-performing employees, unlike the lower performing companies. Of course, skeptics might argue that successful organizations can simply *afford* to follow a practice of pay differentiation. Towers Perrin acknowledged that their survey did not permit drawing causal inferences. Nonetheless, their data are, at minimum, suggestive.[90]

In 2014, a Towers Watson consultant noted, "a manager trying to get even five percent [raise, for one employee] requires some tough decisions for the rest of the population." Even average performers might not get the average 3%percent increase. In Towers Watson's study of 337 U.S. companies, the highest performers receive merit increases differentiated at 170%, while annual incentives are differentiated at125%.[91]

Less rigorous evidence as to the utility of differentiation in pay consists of the opinions of executives at successful companies. Andy Grove, cofounder and CEO of Intel Corporation for 30 years, stated:

> In spite of the criticisms [of performance appraisal and merit pay], I remain steadfast in my conviction that if we want performance in the workplace, somebody has to have the courage and confidence to determine whether we are getting it or not. We must also find ways to enhance what we are getting. … We are paid to manage our organizations. To manage means to elicit better performance from members of our organization. We managers need to stop rationalizing, and to stiffen our resolve and do what we are paid to do."[92]

Along the same lines, T. J. Rodgers, the founder (and still CEO) of Cypress Semiconductor, offered this comment in his *Harvard Business Review* article entitled "No Excuses Management." In his words, companies should "reward people in ways to encourage superior performance rather than demotivate superior perfomers."[93]

In a recent interview, Barney Harford, CEO of Orbitz Worldwide, offered a similar take:

> We believe passionately in the importance of performance management, and the benefits it can give over a sustained period in terms of the quality of an organization. I'll look at a merit increase budget or an equity budget and you've got a certain amount you can give out. The completely wrong approach is to spread these budgets across the organization like peanut butter. You need a really good process to make sure you're allocating compensation based on people's career trajectory—their performance and their potential.[94]

Indispensable to the use of performance-contingent pay is willingness to fire non-performing employees. In an article that attempted to put a better light on the management practices of Steve Jobs, the author, Walter Isaacson, noted that Jobs would only work with outstanding employees. Jobs worried about managers who are so polite that "mediocre people feel comfortable sticking around," which would ultimately lead to a "bozo explosion."[95] Of course, other managers before Jobs had similar concerns. When Jack Welsh was CEO of General Electric Company he introduced the concept of a 20-70-10 vitality curve, and recommended that organizations should "differentiate" and give the bottom 10% of performers "a chance to move on."

The tough performance-driven management philosophy at Netflix was powerfully captured in a PowerPoint deck that, according to Sheryl Sandberg (COO of Facebook), was one of the most important documents ever to come out of Silicon Valley. (As of 2014, the deck was viewed more than 5 million times.[96]) Patty McCord, the Chief Talent Officer at Netflix and coauthor of the Netflix PowerPoint deck stated, in a *Harvard Business Review* article, that Netflix's approach starts "with a built-in expectation of high performance, radical honesty, and the motto 'we're not family.'"[97] McCord noted at a First Round Capital CEO Summit talk that, "maintaining a 'high performance' team is all about instilling people with a sense of freedom and responsibility. But when you do, you might also need to have some tough conversations."[98]

Although incentive plans primarily focus on financial rewards, non-financial rewards can also lead to high levels of performance. As Mary Kay Ash (the founder of Mary Kay Cosmetics Inc.) put it: "There are two things people want more than sex and money: recognition and praise."[99] In their article "Singing the Praises of Praise," Blanchard and colleagues cite a Gallup survey that concluded that a lack of recognition or praise for doing good work is responsible for a 10 to 20% reduction in revenue and productivity. The authors claim that employees who report not being adequately recognized are three times more likely to quit during the following year.[100]

A *Harvard Business Review* blog cited a study of 60 teams. The factor that made the biggest difference between the most and least successful teams was the ratio among teammates of positive comments to negative ones. Among top-performing teams, members provided more than five positive comments for every criticism; among the lowest-performing teams, there were three negative comments for each positive comment.[101]

The body of research pertinent to the effects of recognition programs is small. A report by Bersin & Associates claimed that employers that excel at employee recognition are 12 times more likely to generate strong business results—a relatively vague criterion. The principal analyst for the report, Stacia Garr, noted that employers often underestimate just how much a strong recognition program can accomplish. The best programs boost employee engagement, reduce turnover, and "ultimately drive business performance."[102] More specifically, Garr claims that good recognition programs do a lot more than make employees feel better about their job. Based on a survey of 261 companies, companies with programs considered "excellent" had 31% lower voluntary turnover compared to companies with poor recognition programs.[103]

Although many organizations recognize years of service (and some companies award the traditional wristwatch after 25 years), relatively few companies recognize outstanding work on projects that have boosted organizational performance or customer satisfaction. A 2011 survey by WorldatWork (formerly the American Compensation Association) found that 34% of companies recognize employees for exemplary work behaviors. This was an increase of nine percentage points from data collected by World at Work in 2008.[104]

What is particularly noteworthy is that while 57% of CEOs reported that employees were regularly recognized, only 9% of employees strongly agreed that they were regularly recognized.[105] This finding confirms one of the fundamental premises of the Cube One framework: accurate data on employee- or enterprise-directed practices (as distinct from stated policies) needs to be obtained from employees.

Molina Healthcare Inc., a $6.4 billion company in the healthcare industry, provides a case study pertinent to employee recognition. Prior to 2012, the company distributed gift cards and on-the-spot rewards in a piecemeal fashion, many managers not bothering to provide rewards or recognition. In 2012, Molina implemented a systematic recognition program whereby Molina's 5,300 employees could send online "shout-outs" to colleagues, and supervisors could reward employees with points used toward purchases from a catalog with 50,000 items. The items ranged from movie tickets, to an iPad, to a rafting trip.[106] (A survey conducted by the Incentive Travel Foundation found that 96% of employees said they were motivated by travel incentives, and 72% who earned travel rewards said they felt increased loyalty to the company.[107])

Castle Medical Center in Hawaii uses point-based awards where points are only convertible into tangible items such as store gift cards or flat-screen TVs. Employees who sign up to work a less desirable shift receive points that they can save to make a purchase that, arguably, will be more memorable than extra cash.[108]

Another example is that of a recognition-based program implemented by a large public business school. The school's Service Excellence Initiative (SEI) was developed solely to recognize administrative assistants—individuals who had never previously received any accolades at annual award ceremonies. Electronic polling of thousands of students, faculty, and staff served to provide nominations, which often were accompanied by specific examples of excellent performance, (i.e., critical incidents). At the Annual Awards ceremony, the Dean read vignettes describing the specific work behaviors of each administrative assistant who received the SEI award; the names of the recipients were included in the Award ceremony brochure; the recipients received a personalized plaque and a check for $1,000. During the week prior to the ceremony, the Dean visited each award recipient at his or her workstation to give personal thanks. Subsequent to the ceremony, the first page of the College's website featured a photo of the recipients, and the winners were mentioned in the College's two student newspapers. An encased display of brass plaques with recipients' names was placed outside the Dean's office (with new names added each year). Evidence of effectiveness was obtained in two manners: first, by querying administrative assistants as to their reaction to the SEI process (90% approved); second (and more related to job performance), before and after faculty ratings of their satisfaction with "secretarial assistance" were examined, using data independently collected by the Educational Benchmarking Institute's bi-annual survey of about 100 work-related factors. After implementation of the SEI, the focal metric improved significantly.[109]

While incentives typically have positive effects on work behavior and job performance, some incentive plans have been found counterproductive. A small manufacturing company decided to issue a reward to all employees with perfect attendance during a three-month period (a calendar quarter). But if an employee had one absence during a quarter, the person tended to take extra days off in that quarter. Thus, in the final analysis, the company paid financial awards using an incentive plan that *increased* absenteeism.[110]

6. Measurement

The use of measurement in HPWS invariably takes the form of performance appraisals, often classified as part of the practice of performance management—which is based on an appraisal of the entirety of someone's job performance, as well as appropriate actions and interventions. A less encompassing form of measurement pertains to accomplishment of specific tasks or objectives.

Robert Pritchard and his colleagues have developed an impressive stream of research pertinent to measurement called ProMES, the Productivity Measurement and Enhancement System. Teams of subject matter experts identify four to six key objectives, which are then measured, typically, with a total of eight to 12 quantifiable measures, or "indicators." To illustrate, for the position of a photocopier repair technician, key objectives would include quality, cost, administration, attendance, and ambassadorship. These five objectives would then be measured by ten specific metrics including the cost of parts per service call, labor time per service call, and percentage of repeat service calls caused by a lack of spare parts. Per the ProMES protocol, after development and use of the measurement system, results are fed back to participants.[111]

A review of 83 studies that used the ProMES methodology examined results of interventions in seven countries: Australia, Germany, Hungary, Netherlands, Sweden, Switzerland, and the U.S. The mean result was that the change in performance from before ProMES to after its administration was d = 1.16, which means that, on average, the increase in productivity upon implementation of ProMES was 1.16 standard deviations higher than before the intervention. (Another way to look at this is that the typical company that underwent such intervention did better than 88% of companies without an intervention.) Two matters are especially noteworthy. Not only were the results very strong, they reflected a combination of the measurement of objective task indicators and the provision of objective feedback.[112]

Another line of research that has incorporated measurement of work behaviors is the AMC paradigm developed by Judi Komaki. In her book, *Leadership from an Operant Perspective*, results from more than a dozen studies support the conceptual framework that undergirds her work. She notes three central variables: antecedents, monitors, and consequences.[113] Antecedents are typically statements that correspond to goals. For example, a manager may state, repeatedly, "Remember that I need the 30-day summary report by Monday the 17h." (As an aside, Komaki demonstrated how the frequency of a manager's AMC behaviors can be charted, somewhat akin to musical notation. Ineffective managers repeatedly provided antecedents, [e.g., "don't forget to get the proposal to me ASAP"] and then there would be long pauses [denoted as rests], with the musical score sometimes never getting to the step of monitoring.)

Monitors are defined as attempts to get information about work behavior either by direct on-the-spot observations or indirectly via queries such as, "What is the status of your report?" Komaki found that monitoring has a profound effect on performance. Comparing average versus excellent managers, the difference in monitoring might be characterized as the "one percent effect." Excellent managers tended to devote 3% of their work behaviors to monitoring, frequently via in-person observations and discussions. Average managers would spend about 2% of their time monitoring performance.[114] Although the absolute difference is small, it represents 50% more time spent monitoring.

Komaki focused on the performance of a limited range of tasks, not on a comprehensive assessment of job performance. She found that monitors were more influential in terms of task performance than either antecedents or consequences. This seeming anomaly—given that incentives typically have had a stronger effect on performance than goals or feedback—may be explained by the fact that the primary consequences Komaki administered were oral: praisings or reprimands. Komaki concludes: "Managers usually get what they expect; they virtually always get what they inspect."[115]

Monitoring can become too close or intense. In the early days of Microsoft's founding, Bill Gates worked weekends and commonly pulled all-nighters. In a recent radio interview, Gates acknowledged that he did not believe in vacations. "I had to be a little careful not to try to apply my standards to how hard [others] worked," he said. "I knew everybody's license plate so I could look out at the parking lot and see, you know, when people came in."

Around this time, Bob Greenberg, a Harvard classmate of Gates, put in 81 hours in four days, working Monday through Thursday to finish a milestone. Late on Thursday, Gates asked Greenberg "What are you working on tomorrow?" Greenberg said he was planning to take the day off. Gates asked, "Why would you want to do that?"[116]

One company received some bad press recently because it required all employees to download an app on their cellphone that tracked employees' whereabouts 24/7. One employee, a salesperson, felt that her boss even knew how fast she was driving. After she deleted the app, she was fired. Her attorney claimed the policy was "akin to a felon's ankle bracelet."[117]

However, *self-monitoring* of progress increases goal attainment. In a meta-analysis of 138 studies with a total sample of nearly 20,000 individuals, self-monitoring of progress on goal attainment had a substantial impact. The result was stated in terms of the d statistic, i.e., mean standard deviation between individuals who (based on random selection) participated in self-monitoring of goals versus those who had goals but did not self-monitor. The resulting effect size was $d = 1.97$. According to well-established criteria, a d of 0.50 is "medium" and a d of 0.80 or above is "large." Hence, the result ($d = 1.97$) could most aptly be described as "immense." The effects were further enhanced when progress was made public or physically recorded (i.e., written down).[118]

However, the form of measurement typically incorporated in HRM research consists primarily of annual performance appraisals, which often introduce numerous measurement and administrative problems. As discussed below under the HRM practice of performance management, some scholars and consultants have virtually given up on the use of performance appraisals as a means of improving organizational job performance.

7. Accountability (and GMFAC)

When it comes to effective management of task performance, research and writing have identified five essential ingredients. Absent any one of these five components, and it will be difficult to attain excellent organizational (or individual) performance.[119] The five essential ingredients are: Goal, Measurement, Feedback, Accountability, and Consequences (GMFAC).

A goal, of course, is a standard of performance, akin to what F.W. Taylor a century ago referred to as "a fair day's work." Further, it is widely recognized that an effective goal should be a SMART goal: Specific, Measurable, Attainable, Relevant, and Time-defined. As Pulakos notes in, *Performance Management*, "specific" means no injunctions such as "do your best" or "try your hardest." Goals should be measurable (which is why in religious organizations, the objective of saving souls may be problematic.) If the goal is unrealistically difficult, performance will likely decline; people will metaphorically throw their hands up and think, "This is ridiculous." Some commentators define the A in SMART as "Agreed-upon. Others say the A stands for Achievable. The R component refers to relevant, and T to time defined (e.g., clean eight blocks daily).

Having a goal is step one. A budget is a goal, as is a work timeline with milestones. However, accomplishments must be measured in the metric of the goal. What good is a budget or a timeline if they merely reside in a computer file, a testament to the completion of a perfunctory but ultimately useless activity? Pritchard and Komaki have demonstrated the need for measurement—which unfortunately, in practice, often consists of a relatively subjective assessment of overall job performance, often incorporated in an annual review.

Feedback is essential to HRM practices. However, not all forms of feedback are equal. Feedback should be as objective as possible, and provided using the metric of the goal(s). It would appear, though, that surprisingly few organizations provide timely and useful feedback. As noted above, the Aer Lingus reservationists were astonished to discover how frequently they interrupted callers and how infrequently they used callers' names.[120]

Accountability pertains to answerability. Employees should be responsible for their work behaviors and answerable for outcomes with respect to goal attainment. The failure to achieve a goal may indicate poor performance; but extenuating circumstances may exist. That is why an apt definition of task performance is not isomorphic with results; but rather Performance = f (results, considering). If, for example, despite substantial and uncontrollable (exogenous) impediments, a goal is almost achieved, performance might be deemed exemplary. High Performance Work Practices rarely include holding employees accountable for performance. This may be because "count" is central to accountability. Unless specific work behaviors or outcomes are tracked (or counted), accountability is largely a façade.[121]

Consequences are widely used in organizational settings, but not always contingent on appropriate factors. Sometimes consequences are unrelated to work behaviors and job performance, based instead on longevity or personal connections. Per the classic article "On the Folly of Rewarding A and Hoping for B," it is not uncommon for high performers to be "rewarded" with additional work to accomplish, while their less industrious peers are often ignored, or in some settings promoted, that being the only way to get rid of a non-performer.[122]

The GMFAC paradigm has been employed to improve performance in work settings. In "The Case of the Missing Charts" the percentage of unavailable medical records (charts) at a large urban hospital was reduced by more than 50%, a reduction accomplished within 100 days at a minimal cost.[123] Similarly, use of the GMFAC paradigm reduced patient waiting time in an emergency room by more than 50% in 100 days, again at minimal cost.[124] (Parenthetically, the medical director of the hospital at the outset told the consultants/trainers that if they could solve the emergency room problem they would deserve a Nobel prize. Nearly two decades later, the consultants/trainers continue to await their prize.)

The GMFAC paradigm can also be used to analyze instances of managerial failure. In the case "I Follow a Garbage Truck," sanitation workers devoted only 97 minutes in an eight-hour workday to performing work (pickup up refuse and/or sweeping streets). An examination of the facts of the case indicates the absence of all five components: goal setting, measurement, feedback, accountability, consequences.[125]

A study by Nicholas Bloom and colleagues parallels the GMFAC framework. The study measured the frequency and effects of three management practices in large samples of organizations in 20 countries: (1) performance monitoring (M); (2) target setting (G); and (3) incentives (C). Data were collected from more than 10,000 organizations.[126] In manufacturing organizations, the primary outcome variables examined were productivity, profitability, and growth. For hospitals, a key outcome variable was the risk-adjusted survival rate after an emergency heart attack admission. With respect to schools, educational achievement was ascertained by examining multiple indicators, including math exam scores and average exam marks.

In the words of the Bloom and colleagues, management practices explained "the astounding differences in performance across firms and countries." There were substantial differences in the use of the three key management practices across countries—see Table 2.1. The top five countries in terms of composite management scores (in the manufacturing sector) were the U.S., Japan, Germany, Sweden, and Canada. The countries with the lowest management scores were India, Brazil, China, Greece, and Argentina. A one standard deviation increase in the management score was associated with a 45% increase in labor productivity.

Furthermore, the researchers found a remarkably high correlation between overall management practice scores and per capita gross domestic product (GDP). Specifically, they found a correlation of 0.90. This extraordinarily large correlation substantiates the researchers' (unduly cautious) claim that management practices may contribute to national productivity and per capita GDP.

The irreverent Andy Kessler commented on the findings reported by the Economic Policy Institute: "The level of productivity is the single most important determinant of a country's standard of living, with faster productivity growth leading to an increasingly better standard of living." In Kessler's inimitably provocative

TABLE 2.1 Management Practices Scores by Country

Country	Monitoring	Targets	Incentives	Overall	Percentile Rank
Argentina	3.08	2.67	2.56	2.76	20
Australia	3.27	3.02	2.75	3.02	60
Brazil	3.06	2.69	**2.55**	2.71	5
Canada	3.54	3.07	2.94	3.17	8
Chile	3.14	2.72	2.67	2.83	25
China	**2.90**	**2.62**	2.69	2.71	5
France	3.41	2.95	2.73	3.02	60
Germany	3.57	3.21	2.98	3.23	90
Greece	2.97	2.65	2.58	2.73	15
India	2.91	2.66	2.63	**2.67**	0
Italy	3.25	3.09	2.76	3.02	60
Japan	3.50	**3.34**	2.92	3.23	90
Mexico	3.29	2.89	2.71	2.92	45
New Zealand	3.18	2.96	2.63	2.93	50
Poland	3.12	2.94	2.83	2.90	40
Portugal	3.27	2.83	2.59	2.87	30
Republic of Ireland	3.14	2.81	2.79	2.89	35
Sweden	**3.63**	3.18	2.83	3.20	85
U.K.	3.32	2.97	2.85	3.02	60
U.S.	3.57	3.25	**3.25**	**3.35**	**100**
Average	3.28	2.94	2.82	2.99	55

Scores on each practice ranged from 1 to 5. Bold numbers denote the highest and lowest scores for each variable. Percentile rank data were computed by this author based on overall scores; for example, the percentile rank of 60 for a country would indicate it scores higher than 60% of other countries surveyed in terms of overall management practices.

manner, he succinctly summed up the relationship: "Increase productivity = better living. Bingo."[127]

8. Delegation, Decentralization, Participation

In a study of HPWPs in rural electric industry companies, Luthans and Sommer examined 11 different HPWPs. Two of the 11 were job design programs (including job enlargement and job enrichment) and participation programs (which included quality circles and self-managed work teams). Whereas data are usually analyzed across the composite of all HPWPs, or for the three widely adopted categories of practices (Motivation, Ability, and Opportunity), Luthans and Sommer have presented results separately for each of the 11 practices. With regard to the organizational performance criterion of distribution efficiency, job design and participation were the second and third most highly related HPWPs. (Internal advancement opportunity was the most highly related HPWP.)[128]

In his text, *Control in Organizations*, Arnold Tannenbaum, an early researcher on delegation and decentralization presents abundant evidence that managers gain power "by giving it away." Per what he calls the "paradox of control," power and influence in organizations do not constitute a zero-sum game. Rather, Tannenbaum demonstrates a sizable association between perceived (and actual) power on the part of employees and organizational performance (with $R = 0.65$).[129]

Jiang and colleagues looked at the three categories of HPWPs, one being the opportunity-enhancing practices of flexible job design, employee involvement, and participation in work teams. All three categories of HPWPs were examined in terms of their relationships with human capital, motivation, operational outcomes, and financial outcomes. As predicted, opportunity-enhancing practices were positively associated with human capital, motivation, operational, and financial outcomes. The authors concluded that investing in opportunity-enhancing practices would yield "substantial financial benefits."[130]

A study conducted among employees of the English National Health Service (NHS)—the world's largest publicly funded health service—examined employee perceptions of five HR dimensions. Two of the dimensions related to employee involvement and job design. Although financial results (the key dependent variable) were not broken down by category of HR practice, overall HR practices were significantly related to customer satisfaction (0.26) and financial performance (0.16).[131]

Chang and colleagues identified a number of practices that have been widely seen as consistent with High-Commitment Work Systems (a term analogous to HPWPs. Among the practices Chang et al. identified were job rotation, job design (which expanded job scope), and participative leadership. Analyzing data from 102 firms in China, it was found that HCWSs were associated with a higher level of individual creativity, especially within cohesive teams.[132]

Organizing employees into self-managed teams is a central component of HPWPs—and it pays off. The Honeywell defense avionics plant achieved an increase in on-time delivery (from less than 40% to as high as 99%) and attributed the result to the implementation of teams.[133] In another manufacturing company, work teams achieved a 38% reduction in the defect rate and a 20% increase in productivity.[134] Similarly, Proctor & Gamble reported that productivity increased in various facilities by up to 40% when plants used team-based production.[135]

Pfeffer explains why self-managed teams are generally effective. First, employees are often more concerned about peer pressure than pressure from their supervisor. A coworker's absence falls on his or her teammates. Second, teams can facilitate cross-training, the delegation of authority, and a concomitant increase in responsibility and accountability. The Ritz-Carlton Hotel chain provides each employee the discretion to spend up to $2,500 with no approval needed, in order to respond to guest complaints.[136]

Third, teams can help elicit creative solutions to problems, and superior ways to perform tasks. Teams have found ways to provide superior customer service, and have participated in the selection of new employees (future teammates). Fourth, to the extent teams are given the authority to make decisions, organizations are flatter and less bureaucratic.

An example of a truly flat organization is ContextMedia, which creates and distributes health-focused programming. The two founders have 12 department heads, the only layer in a 160-person company. Part of the selection process includes an inquiry as to whether candidates have previously organized volunteer groups for their school, community, or house of worship—activities consistent with working in a flat organization.[137]

Mike Curtis, vice president of engineering at Airbnb, insists that bureaucracy is not inevitable. Instead of enforcing lots of rules and procedures, he prefers to trust employees' discretion, thereby chopping through red tape.[138] For example, whereas the old rule was that all expenses required pre-approval, Curtis told employees that they should treat expenditures as if they were spending their own money. Only if they might think twice about a particular expenditure should they "gut-check" it with their manager.[139]

At QuikTrip, an $11 billion company with 722 stores, employees are expected to solve problems themselves, and make merchandising decisions for their own stores. Zeynep Ton, a professor at MIT and author of *The Good Jobs Strategy*, notes that QuikTrip provides good pay and considerable employee discretion. At QuikTrip, products do not remain in the back room. Employees are empowered and encouraged to run in-store promotions to sell off inventory that would otherwise languish on the shelves.[140]

A prominent management theorist who promoted the practice of delegation was Douglas McGregor. In his classic 1960 book, *The Human Side of Enterprise*, McGregor argued that managerial assumptions about employee capabilities can become self-fulfilling prophecies. The manager who assumes employees are lazy, irresponsible, and lacking useful ideas will closely supervise employees and not delegate any authority. The employee finding no satisfaction in the job besides his/her (meager) paycheck, will show little enthusiasm or engagement. Then the manager (ironically) may complain to a colleague "you can't get good help anymore"—with the manager completely unaware that he/she has engineered the lack of motivation that is lamented. McGregor asserted that with good management (including a positive set of attitudes and corresponding behaviors), employees will demonstrate unimaginable levels of creative human energy.[141]

An illustration of McGregor's theorizing and its pertinence to organizational performance includes the following interview with a successful executive:

Q. Any managers you've had who influenced you?
A. One of them had this belief in people—that you can do more than you think you can. To me, that's so powerful. If you believe in someone, even

more than they believe in themselves, they will do anything to succeed. They will do everything they can not to let you down.[142]

Consistent with the mindset (or cosmology) of McGregor is the comment of J.W. Marriott, who stated: "The four most important words in the English Language are, 'What do you think?' Listen to your employees and learn."[143]

9. Performance Management

Perhaps the most central single HPWP is performance management, to which the performance appraisal and review process are basic. However, the measurement of job performance is widely considered the single biggest problem in I/O psychology. Years of research have focused on such issues as the format of rating scales, e.g., whether to use graphic rating scales (e.g., "meets expectations"), or behavior-based ratings (e.g., the frequency of greeting a customer with a smile), or narrative examples of exemplary or poor performance (i.e., critical incidents). On this first issue, a 15-year research program conducted by Tziner and colleagues has led to the conclusion that performance measures employing a behavioral observation scale (BOS) are superior in many regards to the more conventional graphic rating scale (GRS) format. BOS ratings are based on the observed frequency of specific, "pinpointed" actions (e.g., "the sales assistant straightens the racks and shelves when necessary" or "the ratee completes all sections of the crime report"). GRS ratings identify relatively broad, and hence more subjective, performance dimensions (e.g., "the sales assistant provides good customer service," or "the ratee is attentive to details." Evidence from six field studies indicates that the BOS format has multiple advantages. It improves rater-ratee communication; goal setting (i.e., greater goal clarity, goal acceptance, and goal commitment); ratee acceptance of the feedback received; ratee satisfaction with the appraisal process; ratee job performance over time; and rater satisfaction, as there is less fear of confrontations.[144]

Unfortunately, rating format is just one of many issues that complicate the performance appraisal process. Others include whether to use ratings, results, or rankings, the latter being based on peer comparisons—which in many ways are problematic.[145] Further, I/O psychologists have also long been concerned with issues such as rater errors (e.g., halo error, recency error, and leniency vs. harshness), rater bias, rater experience, frequency of observations, the use of "forced distributions," and the best source (e.g., peers, subordinates, supervisors) and number of people providing ratings.

As noted above, a performance assessment should be based on a systematic job analysis, and the validity of performance ratings must be established using independent criteria. Furthermore, the number of issues concerning performance appraisals has consistently expanded over time. Besides the technical problems, there are questions as to how performance rating information should be communicated to the focal employee, and whether the rater should encourage ratee self–evaluations. Should positive feedback precede the discussion of areas where improvement is necessary? What should the rater do if the ratee disagrees with the areas for improvement or with the overall rating?

Even more vexing are the practical difficulties associated with performance appraisals such as the potential for ratings to reflect non-performance criteria, e.g., political considerations. As Alan Patz noted, "the most obvious barrier to effective performance appraisal is [employee] suspicion (if not certainty) that data falsification for selfish purposes actively persists." According to Patz, employees believe that managers "game" the system to their own advantage, reporting false evaluations of their direct reports.[146]

Less sinister, perhaps, is that the performance appraisal process may be carried out with insincerity and cynicism—many managers viewing the performance appraisal process as a pointless activity that must be completed at least annually. Moreover, assessing the performance of every direct report's performance on multiple dimensions, and preparing to defend these judgments, take time. As Murphy and Cleveland have noted, "if the appraisal system is seen by most raters and ratees as a waste of time, it is hard to see how the appraisal system will accomplish worthwhile goals."[147]

According to Felix Lopez, more often than not, managers report that the performance review process produces negative emotions, and because criticism is generally not well received, subsequent performance actually gets worse.[148] Consequently, many managers dread the performance review process far more than a visit to the dentist. Tim Hall and Ed Lawler have labeled this phenomenon the "vanishing performance appraisal." Because so many managers have found that performance reviews yield negative results, managers frequently attempt to avoid performance reviews altogether; but if this is not possible, they postpone them, and then hurriedly give brief comments on the way out the door to catch a plane.[149]

Ratee reactions to the performance appraisal and review process have seen intense research attention since the 1990s.[150] Two factors in particular have been found to improve ratee acceptance. First, as noted above, the use of ratings based on absolute standards (such as facilitated by BOS metrics) are viewed by ratees as much fairer than those that are relative to peers.[151] Peer-based evaluations (rankings) are outside the control of the ratee; and they tend to be subjective as 50% of ratees inescapably wind up in the bottom-half of the performance distribution (even in companies with high performing workforces).

Second, when raters receive frame of reference (FOR) training rather than rater error training (RET)—the latter having practically disappeared from the literature over the past two decades—the process becomes fairer.[152] FOR training provides a definition of job performance, which is paralleled by developing categories of behaviors that constitute effective job performance.[153]

Two scholars with extensive practical experience have each authored authoritative books on performance management.[154,155] Their texts address the problems associated with performance management, and they provide detailed practical guidance to address the salient issues. The biggest challenges include the difficulties associated with implementing a complex, time-bound, and inevitably increasingly bureaucratic system.

In 2011, two years after the publication of her text on performance management, Elaine Pulakos coauthored an article published in an eminent journal entitled "Why is performance management broken?" In essence, the article emphasized two major problems associated with implementing performance management: (1) it is difficult to develop cascading goals that funnel through the entire organization, being translated into divisional, departmental/functional levels, all the way down to individuals; and (2) political problems arise, associated with inflated ratings provided by managers hoping to gain added resources for their work team. Her article concluded that "the formula for effective performance management is yet to be discovered."[156] She advised scaling down the performance management process to focus on building trust through informal relationships, and providing ongoing feedback at a granular (i.e., specific task) level.

Along these lines, a 2015 article in *Harvard Business Review* reported that the 65,000+ employee consulting firm, Deloitte Consulting, has "radically redesigned" its own performance management system. Deloitte has abandoned such widely advocated practices as cascading objectives, annual performance reviews, and 360-degree feedback. Rather, they emphasize day-to-day management feedback, and have managers conduct weekly check-ins with their team members.[157]

In the most recent "chapter" in the performance management saga, Pulakos and colleagues reiterated that performance management (PM) "is profoundly broken;" that virtually all managers (95%) dislike the process; and most employees (59%) see the review process as not worthwhile.[158] Yet, the title of their piece is "Performance Management Can Be Fixed." They argue that PM needs to shift from focusing on the formal system of cascading goals and the accompanying detailed bureaucratic procedures (often confounded by the subjective and idiosyncratic ratings that managers provide), to a more collaborative, streamlined process that directs attention to critical day-to-day PM behaviors. They recommend scaling back the scope of PM focusing on the enterprise task performance, and building trusting relationships that enhance employee growth, engagement, and job performance. Consistent with the Deloitte approach is the process described next.

An effective performance management review process

According to Lenny Rachistky, a former project lead at Airbnb, performance reviews are severely underutilized, and often done badly. From the perspective of direct reports they are more likely to spark dread than hope; and on the part of managers they're often treated more as a chore than an opportunity. "Done well, performance reviews improve the performance of direct reports, align expectations, and accelerate a report's career. Done poorly, they accelerate their departure."

Rachitsky recommends a three-step, end-to-end system that can systematically develop star performers, turn big trouble spots into super-strengths, and build a stellar team. The first step is thorough preparation. This entails obtaining detailed, specific performance information from five to eight knowledgeable people to provide input about the performance of a direct report. They should be asked to specify: the two to three things the focal person (FP) should start doing; the two to three things FP should continue doing; and the two to three things FP should stop doing.

The second step is to provide detailed and specific feedback to the direct report. At least two-thirds of the review process should be devoted to development. According to Rachitsky, ambitious people want to know not just how to get better, but how to "blow it out of the water." The manager should paint a picture for direct reports as to what "killing it" looks like, and how this can be accomplished by the next performance review. (The second step is consonant with the process of AI.)

The third step entails continuous follow up. It is unrealistic to think that "carefully chosen words of wisdom" are all that is needed to create a star performer. If a manager cannot find a dozen hours, annually, to focus on a direct report's career, this means that the manager either has too many reports, or shouldn't be a manager.[159]

10. Less Conventional People-Based Practices

More than 100 organizations have carried delegation and decentralization to the level of Holocracy, an avant-garde management approach that eliminates titles, bosses, and hierarchy. One of the chief advocates of Holocracy is Tony Hsieh, the CEO of Zappos, now a division of Amazon. According to a company that provides training in Holocracy, a full transition can take companies years, and many group meetings, to achieve. The 67 new employees who joined Zappos in June 2015 participated in about 200 extra meetings during the first year.[160]

Researchers at the University of Missouri studied meetings conducted by 555 undergraduate students assigned to 111 groups. The groups required to hold meetings while standing (as opposed to sitting) took 34% less time to make decisions. Pfeffer and Sutton noted that if Chevron, a company with over 50,000 employees, required that their annual 20-minute meetings were conducted in a stand-up fashion, Chevron would save about seven minutes per meeting—or nearly 6,000 hours per year.[161]

When team productivity data were analyzed, Alex "Sandy" Portland and colleagues found that among the best predictors of productivity was employee engagement with colleagues outside of formal meetings. So, at a bank's call center, management revised employees' coffee break schedules to enable everyone on a given team to take a break at the same time. This allowed more time to socialize with teammates. Subsequently, average handling time fell by more than 8%t overall, with lower performing teams showing the biggest improvement. Extrapolating results across all ten of the bank's call centers (which employed 25,000 people), the bank anticipated a savings of $15 million annually due to increased productivity.[162]

At Gerson Lehrman Group, all 250 employees can choose on a daily basis where to locate their workspace. Equipped with laptops and telephone headsets, employees can sit in an office, or a cubicle, or in the sun-splashed atrium furnished with comfy chairs. According to Erik Veldhoen, author of *The Demise of the Office*, this flexibility prompts employees to structure their days more productively. Some managers, however, find that the practice of "musical chairs" is a hard sell. They have to cope with people not being in their line of sight.[163] Along these lines at the UN headquarters in New York City several departments now encourage members to use lounges and other public areas (often beautiful spaces sponsored by country delegations) to conduct their daily work tasks as well as some meetings.

Going in the opposite direction, Sophie Kelly, CEO of the Barbarian Group, wants her 125-person digital ad agency to sit at *one* table. So she had a 4,400 square-foot desk constructed. The "superdesk" can presently accommodate 175 people, giving the Barbarian Group plenty of room to grow. No evidentiary support has been provided regarding the efficacy of this seating arrangement.[164]

Dan Hill, a face reader, uses his skill to predict the performance of basketball players. Employing the psychologist Paul Eckman's widely accepted Facial Action Coding Systems (FACS), Hill is able to ascertain which of the face's 43 muscles are working at any moment. Working for the Milwaukee Bucks and other teams, Hill has provided some impressive effectiveness evidence. Among "successful" players, positive emotions (e.g., joy, pleasure, curiosity) are present 39% of the time. In contrast, among "problem players," positive emotions are only visibly present 9% of the time. It is unclear, though, if basketball success evokes particular facial muscles or facial muscles predict performance. Further, it is unclear whether Hill's methodology can be usefully employed for employee selection.[165]

High Performance Work Practices: A Review of Selected Research Evidence

In light of the abundant evidence reviewed thus far, the next section summarizes the findings of six large-scale studies that present evidence of the effects of HPWPs.

- Mark Huselid, in an initial demonstration of "bottom-line results," found that a one standard deviation improvement in HPWPs was associated with a 7% decrease in turnover; increased sales per employee of $27,000 a year; an annual per employee increase in profits of $4,000; and an increase in firm market value of $18,000 per employee.[166] This research was conducted in 1995, and today's financial impact would certainly be larger in terms of dollar amounts.

- Huselid and colleagues found that a one standard deviation increase in HRM effectiveness corresponded to an annual 5.2% increase in sales per employee; an estimated 16.3% increase in cash flow per employee; and an estimated 6% increase in market value.[167]
- Jiang and colleagues found that motivation-, skill-, and opportunity-enhancing practices all have positive associations with financial outcomes (correlations being 0.27, 0.26, and 0.20, respectively).[168]
- Stajkovic and Luthans found that the combined effects of money, feedback, and social recognition were sizable ($d = 0.47$) which corresponded to a 16% improvement in performance.[169]
- Rabl and colleagues examined data from 29 countries and found a significant correlation (.29) between HPWS practices and business performance. Surprisingly, results were stronger where there was low cultural consistency per traditional cultural perspectives.[170]
- Aryee and colleagues examined data from 37 branches of banks in Ghana. They found that individual-level perceptions of HPWS practices exert a sizable influence on branch-level service performance.[171]

Productivity Improvement through Operations Management

Enterprise-directed practices encompass a number of disciplines related to finding superior methods of operating an enterprise. In addition to the HPWS practices reviewed above, there is another major category of interventions including the adoption of new operational strategies, the implementation of new technologies, organizational reengineering through lean management and Six Sigma, supply chain management, and what has been called the Toyota Way/Toyota Production System (TPS).

Productivity Improvement from Operations Strategy

Superior operational results can be attained through strategies that depart from industry norms. Consider, for example, the strategic innovations introduced by Southwest Airlines, which greatly affected the airline industry. Southwest relied on five key strategic initiatives: (1) rapid turnaround of incoming planes (the goal being ten minutes—because a plane sitting idle makes no money); (2) only point-to-point flights (eliminating hubs and the complexities and potential negative repercussions associated with connecting flights); (3) the use of only one aircraft model (so pilots, the flight team, and mechanics can develop exceptional expertise); (4) the use of secondary airport terminals to avoid congestion, reduce costs and delays, and provide room for expansion; and (5) charging relatively low prices (as the company sees itself competing on price with automobiles and buses, not other airlines).[172]

McDonalds has revolutionized the fast-food industry by enabling customers to be served in three minutes. Sandwiches are prepared in anticipation of demand, which both reduces costs and customer waiting time. The restaurant chain Subway charges a small premium for food that is always made-to-order, and customers wait longer. Starbucks charges an even higher premium for a wide array of coffee products and an ambiance that encourages customers to linger. More importantly, it allows customers to self-price-target by selecting a beverage that is only a mild variation of a basic coffee (e.g., a cappuccino), and differentiate themselves from other customers through their choice and (self-selected) upcharge. The company had six stores in Seattle in 1986; it had more than 24,000 in 70 countries in 2016.[173]

Productivity Improvement from New Technology

New technologies also bring rapid productivity improvements. A fascinating early example of the implementation of a new technology resulted from a book published in 1202 by Leonardo de Pisa (nicknamed Fibonacci). The book *Liber Abaci* (or *The Book of Calculations*) introduced Arabic numerals to the European commercial world. Previously, Roman numerals were commonly used—but were agonizingly difficult to use for computational calculations. To get around the Roman numeral problem, skilled and highly paid clerks used table-sized abaci. (Lacking a way to check on the accuracy of a computation, calculations needed to be performed twice to see if the same answer emerged.) Bankers and merchants relied heavily on the abacus technicians. After being rendered obsolete by Arabic numerals, though, the abacus technicians went to the government for help. Several Italian city-states passed laws requiring the use of Roman numerals and forbidding the Arabic system.[174]

In the industrial age, Henry Ford achieved a dramatic increase in productivity when he adopted the continuously moving assembly line. In 1908, prior to the adoption of the new technology, 28 employees produced 175 assemblies per day or 6.3 assemblies per person per day (i.e., CLXXV ÷ XXVIII). By 1914, eight employees assembled 2,600 cars per day, or 325 per employee.[175]

The development of containerized shipping created an impressive gain in productivity. Prior to 1955, no one had designed a containerized ship with a special crane so that containers could easily move from a truck or train to a ship. Malcolm McLean's first containerized ship sailed from Newark to Houston, ignoring the warnings of skeptics such as The *New York Times*, which predicted that the boat would never work and would sink. By the 1960s, containerization had reduced the cost of loading a ship from $5.86 to 16 cents a ton, a 97% reduction. As containerized shipping caught on, global exports rose from

$127.3 billion in 1960 to $22.6 trillion in 2012, according to a United Nations yearbook of statistics.[176]

A more recent technology, data science, is driving operational productivity today. Consider, for example, a small-budget housing rental company that employed predictive modeling software from SAS business tools analytics. By culling information from years of spreadsheets, along with market conditions, seasonal trends, the size and location of a home, among other criteria, they achieved an increase in bookings of more than 10% plus an increase of profits/booking of 15%. The company hoped that the gains from data analytics would pay off in three years; in fact the payoff took less than ten months.[177] Similarly, companies such as Uber have achieved high efficiency in their operations using data analytics that matches customers (riders) to service providers (drivers)—allowing them to match the two even before drivers have concluded their current trips, thus increasing the number of trips accepted and dollar commissions achieved.

Consider how a zoo management company collaborated with IBM to parse historical attendance records along with years of climate data provided by the National Weather Service. Predictive models led to new insights that helped the zoo anticipate with surprising precision how many customers would show up on a given weekend. This, in turn, enabled the zoo to determine, down to the hour, how many employees should be staffing the gates, carousels, and other positions. Additionally, knowing the times of day when customers booked online, the company was able to increase online ticket sales by 770% and new memberships by offering—at specified times—time-limited deals. Says Donna Powell, the zoo's business and administrative services manager: "for a minimal investment of less than $4,000, we sold $60,000 worth of memberships."[178]

In addition to predictive analytics, prescriptive optimization models from the field of Operations research have yielded big savings. For example, UPS's ORION (On-Road-Integrated Optimization and Navigation) truck-routing software system was developed in 2015 by a 500-person think tank, and was set to launch in 2017. Based on a test with 10,000 drivers, UPS claimed that ORION would save about 45 million gallons of fuel annually using an algorithm that solves the venerable "traveling salesman problem" that every UPS driver faces daily. UPS claims that the number of ways a driver can deliver a day's parcels, i.e., the possible route combinations a driver can make in a day is "far greater than the number of nanoseconds the earth has existed." Concomitant with the fuel savings are sizable financial savings. A reduction in travel of just one mile a day saves the company about $50 million a year.[179] Fed Ex uses similar advanced analytics to save time and fuel. Their Route Optimization and Decision Support system (ROADS) tries to make as many right turns as possible, because left turns take more time.[180] While the idea of realizing efficiency through the prediction of future demand (based on historical data) certainly isn't new, cheap and readily available computing power means that "big data" (these and other large data sets) can be deployed much more easily to make business decisions in real time.

Productivity Improvement from Improved Processes

Upon leveraging sound operational strategies, and adopting new technologies, manufacturing and service firms can further improve productivity by improving operational processes incrementally. In the 1990s, the most popular framework for improving productivity was known as Total Quality Management (TQM), but the term lost favor by 2000.[181]

The techniques that replaced TQM remain popular today: lean management that eliminates waste, and Six Sigma, which reduces process variability. (Both trace their roots to the same foundations as TQM.) In the 1950s, the methods of two prominent U.S. consultants, W. Edwards Deming and Joseph Juran, were widely adopted in Japan. One company that quietly adopted quality improvement methods was Toyota, which developed what is known today as the Toyota Production System (TPS), or alternately as the Toyota Way.

Lean Management, Six Sigma, and TPS not only share the same roots. They capitalize on the fact that repetitive processes can be broken into steps that can be reengineered to improve system performance. Two key questions are, "How should workers specialize?" and "Does an assembly-line process necessarily yield optimal results in terms of productivity?"

The advantages of specialization and the implementation of an assembly line were vividly demonstrated by Adam Smith in *The Wealth of Nations* (1776). Smith estimated that one experienced pin production employee—working alone— could at most produce 20 pins in a day. Smith noted, however that with specialization the process is as follows:

> One worker draws out the wire, another straightens it, a third cuts it, a fourth points it; a fifth grinds it at the top for receiving the head; to make the head requires two or three distinct operations; to put it on is a distinct business, to whiten the pins is another; it is even a trade by itself to put them into the paper.

There were 18 specialized tasks with inherent delays between necessary steps. However, ten specialized workers assembled in an assembly line (that minimized delays inherent in the production process), could produce 48,000 pins in a day. Thus, the daily output of pins per employee increased from 20 to 4,800.[182]

Fast-forward 217 years. In their work on reengineering, Michael Hammer and James Champy have shown how the assembly line approach to clerical work is often very inefficient.[183] In Hammer's words: "It is time to stop paving the cow paths … [rather] we should obliterate them" by reengineering businesses using the power of information technology. Hammer has described how reengineering helped Mutual Benefit Life dramatically improve the processing of insurance applications, where typical turnarounds ranged from five to 24 days. Mutual identified 30 discrete steps, spanning five departments (e.g., credit checking, quoting, rating, underwriting), most of the time being spent passing information from one department to the next. Mutual created the position of case manager, who had total responsibility for an application from the time it was received to the issuance of a policy. Processing time shrank to four hours. Customers were pleased and sales agents delighted, because customers no longer had to wait up to 24 days—during which time they could change their minds. The result was better service and increased efficiency as there was no need for supervisors to monitor clerks.[184] Another insurance company estimated that while an application spent 22 days being processed, it was actually worked on for just 17 minutes.[185]

Henry Ford was, arguably, the first to demonstrate the efficacy of the assembly line approach coupled with the concepts of Just-In-Time (JIT) inventory and the assembly-line transportation system—as described in his 1922 autobiography, *My Life and Work*.[186]

Toyota subsequently elaborated on Ford's ideas regarding JIT manufacturing to change the production system used in auto assembly. Traditional auto manufacturers employed assembly lines with big-batch systems that entailed slow-moving streams of materials and parts meandering through warehouses and factories. In contrast, Toyota factories featured smooth, narrow, fast-moving streams from suppliers to customer. JIT at Toyota relied on two rules: (1) Make only what is needed, when and in the amount needed; and (2) defects do not flow (production must be stopped until the source of a problem is identified and fixed.)[187] Of course, in-depth predictive analyses of consumer demand must accompany the JIT process. Toyota learned this the hard way when wait times for Prius hybrid models averaged several months in the early- and mid-2000s.

The company Lolly Wolly Doodle provides a fascinating, modern-day example of JIT. Its founder, Brandi Temple, went from sewing dresses for her daughters in order to make ends meet, to running one of the most talked about e-commerce companies, with revenues rising from zero in 2008 to more than $11 million in 2013. Her business model was simple. Temple, who never held a corporate job, started making single (one-off) copies of several dolls and posted photos of them several times a day on her Facebook page. Over time she developed 900,000 fans (a feat that astonished an executive at Zappos, a company with 1.5 million followers at the time). Fans would order by leaving details as to sizes and monograms and simply commenting on Temple's post while leaving their email address and product specifications. The company would "scrape" customer contact information from the Facebook Wall and start production only after receiving payment. Lolly would make only as many products as were ordered—thereby having no excess inventory. Temple obviated the traditional paradigm of manufacturing and stocking multiple models in various colors and sizes.[188]

As Toyota perfected its production methods, efficiencies were the result of more than its JIT methodology. The paradigm shift at Toyota was initially described merely as lean management. The focus shifted to systematically identifying and removing seven types of waste—transport, inventory, motion, waiting, overproducing, overprocessing, and defects (or the acronym TIMWOOD for short).[189]

By removing waste, an organization removes non-value-added activities from the business process. This enhances the benefits associated with improved productivity: improved customer satisfaction due to quicker service, reduced costs (and potentially reduced prices), and capability of providing better outcomes for employees.

Consider, for example, a non-value-added activity as simple as motion. Katsuaki Watanabe, a past president and CEO of Toyota expressed—with passion—his dedication to curtailing motion. As he put it,

> Take the movements of parts in a factory. Moving components doesn't add to their value; on the contrary, it destroys value, because parts may be dropped or scratched. So the movement of components should be as limited as possible. I want our production engineers to take on the challenge of ensuring that things move as little as possible—close to the theoretical limit of zero—on shop floors. Doing this requires courage and radical thinking.[190]

Most illustrations of the application of lean management techniques exist in the form of the write-ups or case studies of a single organization. However, a comprehensive study examined 13 lean management techniques enacted across 187 companies in Thailand, thereby providing systematic effectiveness evidence.[191] The 13 practices (which included implementing preventive maintenance; reducing inventory; using new process equipment or technologies; removing bottlenecks; and eliminating waste) clustered, statistically, into three factors: JIT, waste minimization, and flow management. All three factors were related (based on survey data) to four indicators of organizational performance: quicker delivery compared to competitors; lower unit costs compared to competitors; overall productivity; and customer satisfaction. Results were independent of ownership (Thai, foreign, or joint), and stronger in enterprises with more than 200 employees.[192]

The development of lean management and the TPS have been attributed to Taiichi Ohno, and trace back to the 1950s.[193] An extensive amount of literature has developed regarding the principles that comprise the "Toyota Way," and delineation of the number of principles depends on the level of detail addressed. The Toyota Way consists of 14 management principles.[194] However, at a less detailed level of analysis, Katsuaki Watanabe, a past CEO, identified five management principles.[195] Examined on a still broader basis, three fundamental principles can be discerned.

One of the three key TPS principles is the philosophy of *kaizen*—a management approach characterized by the unrelenting and unremitting quest for continuous improvement—and this principle is clearly central. The roots of the term appear in the Japanese words *"kai"* (meaning change) and *"zen"* (meaning good).

With regard to historical provenance, kaizen is arguably similar to F. W. Taylor's "search for the one best way" as delineated in his 1911 book, *The Principles of Scientific Management.*[196]

A powerful illustration of the centrality of *kaizen* to Toyota appears in Charles Fishman's *Fast Company* article, "No Satisfaction at Toyota." Unlike most U.S. manufacturers, which episodically roll out improvement programs under the direction of an engineering team (accompanied by much fanfare, PowerPoint slides, and elaborate celebrations of occasional achievements), Toyota's insatiable competitiveness is quiet, internal, self-critical, and rooted in an institutional obsession with improvement. Complacency regarding yesterday's accomplishments is not allowed. In fact, the process of continuous improvement is so paramount that Toyota has developed a process for teaching how to improve the process.[197]

James Wiseman, an experienced factory manager, joined the Toyota plant in Georgetown, Kentucky in 1989, one year after it opened. Wiseman was attending a weekly Friday staff meeting of senior executives run by Fujio Cho, who subsequently became the chairman of Toyota worldwide. Wiseman recalls:

> One Friday, I gave a report of an activity we had been doing … and I spoke very positively about it. I bragged a little. After two or three minutes I sat down. And Mr. Cho kind of looked at me. I could see he was puzzled. He said "Jim-san, we all know you are a good manager otherwise we would not have hired you. But please talk to us about your problems so we can all work on them together."
>
> It was like a lightning bolt. Even with projects that had been a general success, we would ask, "What didn't go well so we can make it better?"
>
> At Toyota I have come to understand what they mean when I hear the phrase, "Problems first."[198]
>

Wiseman continues,

> You cannot solve problems unless you admit them. At Toyota there is a presumption of imperfection. Perfection is a fine goal, but improvement is much more realistic, much more human. Not a [probably unrealistic] 15 percent improvement by the end of the quarter: a one percent improvement by the end of the month.[199]
>

In a prescient article, *Business Week* asked the following question in its November 17, 2003 cover story: "Can Anything Stop Toyota?" After reviewing data, *Business Week's* answer was clear: "No." No competitor can match Toyota's passionate quest for continuous improvement. A dramatic example is Toyota's rapid improvement of its 2003 Sienna minivan. In 2003 it took U.S. auto companies four years to introduce a substantially modified version of a given model. Toyota replaced its 2003 model with a new model in 2004. The 2004 Sienna had a bigger, more powerful engine; improved gas mileage; a five-speed transmission instead of four; a turning diameter of 26.8 feet, versus 30 feet in the 2003 model; a longer and wider body with more leg room, headroom, and 12% more cargo space; a third-row seat that folded into the floor (not having to be removed manually as per the 2003 model); and a $920 lower sticker price—all accomplished in 14 months.[200]

Toyota encourages employees to search for improvements in every aspect of their jobs, even if it means eliminating their own functions. Each employee is assured that "you cannot *kaizen* yourself out of a job." Rather, Toyota promises employees that if they identify ways to eliminate their roles, they will get a job of equal or greater value.[201] This promise, a bold move rarely seen in a global corporation, has paid dividends in terms of conflicts of interest with respect to efficiency. (Employment security is classified as an employee-directed practice in Chapter 3; but it clearly affects both the interests of the enterprise and employees.)

Related to the quest for improved efficiency is Toyota's frugality. Not only does Toyota try to save a few pennies on each component (as highlighted in the aforementioned *Business Week* article): at Toyota penny-pinching is the norm in all aspects of its operations. In Japan, Toyota turns off the lights in their offices at lunchtime to save on energy expenses. The lack of partitions between workers' desks has been attributed to the high cost of office space in Japan.[202] Frugality also extends to the pay of company executives. In 2005, Toyota's top executives received only *one-tenth* the pay of Ford's top executives (despite Toyota having higher company earnings than Ford). The compensation of Toyota's top executives was lower than their counterparts at the ten largest automobile companies worldwide, excepting Honda.[203]

Another organization that has adopted the philosophy of *kaizen* is Dr. Pepper Snapple Group. Although sales in the soda industry have declined for 11 straight years, they have risen consistently for Dr. Pepper for the past five. During this period profits rose more than 50% and the stock price roughly doubled from 2013 to 2015. One contributing factor is that from 2011 through 2015, Dr. Pepper used *kaizen* to improve productivity by $270 million annually, and operating income rose from 18% of sales to 21%.[204]

At Dr. Pepper's headquarters in Plano, Texas and in manufacturing plants in the U.S. and Mexico the company's mantra is "RCI," rapid continuous improvement. Dr. Pepper has held some 575 *kaizen* events where teams of employees spend several days dissecting every step of their work flow in search of waste. The company has issued 6,500 certificates for participating in *kaizen* events, and top management is forcefully supportive of these events. In the words of Marty Ellen, the CFO, "if you don't raise your hand when I ask, 'have you been on a *kaizen*?' you will soon be an outcast in the company."[205]

At Dr. Pepper, the sanitizing lines before starting a new flavor used to take an average of 32 minutes. The company figured out how to do it in 13 minutes. Some of the changes were as simple as not walking away from a machine to get a tool, but having the tool at the machine. The accounts payable process became less expensive to execute in Plano than to outsource it to a firm in India. It was discovered that boxes used by suppliers, but never seen by customers, had the Dr. Pepper logo imprinted on them. By not using boxes with the company logo, the company saved $60,000.[206]

Toyota was not the first automobile company to focus on continuous improvement. Henry Ford reputedly had a defining principle: "Everything can always be done better than it is being done."[207] Ford's "relentless pursuit of manufacturing efficiency" is illustrated by the company's piston-assembly operation. It only took three minutes to assemble a piston rod using a 28-person operation, and the company assumed that this operation "did not seem to be one to bother about." But a time and motion study revealed that workers spent four hours daily taking small steps to gather materials. By rearranging the operation so that each worker performed tasks without taking steps, productivity soared. The old record for the 28-person operation was 175 assemblies a day. Ford wrote that subsequently seven workers could turn out 2,600 assemblies in eight hours. That works out to one-quarter as many workers accomplishing about 15 times more work.[208]

Between 1907 and 1914, Ford Motor Company's output increased 30-fold; profits increased 27-fold; the price of the Model T was reduced from $950 to $550; durability was enhanced; the daily wage paid to employees increased more than 100% with a shortened workday. Employee turnover was reduced from as high as 370% annually to 40%.[209] Increased efficiency provided greater returns to the enterprise, while customers and employees also benefited. This exemplifies the interdependencies among practices and three key sets of outcomes specified by the Cube One framework.

A second fundamental practice that Toyota adopted is its ability to focus not just on day-to-day efficiencies but on long-term radical innovation. In a six-year study of Toyota that entailed visits to facilities in 11 countries, attendance at numerous meetings, and 220 interviews, the researchers concluded that Toyota's success lies in its ability to embrace contradictions.[210] This has enabled Toyota not only to focus on the present, but to implement radical changes over the long term: a philosophy called *kaikaku*.

Toyota's first hybrid car, the Prius, was first mass-produced and sold in Japan in 1997. In 2016 it was sold in more than 40 countries and was the most fuel efficient vehicle on the market according to the U.S. Environmental Protection Agency.[211]

Also illustrative of Toyota's ability to enact radical change is its hydrogen fuel cell hybrid vehicle, the Mirai. The 2016 model was available for purchase in California for a net price of $50,000, after a rebate. The vehicle, which has undergone development and testing for 20 years—with the obvious central concern being safety—uses hydrogen and air to power its electric motor. The only by-product of creating electricity with hydrogen and air is water, which exits the vehicle through the tailpipe. The car produces zero carbon emissions and can be fully refueled in five minutes.[212] It will be fascinating to see which new technology becomes dominant: the entirely electric vehicle (with Tesla providing the most attractive offering), or the hydrogen-powered vehicle offered by Toyota and Hyundai.

The third fundamental practice associated with TPS relates to the treatment of employees. Toyota believes that all people associated with the company should be treated with the utmost respect, and this includes leaders, managers, non-managers, and the extended network of suppliers and, of course, customers. Indicative of the company's respect for employees, Toyota rarely weeds out underperformers, preferring to upgrade their capabilities. Unlike many companies where career outcomes are binary—employees are either promoted or terminated—Toyota is committed to long-term employment. (This practice, also categorized as an employee-directed practice, can have multiple effects, as discussed in Chapter 3.)

During the 1997 Asian financial crisis, Toyota's Thailand operation endured four consecutive years of losses with no job cuts. The order from then president Hiroshi Okada stated, "Cut all costs, but don't touch any people." In August 1998, Moody's lowered Toyota's credit rating from AAA to AA1, citing Toyota's guarantee of lifetime employment. Although Toyota's interest expense had increased by $220 million annually as a result of no layoffs, executives told the rating agency that the company would not abandon its commitment.[213]

Eleven years later, Toyota showed the same concern for its employees, when global automobile demand dropped by 30 during the 2008–2009 recession. Toyota had substantial overcapacity. When Toyota's first loss in 70 years was front-page news in December 2008, Watanabe insisted, "in keeping with its corporate culture, Toyota hasn't laid off workers but has made them make improvements to their work areas and attend seminars aimed at boosting their skills."[214] Toyota ultimately offered buyouts to certain North American factory workers in February 2009, but refused to lay off people outright.[215] Such support for an organization's employees is remarkable when one considers the loss of jobs across the U.S. economy in 2009, resulting in the highest level of unemployment in two generations.

Toyota promotes a corporate culture of humility. The "power of humility" captures the equality of all employees (managers and non-managers). Status distinctions are not associated with differences in hierarchical levels.[216] On the production line, everybody has the right and the obligation to pull the "stop cord" wherever a quality problem is observed. Consistent with this philosophy is the company's training of workers so that they think as though they were two levels higher in the organization. Employees are trained in problem-solving techniques and are encouraged to express their ideas, even if contrary to the ideas of their managers. This openness of communication leads to greater understanding and conveys a willingness to learn from each other. This culture promotes teamwork and leads to growth of individuals as well as teams. In Eiji Toyoda's 1986 book, *Kaizen*, he stated that Toyota workers provided 1.5 million suggestions a year, and 95% were put to practical use.[217]

In *Lean Six Sigma for Service*, Michael George provides a number of success stories. One entailed the city of Fort Wayne, Ind., which during a three-year rollout provided extensive training in Six Sigma to all managers and trained 20 Black Belts and 40 Green Belts. Sixty projects were launched, yielding a cumulative savings of nearly $3 million in direct savings or avoidance of expected costs. Previously, 77% of potholes were repaired within 24 hours; afterward, 98% were repaired within 24 hours, the mean time being 10 hours[218]

Stanford Hospital and Clinics implemented Lean Six Sigma over a two-decade period and achieved annual cost savings of $25 million. Savings in cardiac surgery were about $1.8 million annually; cardiology reported saving $4.4 million; and cardiac bypass surgery achieved a savings of greater than $2,400 per case.[219]

A very widely used approach to improving organizational effectiveness is supply chain management. The scope of supply chain management includes all stages of the production process. Sources of improvements include the design of products; materials purchased; manufacturing, including packaging, equipment, cutting, and/or assembly techniques; inventory levels; transportation expenses; information management; quality inspection; storage, which includes material handling, loading, and temperature control; and marketing, with associated branding and trademarking along with customization.[220]

The conventional paradigm in retailing has entailed four key components: manufacturer, distributor, dealer, and retailer. "Big box" stores such as Best Buy and Walmart have been able to compete in the Internet era by eliminating the distributor and dealer links, getting direct shipments from manufacturers in large lots. The companies then redistribute the products to their various stores. Package delivery companies such as UPS will break down shipments at the port of entry and ship directly to retail outlets and distribution centers.[221]

When product designs change rapidly, such as in the fashion industry, where tastes are fickle, clothing retailers such as Zara and H&M have fully integrated their supply chains. At Zara, the process of design (starting with a sketch pad), manufacturing, logistics, merchandising, and retailing can be accomplished in as little as 15 days; thus new (and trendy) designs can be quickly drawn, manufactured, and distributed. In broad terms, characteristics of the supply chain should be congruent with product/service properties.[222]

In 2016, both Ford and General Motors announced plans to double production in Mexico by 2018. Ford announced it would spend more than $1 billion to increase assembly operations—after investing $2.5 billion to build an engine and transmission plant in Mexico. General Motors planned to invest $5 billion to double Mexican capacity by 2018.[223]

Circa 2010, the chain of hospitals then called the North Shore Long Island Jewish Health System approached supply chain management with "an emphasis on aligning core business processes, workflow (procurement, distribution, inventory management, etc.) pricing, contract management, value analysis, and product standardization through a clinically focused team environment."[224] The organization achieved an annual cost reduction of more than $80 million, in an environment of dramatically increasing medical costs. One component of the transformation entailed replacing 18 warehouse/distribution centers, each previously associated with a single hospital, with one immense warehouse that saved money by making large-scale purchases and delivering to every hospital floor twice daily.[225]

General Mills' Ingredient Overusage Reduction Program (IORP) provides a fascinating example of a rigorous supply chain management analysis and intervention. The company had attributed many of its losses to physical downtimes resulting from equipment or process failures—but it turned out that 75% of losses occurred when a plant was seemingly running well. The major source of loss was extra product going into a package. A single Cheerio, for example, might seem trivial. But multiplied by a billion packages, Cheerios add up. The decrease in overuse resulting from improving operational performance (IORP) amounted to $10 million in the first two and a half years, and 90% of the changes entailed low or no capital expenditures. To achieve waste reduction, schedules had to change, with some tasks performed on a daily rather than monthly basis.[226]

On a far smaller scale, in 2015, the 158-employee privately held ATS Corporation won Industry Week's Best Plant Award. In 2014, ATS had an intellectual understanding "of lean methodologies and basic six sigma tools, but little work had been completed to apply them to production." As the engineering manager at ATS put it, "there was a lot of chaos in what we did then." In early 2014, ATS hired a Master Black Belt, Don Doody, to turn things around. In "an insane two-year frenzy," Doody trained Black Belts and implemented a Lean Thinking program. In 2015, ATS increased its first-pass yield rate by 50% and saved more than $73,000 in that year alone. A key facet of the ATS intervention was rigorously attending to details in actual day-to-day operations.[227]

A survey of ten enterprise-directed practices that organizations can use as a diagnostic tool appears at the end of this chapter. The best source of data about the extent to which practices are actually enacted, versus merely espoused, is employees who frequently put practices into action.

Improving Enterprise Results via Financial Management

One financial management technique relates to aligning costs to product/service offerings. For example, consider the application of rational financial considerations undertaken at Continental Airliners. When Gordon Bethune became CEO of the twice-bankrupt airline, he brought in Greg Brenneman, a former Bain turnaround consultant, as president. Brenneman noticed that nearly 20% of all flights were cash-negative. Indicative of the poor alignment of capacity and demand were the six flights daily from Greensboro, North Carolina to Greenville, South Carolina. Brenneman dryly asked the scheduling team, "Why are we flying that route six times a day when both customers who want to fly that route are on the first flight?"[228]

In 2015, *The New York Daily News* was losing nearly $30 million a year. At one time each of its 106 trucks carried approximately 400 bundles of the newspapers. In 2015, some trucks handled as few as 10 to 15 bundles, reflecting the 43% drop in circulation from March 2012 to September 2015. The newspaper planned to reduce the number of trucks to about 50, eliminating 220 jobs.[229]

Several years ago, Walmart initiated a visible cost-saving move, eliminating the "greeters" at its front entrances. More recently it reintroduced greeters, but not just to provide a friendly person at the beginning of a shopping experience. Walmart viewed the greeters as cost effective. They performed other tasks such as directing shoppers, opening registers, and tidying shelves—and their presence deterred theft.[230]

Improvements in product/service offerings via disintermediation can take many forms, including lower prices, quicker service, increased options regarding offerings. Hotels and airlines now allow guests and passengers to book their stays and flights directly. This has largely reduced the role (and built-in costs) of travel agents. Likewise, the Internet has started to make inroads into the real estate market with the emergence of firms like Zillow. Consumers are able to obtain extensive information about available properties and asking prices.

Consumers can hail one of several types of cars directly via Uber or several competitors. This reduces the need for taxi dispatchers, and the built-in costs of taxi medallions no longer need be indirectly absorbed. Direct hailing also evidently seems to result in increased customer satisfaction.

eBay and Alibaba need no warehouses to store the millions of products they facilitate selling (and purchasing)—transactions that total tens of billions of dollars. They're not moving products or services, but rather electrons.

The Internet has allowed people to trade stocks and bonds, in transactions of almost any size, for less than $5 and receive confirmation within a second. Consider how the process played out up to about 1980. The buyer (or seller) would call a broker, who would handwrite a ticket, with a carbon copy. The broker would then walk the original copy to the back office where it would be keyed in by back office personnel and sent by teletype to the appropriate stock exchange. There, a printed copy would be placed in a pneumatic tube system (at the time "high tech") that physically moved the document to the station of a "runner" for the specific brokerage firm. The runner then physically carried the order to the trading booth where the transaction was effected. A few days later, the buyer/seller would receive a printed confirmation by mail. Clearly, many of the jobs in the execution of financial transactions have been disintermediated by the Internet.

(Around that same time, when a family was planning a vacation it would contact the American Automobile Association and receive by mail a "trip-tick" that provided recommended travel routes and destinations. And a personalized brochure would arrive by mail within ten days.)

Another financial management technique, most often employed by publicly traded companies, is the buying back of shares. Although the repurchase of stock is sometimes seen as controversial, it can be justified if investing in the expansion of operations is viewed as too risky. A short-term advantage of share buybacks is that financial metrics improve and can lead to both higher stock prices and dividends per share. These results, while beneficial to parties focused in the short-term (e.g., executives with performance-based stock options, or investors seeking a rapid gain), may not inure to the long-term benefit of the company.

Some companies choose a domicile based on tax considerations. In 2015, John Tamny wrote a relevant book, *Popular Economics: What the Rolling Stones, Downton Abbey, and LeBron James Can Teach You About Economics*. Tamny noted that in the 1970s, when the Rolling Stones were "minting" money, the top tax rate in Britain was 83%. Keith Richards, lead guitarist (and financial guru) observed, "That's the same as being told to leave the country." The Stones moved to France, allowing Britain to collect 83% of none of their income.[231] More recently, some companies have merged with the acquiring company, often smaller in size, domiciled in a nation with a lower tax rate.

Enterprise-Directed Practices

As noted previously, there is an extensive, and virtually infinite, list of enterprise-directed practices that have been found to improve productivity and organizational performance. The present chapter has examined three major categories of practices: those based on human resource management, operations management, and financial management. To provide a view as to how organizations can apply the Cube One framework provided below is a slightly tweaked version of the original list of ten enterprise-directed practices used in survey research. The original list of practices is provided in Chapter Five. Because the survey below was developed prior to extending the conceptual analysis beyond people-based management practices, it does not fully map the later part of this chapter. However, it provides a starting point for using the Cube One framework for diagnostic and intervention purposes. (As noted previously, there is no "set in stone" list of practices for any of the three dimensions.)

The short ten-item survey below includes virtually all of the behavioral (people-based) techniques associated with HPWS: systematic selection, training, goal setting (and accountability), feedback, incentives (at individual and group levels), measurement, delegation, accountability, and GMFAC. Missing are practices pertinent to operations management (TPS, Six Sigma, lean management, *kaizen*, and supply chain management) and financial management. A few of the latter practices might well be added to the survey of enterprise-directed practices, even though normative data are presently unavailable.

Enterprise-Directed Practices: A Short Ten-Item Survey

Actual Practices

The purpose of this section is to ascertain the *actual practices* (as distinct from stated or printed policies) in the organization where you work (or most recently worked). If you work in a subsidiary of a larger organization, focus on the local organization where you work (or worked). Please use the following scale to record your responses to the ten statements that follow:

1 = Never or Almost Never (or Not Applicable)
2 = Infrequently
3 = Occasionally or Sometimes
4 = Frequently
5 = Always or Almost Always

(1) **Selection.** Individuals are selected for employment based on objective criteria (e.g., written tests, performance tests, work samples, etc.) _____
(2) **Training.** Training is provided to upgrade employees' job-related knowledge and skills. _____
(3) **Goal Setting and Accountability.** Individuals are held accountable for accomplishing specific (quantifiable) goals. _____
(4) **Feedback.** Individuals receive specific performance feedback that is useful for improving their performance. _____
(5) **Individual Incentives.** Salary increases (e.g., raises, bonuses) are proportionate to an individual's job performance. _____
(6) **Group–Based Incentives.** Performance improvement is financially rewarded by a group incentive plan (e.g., gainsharing, profit-sharing, etc.). _____
(7) **Promotions.** Promotions are based almost entirely on job performance. _____
(8) **Measurement.** Where possible, the performance of individuals and groups is quantifiably measured and monitored over time. _____
(9) **Delegation.** Management encourages the delegation of decision-making authority to lower-level employees (i.e., real empowerment). _____
(10) **Job Growth.** Individuals are encouraged to perform a wide variety of tasks whenever possible. _____

Notes

1 Truss, C. (2001). "Complexities and controversies in linking HRM with organizational outcomes." *Journal of Management Studies*, 38(8), 1121–1149.
2 Christensen, C. M. (1997). *The innovator's dilemma: When new technologies cause great firms to fail.* Boston: Harvard Business School Press.
3 Becker, B. E., and Gerhart, B. (1996) "The impact of human resource management on organizational performance: Progress and prospects." *Academy of Management Journal,*

39(4), 779–801; Cascio, W. E. (2006). "The economic impact of employee behaviors on organizational performance." *California Management Review*, 48(4), 41–59; Delaney, J. T., and Huselid, M. A. (1996). "The impact of human resource management practices on perceptions of organizational performance." *Academy of Management Journal*, 39(4), 949–969; Latham, G. P. (2007). *Work motivation: History, theory, research and practice.* Thousand Oaks, CA: Sage Publications; 1996. (It has been argued among scholars whether the term "high performance work systems" (HPWS) is presumptuous insofar as it implies a certainty of performance outcomes; yet alternative labels such as "high commitment" or "high involvement" also are similarly presumptive. So for this reason, the widely adopted term HPWS—analogous to a collection of High Performance Work Practices—is adopted here.)

4 Nelson, B. (2005). *1001 ways to reward employees.* New York: Workman Publishing.

5 Drucker, P. F. (2005). *Managing the non-profit organization.* New York: HarperCollins.

6 Combs, J., Yongmei, L., Hall, A., and Ketchen, D. (2006). "How much do high-performance work practices matter? A meta-analysis of their effects on organizational performance." *Personnel Psychology*, 59(3), 501–528.

7 Jiang, K., Lepak, D. P., Hu, J., and Baer, J. C. (2012). "How does human resource management influence organizational outcomes? A meta-analytic investigation of mediating mechanisms." *Academy of Management Journal*, 55(6), 1264–1294. (The data were drawn from 120 independent samples that included more than 31,000 organizations.)

8 Rabl, T., Jayasinghe. M., Gerhart, B., and Kuhlmann, T. M. (2014). "A meta-analysis of country differences in high-performance-work system—business performance relationship: The roles of national culture and managerial discretion. *Journal of Applied Psychology*, 99(6), 1011–1041. (The data were drawn from 156 studies comprising more than 35,000 firms in 29 countries.)

9 Pfeffer, J. (1998). "Seven practices of successful organizations." *California Management Review*, 40(2), 96–124.

10 Bock, L. (2015). *Work rules! Insights from inside Google that will transform how you live and lead.* New York: Hachette Book Group. For the data on selection rates at Proctor & Gamble and NASA see Reed, S., and Gibby, R. E. (2012). Selecting top talent at Procter & Gamble. Presentation at the DDI Summit. Slides. Retrieved at http://www.ddiworld.com/ddi/media/ddi-summit/2012/pg_techtoselecttalent_ddisummit2012.pdf. Accessed on September 2015.

11 According to Michael Campion, a former editor of *Personnel Psychology*, research has shown repeatedly that the unstructured "shoot-the-bull" interview is "pretty much useless." Further he claims that "[a} structured interview can predict future job performance better than many medical tests can predict the probability of someone getting a disease." See Freeman, L. L. (April 4, 1996). "Surviving the job interview meat grinder: New "structured" assessments put candidates on the spot," *Investor's Business Daily*, pp. 1–2.

12 It cannot be overemphasized that all tests must be validated, and ideally, tests should be used that have been independently and professionally validated. As Michael McDaniel, an expert on selection methods cautions, test users should be skeptical of validity evidence that comes from firms that sell tests. The test preparers may only share positive results and withhold poor results. The use of any test is fraught with risks, including those associated with adverse treatment, and even more commonly, adverse impact. A brief introduction to these issues is provided in Chapter 6 of the book by Elaine Pulakos, (2009). *Performance management.* West Sussex, UK: Wiley-Blackwell, pp. 123–131.

13 Latham, G. P., and Sue-Chan, C. (1999). "A meta-analysis of the situational interview: An enumerative review of reasons for its validity." *Canadian Psychology*, 40(1), 56–67.

14 Ibid.

15 Gary Latham provided this example of a structured interview many years back.

16 Ruiz, G. (2006). "Traditional recipe." *Workforce Management*, 85(8), 1, 22, 29.

17 Terpstra, D. E., and Rozell, E. J. (1993). "The relationship of staffing practices to organizational level measures of performance. *Personnel Psychology*, 46(1), 27–48. For acomprehensive review of data on biographical data, see Rothstein, H. R., Schmidt, F. L., Erwin, F.W., Owens, W.A., and Sparks, C. P. (1990). "Biographical data in employment selection: Can validities be made generalizable?" *Journal of Applied Psychology*, 72(2), 175–184.

18 Inc. (July/August, 2015) "Get out of employees' way: One layer of bosses drives staff creativity and sales." p. 24.

19 Pfeffer, p. 101.

20 Chang, S., Jia, L., Takeuchi, R., and Cai, Y. (2014). "Do high-commitment work systems affect creativity? A multilevel combinational approach to employee creativity." *Journal of Applied Psychology*, 99(4), 665–680.

21 Buchanan, L. (June 2015). "The fine art of people." 56–61. (Reflective of the non-traditional nature of the company, the president has also been known to ask, "How would you keep this company weird?")

22 Rafter, M.V. (2008). "Get your 'A' players here!" *Workforce Management*, 87(4), 1, 20–28.

23 Ibid.

24 Bock, op. cit., 81–85. (The Aarhus team built the JavaScript engine in Chrome.)

25 Silverman, R. E. (May 29, 2013). "First day on the job: Not just paperwork." *Wall Street Journal*, B10.

26 Whitney, D., and Trosten-Bloom, A. (2003). *The power of appreciative inquiry: A practical guide to positive change*. San Francisco: Berrett-Koehler. Cooperrider, D. L., Whitney, D., and Stavros, J. M. 2003. *Appreciative inquiry handbook: The first in a series of AI workbooks for leaders of change*. Bedford Height, OH: Lakeshore Communications and San Francisco; Berrett-Koehler.

27 Gould, D. (May 14, 2015). "Where talent and tech meet: Like other business systems before it, personnel recruiting have become data- and tech-driven. Human resource departments will never be the same." *Bloomberg Businessweek*, pp. S1–S6.

28 For example, in their study of the relationship between High Commitment Work Systems and creativity, Chang et al. (2014), included extensive training as one of 12 practices. Further, they found that training is central to the Ability-Motivation-Opportunity framework—see Jiang et al. (2012).

29 Pfeiffer, op. cit., 112–116.

30 Roadmaps. (November 2014). "Learning & development orientation guide: How to build a training program that aligns talent development with strategic business goals." *Workforce Management*, 93(11), 24–26. Arthur Jr., W., Bennett Jr., W., Edens, P. S., and Bell, S. T. (2003). "Effectiveness of training in organizations: A meta-analysis of design and evaluation features." *Journal of Applied Psychology*, 88(2), 234–245. doi:10.1037/0021-9010.88.2.234

31 See Jiang et al., op. cit. It might be noted that Jiang et al. cite the perspective on HRM advanced by Jackson, Schuler, and Rivero (*Personnel Psychology*, 1989) and also by Becker and Huselid, 1998 (*Research in Personnel and Human Resources Management*, 1998) that "organizations do not perform themselves, but instead HR practices encourage productive behaviors from employees and thus achieve desirable operational and financial results." In essence, this perspective suggests that individual level outcomes can be extrapolated to group and organizational levels. The view that it is possible to extrapolate across levels has been discounted during the past two decades by researchers who advocate a multilevel perspective.

32 Stajkovic, A. D., and Luthans, F. (2003). "Behavioral management and task performance in organizations: Conceptual background, meta-analysis, and test of alternative models." *Personnel Psychology*, 56(1), 155–194.

33 For example see, Lawler, EE III. (1981). *Pay and organization development*. Reading, MA: Addison-Wesley; and Lawler, EE III. (1990). *Strategic pay*. San Francisco: Jossey-Bass.

34 Berfield, S. (February 19, 2015). "The clutter in Kip Tindell." *Bloomberg Businessweek*, 40–45.

35 Davenport, R., and colleagues. (September 2015). "A higher level of learning." *T + D*, 32–41. Quoted material reprinted with permission of the American Society for Training and Development. © 2015 *T + D*.

36 Ibid., p. 35.

37 Meister, J. (December 11, 2006). "Universities put to the test: Amid pressure to demonstrate strategic results corporate education programs are becoming more astute customer of education and placing greater demands on academic partners." *Workforce Management*, 27–30.

38 Ibid.

39 *The Economist*. (March 7, 2015). "The quantified serf."

40 Katzell, R. A., and Guzzo, R. A. (1983). "Psychological approaches to productivity improvement." *American Psychologist*, 38(4), 468–472; also Locke, E. A., Feren, D. B., McCaleb, V. M., Shaw, K. N., and Denny, A. T. (1980). "The relative effectiveness of four methods of motivating employee performance." In K. Duncan, M. Gruneberg, and D. Wallis eds. *Changes in work life*. New York: Wiley. (pp. 363–388).

41 *The Economist*, op. cit.

42 Ibid.

43 Terpstra, D. E., and Rozell, E. J. (1994). "The relationship of goal setting to organizational profitability." *Group & Organization Management*, 19(3), 285–294.

44 Kleingeld, A., van Mierlo, H., and Arends, L. (2011). "The effect of goal setting on group performance: A meta-analysis." *Journal of Applied Psychology*, 96(6), 1289–1304.

45 Gollwitzer, P. M. (1999). "Implementation intentions." *The American Psychologist*, 54(7), 493–503.

46 Harvey, P. D., and Snyder, J. D. (January–February 1987). "Charities need a bottom line too." *Harvard Business Review*, 65(1), 15–18.

47 Gawande, A. (December 10, 2007). The checklist: If something so simple can transform intensive care what else can it do? *The New Yorker*. Retrieved at http://www.newyorker.com/magazine/2007/12/10/the-checklist. Gawande has provided an expanded discussion in Gawande, A. (2010). *The checklist manifesto: How to get things right*. New York: Metropolitan Books.

48 Kopelman, R. E. (1982). "Improving productivity through objective feedback: A review of the evidence." *National Productivity Review*, 2, 43–55.

49 Locke, E. A., and Latham, G. P. (1984). *Goal setting: A motivational technique that works!* Englewood Cliffs: Prentice-Hall.

50 Locke, E. A., and Latham, G. P. (1990). *A theory of goal setting & task performance*. Englewood Cliffs: Prentice-Hall.

51 Kopelman, R. E. (1986). "Objective feedback." chapter in E. A. Locke, ed. *Generalizing from laboratory to field settings*. Lexington, MA: Lexington Books (pp. 119–145).

52 Allen, S.A. (1976). *Aer Lingus—Irish (B) case*. Boston: Intercollegiate Case Clearinghouse 9-477-640, pp. 1–20. The feedback intervention resulted in a 66.5% reduction in interruptions; an 84.4% increase in the use of caller's name; with the overall effect being a 77.9% improvement in the three criteria over three months.

53 McNees, P, Gilliam, S. W., Schnelle, J. F., and Risley, T. (1980). "Controlling employee theft through time and product identification." *Journal of Organizational Behavior Management*, 2(2), 113–119. Regarding the issue of "pinpointing," the situation is analogous to the classic article by Steven Kerr, (updated in 1995), "On the folly of rewarding A, while hoping for B." *Academy of Management Executive*, 9(1), 7–16.

54 Karan, B. S., and Kopelman, R. E. (1986). "The effects of objective feedback on vehicular and industrial accidents: A field experiment using outcome feedback." *Journal of Organizational Behavior Management*, 8(1), 45–56. Reductions in vehicular accidents and injuries were 26% and 17%, respectively. That the improvements were relatively

modest was partly attributed to the fact that drivers reported to work at varying times. Drivers, therefore worked on more than one tour, and felt limited identification with a single tour. Moreover, accidents and injuries were associated with the tour when they occurred, so a driver might contribute to accidents on more than one tour.

55 Berfield, S. (February 19, 2015). "The clutter in Kip Tindell." *Bloomberg Businessweek*, pp. 40–45. (For the reader who is interested in exploring the complexity of parsing the relative effects of different enterprise-directed practices, it is notable that both the Container Store and Nordstrom illustrate how goal setting, feedback, and financial incentives, especially in concert, can positively affect organizational performance. Complicating matters, a "second derivative" of goal setting, objective feedback, and incentive compensation is that sales associates are typically highly motivated to provide outstanding customer service, which is a component of customer-directed practices. However, in isolation, most practices are primarily directed toward one constituent stakeholder—i.e., the enterprise, employees, or customers. That there is relatively little disagreement, empirically, as to the primary intended beneficiary of specific practices is addressed in the chapter on survey research (Chapter 5.)

56 Stajkovic, A. D., and Luthans, F. (2003). "Behavioral management and task performance in organizations: Conceptual background, meta-analysis, and test of alternative models." *Personnel Psychology*, 56(1), 155–194. It should be noted that the use of an observable, measureable, behavior-based indicator of task performance essentially made the feedback measure a form of objective feedback.

57 Ibid.

58 Caruso, K. (June 11, 2014). "You rock!—5 ways to transform positive performance feedback." Retrieved at http://web.viapeople.com/viaPeople-blog/bid/100744/You-Rock-5-Ways-to-Transform-Positive-Performance-Feedback. Accessed on July 12, 2014.

59 Kluger, A. N., and DeNisi, A. (1996). "The effects of feedback interventions on performance: A historical review, meta-analysis, and a preliminary feedback intervention theory." *Psychological Bulletin*, 119(2), 254–284.

60 Raver, J. A., Jensen, J. M., Lee, J., and O'Reilly, J. (2012). "Destructive criticism revisited: Appraisals, task outcomes and the moderating role of competitiveness." *Applied Psychology: An International Review*, 61(2), 177–203.

61 Along these lines, employees are more receptive to performance feedback, including performance appraisal reviews, that are based on behavioral observations (e.g., frequency of cleaning counter tops when dirty), compared to feedback based on relatively broad traits or job characteristics (e.g., conscientiousness, service quality). See Tziner, A., and Kopelman, R. E. (2002). "Is there a preferred rating format? A non-psychometric perspective." *Applied Psychology: An International Review*, 51(3), 479–503.

62 Meyer, H. H., Kay, E., and French, J. R. P., Jr. (1965). "Split roles in performance appraisal." *Harvard Business Review*, 43(1), 123–129.

(As a source of anecdotal evidence, the reader might perform the following thought experiment. How often have you seen people at work walking around muttering "It is true, in fact I am a total loser"?)

63 Cross, K. P. (Spring 1977). "Not can but will college teachers be improved? *New Directions for Higher Education*, 17, 1–15.

64 Kemmerer, F. N., and Thiagarajan, S. (1992). "Incentive systems." In H. D. Stolovitch, and E. J. Keeps, eds. *Handbook of human performance technology: A comprehensive guide for analyzing and solving performance problems in organizations*. San Francisco: Jossey-Bass. (pp. 312–330).

65 Pfeffer, J. (1998). "Seven practices of successful organizations." *California Management Review*, 40(2), 96–124.

66 Deci, E. I., Koestner, R., and Ryan, R. M. (1999). "The undermining effect is a reality after all—Extrinsic rewards, task interest, and self-determination: Reply to

Eisenberger, Pierce, and Cameron (1999) and Lepper, Henderlong, and Gingras (1999). *Psychological Bulletin*, 125(6), 692–700.

67 Cerasoli, C. P., Nicklin, J. M., and Ford, M. T. (2014). "Intrinsic motivation and extrinsic incentives jointly predict performance: A 40-year meta-analysis." *Psychological Bulletin*, 140(4), 980–1008. The authors' conclusion appears on page 1001. (It might be noted that of the total sample of 210,000 individuals, 185,000 were children or adolescents. This is meaningful because evidence of negative effects of incentives has primarily been found in elementary school settings and among parents of children.) Although not noted by the authors of the meta-analysis, it is problematic to generalize the results of children and adolescents participating in brief experiments to adult employees in the world of work. Yet, notwithstanding the nature of the sample, the authors still found that extrinsic rewards were effective insofar as they "crowded out" the motivational impact of intrinsic rewards when incentives were directly tied to performance.

68 Kohn, A. (1993). "Why incentive plans cannot work." *Harvard Business Review*, 71(5), 54–63. The primary evidentiary basis for Kohn's argument has been studies of schoolchildren, and anecdotes regarding parenting. He has argued (reasonably) that using gold stars and praise ("Good job!") as rewards may be somewhat akin to employing bribes. However, Kohn goes even further, suggesting that grades in school are "degrading." Based on his evidence, mostly from schools and parenting, Kohn concluded that in the world of work, incentives "cannot work." It is notable that after Kohn's article in *Harvard Business Review*, there was an outpouring of commentary in subsequent issues. As Kohn himself noted in the revised (1999) edition of his book, *Punished by rewards*, his *Harvard Business Review* article "generated dozens of letters; their tone ranged from highly critical (at one end of the spectrum) all the way to downright nasty (at the other.)" With regard to the content of the comments, several writers stated that it makes no sense to pay all employees the same. One concluded: "Indeed his [Kohn's] assertions are being tested on the firing line and disproved by a persuasive cross section of U.S. businesses."

Reflective of Kohn's viewpoint, an essay directed to human resource managers that argues against merit pay was advanced by Hughes, C. (June 1986) "The demerit of merit." *Personnel Administrator*, 30(6), 40. According to Hughes, if low performers are paid less than high performers, some low performers may experience pay inequity. Kopelman, R. E. provided a rejoinder (January 1987) "Is it better to inherit?" *Personnel Administrator*, 32(1), 30, 32. He argued that if all performers are paid the same, then many high performers will experience pay inequity—as equal increases in pay will not be seen as equitable. Further, how can a company retain and motivate its best employees, especially if competitors recognize and reward excellent performance? In short, by employing equal pay organizations will be investing in the retention and satisfaction of low performers.

69 Nash, A. N., and Carroll, S. J., Jr. (1975). *The management of compensation*. Belmont, CA: Wadsworth Publishing Company, Inc. (The summary of incentive effectiveness studies appears on page 199.)

70 Locke, E. A., Feren, D. B., McCaleb, V. M., Shaw, K. N., and Denny, A. T. (1980). "The relative effectiveness of four methods of motivating employee performance." In K. D. Duncan, M. M. Gruneberg, and D. Wallis, eds. *Changes in working life*. London: John Wiley & Sons, Ltd. (pp. 363–388). Consistent with the findings of Locke and colleagues is the review of the effects of groups incentive plans provided by Kopelman, R. E. (1986). *Managing productivity in organizations*. New York: McGraw-Hill. Improvements in performance have typically averaged 16% using one of the three versions of the Scanlon plan, and 20% using the Improshare plan developed by Mitchell Fein, where gains resulting from improved productivity are shared 50–50 between workers and the company.

71 Katzell, R. A., Bienstock, P., and Faerstein, P. H. (1977). *A guide to worker productivity experiments in the United States 1971–1975*. New York: New York University Press.

72 Miner, J. (1978). "Performance appraisal: The barrier to pay for performance." In *Proceedings*, American Compensation Association, p. 46.

73 Lazear, E. P. (2000). "Performance pay and productivity." *The American Economic Review*, 90(5), 1346–1361.

74 Peterson, S. J., and Luthans, F. (2006). "The impact of financial and nonfinancial incentives on business-unit outcomes over time." *Journal of Applied Psychology*, 91(1), 156–165.

75 Luthans, K. W., and Sommer, S. M. (2005). "The impact of high performance work on industry-level outcomes." *Journal of Managerial Issues*, 17(3), 327–345.

76 Lawler, E. E. III. (1977). "Reward systems." In J. R. Hackman, and J. L. Suttle, eds. *Improving life at work*, Santa Monica, CA: Goodyear. (pp. 162–225).

77 Marquez, J. (2005). "Premium on productivity." *Workforce Management*, 84(12), 22–30. Nucor has grown from 9,000 employees in 2004 to nearly 24,000 employees in 2014. Over the past fifty years Nucor has only lost money in one year: 2009.

78 *The Economist*. (March 19, 1996). "Managing People: Nicely does it." p. 84. More recent data are provided by Milkovich, G. T., Newman, J. M., and Gerhart, B. (2014). *Compensation* (11th Edition). New York: McGraw-Hill/Irwin. Also see, Shin, H. Y., and Lee, W. "How can we introduce the most effective incentive plan for non-exempt employees?" (2013). Retrieved at http://digitalcommons.ilr.cornell.edu/student/18/

79 Kopelman, R. E. "Organizational control system responsiveness, expectancy theory constructs, and work motivation: Some interrelations and causal connections." *Personnel Psychology*, 29(2), 205–220. Respondents in the company with a moderate to strong performance-pay correlation (0.45) reported working an additional 2.84 hours per week compared to respondents in the company where there was a modest (0.25) performance-pay correlation.

80 Kopelman, R. E., and Reinharth, l. (1982). "Research results: The effect of merit-pay practices on white collar performance." *Compensation Review*, 14(4), 30–40. Note that the results were restricted methodologically (artifactually) because the measure of branch performance was the mean level of *individual* performance. The methodological problem is that if individual performance scores were exceptionally high, (i.e., if all employees in a branch received the maximum performance rating), there could not be a within-branch high pay-performance correlation. In fact, the correlation could not be calculated. This built-in ceiling on results would have been obviated had there been an independent measure of overall branch performance, but none was available to the researchers.

81 Kopelman, R. E., Rovenpor, J. L, and Cayer, M. (1991). "Merit pay and organizational performance: Is there an effect on the bottom line? *National Productivity Review*, 10(3), 299–307. Also see Cayer, M., Kopelman, R. E., and Greenberg, J. L. (1991). "Merit pay: Road to the bottom line or bottom of the barrel?" Chapter 40 in J. W. Jones, B. D. Steffy, and D. W. Bray, eds. *Applying psychology in business: The handbook for managers and human resource professionals*. Lexington, MA: Lexington Books. (pp. 390–407).

82 Jiang, K., Lepak, D. P., Hu, J., and Baer, J. C. (2012). "How does human resource management influence organizational outcomes? A meta-analytic investigation of mediating mechanisms." *Academy of Management Journal*, 55(6), 1264–1294. (As noted above, the data were drawn from 120 independent samples including more than 31,000 organizations.)

83 Rabl, T., Jayasinghe, M., Gerhart, B, and Kuhlmann, T. M. (2014). "A meta-analysis of country differences in high-performance-work system—business performance relationship: The roles of national culture and managerial discretion. *Journal of Applied Psychology*, 99(6), 1011–1041. (The data were drawn from 156 studies comprising more than 35,000 firms in 29 countries.)

84 Neal, A., West, M. A., and Patterson, M. G. (2005). "Do organizational climate and competitive strategy moderate the relationship between human resource management and productivity?" *Journal of Management*, 31(4), 492–512. The data for this research, which supported the "spare capacity" interpretation, were obtained from 92 U.K. manufacturing firms.

85 Trevor, C. O., Reilly, G., and Gerhart, B. (2012). "Reconsidering pay dispersion's effect on the performance of interdependent work: Reconciling sorting and pay inequality." *Academy of Management Journal*, 55(3), 585–610.

86 Ibid.

87 Byron, K, and Khazanchi, S. (2012). "Rewards and creative performance: A meta analytic test of theoretically derived hypotheses." *Psychological Bulletin*, 138(4), 809–830.

88 Young, G. J., Beckman, H., and Baker, E. (2012). "Financial incentives, professional values and performance: A study of pay-for-performance in a professional organization." *Journal of Organizational Behavior*, 33(7), 964–983.

89 Jenkins, G. D., Jr., Miitra, A., Gupta, N., and Shaw, J. D. (1998). "Are financial incentives related to performance? A meta-analytic review of empirical research." *Journal of Applied Psychology*, 83(5), 777–787.

90 Gherson, D. J. (2000). "Getting the pay thing right." *Workspan*, 43(6), 47–51.

91 Sammer, J. (September 2014). "Making rewards count: Despite tight budgets, it's important to carve out rewards for top performers." *HR Magazine*, 59(9), 59–61.

92 Grove, A. S. (February 27, 1984). "Keeping favoritism and prejudice out of evaluations." *Wall Street Journal*, p. 26. Quotation reproduced with permission of Dow Jones and Company, Inc. © 1984 Dow Jones and Company, Inc.

93 Rodgers, T. J. (July–August 1990). "No excuses management." *Harvard Business Review*, 68 (4), 84–98. Further, in his book, also entitled *No excuses management*, New York: Doubleday. Rodgers reports that if high, middle, and low performers are awarded pay increases of 5%, 3%, and 1%, respectively, the low performers will be displeased. Given that the 1% pay increase merely produces dissatisfaction among low performers, Rodgers made it a practice of zeroing-out the low performers, distributing increases of 6%, 3%, and 0% instead.

94 Bryant, A. (August 15, 2014). "Finding a team that fits to a 'T'." *The New York Times*, B2.

95 Isaacson, W. (April 2012). "The real leadership lessons of Steve Jobs." *Harvard Business Review*, 90(4), 92–102. Information about the forced distribution plan at GE is provided by Jones, D. (April 18, 2005) "Let people know where they stand, Welch says: Ranking workers pays, former GE chief says." *USA Today*, p. 5B.

96 McCord, P. (February 2014). "How Netflix reinvented HR: Trust people, not policies. Reward candor. And throw away the standard playbook." *Harvard Business Review*, 90(3), 71–76.

97 Ibid.

98 First Round Review (June 29, 2013). "The woman behind Netflix culture doc." *First Round Review*. Retrieved at http://firstround.com/review/The-woman-behind-the-Netflix-Culture-doc/

99 Schleier, C. (August 28, 2007). "Mary Kay Ash cared about beauty and her workers." *Investor's Business Daily*, p. A3.

100 Blanchard, K., Stanford, V, and Witt, D. (April 2014). "Singing the praises of praises: If managers want to create a workplace environment where people thrive, tap into the benefits of praise. It costs nothing and pays big dividends to both giver and receiver." *Workforce*, 93(4), 36–39. (According to the authors, the biggest factor that explains the difference between the most and least successful firms is the ratio of positive to negative comments. Purportedly, the "magic ratio" is 5:1.

101 Blanchard et al., op. cit. The *Harvard Business Review Blog* posting was published March 15, 2013 by Professors Zenger and Folkman. Their blog referenced research by Heaphy and Losada that was published in 2004 in *American Behavioral Scientist*.

102 Breslin, M. M. (January 2013). "Solid rewards program can be rewarding for businesses: The best worker rewards programs boost engagement, reduce turnover and drive business performance an expert says." *Workforce Management*, 2(1), 8.

103 Breslin, M. S. (August 2012). "Properly rewarding workers could reward employers, too." (August 2012), *Workforce Management*, 1(8), 8. As noted by Laabs, J. (November 1998), "Satisfy them with more than money." *Workforce*, 77(11), 40–43, employees want more than money. They want to be needed, valued, and appreciated, something a paycheck alone cannot accomplish.

104 Breslin, M. S. (January 2013), op. cit.

105 Breslin, M. S. (August 2012), op. cit.

106 Ibid.

107 The Build Quarterly Report. (December 2013/January 2014). Talent management. *Inc*, 35(10), 2–3. Retrieved at http://remote.baruch.cuny.edu/login?url=http://search.e bscohost.com/login.aspx?direct=true&db=f6h&AN=92770346&site=ehost-live

108 Lackey, S. (April 2009). "Fill those unpopular shifts: Point-based awards and incentives drive employee behavior in positive ways, provide administrative efficiency and reduce cost." *HR Magazine*, 54(4), 63–66.

109 Kopelman, R. E., Gardberg, N. A., and Brandwein, A. C. (2011). "Using a recognition and reward initiative to improve service excellence: A quasi-experimental field study in a public higher education institution." *Public Personnel Management*, 40(2), 133–149.

110 Schneller, G. O. IV, and Kopelman, R. E. (1983). "Using incentives to *increase* absenteeism: A plan that backfired." *Compensation Review*, 15(2), 40–45.

111 Pritchard, R. D., Harrell, M. M., DiazGranados, D., and Guzman, M. J. (2008). "The productivity measurement and enhancement system: A meta-analysis." *Journal of Applied Psychology*, 93(3), 540–567.

112 Scaduto, A., Hunt, B., and Schmerling, D. (2015). "A performance management solution: Productivity measurement and enhancement system (ProMES)." *Industrial and Organizational Psychology*, 8(1), 93–100.

113 Komaki, J. (1998). *Leadership from an operant perspective*. London: Routledge.

114 Ibid.

115 Komaki, J. (1984). Comment at the I/O Psychology Division of the American Psychological Association Professional Development Workshop.

116 Holley, P. (February 3, 2016). "The crazy things Bill used to do to monitor workplace productivity." *The Washington Post*. Retrieved at https://www.washingtonpost.com /news/on-leadership/wp/2016/02/03/the-crazy-thing-bill-gates-used-to-do-to-monitor-workplace-productivity/?hpid+hp-more-top-stories_gates-650am percent-t3Ahomepage percent2Fstory

117 Streitfeld, D. (August 19, 2015). "The 24-hour timecard." *The New York Times*, pp. B1–2. More rigorous evidence that excessive monitoring can create stress and increase turnover is provided by the research of Batt, R., and Colvin, A. (2011). "An employment systems approach to turnover: Human resources practices, quits, dismissals, and performance." *Academy of Management Journal*, 54(4), 606–717.

118 Harkin, B, Webb, T. L., Chang, B. P. I., Prestwich, A., Conner, M, Kellar, I. Benn, Y., and Sheeran, P. (2016). "Does monitoring of goal progress promote goal attainment? A meta-analysis of the experimental evidence." *Psychological Bulletin*, 142(2), 198–229.

119 Kopelman. R. E. (2003). "GMFAC: How a simply successful approach to organizational improvement worked in a large city hospital." *Journal of Organizational Excellence*, 23(1), 37–42.

120 Allen, S. A. (1976). *Aer Lingus—Irish (B) case*. op. cit.

121 Kopelman, R. E. (1990). "Accountability with the emphasis on count." *National Productivity Review*, 9(2), 127–129. Note that the formula Performance = f (results, considering) suggests that, in broad terms, life can be viewed as a series of multiple regression equations.

122 Kerr, S. (1995). "On the folly of rewarding A, while hoping for B." *Academy of Management Executive*, 9(1), 7–16. Along these lines, if the path to pay increases is not work via behavior and/or job performance, but rather almost entirely through seniority, employees will be primarily motivated to take their vitamins and minerals, so they can reach the top of the pay scale.

123 Kopelman, R. E. (2003). "GMFAC: How a simply successful approach to organizational improvement worked at a large city hospital." *Journal of Organizational Excellence*, 23(1), 37–42.

124 Olivero, G., and Kopelman, R. E. (1998). "Reducing patient-flow cycle time in the emergency room of an inner city hospital." *National Productivity Review*, 17(4), 5–12.

125 Fiuchette, H. H. with copyright by Ross, P. (1978). "I follow a garbage truck." 4pp.

126 Bloom, N, Genakos, C., Sadun, R, and Van Reenen, J. (2012). "Management practices across firms and countries." *Academy of Management Executive*, 26(1), 12–33. Regarding the methodology, 18 statements assessed the three sets of management practices, six directed to each of the three categories, G, M, and C. The researchers addressed the possibility that the exceptionally high association between management practices and GDP was an artifact of inaccurate measurements. Specifically, they had independent raters score management practices. The two sets of ratings of the practices correlated at 0.89, providing evidence of their validity.

127 Kessler, A. (2011). *Eat people: And other unapologetic rules for game-changing entrepreneurs.* New York: Portfolio/Penguin, p. 87.

128 Luthans, K. W., and Sommer, S. M. (2005). "The impact of high performance work on industry-level outcomes." *Journal of Managerial Issues*, 17(3), 327–345.

129 Tannenbaum, A. S. (1968). *Control in organizations.* New York: McGraw-Hill. Data were collected from multiple divisions of the same organization, (e.g., 33 automobile sales agencies, 40 life insurance agencies) so that performance metrics were comparable. It is notable that as employees gained power/influence, managers gained power/influence—in addition to there being significantly higher unit performance.

130 Jiang, K., Lepak, D. P., Hu, J., and Baer, J. C. (2012). "How does human resource management influence organizational outcomes? A meta-analytic investigation of mediating mechanisms." *Academy of Management Journal*, 55(6), 1264–1294.

131 Piening, E. P., Baluch, A. M., and Salge, T. O. (2013). "The relationship between employees' perceptions of human resource systems and organizational performance: Examining mediating mechanisms and temporal dynamics." *Journal of Applied Psychology*, 98(6), 926–947.

132 Chang, S., Jia, L, Takeuchi, R, and Cai, Y. (2014). "Do high-commitment work systems affect creativity? A multilevel combinational approach to employee creativity." *Journal of Applied Psychology*, 99(4), 665–680.

133 Pfeffer, J. (1998). "Seven practices of successful organizations." *California Management Review*, 40(2), 96–124.

134 Ibid.

135 *The Economist.* (March 19, 1994). "Managing people: Nicely does it." Issue 7855, p. 94.

136 Pfeffer, J. op. cit.

137 Lehoczky, E. (July/August, 2015). "Get out of the employees' way. One layer of bosses drives staff creativity and sales." *Inc.*, 37(6), 24.

138 *First Round Review.* (May 14, 2015). "Bureaucracy isn't inevitable—Here's how Airbnb beat it." Retrieved at https://growthhackers.com/posts/httpfirstround-comrevie wbureaucracy-isnt-inevitable-heres-how-airbnb-beat-it

139 Ibid. Regarding bureaucracy, and in contrast to the management approach at Airbnb, in my graduate courses I seek to develop professional bureaucrats. Therefore, I share excerpts from the bureaucrat's bible by Boren, J. H. (1972). *When in doubt, mumble: A bureaucrat's handbook.* New York: Van Nostrand Reinhold. I (facetiously) instruct prospective future bureaucrats in the proper way to cut red tape—lengthwise—so that it

is challenging to get through it. Moreover, I hold out the tantalizing possibility that with further practice and instruction, they might attain a higher level than merely a *professional* bureaucrat. They might become a *visionary* bureaucrat—able to author complex regulations that are virtually impenetrable, and internally contradictory.

140 Nocera, J. (July 7, 2015) "The good jobs strategy." *The New York Times*. Retrieved at www.nytimes.com/.../joe-nocera-the-good-jobs-strategy.html

141 Kopelman, R. E., and Prottas, D. J. (2013). "Douglas McGregor's Theory X and Theory Y." Chapter in E. H. Kessler, ed. *Encyclopedia of management theories*. Thousand Oaks, CA: Sage Reference Publications. (pp. 874–878).

142 Bryant, A. (June 2, 2013). Here's my vision. And here's yours. Let's make it work. (Interview with Jenna Fagnan). *New York Times*. p. B2. Quoted material reproduced with permission of *The New York Times*. Copyright © 2013 *The New York Times*. Although Steve Jobs has received "bad press" about his being at times a brutal bully, Isaacson in his April 2012 *Harvard Business Review* article, "The real leadership lessons of Steve Jobs" noted that Jobs could also bring out the best in people by believing in them. In Jobs' words, "I've learned over the years that when you hire really good people you don't have to baby them. By expecting them to do great things, you can get them to do great things." p. 100.

143 Wisdom to live by. (January 8, 2015). "Marriott on collaboration." *Investor's Business Daily*, p. A3.

144 Tziner, A., and Kopelman, R. E. (2002). "Is there a preferred performance rating format? A non-psychometric perspective." *Applied Psychology: An International Review*, 51(3), 479–503. The primary "downsides" to the use of BOS in comparison to GRS assessments, are the increased costs of scale development and the need to provide rater training.

145 As noted in connection with feedback, the majority of employees see themselves as performing at an above-average level. So the provision of ranking performance feedback necessitates that one-half of all rates receive below-average performance scores. Although rankings fully obviate the problem of leniency, they can be demoralizing. The switch at Microsoft from rankings to ratings was reported to have increased employee output by 11%. See McGregor, J. (August 27, 2013). "With Steve Ballmer's departure, a look at Microsoft's flawed system of performance reviews." *The Washington Post*. Retrieved at https://www.washingtonpost.com/news/on-leadership/wp/20 13/08/27/with-steve-ballmers-departure-a-look-at-microsofts-flawed-system-o f-performance-reviews/

146 Patz, A. I. (May–June 1975). "Performance appraisal: Useful but still resisted." *Harvard Business Review*, 53(3), 74–80. Additional examples of raters' deliberate distortions of ratings to advance the rater's personal goals include giving low ratings because of fear that an employee may be promoted, or high ratings due to fear of violence by the ratee. See Tziner, A., and Roch, S. G. (2016). "Disappointing interventions and weak criteria: Carving out a solution is still possible." *Industrial and Organizational Psychology*, 9(2), 350–356.

147 Murphy, K. R., and Cleveland, J. N. (1995). *Understanding performance appraisal: Social, organizational and goal-based perspectives*. Thousand Oaks, CA: Sage, p. 314.

148 Lopez, F. M. (1975). *Personnel interviewing: Theory and practice*, 2nd ed. New York: McGraw-Hill.

149 Hall, D. T., and Lawler E. E. III. (1969). "Unused potential in research and development organizations." *Research Management*, 12(5), 339–354. Also see Hall, D. T. (1976). *Careers in organizations*. Santa Monica, CA: Goodyear, pp. 68, 155.

150 Levy, P. E., and Williams, J. R. (2004). "The social context of performance appraisal: A review and framework for the future." *Journal of Management*, 30(6), 881–905.

151 Roch, S. G., Sternburgh, A., and Caputo, P. (2007). Absolute versus relative performance rating formats: Implications for fairness and organizational justice. *International Journal of Selection and Assessment*, 15(3), 302–316.

152 Roch, S. G., Woehr, D. J., Mishra, V., and Kieszczynska, U. (2012). "Rater training revisited: An updated meta-analytic Frame-of-Reference Training." *Journal of Occupational and Organizational Psychology*, 85(2), 370–395.

153 Tziner and Roch, op. cit.

154 Aguinis, H. (2009). *Performance management*, 2nd ed. Upper Saddle River, NJ: Pearson Prentice-Hall. (Dr. Aguinis has extensive consulting experience.)

155 Pulakos, E. D. (2009). *Performance management: A new approach for driving business results.* West Sussex, UK and Malden, MA: Wiley-Blackwell. Indicative of her hands-on experience, in 2009, Dr. Pulakos was the Chief Operating Officer of the prominent consulting firm PDRI (Personnel Decisions Research Institute), and held highest academic designation, being a fellow of APA and SIOP.

156 Pulakos, E. D., and O'Leary, R. S. (2011). "Why is performance management broken?" *Industrial and Organizational Psychology: Perspectives on Science and Practice*, 4(2), 146–164. Thirteen articles were written in response to Pulakos and O'Leary's focal article, most acknowledging that the performance management process is difficult and needs careful attention.

157 Buckingham, M., and Goodall, A. (2015). "Reinventing performance management: How one company is rethinking peer feedback and the annual review, and trying to design a system to fuel improvement." *Harvard Business Review*, 94(4), 40–50.

158 Pulakos, E. D., Hanson, R. M., Arad, S., and Moye, N. (2015). "Performance management can be fixed: An on-the-job experiential learning approach for complex behavior change." *Industrial and Organizational Psychology*, 8(1), 51–76.

159 Rachitsky, L. (July 20, 2019). "The power of performance reviews: Use this system to become a better manager." *First Round Review*. Retrieved at https://firstround.com/review/the-power-of-performance-reviews-use-this-system-to-become-a-better-manager/. Accessed on July 20, 2019.

160 Greenfield, R. (July 13, 2015). "The future is bossless: Skeptical professionals adopt a guru's convoluted management system." *Bloomberg Businessweek*, Issue 4434, p. 63. According to Greenfield, "after Zappos realized new hires were perplexed, the company added a three-day Holocracy session. … Anyone who shows up late for the daily 7am start is fired on the spot. New hires take a final exam—and must score 90 percent or they are let go."

161 Bluedorn, A. C., Turban, D. B., and Love, M. S. (1999). "The effects of stand-up and sit-down meeting formats on meeting outcomes." *Journal of Applied Psychology*, 84(2), 277–285. The idea of applying this intervention at Chevron was developed by Pfeffer, J., and Sutton, R. I. (January, 2006). "Evidence-based management." *Harvard Business Review*, 84(1), 63–74.

162 Grantham, V. (June 1, 2015). "Desk jockey: Ad guru Sophie Kelly takes the open office plan to winding new heights." *New York Post*, p. 31.

163 Pavlus, J. (September 22–28, 2004). "Don't get too cozy: A musical-chairs approach to an office may improve efficiency: People are more aware of 'what they're going into the office to do.'" *Bloomberg Businessweek*, pp. 51–52.

164 Grantham, V. (June 1, 2015). "Desk jockey: Ad guru Sophie Kelly takes the open office plan to winding new heights." *New York Post*, p. 31.

165 Randall, K. (December 26, 2014). "Teams turn to a face reader, looking for that winning smile." *The New York Times*, pp. A1, B7. Pertinent to the generalizability of Hill's methodology, he has being conducting facial analyses for 16 years, mostly for companies developing advertising campaigns or new products. Hill claims that his analysis is especially useful in focus groups whose members are often unwilling or unable to speak frankly and convey their true opinions.

166 Huselid, M. (1995). "The impact of human resource management practices on turnover, productivity, and corporate financial performance." *Academy of Management Journal*, 38(3), 635–672.

167 Huselid, M., Jackson, S, and Schuler, R. (1997). "Technical and strategic human resource management effectiveness as determinants of firm performance." *Academy of Management Journal*, 40(1), 171–188.

168 Jiang, K., Lepak, D. P., Hu, J., and Baer, J. C. (2012). "How does human resource management influence organizational outcomes? A meta-analytic investigation of mediating mechanisms." *Academy of Management Journal*, 55(6), 1264–1294.

169 Stajkovic, A. D., and Luthans, F. (2003), "Behavioral management and task performance in organizations: Conceptual background, meta-analysis, and test of alternative models." *Personnel Psychology*, 56(1), 155–194.

170 Rabl, T., Jayasinghe, M., Gerhart, B., and Kuhlmann, T. M. (2014). "A meta-analysis of country differences in the high-performance work system-business performance relationship: The roles of national culture and managerial discretion." *Journal of Applied Psychology*, 99(6), 1011–1041.

171 Aryee, S., Walumbwa, F. O., Seidu, E. Y. M., and Otaye, L. E. (2012). "Impact of high-performance work systems on individual- and branch-level performance: Test of a multilevel model of intermediate linkages." *Journal of Applied Psychology*, 97(2), 287–300.

172 Freiberg, K., and Freiberg, J. (1998). *Nuts! Southwest Airlines' crazy recipe for business and personal success*. New York, NY: Crown Business.

173 Cachon, G, and Terwiesch, C. (2017). *Operations management*. New York, NY: McGraw-Hill. Details on the growth of Starbucks can be accessed at the company's website: http://www.starbucks.com/about-us/company-information/starbucks-company-profile. Accessed on June 9, 2016.

174 Gordon, J. S. (August 14, 2015). "The man behind modern math." *Barron's*, p .45.

175 Part of the data are from a website called "this day in history" Retrieved at http://www.history.com/this-day-in-history/moving-assembly-line-at-ford/print

176 Smith, S. S. (June 126, 2014). "The father of containers made big shipping waves." *Investor's Business Daily*, p. A3.

177 Kelleher, K. (July/August, 2014), "Big data, small budget. So you think Big Data is just for the giants? So did these companies—once." *Inc*. 36(6), 68–72.

178 Ibid.

179 Howeel, D. (December 26, 2013), "Tech at UPS, FedEx focuses on humans." *Investor's Business Daily*, pp. 1, 4.

180 Ibid.

181 Dvorak, P. (June 26, 2006). "Why management trends quickly fade away." *The Wall Street Journal*. Retrieved at http://www.wsj.com/articles/SB115127414542190162. Accessed on June 8, 2016.

182 Smith, A. (1776/2003). *The wealth of nations*. New York, NY: Bantam Dell. The description and analysis of the pin factory appears on pp. 10–13.

183 Hammer, A., and Champy, J. (1993). *Reengineering the corporation: A manifesto for business revolution*. New York: HarperCollins.

184 Hammer, M. (July/August 1990). "Reengineering work: Don't automate, obliterate." *Harvard Business Review*, 68(4), 104–112.

185 Shell, R. W. (Spring, 1992). "Cashing in the chips." *Wharton Alumni Magazine*, pp. 9–13.

186 Levinson, W. A. (2003). "The true origin of Just-In-Time manufacturing." Web blog posting, Retrieved at http://www.ct-yankee.com/lean/mlw/jit.html. Accessed on June 8, 2016.

187 Stahl, F. (2015). "Managing for productivity in the 21st century." *Perspectives on Work*, 19, 10–13.

188 Foster, T. (June, 2014). "Along Came Lolly: From the unlikeliest of places, an e-commerce revolution—with ruffles." *Inc.*, 36(5), 24–36. Indicative of the promise of Lolly Wolly Doodle, in June 2013, the company received a capital investment of $20 million

from the fund started by Steve Case, the founder of AOL. Case "aims to make it [Lolly Wolly Doodle] a multibillion–dollar brand." p. 26.

189 Schachter, K. (July 15, 2015), "Kaizen: Merger brings a new management philosophy to Pall Corp." *Newsday*, pp. A33–A37.

190 Stewart, T. A., and Raman, A. P. (July–August, 2007). "Lessons from Toyota's long drive: An Interview with Katsuaki Watanabe." *Harvard Business Review*, 85(7/8), 74–83.

191 Rahman, S., Laosirihongthong, and Sohal, A. S. (2010). "Impact of lean strategy on operational performance: A study of Thai manufacturing companies." *Journal of Manufacturing Technology Management*, 21(7), 839–852.

192 Ibid.

193 Liker, J. K. (2004). *The Toyota way: 14 management principles from the world's greatest manufacturer*. New York: McGraw-Hill.

194 Ibid.

195 Stewart, and Raman, op.cit.

196 Taylor, F. W. (1911). *The principles of scientific management*. New York and London: Harper & Brothers.

197 Fishman, C. (December, 2006). "No satisfaction at Toyota." *Fast Company*, 111, 82–92.

198 Ibid., p. 88–89. Quotation reproduced with permission of Fast Company©2019. All rights reserved.

199 Ibid., p. 89. Quotation reproduced with permission of *Fast Company* © 2019. All rights reserved.

200 Bremner, G. M., and Dawson, C. (November 17, 2003). "Can anything stop Toyota?" *Business Week*, 1, 114–122.

201 McGee, M. reporter. (2006). "Toyota production system in the news," video from the Canadian cable channel Report on Business Television (renamed Business News Network in 2007). Retrieved at www.youtube.com/watch?v=jlcrqb2qMAA. Accessed on June 8, 2016.

202 Takeuchi, H., Osono, E., and Shimizu, N. (2008). "The contradictions that drive Toyota's success." *Harvard Business Review*, 86(6), 96–104.

203 Ibid.

204 Estrel, M. (February 22, 2016). "How Dr. Pepper cuts costs. And then cuts costs some more." *The Wall Street Journal*, p. R4.

205 Ibid.

206 Ibid.

207 Graham, J. (April 9, 2010) cites the book by Charles Sorenson, *My forty years at Ford* for this quote, p. A3.

208 Graham, op cit., citing the book by Henry Ford, *My life and work*, p. A3.

209 Graham, op. cit., p. A3.

210 Takeuchi et al., op. cit.

211 "Toyota Prius: A brief history in time." Retrieved at http://www.greencarreports.com/news/1014178_toyota-prius-a-brief-history-in-time. Accessed on January 31, 2016.

212 "Toyota Mirai—The turning point." Retrieved at http://22l.toyota,com.mirai/fuel.html. Accessed on January 31, 2016. (This article was removed from their blog, but replaced by a 2018 entry: http://upcomingtoyota.us/read-toyota-mirai-the-turning-point) More details can be found in the Google entry: Toyota-Marai The Turning Point for Zero Emission Cars. See: www.vroomgirls.com/toyota-mirai

213 Takeuchi et al., op. cit.

214 Yakahashi, Y., and Linebauch, K. (December 23, 2008). "Toyota sees first loss in 70 years: Global plunge in car demand creates an 'emergency that we've never experienced'". *Wall Street Journal*. Retrieved at http://www.wsj.com/articles/SB12299 2788012825897. Accessed on June 8, 2016.

215 Maynard, M. (February 12, 2009). "Toyota's cost-cutting plan to include buyouts for factory workers." *Wall Street Journal*, p. B1, and Linebaugh, K. (February 13, 2009). "Facing a loss, Toyota offers job buyouts, end bonuses." *Wall Street Journal*, p. B1.

216 Scarbrough, D., and Alpenberg, J. (2009). "Culture and the Toyota production system archetype: A preliminary assessment." Chapter in K. Jonnergard and R. G. Larson, ed. *Från barkbröd till ciabatta: kreativitet och kontroll inom ekonomistyrning : en generationsväxlingsbok tillägnad Lars-Göran Aidemark, Göran Andersson, Torbjörn Bredenlöw och Tomas Prenkert.* Goteborg, Sweden: Vaxjo University Press.

217 Tabuchi, H., (September 18, 2013). "Eiji Toyoda, promoter of the Toyota Way and engineer of its growth dies at 100." Obituary in *The New York Times,* p. B17.

218 George, M. L. (2003). *Lean Six Sigma for service.* New York: McGraw-Hill.

219 Ibid.

220 Desai, K. J., Desai, M. S., and Ojode, L. (Summer 2015), "Supply chain risk management framework: A fishbone analysis approach." *SAM Advanced Management Journal,* 80(4), 34–56.

221 Das, A. (2017). *An introduction to operations management: The joy of operations.* New York and London: Routledge.

222 Capwell, K. (October 20, 2008). "Zara thrives by breaking all the rules." *Business Week,* 4104, 66.

223 Rogers, C. (February 8, 2016). "Ford to more than double Mexico production capacity in 2018." *The Wall Street Journal.* Retrieved at http://wsj.com/articles/ford-to-more-than-double-mexico-production-capacity-in-2018-1454857923. Of course, Ford and G.M. are not the only foreign auto manufacturers with plants in Mexico. Others include BMW, Honda, Volkswagen, Kia, Nissan, and Mazda. See *Wall Street Journal,* March 4, 2016, p. A12.

224 Drummond, D., and Hamilton, P. (2010). "Supply chain transformation case study: NSLIJHS." PowerPoint slides were retrieved at http://www.google.com/url?sa =t&rct=j&q=&esrc=s&source=web&cd=1&ved=0ahUKEwiUj9SozJvLAhWB kx4KHS_rBHsQFggcMAA&url=http percent3A percent2F percent2Fwww.hfma-metrony.org percent2FPortals percent2F0 percent2FA1-Mapping-the-Future.... ppt&usg=AFQjCNHhOZuCiT05k_Z0DWXCCyPSuCVMbQ&bvm=bv.1153392 55,d.dmo

225 Ibid.

226 Jusko, J. (October 6, 2015). "General Mills' big loss." *Industry Week.* Retrieved at http: //www.industryweek.com/supply-chain/top-25-supply-chains-2015#slide-4-field _images-167391

227 Hessman, T. (February 17, 2016). "2015 IW Best Plants winner: Lean thinking in action at ATS Corp." *Industry Week.* Retrieved at http://www.industryweek.com/in dustryweek-best-plants/2015-iw-best-plants-winner-lean-thinking-action-ats-corp. Analogous to the prior situation at ATS in 2014 would be an organization that was intellectually aware of the need for a budget, but then ignored budgetary issues.

228 Brenneman, G. (1998). "Right away and all at once: How we saved Continental." *Harvard Business Review,* 76(5), 162–179. Bethune (in *From Worst to First*) points out that there is a limit to which a company can cut costs and remain in business. A pizza maker can make a very inexpensive pizza by leaving off the cheese.

229 Kelly, K. J. (November 12, 2015), "Truck stop: Zuckerman hands News drivers digital threat." *New York Post,* p. 45.

230 Nassauer, S. (June 18, 2015). "Welcome back, Wal-Mart greeters." *The Wall Street Journal.* Retrieved at http://www.wsj.com/articles/wal-mart-ushers-greeters-ba ck-to-the-front-1434651944

231 Will, G. F. (March 26, 2015). "Economics isn't hard: Just ask Keith Richards." *Investor's Business Daily,* p. A13.

3

EMPLOYEE-DIRECTED PRACTICES

As noted in Chapter 2, 14 High Performance Work Practices (HPWP) have been identified and conventionally classified into three categories: ability-related practices; motivation-related practices; and opportunity-enhancing practices. The first two (increasing ability and motivation) primarily enhance individual and organizational performance and are thus considered enterprise-directed practices in the Cube One framework. Opportunity-enhancing practices primarily concern employees and their careers.

Four of the 14 HPWP focus on enhancing employee loyalty, engagement, satisfaction, and performance of tasks outside of employees' core job responsibilities (sometimes referred to as organizational citizenship behaviors—OCB). The four employee-directed practices are employment security, information sharing, extensive benefits, and work teams. These four practices have motivational and ability-related side effects but are mainly promotive of employee attitudes of loyalty and satisfaction. The Cube One framework entails some complexity in that practices often do not exclusively affect just one of the three dimensions or domains. Extensive benefits and job security may increase the size of the pool of potential applicants for a position, and thereby indirectly increase the likelihood of attracting and selecting talented and motivated employees who will be high performers.

Well-managed organizations tend to consider the interests of all three primary parties: the organization, employees, and customers. Consider the Toyota Way discussed in the previous chapter. In addition to Toyota's emphasis on *kaizen* and frugality (which enhance productivity and profitability), the company is dedicated to long-term product planning (which provides new and improved products for customers). Toyota provides respectful treatment of all involved parties. Toyota emphasizes the equality of its personnel, a high commitment to teams, and sharing information—which are conducive to increasing employee (and supplier) loyalty, satisfaction, and commitment. One can parse the components of the Toyota Production System into categories of practices in terms of the Cube One framework: Toyota emphasizes product and service quality and innovativeness which translate into customer satisfaction. Toyota pays special attention to efficiency and demonstrates high concern for employees. In essence, the success of Toyota can be explained in terms of practices promotive of the three dimensions of the Cube One framework.

The levels of enactment of the three sets of practices are not independent across organizations. Well-managed organizations tend to attend to all three causal dimensions. Hence, when examining organizational practices and performance data across organizations, it is difficult to isolate the exclusive effects of each set of practices, (a phenomenon that parallels what statisticians refer to as multicollinearity.) Chapter 5 of this book presents empirical research across more than 1,000 organizations that makes this case persuasively.

In addition to the four employee-directed HPWP, there are at least an additional half-dozen sets of employee-directed practices that might also be adopted, yielding a collection of ten categories of practices. Such categories are, by definition, broad collections of specific actions, which evolve over time as organizations find new ways to enhance employee loyalty and satisfaction.

In contrast to the relatively clear-cut financial effects of enterprise-directed practices—which directly relate to productivity, efficiency, and profitability—the effects of employee-directed practices on an organization's bottom line are less directly evident. However, evidence of the effects of employee-related practices does exist with respect to specific jobs, and across organizations.

Job-Level Financial Impact

Excessive employee turnover can create four types of costs which can be classified as related to separation, replacement, training, and lost productivity or business. Separation costs include those associated with exit interviews; the administrative tasks associated with termination, possible separation payments; and increases in unemployment taxes. Replacement costs include costs associated with communicating job availability, processing applications, conducting interviews, holding staff meetings, testing or other assessment procedures, post-hiring administrative activities, and possible medical examinations.

Training costs include informational literature (e.g., an employee handbook), organizational orientation (or more broadly "on-boarding"), formal training programs, and the costs of employees involved in on-the-job training. Finally, costs associated with lost productivity include overtime pay to cover a vacancy, additional temporary employees, lost productivity associated with the learning curve ("time to full performance"), and the customers, sales, and profits that might be lost due to an employee's departure.[1]

The combined costs of unplanned turnover can easily exceed 150% of the departing person's salary (as reported by Ernst & Young in connection with filling a position vacated by an entry-level auditor). Costs increase with the complexity of a job, as recruiting, selecting, and training new employees becomes more resource intensive. At pharmaceutical giant Merck, costs associated with turnover reportedly ranged from 150% to 250% of annual salary, depending on the job.[2]

Organizational-Level Financial Impact

The financial results of companies in the *Fortune* "100 Best Companies to Work for in America" provide a broader-gauged analysis of the effects of employee-directed practices. Membership in this elite group is restricted to organizations at least 10 years old, with a minimum of 500 employees—and the willingness to devote at least 300 hours annually to completing the application process. The 100 Best is based on results of surveys sent to 225 employees from each eligible organization. The surveys tap a number of key domains of employee-directed practices:

- keeping employees informed via open and two-way communication;
- concern for individuals in the broader scope of their personal lives, including issues of work/family balance;
- creating a feeling or sense of belonging to a "family" or "team";
- perceived fairness as manifested by impartiality and justice;
- providing opportunities for personal as well as professional growth;
- integrity as manifested by consistency of statements and actions.[3]

Among public, for-profit organizations, members of the 100 Best have achieved superior financial results compared to their peers. Comparing the 100 Best with a set of matching companies, the former had a higher Return on Assets (ROA) each year of a six-year period. Comparative stock market performance found a gain of 376% for the 100 Best versus 193% for a broad market index, an advantage of 183% points.[4]

Organizations selected for inclusion in the 100 Best list have gained, thereby, a human capital or reputational strategic asset.[5] According to an analysis by Great Place to Work®, voluntary turnover among the 2016 *Fortune* 100 Best was 50% lower than among industry peers.[6]

The brokerage firm Edward D. Jones & Company provides an impressive example. The year before the company made the 100 Best list it received 7,000 applications for employment. Five years after inclusion (in 2003), Edward D. Jones received 400,000 employment applications. Assuming a fixed number of about 35,000 employees (Edward D. Jones recently had 43,000), and assuming a low annual turnover rate of 10% prior to inclusion in the "Top 100" list, Edward D. Jones would have hired about 3,500 individuals annually—equivalent to a selection ratio of 50%. Being able to select from 400,000 applicants means a selection ratio of less than 1%. This translates into new hires being about two standard deviations more qualified than under the prior (7,000-applicant) scenario. Assuming an average annual salary of $35,000 (conservative in the financial services industry), the productivity gain would be worth more than $30 million annually. In other words, the 300 hours of time required to apply for the 100 Best yielded about $30,000,000 annually.

A small downside: each year applicant companies must apply from scratch, and it does not look good to "fall off" the list. Thus, as in other performance domains, performing well in terms of employee-directed practices creates further pressure to maintain the same performance level. As Robert Sobiech, director of human resources for the Midwest Cluster of Deloitte & Touche, has noted, "The bar is always getting higher. It's just because other employers continue to roll out imaginative benefits. [So] you're always wondering, what is the next thing and how can we keep up?"[7]

Three Companies with Excellent Employee-Directed Practices

Reviewing case studies of companies with excellent employee-directed practices resembles stamp-collecting. How many of the spaces in the album have been filled? Thus, it helps to think of these practices in terms of the ten specific categories. This brings order and simplicity to the examination of practices. The three companies discussed below have demonstrated extraordinary concern for employees and addressed every—or nearly every—category.

Costco is famous for how well the company treats employees. A 2013 article entitled "How Cheap is Craig Jelinek?" notes that Costco reveals few signs of status differentials. For example, at Costco's headquarters outside of Seattle, the floor of the executive wing is covered with faded blue carpeting. Inside the boardroom are six faux-wood tables jammed together, resembling a primary school lounge. The artwork on the boardroom walls consists of copies of Van Gogh and Picasso prints that can be purchased for less than $15. Costco has no public relations staff. The Chief Financial Officer gives journalists his cell phone number and returns calls on a Saturday.[8]

Costco's inherent thriftiness and no-frills culture is not manifested in the way employees are treated, though. Job security is paramount, and in 2009, at the height of the last recession, Costco eschewed job or pay cuts (implemented by most competitors). Moreover, that year Costco announced that hourly employees would receive a pay increase of $1.50 per hour, spread over three years.[9]

Costco's benefits include matching 401k pension plans; up to five weeks of vacation a year; and company-paid health insurance which is provided for 88% of employees. Only 4% of Costco's workers are temporary, primarily employees paid directly by contractors who give away samples or sell cell phones. Costco pays for undergraduate and graduate school education for its warehouse workers.[10]

How can Costco be so generous in comparison to other prominent retailers? A key facet of their business model is that shoppers must purchase an individual membership for $60 or a family or Executive membership for $120. One factor contributing to its 90 million-strong membership is Costco's refusal to mark up a product more than 14%. At least two-thirds of the company's net profit comes from membership fees.[11] Walmart also has a membership division—Sam's Club—but Sam's sales amount to only 12% of Walmart's total revenues.[12]

The average hourly pay at Costco has recently been reported at about $20, whereas the average pay at Walmart is usually cited at around $13/hour. The difference is largely an artifact of the way average salaries are calculated. Walmart weights average salaries by the number of people in different titles. Costco calculates an average of the pay levels associated with different positions, weighting each position equally (despite there being a lot more clerks than supervisors).[13]

Patagonia is primarily an outdoor clothing and equipment company headquartered in Ventura, Calif. The company, founded in the late 1970s, has had since its inception a very strong commitment to the environment, donating 1% of sales to grassroots environmental organizations. Patagonia's annual sales in 2013 were $600 million, and its profits tripled from 2008 to 2013, in part reflecting the employees' team spirit and passion for the company. Patagonia has enacted at least eight of the ten sets of employee-directed practices described below. Note that company size is not determinative of the enactment of employee-directed practices. Patagonia's revenues were one-half of 1% of Costco's annual revenues of approximately $120 billion in 2016.[14]

An employee turnover level at least 40% below the industry average (according to the U. S. Bureau of Labor Statistics) contributes to Patagonia's profitability and reflects its practices enacted. At company headquarters the café serves organic food, and one of the café windows looks into the childcare room. Benefits include two months of paid leave for new parents and flexible work hours. If an employee has a family member who is ill, Patagonia will tell the employee to take off whatever time is needed. The founder, Yvon Chouinard, encourages workers to go surfing when the waves are up. Describing his company's policy on National Public Radio, he stated "I don't care when you work as long as the job gets done."

In Patagonia's Boston store—where the interior echoes the company's lodge-like feel—employees feel that they belong to a team. According to the store manager, employees both work and play together. "As a result, people stay around longer because they feel supported and understood." Employees are encouraged to make suggestions to management. Managers are coached to trust employees and treat them with respect. Quarterly meetings where executives review financial results are open to all employees.

Patagonia has only had one large-scale layoff—during the recession in the early 1990s. After two years of service, employees can apply for a two-month internship with environmental nonprofits, and concurrently be paid by Patagonia. To downplay status differentials at the company's headquarters, no one has a private office.

To summarize, Patagonia's employee-directed practices mitigate work–life conflicts; encourage teamwork; grant employees considerable autonomy; keep employees informed; encourage employees to share ideas; provide a high level of job security; and minimize hierarchical status differences.

Mitchells was founded in 1958 with first-year annual sales of $50,000. In 2008, when Jack Mitchell published *Hug Your People*, his three-generation family-owned business operated three stores. At that time, Mitchells was the largest independent family-owned high-end specialty clothing store in the U.S. with approximately $100 million in revenues (about one-sixth the sales of Patagonia, and less than 0.01% the sales of Costco). Despite its small size, Mitchells implements almost all the major categories of employee-directed practices.[15]

Because it is a third-generation privately held firm, the company is particularly sensitive to minimizing status differences. All employees are "associates," and no ostensible perks go to family members and management: there are not even assigned parking spaces or an executive dining room. The president will serve coffee and empty the trash.

Mitchells reports sales information to all 250 associates. Data are available on a real-time basis. Any associate can log on to a store computer and not just get quarterly or annual sales, but sales figures by the week, day, hour, and department compared to the prior year. As Jack Mitchell noted, there is no point urging better results if people don't know the score, i.e., if they are above or below the previous year. At monthly meetings called "State of the Store," store sales and other financial results are shared with all associates.

In addition to financial transparency, CEO/Chairman Jack Mitchell sends out an email with a "Hug of the Week story" to all associates. Hug stories come about when someone does something special: then the act is shared (hugged) in an email to all. Information is not just disseminated on a need-to-know basis but on a want-to-know basis—including poor results. In Mitchell's words "associates see through distortions and spin, so they are never insulted with phony information." Managers encourage suggestions from associates: "Mark, what do you think we should do?" And managers give credit to associates for their ideas; they don't steal them.

Many managerial practices relate to creating a feeling of belonging. Paraphrasing Jack Mitchell, the company wants associates to see themselves as part of an extended family. Managers know associates' names (and nicknames), as well as interests.

After work, a store will have a Texas hold em' night; or everyone will be invited to a bowling party, or take a trip to Foxwoods Resort and Casino. Birthday cakes and store picnics are common. On every associate's birthday and employment anniversary, Jack Mitchell handwrites a personal note. In his words:

> When you connect with someone you often see an immediate impact. I'll always remember Joe [last name withheld] coming to see me and in a warm

> way thanking me for the card marking his tenth anniversary with us, and for the words I wrote. Joe's eyes filled with tears when he told me that he [left the card out] and his wife saw it. When she read it, she was blown away by the appreciation.[16]

A manager might say, "Stephen, go home early. I know it's your son's birthday and I'll cover for you." Flexible work schedules are permitted for various reasons. For example, one associate's husband opened up a business in Atlanta. The associate was allowed to work a four-day week and have a 900-mile commute. Another associate got a few days off to go on a college hunt.

Benefits include company-contributed health insurance. To foster professional growth, sales associates may become specialists in a product line such as jewelry or handbags and will go to market with buyers.

Mitchells also attempts to minimize fear and job-related anxiety. They communicate the idea that everyone makes mistakes, and punishment is avoided (except when there is dishonesty, which is never tolerated). By not punishing honest mistakes, management promotes integrity and reduces subterfuge.

Management responds to employee concerns with actions, and not just words. A trivial example: one associate commented that during the summer the store is hot and it would be nice to have a refrigerator with soft drinks. A couple of days later a mini-refrigerator materialized stocked with assorted drinks. On a broader scale, if a manager's words are not consistent with his/her actions, trust will quickly be eroded.

At Mitchells, conflicts are neither ignored nor swept under the rug. They are addressed, with associates encouraged to seek resolution—with a facilitator if necessary.

A review of the employee-directed practices enacted at Mitchells indicates that all or almost all of the categories have been covered.[17] What follows is an expanded and more detailed description of practices that comprise the ten categories.

1. Employment Security

Perhaps the most important employee-directed practice is employment security. It affects loyalty, commitment, and retention, and to a substantial degree employee ability, initiative, and motivation. It affects both employees and the enterprise.

In the classic Hawthorne Studies conducted at the Western Electric Company (1924–1932), a group incentive plan yielded increased performance levels among the Relay Assembly Test Room workers over a two-year period. However, a similar plan was ineffective in the Bank Wiring Room during the Depression, a time when customers returned more telephones than they bought. Employees (rationally) were fearful of job loss and withheld production from 1931 until May 1932, when the study ended because the Bank Wiring Room operation was closed down.[18]

Lincoln Electric has long had a successful performance-based incentive plan. As of 2015 it had not had a layoff in 67 years. James Lincoln noted in 1951 that workers will not acquire skills and apply imagination to work more efficiently if they fear unemployment will result due to work progress. In his speech at the Academy of Management in 1996, the CEO of Lincoln Electric called downsizing "dumbsizing."[19] The company's commitment to providing job security to all its workers has been a major contributor to its success.

Western Electric and Lincoln Electric were both concerned with job security—a person keeping one's own job—versus employment security, where a company makes an effort to keep people employed by a variety of techniques, such as shifting employees to different jobs. Illustrative of this distinction, when Honda opened its first U.S. plant in Marysville, Ohio, applicants were only considered if they were willing to move from job to job at management's discretion. Applicants were told that this flexibility was necessary to minimize layoffs during business downturns.[20]

The primary effects of job security at Western Electric and Lincoln Electric relate to employees' willingness to acquire new skills, apply creativity, and work hard.[21,22] Thus, the effects of job security are ability- and motivation-related, and therefore enterprise-directed. While job security leads to increased satisfaction among employees, the accretion in human capital ultimately shows up on an organization's bottom line. This point is underscored by Mitchell Fein, the developer of Improshare® (an incentive program that shares the value of productivity increases 50–50 between workers and organizations) and asserts that job security should be a *management demand* in labor relations. In his words:

> Since job security is such an important component of the work environment, management must look upon job security as *an essential precondition to enhancing the will to work* … In plants without job security workers will stretch out the work if they do not see sufficient work ahead of them. They will not work themselves out of their jobs.[23]

Broader in scope than job security, employment security can promote employee commitment and loyalty. Consider Toyota's refusal to back down on its guarantee of lifetime employment at its plant in Thailand, despite four consecutive years of losses (see Chapter 2). Toyota absorbed an annual increase in interest expenses of $220 million to keep its commitment.

Sadami Wada, a vice president at Sony, offered the following poignant comment: "I understand why some American companies fail to gain the loyalty and dedication of their employees. Employees cannot care for an employer who is prepared to take their livelihood away at the first sign of trouble."[24]

Even among companies that provide a commitment to lifetime employment, such as Toyota, employment security does not preclude organizations from firing people who consistently perform poorly. Nor does it preclude layoffs if a division or an entire enterprise that offers an obsolete product/service, or has adopted an unsustainable business model. An example of the latter is the sad case of Borders, the bookstore chain that outsourced its Internet business to Amazon. In 2008, Borders tried to reclaim its Internet business (three years after Amazon's Kindle, Barnes & Noble's Nook, and Apple's iPad were released). Despite (or perhaps thanks to) four CEOs in three years, and multiple business plans, Borders had to close 642 stores and lay off 19,500 employees when no buyer was interested in acquiring it.[25]

The threshold for poor performance may be lower at companies in dynamic, technology-based companies. Management at Netflix claims that employees generally know when their skill sets do not match what is required. When people enter this "death zone," terminations need not become a tragic, dragged-out drama. Rather, employees receive a generous severance package, a glowing reference, and thanks for making everything up to the present possible.[26]

According to "The Real Leadership Lessons of Steve Jobs," Jobs' primary concern was preventing a "bozo eruption." In Jobs' (edited) words: "I don't think I run roughshod over people, but if something [is poor] I tell people to their face. It's my job to be honest."[27]

High-tech companies are also concerned about retaining present employees. Intel uses a sentiment-processing algorithm developed by San Francisco-based Kanjoya to gain more insight into the 50,000 open-ended comments provided by employees on company surveys. Purportedly, sentiment-analysis software helps identify and resolve issues before talent starts to leave.[28] Most Fortune 500 companies use annual employee surveys to measure employees' job attitudes and predict, among other outcomes, the likelihood of employee turnover.

Maintaining employment security is a valuable employee-directed practice in part because it encourages employees to take a longer-term perspective. A study of 192 banks showed a significant relationship between employment security and the financial outcome of ROA. With employment security, loan officers were concerned not just with increasing the dollar amount of loans they arranged (and their pay), but also with the longer-term matter of repayment prospects.[29]

One of the most famous U.S. companies to have a policy of employment security is Southwest Airlines. Even after the near halt in air traffic after September 11, 2001, and during the depth of the recession in 2009, Southwest Airlines never had a layoff. As the founder and past CEO, Herb Kelleher, put it: "Certainly there were times when we could have made substantially more profits in the short term if we had furloughed people, but we didn't. We were looking at our employees' and our company's longer-term interests." Kelleher notes that if employment security is your goal, it imposes additional discipline—because to avoid layoffs you must hire carefully and sparingly.[30]

2. Open Two-Way Communication

An organization builds trust and minimizes rumors by sharing information with employees. As Frederick Reichheld, a management consultant at Bain & Company put it: "Loyalty is impossible without trust. And trust is impossible without accurate, reliable information."[31]

At Zappos, the presence of open two-way communication is an important facet of the corporate culture. In the company's monthly newsletter, *Ask Anything*, answers are provided to employees' anonymous questions. Zappos' founder and CEO, Tony Hsieh, sends emails to all employees when he has an important announcement to pass along. The company has even shared inventory, sales, and profitability data with vendors.[32]

At Four Seasons, the luxury hotel chain, founder and past CEO Isadore Sharp communicated directly with all employees on important occasions. Four Seasons frequently administers traditional-style employee surveys and shares quarterly results for each hotel. Employees from each unit of a hotel elect a representative who participates in monthly meetings with the general manager, sharing ideas and problems.[33] The company's transparency and communication strategy shone during the crisis resulting from 9/11, when Sharp wrote two letters to all employees outlining the company's strategy in response to the disaster.

A survey of Canadian Information Technology professionals found that they associated sharing information with heightened organizational commitment and greater willingness to engage in organizational citizenship behaviors. Organizational commitment is one of the strongest predictors of employees' intention to remain with their current employer. Hence, information sharing tends to reduce employees' intention to quit.[34]

Sharing information can also increase work motivation (serving as an enterprise-directed practice). The owner of a hotel in Memphis, Tenn. told a friend that his critical number was room capacity, and that break-even was achieved at 76%. The owner lamented that his 180-employee hotel was currently at 67%. The friend asked, "How many of your 180 employees know that your break-even is 76%?" The owner said: two people. The friend asked, "What would happen if all 180 people knew?" So, the owner informed his employees of the crucial role of capacity and set operating and financial goals. The hotel subsequently achieved 80% occupancy, in part because maids gave out business cards to guests, and chefs prepared special meals on request.[35]

Although at one time (1996), Whole Foods Markets made all sorts of financial data available to all employees, by 2013 this degree of transparency was not seen as helpful. As noted in *Conscious Capitalism*, Whole Foods currently is "afraid the information would cause more harm than good if it were known … [and] discretion is necessary to protect important organizational information from being leaked to competitors or others who mean harm."[36,37] It remains to be seen whether such practices will change after the 2017 acquisition of the company by Amazon—a company that values information, but not necessarily transparency.

Concern about the leaking of confidential information through the use of "open-book management" seems less of a concern at small companies. A pool cover installation company, Pool Covers, Inc., in Fairfield Calif., used open-book management from 1997 to 2007. During that time, the assessed value of the company grew by 24% annually. However, when Pool Covers shared the financial results for September, 2008, with employees, the need for layoffs became evident.

Employees recognized that it was no one's fault that the sales of pool covers plunged 49% in September 2009, two months ahead of the typical seasonal drop-off. Seeing the results made it easier for seven installers to volunteer for a layoff.[38]

Likewise, the rapidly growing new e-commerce startup, Jet.com, shares its financial information. In the reception area at the company's headquarters (in Hoboken, N.J.), a screen posts constant updates of daily sales by number of shipments and dollar volume. The company shares even more information on a daily basis with investors and salaried employees, including data on first-time buyers the previous day, and cash on hand.[39] Will this practice change, now that Jet.com has been acquired by Walmart? How might any changes in this practice impact employee attitudes and related outcomes?

As the term suggests, *two-way* communication means that organizations can benefit substantially by listening. Some listening interventions are problem-driven, not systematic. For instance, when turnover at Guardian Industries (a company that makes automotive glass) reached 80% annually, the plant's HR manager concluded that management needed to understand what the problems were—and this entailed querying workers. Management discovered that the company's use of rotating shifts was interfering with workers' childcare, sleep, and social lives. Guardian switched to fixed 12-hour day and night shifts and turnover fell by 50%.[40]

Similarly, employees at a credit-card processing company disliked the quality of their work lives, notwithstanding good benefits. When a consulting firm surveyed the employees, two complaints emerged. The employees disliked sharing a common office space, and they did not get along well with their peers. They liked their managers even less. The company assigned private work spaces, created work teams, and started training and selecting managers more carefully. Turnover was reduced from 38% to 15% and the savings outweighed the extra real estate costs.[41]

As noted in Chapter 2, the existence of open, two-way communication supports the claim of R. W. Marriott, Jr.: "The four most important words in the English language are 'What do you think?'"[42] But asking that question will not be effective if employees are reluctant (or afraid) to tell the truth. According to Robert Sutton, Professor of Management Science at Stanford, managers need to convey an "attitude of wisdom." As he sees it, it's not just about hearing employees: it's more about getting them to tell you the truth when there is little incentive to do so. Sutton notes that people are less well liked when they share negative news or criticisms, and better liked when they flatter (even if the recipient of the flattery knows they are lying). Given these constraints, why would an employee ever tell a boss the truth? Sutton insists that managers must be able to accept feedback, even when it is not phrased as delicately as it could be. Managers must be careful not to "snap at people" when they provide negative comments.[43] (Humility is key. There is always the remote possibility that the critical feedback might be accurate and helpful.)

Distinct from problem-driven listening interventions, systematic organizational surveys can be useful in several ways, including[44]

1. Opening a communication channel
2. Pinpointing areas of concern
3. Observing long-term trends
4. Driving change initiatives
5. Monitoring the impact of interventions
6. Gaining employee suggestions as to future actions
7. Providing employees with feedback
8. Obtaining descriptive information about actual organizational practices

By initiating a survey process, the meta-communication from management to employees is that management is interested in employee opinions and perceptions. Indeed, the majority of medium-sized firms and about 75% of large firms regularly conduct employee surveys.[45] However, feedback of survey results, alone, will be insufficient for positive results. Feedback, without subsequent actions, is worse than providing no feedback at all.[46] Handled constructively, feedback can serve as the basis for team discussions and managerial actions, especially if survey items focus on practices. The process of participation is integral to developing highly engaged employees.

A multi-branch bank conducted surveys of practices and perceptions within each branch. Employees responded to questions about the adequacy of training; the extent to which cross-training was provided; perceived levels of team cooperation; commitment to quality; the extent to which managers emphasize measurement; the extent to which managers shared data on measured branch results; the overall level of morale among branch employees; and the adequacy of staffing.[47] Collection and use of such detailed data is central to organizational development.

Today, most surveys are conducted electronically, and open-ended questions can be analyzed using more than a dozen analytic and text mining applications.[48] As noted earlier, Intel uses sophisticated sentiment analytic software to detect changes in attitudes and avoid losing technical talent.

As a rule, employees should be assured of anonymity, and responses to open-ended questions should be reworded to protect the identity of a responder (because individuals may employ idiosyncratic expressions). Perhaps worse than revealing the identity of a respondent is a manager mistakenly attributing a particular comment to the wrong person.[49] Open-ended questions can yield particularly valuable suggestions. One consultant recommends asking, "If you were in charge, what would you do differently?"[50] (Delta Airlines asks a single question of its customers after phone interactions with customer service representatives; "If you were managing a call center, would you hire the associate you just talked to?")

Employee happiness is perhaps the primary concern of Marc Lore, founder and CEO of Jet.com. He believes that employee happiness is a prerequisite for organizational success, and he says, "I'm constantly asking people at Jet if they're happy." In 2015, Jet.com hired a survey company to initiate its first "Happiness Pulse." One of the questions asked parallels what Reichheld has called the "Ultimate Question" that is predictive of customer loyalty (more on this in Chapter 4). When Jet.com employees were asked "would you recommend Jet.com as a place to work?" 87% of respondents responded positively.[51]

An organizational survey entails some degree of risk. This is because responsive action is critically important to the survey process, since the process raises employee expectations that changes will follow. As early as 1953, Viteles noted that a survey may do real harm unless actions are taken on the conditions brought to light. Viteles quoted a Conference Board report that said "An attitude survey is like a hand grenade—once you pull the pin you have to do something with it. Otherwise it may hurt you rather than help you."[52] Of course, employees will not expect that all their issues will be resolved, but some actions should result.

The survey process is central to the use of the Cube One framework as a vehicle for organizational diagnosis and change. Employees, by dint of their position, are best able to report on management practices in use, as distinct from policies that are claimed to be in use.

3. Minimizing Status Differences

Through several mechanisms, many organizations have attempted to convey at a symbolic level that all employees have value and deserve respect—on the premise that participants will be more inclined to share their ideas if they feel they have the status to do so. (In legal terms, employees will have "standing" to make suggestions.)

One way to reduce hierarchical and status distinctions is to use more status-bearing titles. For instance, stockbrokers are called financial advisors; employees are called associates (e.g., at Nissan or Mitchells); and the title of administrative assistant has been widely adopted because it has a more positive connotation than secretary.

Several companies insist that all employees, including senior leaders, be referred to by their first names. When Michael Ullman took over as CEO of J. C. Penney in 2004, the corporate culture seemed to evoke the 104-year-old retailer's founding protocols. Senior managers and store managers were referred to as Mr. and Ms., but Mr. Ullman insisted "Call me Mike!" Employee ID cards featured the person's first name in large letters, and the last name in small letters. Strict status-based rules of office décor were no longer enforced by "office police" who previously were on the lookout for too many personal items being displayed (which could lead to a notification being sent to human resources if a violation was observed). While possibly a coincidence, in 2005—one year after Ullman became CEO—profits more than doubled, and within two years stock price surged more than 80%.[53]

Other status symbols can be downplayed as well. Many companies have discontinued their executive dining rooms (e.g., Lincoln Electric, Solectron, Nissan), and reserved parking spaces have become less common. Ko Nishimura, the CEO of Solectron, would often accompany other employees on the shuttle buses used to transport employees from distant parking lots. Mr. Nishimura claimed that he learned more from riding with employees than from almost any other source of information.[54]

Attire can also minimize status differences. At Nissan's plant in Smyrna, Tennessee, all employees, including managers, wear identical work floor clothing.[55] At Jet Blue, it was not uncommon for the founder and CEO, David Neeleman, to help turn around a plane that was 20 minutes late by vacuuming the plane, joining baggage handlers in loading cargo, and using the plane's PA system to apologize to passengers for the delay.[56]

Dennis Barbeau was hired as a consultant to a unionized manufacturing facility that had serious problems with costs and deliveries. Although not on the union's agenda, Barbeau insisted that if the unionized blue-collar workers were required to punch time clocks, so should everyone else in the company. In his view, time clocks conveyed the impression that only the unionized workers were deemed untrustworthy. The time clocks were removed, and workers were reputedly motivated by this demonstration of trust.[57]

John Chambers, CEO of Cisco System, completed 44 acquisitions between 1994 and 2001. Chambers would examine not just the financials and customer references; he would also look at the size, location, and grandeur of the CEO's office suite. Chambers noted that his own office measures 11 by 12 feet and is located in the middle of the floor, so that others can have more light; and he has plain furniture: no mahogany anywhere. The photos on his desk and walls (relatives, not dignitaries) likely make Chambers more approachable to employees and visitors alike. Chambers claims to seek team players, who serve as coaches and focus on team achievements—reflecting "we" rather than "I." Evidently, Chambers has had some success in finding acquisitions that are cultural fits. In an industry where the turnover rate averages 20%, for employees of companies acquired by Cisco, it's only six%.[58]

Starbucks requires all new employees, even those hired for executive positions, to start their company career with a front-line position. Every new Starbucks employee goes through a 24-hour paid training module called First Impressions, which focuses on learning about coffee and creating a positive customer experience. Next comes weeks of in-store experience, making beverages, talking to customers, and pouring lattes, while serving as a barista. Starbucks believes that employees at all levels should have entry-level, hands-on experience.[59]

Many companies require that high-level executives spend a day or two each year in a front-line capacity. Evidently a growing number of big businesses believe that requiring their CEOs and other top executives to work "in the trenches" generates increased empathy and gains accurate information as to what is actually going on. Such companies include Walt Disney, Continental Airlines, Sysco Corp., Amazon.com, Royal Dutch Shell, and Loews Hotels. In the case of Loews, as a result of having 150 executives spend a day at the chain's 18 hotels, the company added handlebars to room service carts, making them easier to push.[60] Although spending a day on the front line may have symbolic (and occasionally pragmatic) value, it is not clear to what extent this practice minimizes status differentials.

4. Work–Life Flexibility

Respondents to Glassdoor.com, a site where employees evaluate their employers, report on their work–life balance, among other organizational features. Glassdoor has developed a list of the top 25 companies in this regard. Employees (and ex-employees) also provide responses to several specific practices in this regard such as: making their own hours; rarely having to work > 40 hours/week; almost always able to be home with family during the evenings; having managers who are supportive of work/life balance; having on-site childcare; being able to work from home (or remotely); being required to take vacation time; and having a high level of time off.[61]

There is reason to believe that the provision of work–life flexibility and support is of financial benefit to employers. As Cascio notes, it should lead to enhanced recruiting and better staffing; lower absenteeism and associated costs; lower turnover and associated costs; improved citizenship behaviors; and therefore improved team performance and service.[62] Cascio noted that when Sysco Corp., the food-service company, reduced its turnover rate among its 10,000 marketing associates from 30% to 18%, it achieved a cost savings of $70 million annually.[63]

While most airlines used traditional call centers, Jet Blue devised a system where employees can work from their homes. This has become one of the airline industry's signature work–life innovations, attracting a sizable pool of motivated employees who find convenience and flexible schedules more valuable than above-average pay. As the founder, David Neeleman put it: "We train them, send them home, and they are happy."[64]

According to a national survey in 2014, 38% of employees in the U.S. can perform some of their work at home on a regular basis, up from 23% in 2008. About 43% of employees were able to work a compressed work week in both 2008 and 2014.[65]

However, Claudia Goldin, an economics professor at Harvard, has cautioned that flexible work hours may have some downsides in terms of employees' pay and career prospects. The existence of flexible work hours does not ensure that employees who avail themselves of this family-friendly benefit will earn the same total level of pay (which includes opportunity for overtime hours), or will achieve the same rate of promotions. Erin Kelly, sociology professor at the University of Minnesota, cautions that many organizations have a culture which implicitly recognizes and rewards people who work in a traditional manner. Employees not working traditional schedules may experience stigmatization or career penalties.[66] In addition, applicants who purposefully seek such arrangements may be disappointed when the rules are changed post-hire—as was the case at Yahoo after the 2012 appointment of Marissa Mayer as CEO.

Some companies, however, have developed a culture that explicitly attaches a positive meaning to flexible work hours. At Manhattan-based M5 Networks, the firm has six rules for retaining key employees. Rule 5 is to allow key players to work from home at least one day a week, if they wish.[67]

The company LivingSocial, launched in 2009, has grown rapidly. By 2016, LivingSocial had more than 46 million members in 25 countries and close to 5,000 employees worldwide. The founder and CEO, Tim O'Shaughnessy, starts work at 5:00 a.m. and is extremely high-wired during the work week, but he has striven to make weekends a time for family. "I try to set the tone by not working on weekends," he says. "Monday morning to Friday afternoon is LivingSocial time. It's really important for people to take breaks and unplug. So unless something's really urgent, I don't send any work-related emails until late Sunday night."[68]

Best Buy initiated perhaps the most ambitious experiment with work–life flexibility, with their introduction of ROWE: Results Only Work Environment. The premise of the intervention was that upon reaching agreement on goals, employees should be given total autonomy to work whenever, and wherever they chose—so long as their goals were accomplished. There would be no such thing as a sick day or vacation day. If, for example, an employee saw that commuter traffic was terrible, she could work from home that day.[69]

Initially instituted by Best Buy in 2005, ROWE was credited with achieving a savings of $2.2 million over the initial three-year period due to increased employee productivity, heightened employee-well-being (e.g., less stress), and decreased turnover.[70] But Best Buy faced many hurdles, most notably the recession of 2008–2009 with the accompanying sharp drop in prices of almost all consumer electronics. These challenges impacted the entire industry and—coupled with the rise of online comparison shopping with retailers like Amazon and Walmart—contributed to the failures of two of BestBuy's competitors, CompUSA and Circuit City. In early 2013, a new CEO was hired at Best Buy, and the Practice of ROWE was discontinued.[71,72]

What the ROWE experiment illustrates is that business success (or more broadly, organizational performance) might most aptly be viewed as a complex multiple regression equation. Many variables, internal and external to the organization, directly and indirectly affect results. Perhaps ROWE might have been successful in a less turbulent industry during a more stable economic environment. But, just as in baseball where fans can argue forever as to whether or not a relief pitcher should have been brought in, life does not often permit controlled experiments where *ceteris paribus* (everything else is equal) applies.

It is safe to conclude that some measure of work–life flexibility will usually be a successful practice given its attractiveness to employees: viz., enhancing an organization's ability to recruit from a larger pool of potential applicants; the motivational and attitudinal benefits associated with heightened employee autonomy; the reduced stress associated with congenial work–life arrangements; the benefits to all parties of reduced turnover. In the highly competitive talent-driven world of Silicon Valley, work–life practices can be a major factor in recruitment and retention. Netflix is giving new parents up to a year of *paid* leave.[73]

Pertinent to both flexible work hours and excellent traditional benefits, is the finding cited by Kabachnick in her book, *I Quit but Forgot to Tell You*. Based on a survey of 1,400 executives, managers, and associates of all ages, 76% would switch jobs for less money in order to work for a company that offers both flexibility and benefits that include opportunities for personal development.[74]

5. Extensive Traditional Benefits

Three types of benefits can be classified as commonplace or traditional: those related to health/medical insurance, retirement plans, and tuition reimbursement for personal growth. Some companies believe that providing not just sizable, but lavish benefits of this type produce a substantial economic payback: a high Return on Benefits (ROB).

At Diamond Pet Foods, a private manufacturer in Meta, Mo., wages are in line with similar manufacturers, but benefits average 35% of total compensation, compared to about 30% for a typical private employer, according to the Bureau of Labor Statistics. The payoff to Diamond Pet Foods includes a voluntary turnover rate of only 3% compared to the industry average of almost 11%.[75] Andrew Brondel, the director of administration, at Pet Foods, employees do not merely stick around. They are also highly productive.

"When employees don't have to worry about health care or financial issues, they can focus on success and growing our business," he says. During the fall when pet food demand peaks, Diamond employees step up production. He has heard people say, "I know this company has my back, so I'm giving them everything I've got."[76]

The benefits at Diamond Pet Food include fully paid health insurance. Related to health, but relatively uncommon, there is a registered dietitian on premises to help improve employee nutrition. Additionally, employees are allowed to take time off, no questions asked, for family emergencies. (The company also provides enterprise-directed practices: bonuses and profit sharing, which contribute to the high ROB, as manifested through employee willingness to work hard.)[77]

The case of Diamond Pet Foods is consistent with survey research based on 1,530 employees from 126 publicly traded U.S. companies. Employees' perceptions that they are "receiving a competitive benefits package," are positively related to company net income and productivity.[78] Although such data cannot prove causality, one can reasonably assume that competitive benefit packages serve the interests of employees and the enterprise.

The Diamond Pet Foods case also supports the claim by Leonard Berry, professor at Texas A&M University, that the best companies are generous companies. Berry argues that all employees are volunteers, in the sense that "a gap exists between the maximum amount of energy an employee can choose to exert, and the amount necessary to avoid being penalized by the employer." Generous companies are more likely to achieve that higher level of motivation.[79]

In 2016, LinkedIn announced disappointing earnings for 2015. The stock price plunged as a result, wiping out nearly $11 billion of market value. The LinkedIn CEO, Jeff Weiner, promptly announced that he was donating his entire annual $14 million stock bonus to employees. The fact that employees who joined the company in 2015 saw their options go "under water" prompted this gesture at least in part.[80] It may not be entirely coincidental that in 2014, a nationwide Glassdoor. com employee poll of large companies found that Jeff Weiner was the highest rated CEO in the U.S.[81]

Health insurance plans are a commonplace employee-directed practice, but are not always provided to entry-level hourly workers. Some companies provide health insurance to virtually all employees. It is available to hourly workers at the Cheesecake Factory who work at least 25 hours a week, after an eligibility period of six months. Turnover at Cheesecake Factory is about 25 percentage points lower than the 106% average in the restaurant industry.[82]

At Costco, 85% of employees have company-sponsored health insurance, with Costco paying 90% of the cost—which amounted to about $6,000 per employee in 2007. The high cost notwithstanding, then-CEO Jim Sinegal stated, "We're 100 percent committed to maintaining this program. It works for us. And our people count on it. We think they're entitled to that security."[83]

Of course, the details of health insurance coverage are crucial. Issues such as employee eligibility, financial participation, threshold for deductibles, co-pays, and the extent of coverage for major medical illnesses, hospitalization, prescription drugs, dental, and vision are all part of the complicated equation. Yet a poignant case brings to mind the crucial importance of health insurance. Consider the situation facing Michael Gill in *How Starbucks Saved My Life*. Gill was forced out (he claimed "aged out") of his high-level executive job at a famous advertising agency. Due to his personal mistakes and misfortune, he became essentially penniless, and then discovered he had a serious brain disease. Fortunately, he was hired by Starbucks and was able to acquire health insurance. In addition to earning a modest income, he gained newfound respect for others, irrespective of their jobs.[84]

Retirement plans are offered by many companies in part due to the favorable tax treatment afforded this benefit. One company with an extraordinarily generous retirement plan is Nucor Steel. As of 2005, the company was profitable for 130 straight quarters (in large measure due to the use of incentive plans—an enterprise-directed practice), despite the cyclicality of the steel industry. Nucor matched individuals' 401(k) retirement contributions, and employees were permitted to contribute in the range of five to 25% of their salary. In practice, the average match amounted to 12.5% of employee income.[85]

The Principal Financial Group achieved an exceptionally high level of employee participation in their retirement plans by employing social science knowledge. People say they want to be responsible when it comes to their retirement, but there is a big gap between what people say and what they do. The key "nudge" that the company employed was the implementation of an auto-enrollment feature, with an option to opt out. (This is very different from the conventional approach of coaxing employees to participate, by teaching them about the value of an employer match, and so forth.) The auto-enrollment feature raised the employee participation rate to 90% from less than 40%of employees. According to Jerry Patterson, senior vice president of retirement investor services, so few people opted out (at least in part) because "when you require people to tell you they are opting out, many won't, perhaps because they do not want to be seen as being irresponsible."[86] Not only does The Principal Financial Group encourage employees to defer a sizable proportion of their income in a matched 401(k) plan; it recommends that they start with a six% deferment and raise the rate by 1% annually so that it reaches 10% in five years. Says Patterson: "If you can get 90 percent of your workforce participating, at an average 10 percent deferral rate, and with 90 percent of them allocating a portion of their accounts into stocks or other non-cash-equivalent investments, you will have a plan that really works."[87]

The HPWP category associated with career opportunity pertains to more than job-related growth. There is an important distinction between training and development conducted to improve employees' job performance or versatility, and development opportunities that target employees' personal growth. Regarding the former, as noted in connection with enterprise-directed practices, companies like Home Depot, Wegmans, and The Container Store provide extensive work-related training, The Container Store providing all employees at least 235 hours annually.

Tina Traster suggests that one of the six rules for retaining key employees is to provide training for a higher-level job that the employee might be able to grow into.[88] Many companies provide tuition assistance toward baccalaureate or graduate degrees, even if unrelated to the employee's current work. One practice on Jeff Haden's list of "10 things extraordinary bosses give employees" is the chance for a meaningful future. Haden states that "exceptional bosses take the time to develop employees for the job they someday hope to land, even if the job is with another company." Haden argues that managers must first show employees that they care about them and their future, if they want employees to care about their current job.[89] Along these lines, for years Verizon provided employees with $8,500 of tuition assistance.[90] More recently, Starbucks in 2014 initiated support to baristas to take online education, and Jet Blue in 2016 initiated company-sponsored education.[91,92]

6. Managerial Integrity

Managers' actions should align with their words or they will be seen as lacking integrity and trustworthiness. If managers tell one group one thing and another group something different they will gain a reputation for untrustworthiness and inconsistency. Integrity relates to managerial practices and actions in infinite ways—and absent integrity and fairness, employees will become distrustful, and believe that ever-changing rules are self-serving and unfair.

Mary Kay Ash, founder of Mary Kay Cosmetics, once observed, "A manager should never make a promise that something will be done unless he is absolutely certain it will be done. A broken promise is devastating for those who have been disappointed, and there is no excuse for it in management."[93]

Management may not always explicitly promise what will be done, but it's usually understood that constructive actions will ensue. Consider the situation at the U.S. Department of Homeland Security, which finished the lowest in the 2014 Best Places to Work in the Federal Government ranking. Afflicted with the lowest morale of any large agency, DHS did what comes naturally to some organizations: study the problem and, years later, study it some more.

The first DHS study cost $1 million, and when it was finished it went into a drawer. The next one cost less but duplicated the first and ended up in another drawer. Then, because Americans were so unhappy with the DHS, in 2014 the department commissioned two more studies. The president of the Partnership for Public Service, a nonprofit group that seeks to make government more effective, stated, "You see study, study, study and no execution or fulfilling of the recommendations. It is time to get moving." After the most recent 268-page Deloitte report was completed, ICF (another consulting firm) started a separate morale study of the DHS Science and Technology Directorate. The study recommended a follow-up survey.[94]

An academic study entitled "When leaders fail to 'walk the talk'" concluded that word-deed misalignment leads to perceptions of supervisory hypocrisy which, in turn, leads to a substantially lower level of trust, lower perceptions of justice, and—due to a heightened uncertainty of treatment—increased intention to quit. The researchers concluded that managers may believe they are doing a good job if they consistently meet performance targets and provide subordinates with the necessary resources to complete assignments. What they may not realize is that "subordinates pay particular attention to whether leaders 'own' their behaviors, such as whether they 'walk the talk' by engaging in behaviors that are consistent with those they verbally encourage." A misalignment creates perceptions of hypocrisy, which lead to unfavorable outcomes.[95]

In *Harmonize: How People-Centric Organizations Succeed in a Social World*, Jamie Notter and Maddie Grant devote a chapter to "How to Be Trustworthy." A sound value statement enhances trustworthiness, and Googling "company values statement" (in 2012), yielded 84 million hits.[96] Here is Microsoft's: "As a company, and as individuals, we value integrity, honesty, openness, personal excellence, constructive self-criticism, continual self-improvement, and mutual respect."[97]

Complete truthfulness may produce conflicts and hurt feelings. These emotions may lead to abrasive and time-consuming political maneuvering. If differences are not addressed and resolved adroitly, the organization could develop a culture of half-truths.

The issue of honesty was subtly framed by Kim Scott, when she introduced the concept of "radical candor":

> I had just joined Google and gave a presentation to the founders and the CEO about how the AdSense business was doing. I walked in feeling a little nervous, but happily the business was on fire. When we told Larry, Sergy, and Eric how many publishers we had added over the previous months, Eric almost fell off his chair and asked what resources they could give us to help continue this amazing success. So ... I sort of felt the meeting went okay.
>
> But after the meeting, Scott's boss Sheryl Sandberg, suggested they take a walk together. She talked about the things she'd liked about the presentation and how impressed she was with the success the team was having—yet Scott could feel a "but" coming. Finally, she said, "But you said *um* a lot." And I thought 'Oh, no big deal. I know, I do that. But who cared if I said *um* when I had the tiger by the tail?'
>
> Sandberg pushed forward, asking whether Scott's *ums* were the result of nervousness. She even suggested that Google could hire a speaking coach to help. Still, Scott brushed off the concern; it didn't seem like an important issue. Finally, Sheryl said, 'You know, Kim, I can tell I'm not really getting through to you. I'm going to have to be clearer here. When you say *um* every third word, it makes you sound stupid.'
>
> Now, that got my attention! Scott says. For all of us raised in a culture that preaches if you can't say something nice ..." that criticism might not sound so *nice*. But Scott knows now that it was the kindest thing Sandberg could have done for her. If she hadn't said it just that way, I would have kept blowing her off. I wouldn't have addressed the problem. And what a silly thing to let trip you up (And Scott did work with a speaking coach.)

Scott has developed a 2 × 2 conceptualization of values where the vertical axis reflects caring for the other party and the horizontal axis reflects honesty. According to Scott, perhaps the worst combination is high caring and low honesty. This she characterizes as "ruinous empathy," where the target person never gets the information needed to improve. One might call the combination of low caring and low honesty "manipulative insincerity," and the combination of low caring and high honesty "obnoxious aggressiveness." Scott advocates that organizations promote a culture of high caring and high honesty—what Scott calls

"Radical Candor."[98] Scott's analysis is logical and perhaps even compelling, but the evidence so far is anecdotal. This would be an excellent, albeit challenging, area for research.

Some organizations address integrity in a straightforward manner. In 1981, N. R. Narayana Murthy cofounded Infosys, and the company set out to be India's Most Respected Company: by delivering to customers what was promised; by treating employees with fairness and dignity; by promising investors transparency and accountability. Infosys has a zero-tolerance policy toward violations of integrity. If someone is accused of a violation, the company investigates the matter and gives the accused parties a chance to argue their case. Infosys has let some extraordinarily bright and contributory people go because of unethical behavior. In Murthy's words: "[f]or instance, we fired a project manager for fudging a taxi bill to the tune of $40. He was a crucial member of the team, but our zero tolerance policy would not allow us to continue to employ him."[99]

7. Respect

In a recent interview, Walt Bettinger, CEO of Charles Schwab Corporation, gave the following response to the question, "What about lessons you learned in college?"

> A business strategy course in my senior year stands out. I had maintained a 4.0 average, and I wanted to graduate with a perfect average. It came down to the final exam, and I had spent many hours studying and memorizing formulas to do calculations for the case studies.
>
> The teacher handed out the final exam, and it was one piece of paper, which really surprised me because I figured it would be longer than that. Once everyone had their paper, he said, "Go ahead and turn it over." Both sides were blank.
>
> And the professor said, "I've taught you everything I can teach you about business in the last 10 weeks, but the most important message, the most important question, is this: "What's the name of the lady who cleans this building?"
>
> And that had a powerful impact. It was the only test I ever failed, and I got the B I deserved. Her name was Dottie. I'd seen her, but I'd never taken the time to ask her name. I've tried to know every Dottie I've worked with ever since. It was just a great reminder of what really matters in life, and that you should never lose sight of the people who do the real work.[100]

Managers, especially if they are just starting out, generally have to earn the respect of the people they are to manage. For example, at age 24, Ashley Goldsmith was hired as an assistant manager of a Home Depot store in Georgia. She had neither retail nor home improvement experience; she had a college degree in Psychology. (At the time, Home Depot had started a fast-track executive leadership program for high-potential employees who would be rotated through managerial jobs in various functions.)

Most employees then at Home Depot did not have a college degree, and they saw it as only appropriate for people to work their way up to obtain a managerial position. The Home Depot workers were suspicious of Ashley Goldsmith.

She made it her mission to earn the respect of her colleagues. She worked in every store department. In merchandising, she volunteered for the overnight shift, which frequently entailed restocking merchandise and rearranging displays—a job much harder than it sounds, Goldsmith said.

> You crawl out from under the racks looking like you just walked out of a chimney. So they would be walking in in the morning, and I'd be walking out at 6 a.m. dirty and looking like I had worked really hard. By far that was the biggest credibility-earner.

By the time she left six months later for her next assignment, she had made some good friends and earned the traditional Home Depot farewell. Everyone in the store signed her orange apron. In her words: "They gave me an apron and it had so many signatures—there were probably 200 people in the store. It was such an overwhelming feeling."[101]

Managers in organizations, upon accepting the concept that all associates should be treated with dignity and respect, need to put these ideas into action. The content and nature of communication are critical in this regard. In the words of the late psychologist Harry Levinson: "Never overestimate the knowledge of others; never underestimate their intelligence." Managers, via their communications, should treat employees as responsible and mature adults, and avoid any hint of condescension. One can convey a great deal of information by both verbal and nonverbal means.[102]

Managers should convey positive emotions via facial expressions, and display warm rather than threatening gestures (such as pounding on a table, or pointing or cutting the air vertically with one's hand as if holding an imaginary sword). If a manager is invariably on time for meetings, that indicates respect for others' time. Consistent lateness conveys the opposite message. Other nonverbal indicators of respect, or its absence, include the use of space, tone of voice, and appearance. Managers can learn many basic human relations skills from the classic book by Dale Carnegie, *How to Make Friends and Influence People*.[103]

8. Minimizing Fear

In the context of employee-directed practices, minimizing fear refers to creating a climate that reduces performance anxiety. The literature on the effects of minimizing employee fear is primarily based on anecdotal evidence such as founders' success stories, or instances where fear was paramount and organizational performance was poor. A predecessor to The Hackett Group conducted a rare empirical investigation on this subject some years ago, labeling companies that adopted specific HRM practices "value-aligned" and those with low HRM practice adoption rates as "non-aligned." The study found that 93% of value-aligned companies regarded failure as a form of learning; only 47% of non-aligned companies treated failure tolerantly. Tolerance of failure was just one of the HRM practices used to classify firms, but the study found that over a five-year period, value-aligned firms produced twice the return to shareholders.[104]

Pat Kelly founded Physicians Sales and Services in 1983, after being fired from his job at a company that sold medical supplies. Within 15 years the company—later called PSS World Medical—had sales of $1.3 billion, achieving a compound annual growth in sales of almost 60%.[105] He emphasized the importance of "driving out fear." Employees who take on higher levels of responsibilities and fail should be provided a "soft landing;" i.e., a return to their previous job. Kelly also claims that the culture at PSS assured no retribution for an employee talking to anyone about anything.[106]

As mentioned at the beginning of this chapter, Mitchells stores also does not punish associates for honest (i.e., non-negligent) mistakes. Joe Albertson, founder of the Albertson grocery chain has espoused a similar philosophy. He would tell his managers to "let your people make a few mistakes." He saw working for his company as akin to driving on a highway with a broken line down the middle. Employees had the latitude to change lanes, so long as they didn't drive off the road.[107] Compare this leadership style with that witnessed by Terri Kabachnick in "*I Quit but Forgot to Tell You.*" In her book, she describes her consultation with a small company that had severe morale problems. She traced the problems to the behavior of the CEO, who "focused on every mistake made by employees"[108] This situation parallels the claim that Ken Blanchard and Spencer Johnson make in *The One Minute Manager* that managers typically spend most of their time trying to catch people doing something wrong.[109]

Management practices in the high-tech world tend to be different from the norm. Reed Hastings, Netflix's CEO, recommends the practice of "hire slow, fire fast," claiming this approach will increase "talent density."[110]

With regard to the presence of employee fear at Amazon, in 2015 the *New York Times* published a lengthy (100+ paragraph), in-depth article based on detailed reporting of the company's HR practices: "Amazon's Bruising, Thrilling Workplace." Amazon does not just encourage—but expects—exceptionally creative achievements. With rapid innovations, myriad things will go wrong and must be rectified promptly. To minimize mistakes, Amazon has fostered a culture where blunt criticism (sometimes harsh, sometimes bordering on confrontational) is encouraged. Amazon has no place for polite praise or quiet clapping for flawed ideas (what Kim Scott has characterized as "manipulative insincerity"). However, unsparing criticism at meetings may make some workers fearful of speaking up.[111]

As Jeff Bezos wrote in an annual report, "You can work long, hard, or smart, but at Amazon.com you can't choose two out of three." A number of ex-Amazonians have given detailed, grim testimony to the sometimes bruising atmosphere at the company. Liz Pearce, who managed projects such as the wedding registry, states that "the pressure to deliver far surpasses any other metric. I would see people practically combust." According to Bo Olson, a former book marketer, "Nearly every person I worked with, I saw cry at their desk."[112]

Perhaps as more industries become high-tech, or as competition intensifies across companies, there may be a trend toward companies being more "brutal" with regard to the consequences of non-performance. From a human capital perspective, such developments would likely be counterproductive. Decades of psychological writing have asserted that fear is a poor way to achieve excellent performance. Consider the apocryphal boss who trumpeted: "there will be no pay increases until morale improves!"

9. Teams and Climate of Belonging

Teams play a major role in most organizations, at least for employees in medium- to high-complexity jobs. Perusing recruitment materials and job ads, one would be hard pressed to find any position that doesn't require some level of teamwork or playing nice with others.

The role of teams can be formalized, as in self-managed work teams, or viewed as more of an informal phenomenon, akin to part of an organization's culture. With regard to self-managed teams, management professor Jeff Pfeffer sees three primary advantages.

First, the process of creating self-managed teams essentially introduces more decentralized decision-making, which increases authority and accountability among associates. That team members can make important decisions is a source of intrinsic satisfaction as well. Indeed, in one survey 75% of associates who were placed in teams stated that they would want to work on a team again; only 10% said they had no interest in "re-upping."[113]

Second, Pfeffer notes that teams can be the source of better work practices, if people engage in brainstorming and problem solving. This insight parallels Adam Smith's observation that the people "doing the work" will ultimately have the most knowledge about task performance. Teams can be a driving factor in organizational knowledge sharing and informal training, as experienced workers serve as mentors to those who are just "learning the ropes."[114]

Third, organizations may save money by reducing at least a portion of one layer of bureaucracy. If self-managed teams are fully autonomous, there will be less need for supervisors giving orders, making decisions, and checking that their orders are carried out.[115] Consistent with these three advantages, Pfeffer cites examples of companies that have improved quality, increased on-time deliveries, and raised productivity and profits by increasing teamwork.

Perhaps the most famous company to advocate self-managed teams is Whole Foods Market, where teams range in size from six to 100 members; the larger teams being grouped into sub-teams. Teams have a good deal of power. Everyone is hired into a particular team for a probationary period of 30 to 90 days, after which a two-thirds positive vote is necessary for the new member to have full team-member status. As Mackay and Sisoda note in *Conscious Capitalism*, anyone can fool a team leader for a while, but it is much more difficult to fool the entire team. If a new hire is not elected to their initial team, they have to join another team (also on a probationary basis) or leave the company.[116]

At Whole Foods, voluntary turnover for full-time team members (who make up 75% of the workforce) is less than 10% per year. Low turnover makes it more economical to invest in a high level of training. Teams compete in the same work area (e.g., produce, meat) across stores, and it's a matter of pride for a department to be the best of its kind in a given region. Teams not only make operating decisions; they also get to vote on their own benefit packages every year—which might include more paid time off or even pet bereavement insurance.[117]

Formally established teams are more "official" than is the case with organically emerging teams. The latter may reflect a shared sense of community and feelings of belonging. Such feelings are notable at Patagonia and at Mitchells, where managers encourage associates to see the company as almost akin to their second family.

The 100 Best Companies to Work For survey asks respondents about the extent to which they experience pride "in the work produced by one's team or work group" and a sense of camaraderie. Survey questions ask about the extent to which respondents experience a "socially friendly and welcoming atmosphere," and a "sense of 'family' or 'team.'"[118]

Salespeople at Nordstrom are famous for the extraordinary lengths they will go to satisfy a customer—including even finding the desired style, size, and color shoe at a store other than at Nordstrom, and then purchasing it and hand-delivering it to the customer's home. Salespeople at Nordstrom are proud to see themselves as "Nordies." (See Chapter 7 for a fuller description of customer-, employee-, and enterprise-directed practices at Nordstrom.)

Much research exists on the characteristics of effective and creative teams. Members know how to disagree in an atmosphere of mutual respect. It has been suggested that if a manager disagrees with a team's idea, the manager should strive especially hard to implement it. That way, if the idea fails, team members will conclude that it was a bad idea, rather than poor implementation.[119]

Recently, Google applied its data-driven capabilities to discern the characteristics of the "perfect team." They found that the perfect team had clear goals and constructive norms. The latter included taking turns talking during team conversations; listening to each other; creating psychological safety for members; having respect for one another; and being sensitive to one another.[120]

10. Manifest Concern for Employees in Other Ways

As noted above, an HR director at Deloitte & Touche has lamented that the bar for inclusion in the "100 Best Companies" is constantly being raised, as employers continuously develop and introduce new employee-directed practices. Especially in competitive industries such as high technology, the list of benefits and perks companies use to compete for the best talent keeps growing (e.g., free snacks, on-site laundry, pet sitters, free bicycle repairs). This final section lists some less commonly implemented benefits. To this point consider the final sentence in Philip Roth's novel *Portnoy's Complaint*. Portnoy's psychoanalyst asks, "So, now ve may perhaps to begin. Yes?"[121]

(a) *Safety.* A powerful demonstration of the importance and utility of safe working practices comes from the Aluminum Corporation of America (Alcoa). After a year of poor financial results, in 1987 the board of directors hired Paul O'Neill, an outsider with prior government experience, as the CEO. At Alcoa's first meeting with financial analysts and investment managers following his hiring, O'Neill took the stage in the ballroom of a posh Manhattan hotel, and declared:

> I want to talk to you about worker safety. …Our safety record is better than the general American workforce, especially considering that our employees work with metals that are 1500 degrees. … But it is not good enough. I intend to make Alcoa the safest company in America. I intend to go for zero injuries.[122]

The audience of analysts and investment managers was confused. They expected to hear about how managerial changes would achieve synergies and record profits. But O'Neill did not mention profits even once; he spoke only about safety. As Charles Duhigg noted in *The Power of Habit*, one investor, knowing about O'Neill's prior work experience, thought, "This guy must have done a lot of drugs."[123]

The analysts and investors almost stampeded out of the ballroom. One investment manager used a payphone in the lobby to call his 20 largest clients. In his words: "I ordered them to sell this stock immediately, before everyone else in the room started calling their clients. … It was literally the worst piece of advice I gave in my entire career." When O'Neill retired in 2000 (after 13 years), the stock had increased in value by 500%, including dividends.[124]

Indicative of O'Neill's concern for safety, he visited the company's facilities in 32 countries. At a smelting plant in Tennessee he told a large gathering of workers that "I'm really glad to be here." He continued: "I'm happy to negotiate with you about anything. But there's one thing I'm never going to negotiate with you, and that's safety. I don't ever want you to say that we haven't taken every step to make sure that people never get hurt. If you want to argue with me about that, you're going to lose."[125]

Why was the intense concern for safety so successful? First, it was warmly received by workers and their union representatives. With their support, and with managers who would not dare balk at any new safety protocols, it was possible to rapidly implement significant operating changes. Employees embraced work rules that the unions had spent decades opposing, such as measuring individual productivity, because such information was necessary to determine when part of the manufacturing process was out of alignment and might pose a safety risk. Policies managers had long resisted, such as giving workers the authority to shut down a production line when the pace was overwhelming, were now accepted.

To emphasize his concern for worker safety, O'Neill gave workers his home telephone number and urged them to call him if management did not follow up on safety issues. But, according to O'Neill, it turned out that workers did not want to talk about accidents or safety. Rather, they mostly wanted to share their ideas about how to operate more effectively.

At Alcoa, the overriding concern for worker safety was accompanied by an increase in operating profitability. Likewise, an increased concern for product/service quality—which one might think would increase costs—often yields increased profitability (see Chapter 4). This finding parallels the conclusion of John Kay in *Obliquity*: goals are often best achieved indirectly.[126]

(b) *Realistic Job Previews*. A survey by Development Dimensions International (DDI), a prominent consulting firm, found that 51% of new employees hired in 2012 were dissatisfied with their jobs ("buyer's remorse"), and 88% were looking to make a job change within six months. With this in mind, AGCO Corporation, an Atlanta-based manufacturer of heavy agricultural equipment, made retention a key goal when the firm hired 1,500 salaried workers in 2012. To achieve this aim, AGCO provided greater detail about each job, including both pros and cons so that applicants could make a better-informed decision.[127]

Lauri Lipka, director of global talent management at AGCO, noted that new hires are most vulnerable during the first three to six months of employment. "If we don't give them a thorough picture of the job before we hire them," she says, "then they're most likely going to feel like, 'Hey, this isn't the job I signed up for.'"[128]

Considerable (although not recent) literature is available on the realistic job preview (RJP). In a meta-analysis of 21 RJP studies, four positive effects appear: higher organizational commitment, job satisfaction, performance, and job survival.[129] All are concomitant with a more recent behavioral construct, job engagement.

(c) *Good Nutrition.* In their book *Leading with Kindness,* William Baker and Michael O'Malley describe the efforts of Pitney Bowes (a $6 billion company in 2008) directed toward encouraging good employee nutrition. Michael Critelli, chairman, noted that unhealthy foods could be eliminated altogether from their cafeterias; but this would not be practicable. Instead the company attempts to create "a social architecture" that "nudges" employees toward a more healthful direction. Healthful foods are sold at a price discount; less healthful foods, at a higher price. The latter are located far from the cashiers; the former are attractively displayed at the entrance to the cafeteria.[130]

As noted above, Diamond Pet Foods employs a registered dietitian on the premises to create personalized nutritional plans for employees. Patagonia serves healthful food in their cafeteria, including free-range organic barbecued chicken. Other companies in the natural-and-organic segment take a similar approach. Aveda, a hair-care and beauty company has been shaped by its founder's mission of environmental and social responsibility, even after its acquisition by corporate giant Estee Lauder Companies in 1997. At its headquarters in Blaine, Minn., the cafeteria serves organic fare, and the corporate campus is an NWF Certified Wildlife Habitat that allows employees to alleviate stress and recharge their batteries.

(d) *Idiosyncratic Practices.* The Cheesecake Factory made it their practice to give each general manager (the person responsible for all aspects of a store), a brand new BMW.[131] Go Daddy supplements traditional mental health and substance-abuse programs for employees with pet-assisted therapy.[132] Several new companies have developed programs particularly attractive to millennial employees who are launching their careers. Student Loan Genius helps in paying off student-loan debt, and PayActiv can increase cash flow to help pay unexpected bills or contribute to savings.[133]

Arguably the most remarkable benefit is the crying room, apparently proposed facetiously by PYRO, a new female comedy channel, and Kathryn Gordon, in their article entitled "So, where exactly should you cry at the office?"

> No need to overshare at your open-plan desk. There's a place just left of the photocopier called the Crying Room, and you can go there and do that. … It's dark. There are no windows—just a couch with throw pillows that work well to muffle the sound of your sobbing, a table, and a box of tissues. Recently, I handled a situation where I was asked to speak expertly about a subject I know nothing about, and which I was only briefed on moments before, with the reminder that my job was on the line. … I simply walked over to the Crying Room, flopped face-down on the couch, grabbed a pillow, and screamed into it at the top of my lungs. It was cathartic and so

efficient. I was actually able to retouch my makeup before I entered the lion's den. My colleague was so amazed that she started using the Crying Room too (bad breakup).[134]

Unfortunately, in light of the bruising work experiences at some high-tech companies, this proposal might not be universally seen as comical.

Employee-Directed Practices

This chapter has identified ten categories of employee-directed practices. It is the contention of the Cube One framework that organizations will have more satisfied and loyal employees, when it frequently engages in the following practices:

1. Providing employment security
2. Enabling two-way communication
3. Minimizing status differences
4. Employing work–life flexibility
5. Providing extensive traditional benefits (e.g., health insurance, pension)
6. Demonstrating managerial integrity
7. Treating all employees with respect
8. Minimizing fear
9. Encouraging a team feeling and possibly employing self-directed teams
10. Manifesting concern for employees in various other ways (e.g., safe work practices, good nutrition, RJPs, etc.

The Cube One framework posits that it is employees' perceptions of these practices that are of paramount importance. Hence, employee surveys are indispensable to obtain accurate information about what is actually "going on." (As noted previously, these ten categories incorporate an almost unlimited variety of specific practices—plus variety in the details, intensity, and efficacy with which they are carried out.) We present the original list of ten employee-directed practices (slightly tweaked) below. This ten-item survey taps virtually all of the aforementioned major categories, except the amalgamation of miscellaneous practices.

These practices have both direct and indirect effects, contributing to the complexity of the Cube One framework. As noted in this chapter, employment security, for example, not only enhances employee loyalty and commitment; it also indirectly elevates employee motivation and creativity. Likewise, employee-directed practices impact customer satisfaction and loyalty (which are direct outcomes of customer-directed practices, addressed in the next chapter). In their book, *The Customer Comes Second*, Rosenbluth and Peters have argued that, especially in a service setting, it is not reasonable to expect employees to treat customers better than they (employees) see themselves as being treated.[135] And in *Employees First, Customers Second*, Vineet Nayar shows how he applied this philosophy at HCL Technologies.[136]

Nonetheless, it is critical that organizations attend directly to customer outcomes via customer-directed practices. We address this, the third and final causal dimension of the Cube One framework, next.

Employee-Directed Practices: A Short Ten-Item Survey

Actual Practices

The purpose of this survey is to ascertain the *actual practices* (as distinct from stated or printed policies) in your organization. If you work in a subsidiary of a larger organization, focus on the local organization where you work. Please use the following scale to record your responses to the ten statements that follow:

1 = Never or Almost Never (or Not Applicable)
2 = Infrequently
3 = Occasionally or Sometimes
4 = Frequently
5 = Always or Almost Always

(1) **Employment Security.** Employee layoffs are avoided where possible, by first attempting to place employees in other jobs within the organization._____
(2) **Open, two-way communication.** All employees are informed about new developments and encouraged to express their ideas and complaints. _____
(3) **Minimizing Status Differences.** Distinctions between hierarchical ranks are minimized. Management downplays status symbols (e.g., executive dining rooms). _____
(4) **Work–Life Flexibility.** Work–life conflicts are minimized by adopting policies such as flexible work hours, daycare assistance, and encouraging managerial tolerance._____
(5) **Extensive Traditional Benefits.** Employees receive assistance with health care and retirement, plus educational support for external training/education. _____
(6) **Managerial Integrity.** Integrity is demonstrated by dealing fairly with employees. All employees are given the same information; promises are kept. _____
(7) **Actions, Not Just Words.** The organization responds to employee concerns by taking appropriate actions, not just by words. _____
(8) **Respect.** Employees are treated with respect as mature adults. Communications are straightforward, not condescending or patronizing. _____
(9) **Minimizing Fear.** Employees know they can make (a few) mistakes. Management attempts to minimize the role of punishment and fear. _____
(10) **Teams and Climate of Belonging.** Management encourages the creation of teams and for employees to feel that they are part of a team. _____

Notes

1 Cascio, W. F. (2016). *Managing human resources: Productivity, quality of work life, profits*, 10th ed. New York, NY: McGraw-Hill. pp. 51–53.

2 Ibid.

3 Fulmer, I. S., Gerhart, B., and Scott, K. S. (2003). "Are the 100 Best better? An empirical investigation of the relationship between being a 'great place to work' and firm performance." *Personnel Psychology*, 56(4), 965–993.

4 Ibid.

5 Ibid.

6 Great Place to Work®. (2016). "Connecting people and purpose: 7 ways high trust organizations retain talent." Retrieved at http://learn.greatplacetowork.com/rs/520 -AOO-982/images/GPTW-Fortune-100Best-Report-2016.pdf. Accessed on May 4, 2006.

7 Cleaver, J. (May 2003). "Lust for lists." *Workforce*, 82(5), 44–48.

8 Stone, B. (June 7, 2013). "How cheap is Craig Jelinek?" *Bloomberg Businessweek*, 55–60.

9 Ibid.

10 Ibid.

11 Niu, E. (November 15, 2015). "How many members does Costco have?" Retrieved at http://www.fool.com/investing/general/2015/11/15/costco-members.aspx. Also see, http://www.costco.com/join-costco.html

12 Comparing the business models of Costco Wholesale and Walmart is a bit more complicated than meets the eye. Although Walmart also has a wholesale division, Sam's Club, that charges membership fees, this division represents a relatively small part (about 12%) of Walmart revenues. See data from Sam's Club retrieved at http://corporate.samsclub.com/about-us/quick-facts

13 When Costco describes the average level of pay it provides, it averages the pay levels associated with each separate job title; it does not calculate the average based on the actual numbers of employees in each job title. Thus, a Sales Assistant gets paid $12.92, a Merchandiser $12.30, an Inventory Auditor gets $20.87, and a Meat Supervisor $25.18. Hence, the average pay of $20.89/hour is a bit misleading. See Ogden, P. K. (February 16, 2015). "Costco and the $20.89 an hour job myth." Retrieved at http://www.ogdenonpolitics.com/2015/02/costco-and-2089-hour-job-myth.html

14 Baer, D. (February, 2014). "How Patagonia's new CEO is increasing profits while trying to save the world." *Fastcompany*. Retrieved at http://www.fastcompany.com/302 6713/lessons-learned/how-patagonias-new-ceo-is-increasing-profits-while-trying-t o-save-the-world

15 Mitchell, J. (2008). *Hug your people*. New York, NY: Hyperion.

16 Op cit., p. 40. Quotation reprinted with permission of Hyperion, a subsidiary of Hachette Book Group, Inc. Copyright © Jack Mitchell, 2008.

17 In the eight years subsequent to the publication of *Hug your people*, Mitchells acquired five additional high-end stores, the company in 2016 being comprised of eight stores.

18 Roethlisberger, F. J., and Dickson, W. J. (1939). Management and the worker Cambridge, MA: Harvard University Press.

19 Koller, F. (2015). "Lincoln electric, 67 straight years without layoffs, 82 straight years of profit-sharing bonuses." Retrieved at http://www.frankkoller.com/2015/12/linco ln-electric-67-straight-years-without-layoffs-82-straight-years-of-profit-sharing-bon uses/

20 Kopelman, R. E. (1986). *Managing productivity in organizations: A practical, people-oriented perspective*. New York: McGraw-Hill. (See p. 55.)

21 Pfeffer, J. (1998). "Seven practices of successful organizations." *California Management Review*, 40(2), 96–124. Nucor has also had a remarkable record of continuous employment and also been consistently profitable. See Marquez. J. (November 2005). "Premium on productivity" (cover story). *Workforce Management*, 84(12), 22–31. Nucor

was profitable for 130 straight quarters up until 2005. From 2006 to 2017, Nucor was profitable every year except 2009.

22 Note that these advantages parallel those noted by Adam Smith, op. cit., in his explanation as to why specialization in a pin factory was so effective. He offered three explanations. First, employees develop greater skill when they perform one job repeatedly. Second, employees are able to translate this skill into higher output (in part via greater motivation). Third, Smith noted that with extensive experience in performing an operation of limited scope, the workers can be the source of new ideas for improved performance.

23 Fein, M. (1977). "An alternative to traditional managing." Unpublished paper, Hillsdale, N.J, p. 40 (italics in original). At SIA, the Subaru plant in Indiana, it is clear that Fein's advice has been followed. Said an automobile analyst, "You get worker commitment to productivity by offering job security." See, Farzad, R. (June 6–12, 2011). "The scrappiest car manufacturer in America." *Bloomberg Businessweek*, pp. 68–76.

24 Tomasko, R. M. (2002). *Downsizing: Reshaping the corporation of the future.* New York, NY: Amacom.

25 Keating, R. J. (August 26–September 1, 2011). "The sad but not surprising end of Borders bookstores." *Long Island Business News*, p. 17a.

26 First Round Review. (June 29, 2013). "The woman behind the Netflix culture Doc." Retrieved at http://firstround.com/review/The-woman-behind-the-Netflix-Culture-doc/

27 Isaacson, W. (April, 2012). "The real leadership lessons of Steve Jobs." *Harvard Business Review*, 90(4), 93–102.

28 King, R. (October 13, 2015; updated version). "How do employees really feel about their companies." Retrieved at http://www.wsj.com/articles/how-do-employees-really-feel-about-their-companies-1444788408

29 Pfeffer, op cit., p. 98.

30 Ibid.

31 Cole, W. (December, 2001). "Suddenly loyalty is back in business: Amid the slump, smart companies are boosting profits by cultivating loyalty among workers and customer alike." *Time Magazine Bonus Section, Your Business*, pp. Y13–16.

32 Hsieh, T. (2010). *Delivering happiness: A path to profits, passion and purpose.* New York, NY: Business Plus.

33 Sharp, I. (2009). *Four Seasons: The story of a business philosophy.* New York, NY: Portfolio.

34 Pare, G., and Tremblay, M. (2007). "The influence of high-involvement human resources practices, procedural justice, organizational commitment, and citizenship behaviors on information technology professionals' turnover intentions." *Group & Organization Management*, 32(3), 326–357.

35 Stettner, M. (March 19, 1997). "Use the bottom line to spur your workers: 'Open-book management' opens employees' eyes to profits." *Investor's Business Daily*, pp. A1, 8.

36 Pfeffer, op cit. describes practices in 1996, p. 118.

37 Mackey, J., and Sisodia, R. (2013). *Conscious capitalism: Liberating the heroic spirit of business.* Boston, MA: Harvard Business Review Press, pp. 223–224.

38 Lorber, L. (February 23, 2009). "An open book: When companies share their financial data with employees, the results can be dramatic." *Wall Street Journal*, p. R8.

39 Streitfeld, D. (December 26, 2015). "Jet.com's strategy: Low prices, fast delivery, happy workers." Retrieved at http://www.nytimes.com/2015/12/27/technology/jetcoms-strategy-low-prices-fast-delivery-happy-workers.html?_r=0

40 Shellenberger, S. (November 19, 1997). "Employers are finding it doesn't cost much to make a staff happy." *Wall Street Journal*, p. B1.

41 Ibid.

42 Wisdom to Live By. (January 8, 2015). "Marriott on collaboration." *Investor's Business Daily*, p. A3.

43 First Round Review. (November 16, 2013). "Fight like you're right, listen like you're wrong and other keys to great management." Retrieved at http://firstround.com/review/Fight-Like-Youre-Right-Listen-Like-Youre-Wrong-and-Other-Keys-to-Great-Management/

44 Kraut, A. (2006). "Moving the needle: Getting action after a survey." In A. I. Kraut ed. *Getting action from organizational surveys: New concepts, technologies, and applications*. San Francisco: Jossey-Bass (a Wiley Imprint). (Chapter 1).

45 Ibid.

46 Church, A. H., and Oliver, D. H. (2006). "The importance of taking action, not just sharing survey feedback." Chapter 5 in Kraut, op. cit., pp. 102–130.

47 Wiley, J. W., and Campbell, B. H. (2006). "Using linkage research to drive high performance: A case study in organization development." Chapter 7 in Kraut, op. cit., pp. 150–180.

48 Church, A. H., and Oliver, D. H., op cit.

49 Kulesa, P., and Bishop, R. J. (2006). "What did they really mean? New and emerging methods for analyzing themes in open-ended comments." Chapter 10 in Kraut, op. cit., pp. 238–263.

50 Herzlich, J. (September 21, 2015). "Gauging satisfaction to keep key talent." *Newsday*, p. A35.

51 Streitfeld, op. cit.

52 Viteles, M. S. (1953). *Motivation and morale in industry*. New York, NY: Norton, p. 394.

53 Byron, E. (March 27, 2006). "'Call me Mike!': To attract and keep talent, J.C. Penney CEO loosens up once-formal workplace." *Wall Street Journal*. Retrieved at http://www.wsj.com/articles/SB114341448122708573. Similarly, the use of first names has been employed by Zappos! as described by Hsieh, op. cit., and also by the Physicians Sales and Services Company (now called PSS World Medical). See Kelly, P. (1998). *Faster company: Building the world's nuttiest turn-on-a-dime home-grown billion-dollar business*. New York, NY: Wiley.

54 Pfeffer, op cit., p. 117.

55 Schnapp, J. (February 22–23, 2014). "The long history of the UAW's failed southern strategy." *Wall Street Journal*, p. A15.

56 Newman, M. (Winter, 2001). "Onward and upward." *GMJ (Gallup Management Journal)*, 4(1), 20–23. Similarly, the founder and CEO of Southwest Airlines, Herb Kelleher, was not infrequently seen visiting maintenance crews at 3 a.m., helping to load baggage and serving peanuts (the only food served) on flights. See Freiberg, K., and Freiberg, J. (1998). *Nuts! Southwest airlines' crazy recipe for business and personal success*. New York, NY: Broadway Books, a division of Bantam, Doubleday Dell Publishing Group.

57 Barbeau, D. (January, 2016). "Taking the time to respond to time and attendance." Reader commentary in *Workforce*, 95(1), 4.

58 O'Neil, W. J. (2004). *Business leaders & success: 55 top business leaders & how they achieved greatness*. New York, NY: McGraw-Hill, pp. 188–191.

59 Erickson, T. J., and Gratton, L. (March, 2007). "What it means to work here." *Harvard Business Review*, 85(3), 104–112. Similarly, at the Container Store, all new hires go through five days of intensive training about products processes and the company's values, and then many apprentice with a star performer before assuming a regular position.

60 Lublin, J. S. (June 25, 2007). "Top brass try life in the trenches: To promote understanding, firms require executives to perform entry-level jobs." *Wall Street Journal*, pp. B1, 3.

61 Glassdoor.com. (August 16, 2013). "Top 25 companies for work-life balance." Retrieved at https://www.glassdoor.com/Top-Companies-for-Work-Life-Balanc e-LST_KQ0,35.htm. In an earlier study of flexible work hours, 18 positive features were identified. See, Kopelman, R. E. (1992). "Alternate work schedules." In W. K. Hodson ed., *Maynard's industrial engineering handbook*, 4th ed. New York, NY: McGraw-Hill. (pp. 10.105–10.121).

62 Cascio, W. F. (2016). *Managing human resources: Productivity, quality of work life, profits*, 10th ed. New York, NY: McGraw-Hill. pp. 54–59.

63 Cascio, W. F. (October, 2006). "The new human capital equation." *The Industrial-Organizational Psychologist*, 44(2), 15–22.

64 Erickson and Gratton, op. cit., p. 109.

65 Bernard, T. S. (May 20, 2014). "For workers, less flexible companies." *New York Times*, pp. B1, 7.

66 Thompson, C. A. (2008). "Barriers to the implementation and usage of work-family policies." In S. A. Y. Poelmans and P. Caligini eds. *Harmonizing work, family, and personal life: From policy to practice*. New York, NY: Cambridge University Press. (pp. 209–234).

67 Traster, T. (February, 14, 2005). "Six rules for retaining a firm's key employees." *Crain's New York Business*, 21(7), p. 17.

68 O'Shaugnessy, T. (March, 2012). "The way I work: If you're not nervous about one or two decisions every day, you probably aren't trying hard enough." *Inc.*, 105–108. Retrieved at http://www.inc.com/magazine/201203/liz-welch/the-way-i-work-tim-o-shaugnessy-living-social.html

69 Stevenson, S. (May, 2014). "Don't go to work: The management scheme that lets workers do whatever they want, as long as they get things done." Retrieved at http://www.slate.com/articles/business/psychology_of_management/2014/05/best_buy_s rowe_experiment_can_results_only_work_environments_actually_be.html

70 Valcour, M. (March 8, 2013). "The end of 'Results Only' at Best Buy is bad news." *Harvard Business Review*. Retrieved at https://hbr.org/2013/03/goodbye-to-flexi ble-work-at-be

71 Peterson, G. (March 12, 2013). "Cutting ROWE won't cure Best Buy." *Forbes*. Retrieved at http://www.forbes.com/sites/garypeterson/2013.03.12/cutting-rowe-wont-cure-best-buy/. After 2005, as many as 40 organizations have experimented with ROWE.

72 The CEO who cancelled ROWE argued that there is no universal management style that is suitable for all organizations or employees. In his words: "Well anyone who has led a team knows that delegation is not always the most effective leadership style. If you delegate to me the job of building a brick wall, you will be disappointed with the results!" See, Bhasin, K. (March 18, 2013). "Best Buy CEO: Here's why I killed the 'results only' work environment." *Business Insider*. Retrieved at http://www.businessi nsider.com/best-buy-ceo-rowe-2013-3

73 Liedtke, M. (August 4, 2015). "Netflix to give workers with babies a year of paid leave." Retrieved at http://bigstory.ap.org/article/4d62ab9a14d04fa28f13fe0ed9a4f 8c2/netflix-give-workers-babies-year-paid-leave. As Tawni Cruz, the chief talent officer at Netflix, wrote in a blog post, "Experience shows people perform better at work when they're not worrying about home."

74 Kabachnick, T. (2006). *I quit, but forgot to tell you*. Dallas, TX: Cornerstone Leadership Institute, see p. 32.

75 Leibs, S. (December, 2013/January, 2014), "You can buy happiness. (But should you?)" *Inc.*, 35(10), 108–112. Companies that offer lavish benefits believe there is a return on their investment. The challenge: Figuring out how to calculate it.

76 Ibid., p. 110.

77 Ibid.

78 Subramony, M., Krause, N., Norton, J., and Burns, G. N. (2008). "The relationship between human resource investments and organizational performance: A firm-level examination of equilibrium theory." *Journal of Applied Psychology*, 93(4), 778–788.

79 Berry, L. L. (July/August, 2007). "The best companies are generous companies." *Business Horizons*, 50(4), 263–269.

80 Cuthbertson, A. (March 4, 2016). "Why LinkedIn CEO Jeff Weiner is donating his $14M bonus to employees." Retrieved at http://www.newsweek.com/why-linkedi n-ceo-jeff-weiner-donated-his-14m-bonus-employees-433345. It might be noted that Weiner became CEO of LinkedIn in 2009, and by 2015 the company had 364 million registered users, with offices in 30 countries and a market capitalization of $26 billion.

81 Vaccaro, A. (March 23, 2014). "The most loved CEOs in America." *Inc.* Retrieved at http://www.inc.com/adam-vaccaro/most-loved-ceos.html

82 Ruiz, G. (April 24, 2006). "Traditional recipe." *Workforce*, 85(8), 1, 22–29.

83 Bary, A. (January 12, 2007). "Everybody's store." *Barron's*, pp. 29–32.

84 Gill, M. G. (2007). *How Starbucks saved my life.* New York, NY: Gotham Books. (This case pre-dated the Affordable Care Act.)

85 Marquez. J. (November 2005). "Premium on productivity." (cover story) *Workforce Management*, 84(12), 22–31. Nucor was profitable for 130 straight quarters up until 2005. From 2006 to 2017, Nucor was profitable every year except 2009.

86 TheBuildNetwork.com. (December, 2013/January, 2014). "Star power: How to recruit, reward & retain top talent." *The Build Quarterly Report*, pp. 1–22. (It might be noted that although it is argued that employees might not opt out because they do not want to be seen by others as financially irresponsible, more fundamentally, they might not want to see themselves in this fashion.)

87 Ibid.

88 Traster, T. (February 14, 2005). "Six rules for retaining a firm's key employees." *Crain's New York Business*, 21(7), p. 17.

89 Haden, J. (August 6, 2013) "10 things extraordinary bosses give employees." *Inc.* Retrieved at http://www.inc.com/jeff-haden/10-things-extraordinary-bosses-do-f or-their-employees.html

90 Verizon (April 22, 2016). "What's there to strike about?" *New York Post*, p. 15.

91 Greenhouse, S., and Strom, S. (July 4, 2014). "Paying employees to stay, not to go." *New York Times.* Retrieved at http://www.nytimes.com/2014/07/05/business/economy/ boloco-and-shake-shack-offer-above-average-pay.html?_r=0

92 Inside Higher Ed. (April 19, 2016). "New employee degree program at JetBlue." Retrieved at https://www.insidehighered.com/quicktakes/2016/04/19/new-emp loyee-degree-program-jetblue

93 Schleier, C. (August 28, 2007). "Mary Kay Ash cared about beauty and her workers." *Investor's Business Daily*, p. A3.

94 Markon, J. (February 20, 2015). "DHS tackles endless morale problems with seemingly endless studies." Retrieved at https://www.washingtonpost.com/politics/homel and-security-has-done-little-for-low-morale-but-study-it--repeatedly/2015/02/20/ f626eba8-b15c-11e4-886b-c22184f27c35_story.html. According to a DHS employee who was familiar with an early study (but who spoke on the condition of anonymity because of fear of retaliation), "It was not a very good light to shine on any of us, so we just hid it."

95 Greenbaum, R. L., Mawritz, M. B., and Piccolo, R. F. (2015). "When leaders fail to 'walk the talk': Supervisor undermining and perceptions of leader hypocrisy." *Journal of Management*, 41(3), 929–956.

96 Notter, J., and Grant, M. (2012). *Harmonize: How people-centric organizations succeed in a social world.*" Indianapolis, IN: Que Publishing. Quote on p. 163.

97 Notter and Grant, op. cit.

98 *First Round Review.* (November 24, 2015). "Radical candor—the surprising secret to being a good boss." pp. 1–15. Retrieved at http://firstround.com/review/radical-candor-the-surprising-secret-to-being-a-good-boss/. Quotation reprinted with permission of *First Round Review.*

99 Murthy, N. R. N., and Anand, P. (November, 2011). "Why don't we try to be India's most respected company?" *Harvard Business Review*, 89(11), 80–86.

100 Bryant, A. (February 7, 2016). "You've got to open up to move up." *The New York Times*, p. B2. Quoted material reproduced with permission of *The New York Times.* Copyright © 2016 The New York Times.

101 Pyrillis, R. (April, 2014). "More doing: From temping at Home Depot to CHRO at tech firm Workday, Ashley Goldsmith's path isn't for the faint of heart." *Workforce*, 93(4), 40–43. Quoted material reproduced with permission from humancapitalmedia. com.

102 Debenham, L. (December 23, 2015). "Communication: What percentage is body language?" Retrieved at http://www.bodylanguageexpert.co.uk/communication-what-percentage-body-language.html. The 55% estimate is based on the classic research undertaken by Albert Mehrabian in 1971.

103 Carnegie, D. (1936). *How to win friends and influence people.* New York, NY: Simon & Schuster. According to Amazon.com, this book has sold more than five million copies since its first publication in 1936.

104 Caudron, S. (December, 2001). "How HR drives profits: Academic research and real-world experience show how HR practices affect the bottom line." *Workforce*, 80(12), 26–31. Among the other employee-directed HRM practices used to ascertain value-alignment were sharing financial information and communicating successes.

105 Kelly, P. (1998). *Faster company: Building the world's nuttiest-turn-on-a-dime home-grown billion-dollar business.* New York, NY: Wiley. Ten years later, in 2008, the company celebrated its 25th year in business and was named in Forbes 400 Best Big Companies list for the second time. In 2013, the company was purchased by the McKesson Corporation for $2.1 billion. It might be noted that Kelly's encouragement of employees "speaking up," reflects an implicit national/societal norm of low power distance. There are many cultures where employees would not even consider speaking out about their managers.

106 Ibid.

107 Mandaro, L. (December 8, 2005). "He put the 'grow' in grocery." *Investor's Business Daily*, p. A3.

108 Kabachnick, T. (2006). *I quit but I forgot to tell you.* Dallas, TX: The Kabachnick Group.

109 Blanchard, K., and Johnson, S. (1981). *The one minute manager.* New York, NY: William Murrow and Company.

110 McKeown, G. (March 3, 2014). "Hire slow, fire fast." *Harvard Business Review.* Retrieved at https://hbr.org/2014/03/hire-slow-fire-fast

111 Kantor, J., and Streitfeld, D. (August 16, 2015). "Amazon's bruising, thrilling workplace." *New York Times*, pp. 1, 20–22.

112 Ibid. As a newspaper write-up, the examples of cruelty are powerful. But Amazon provided a detailed rebuttal, claiming that the *New York Times* did not provide a fair and accurate picture.

113 Pfeffer, J. (1998). "Seven practices of successful organizations." *California Management Review*, 40(2).

114 Ibid.

115 Ibid.

116 Mackjay, J., and Sisoda, R. (2013). *Conscious capitalism: Liberating the heroic spirit of business.* Boston, MA: Harvard Business Review Press.

117 Ibid.

118 Fulmer, I. S., Gerhart, B., and Scott, K. S. (2003). "Are the 100 Best better? An empirical investigation of the relationship between being a 'great place to work' and firm performance." *Personnel Psychology*, 56(4), 965–993.

119 First Round Review. (November 16, 2016). "Fight like you're right, listen like you're wrong and other keys to great management." Retrieved at http://firstround.com/review/Fight-Like-Youre-Right-Listen-Like-Youre-Wrong-and-Other-Keys-to-Great-Management/

120 Duhigg, C. (February 28, 2016). "What Google learned from its quest to build the perfect team: New research reveals surprising truths about why some work groups thrive and others falter." *New York Times*. Retrieved at http://www.nytimes.com/2016/02/28/magazine/what-google-learned-from-its-quest-to-build-the-perfect-team.html

121 Roth, P. (1992 Edition). *Portnoy's complaint*. New York, NY: Random House, p. 274

122 Duhigg, C. (2012). *The power of habit: Why we do what we do in life and business*. New York, NY: Random House, p. 98. Copyright © 2012 by Charles Duhigg. Quoted material reproduced with permission of Random House, and imprint and division of Penguin Random House LLC. All rights reserved

123 Ibid., p. 99.

124 Ibid., p. 100.

125 Ibid., pp. 105–106. Copyright © 2012 by Charles Duhigg. Quoted material reproduced with permission of Random House, and imprint and division of Penguin Random House LLC. All rights reserved.

126 Kay, J. (2010). *Obliquity: Why our goals are best achieved indirectly*. New York, NY: Penguin.

127 Kranz, G. (March, 2013). "New employees feeling jobbed about their jobs." *Workforce Management*, 92(3), 8. The same article reports an even more dismal picture, found in a November 2012 survey of 700 employees by Right Management: only 5% of all employees planned to stay in their current job during the next year. The DDI survey found that 14% of new hires were deemed failures by their employers.

128 Ibid.

129 Premack, S., and Wanous, J. P. (1985). "A meta-analysis of realistic job preview experiments." *Journal of Applied Psychology*, 70(4), 706–719.

130 Baker, W. F., and O'Malley, M. (2008). *Leading with kindness: How good people consistently get superior results*. New York, NY: AMACOM.

131 Ruiz, G. (April 24, 2006). "Traditional recipe." *Workforce Management*, 85(8), 1, 22–29.

132 Supek, S. (April, 2015). "GoDaddy goes to the dogs." *Workforce*, 94(4), 18.

133 Carey, T. W. (May 23, 2016). "Two new employee benefits aimed at millennials." *Barron's*, p. 24.

134 Gordon, K. for PYPO. (February 22, 2016). "So where exactly should you cry at the office? *New York Magazine*. Retrieved at http://nymag.com/thecut/2016/02/where-exactly-should-you-cry-at-the-office.html. See also https://www.pypo.com/the crying room/. Quoted material used with permission of *New York Magazine*, copyright © 2016 PYPO.

135 Rosenbluth, H. F, and Peters, D. M. (2002). *The customer comes second: Put your people first and watch 'em kick butt*. New York, NY: HarperCollins.

136 Nayar, V. (2010). *Employees first, customers second: Turning conventional management upside down*. Boston, MA: Harvard Business School Press. More rigorous research on the linkage between climates that are promotive of employee well-being and customer satisfaction has been provided by Schneider, B., Erhart, Mayer, D., Saltz, J., and Niles-Jolly, K. (2005). "Understanding organization-customer links in service settings." *Academy of Management Journal*, 48(4), 1017–1032. There is also evidence in Brown, S. P., and Lam, S. K. (2008). "A meta-analysis of relationships linking employee satisfaction to customer responses." *Journal of Retailing*, 84(3), 243–255.

4

CUSTOMER-DIRECTED PRACTICES

In Chapter 2, we cited 14 High Performance Work Practices (HPWP) that have been identified and conventionally classified into three practice categories: ability-related; motivation-related; and opportunity-enhancing. Increasing ability and motivation relate primarily to improving individual and organizational performance, which are considered enterprise-directed practices in the Cube One framework. Opportunities primarily concern employees and their careers. However, three of the enterprise-directed HPWP can indirectly but noticeably impact customer satisfaction: selection, training, and reward systems. For example, Cheesecake Factory hires for the smile (or personality), figuring that it is easier to teach people how to set a table than to have an upbeat demeanor. With regard to training, L.L. Bean provides new employees 40 hours of training before they are first allowed to interact with a customer. The commission-based (and publicly posted) reward system at Nordstrom produces salespeople who go to extraordinary lengths to satisfy customers. For more details on the practices enacted at Nordstrom, see Chapter 9.

Four of the 14 HPWP (employment security, information sharing, extensive benefits, and work teams) focus on enhancing employee loyalty, engagement, satisfaction, and performance of non-required tasks (sometimes referred to as organizational citizenship behaviors or OCB). Although those four practices may have motivational and ability-related side effects, they are primarily employee-directed. HPWP often do not exclusively affect just one of the three dimensions or domains. Extensive benefits and job security, for example, may increase the pool of applicants for a position, thereby indirectly increasing the likelihood of selecting talented and motivated high performers, who will provide excellent products and services.

Well-managed organizations attend to the interests of the enterprise, employees, and customers. The Toyota Way's emphasis on *kaizen* and frugality, enhancing productivity and profitability, is *enterprise*-directed. Toyota insists on respect for all employees, customers, and suppliers; a high commitment to teams; and the sharing of information. This tends to increase *employee* (and supplier) loyalty and satisfaction. Toyota is dedicated to long-term product planning, which provides new and improved products for *customers*. Toyota has "nailed" all three dimensions of the Cube One framework.

Other practices primarily enhance customer satisfaction and loyalty. We address that dimension of the Cube One framework next. We classify customer-directed practices into ten categories, shown in the survey at the end of this chapter. Three of the original practice items have been modified to reflect recent phenomena such as the real-time tracking of online preferences, as well as the use of various large data bases (so-called "Big Data").

Surveying Customers

Conceptualizing and measuring customer satisfaction isn't easy. For example, customer loyalty alone is not a good measure of satisfaction. One study showed that between 60 and 85% of customers who switched firms would have been classified as satisfied.[1] According to Reichheld and Markey, "traditional satisfaction surveys just aren't up to the job. They ask too many questions and seem to inspire analyses instead of actions."[2]

Let's start with the issue of measurement. Keiningham and Vavra, in their book *The Customer Delight Principle*, argue for three "zones" of satisfaction: pain (or disappointment); mere satisfaction (perceived adequacy and indifference); and delight (surprise and exceeding expectations).[3] The relationship between satisfaction and organizational outcomes is non-linear, with the point of upward inflection beginning at the zone of delight. If an organization's customer satisfaction scores move up or down a few points in the merely satisfied zone, organizational results will not see an appreciable effect.[4]

The Customer Delight Principle notes many examples of the "disconnect" between satisfaction and business performance. Between 1994 and 1998, the mean American Customer Satisfaction Index (ACSI) for the hotel/motel industry declined from 75 to 71%, while industry profits more than tripled, rising from under $6 billion to over $18 billion. Between 1994 and 1999, ACSI scores for Walmart declined from 81 to 75% but profits more than doubled: from $2.2 billion to $4.5 billion. At Colgate Palmolive, satisfaction scores declined from 86 to 79% between 1995 and 1999 but profits rose from under $200 million to over $900 million. Southwest Airlines, a company deservedly famous for outstanding customer service, saw a consistent decline in satisfaction scores between 1994 and 1999, from 78 to 72%—and profits roughly tripled, from around $150 million to $475 million.[5]

W. Edwards Deming commented, in 1986, "It will not suffice to have customers who are merely satisfied."[6] As Deming implied, customers will want to be more than satisfied. They will seek to be delighted. But as noted by Keiningham and Vavra, delight often results from a surprisingly pleasant experience. But, the authors note, it takes ingenuity to develop a product or service that creates delight—such as the hotel chain that gives new arrivals a warm, fresh-baked cookie at check-in. The element of surprise is hard to retain and creating ever-more surprising experiences is not free.[7]

Strength of customer satisfaction often relates to loyalty, and it can play a central role in customer retention. However, when customer satisfaction is relatively weak, the decline in customer retention falls to about 60%.[8] A problem associated with gauging customer satisfaction by surveys, is that they are often used for marketing research purposes and can be quite lengthy. Research has developed systematic techniques for splitting "massive" surveys into equivalent pairs of surveys.[9]

Another problem: it is difficult to obtain a representative sample of typical or "average" customers. Research has shown that a certain type of customer is more likely to participate in customer-focused organizational research, i.e., a form of selection bias. The act of simply completing a customer satisfaction survey has been associated with substantial positive results, compared to a control group that did not receive a survey. More specifically, survey participants made a greater number of purchases; were more responsive to promotions; had a lower inter-purchase time interval; and had an overall higher level of spending.[10]

Another wrinkle in the use of customer satisfaction surveys appeared in a 2017 issue of *Harvard Business Review*. In surveys conducted by a national retail chain, customers who were asked for a compliment at the beginning of the survey purchased 9% more products and spent 8% more the following year. A study by a B2B software firm found that users of software who were asked to describe the features they particularly liked spent 32% more on the firm's products, compared with users who were not asked for a compliment. Sterling Bone, of Utah State, conjectures that expressing gratitude may increase a customer's sense of well-being. However, Kristen DeTienne, a professor at Brigham Young University, cautions that pushing too hard for positive comments might be seen as gratuitous and over the top.[11]

With regard to both the measurement of customer satisfaction and the implementation of closed-loop learning, Reichheld and Markey, consultants at Bain & Company, provide an important contribution. In their early work, they used 14 questions to assess customer satisfaction. After extensive empirical analyses, they found that a single item—the Ultimate Question—best predicted customer behaviors and organizational outcomes:

"On a zero-to-ten scale, how likely is it that you would recommend us (or this product/service/brand) to a friend or colleague?"

Responders with scores of 9 and 10 were deemed Promoters; respondents with scores of 7 or 8 were characterized as Passives; and respondents with a score of 6 or lower were classified as Detractors. The Net Promoter Score (NPS) was calculated as the percentage of Promoters minus the percentage of Detractors. Abundant evidence has been collected that the NPS is far and away the best predictor of customer loyalty (i.e., repeat purchases), and that the economics of loyalty (discussed below) are financially sizable.[12]

Thousands of organizations have adopted the NPS system, including Apple, Intuit, American Express, Charles Schwab, eBay, Facebook, GE, Jet Blue, Nike, TD Bank, Verizon, and Zappos. Schwab has gone so far as to develop a protocol for tracking NPS every business day for every branch, every call center, and even by team, and employee. (The NPS has even invaded the field of employee—not just customer-surveying. Several Fortune 500 companies now include NPS questions on their annual employee surveys.)

Companies with particularly high NPS metrics include Southwest Airlines, Costco, Trader Joe's, and State Farm. These firms attest to the utility of the NPS system. However, a list of prominent companies alone doesn't explain the widespread use of the NPS system. Let's examine the rationale for the utility of NPS in more detail:

- Promoters have a far higher retention rate, and the financial impact of a long-term loyal customer can be considerable. It costs a lot less to retain a customer than to recruit a new one.
- Promoters usually want the company to prosper and are less price-sensitive. They are not looking for the lowest price possible.
- Promoters spend more and are more receptive to new offerings and brand extensions.
- Detractors can be very costly in terms of legal expenses, as well as demoralizing to frontline employees.
- Promoters provide positive word-of-mouth comments and are responsible for between 80% and 90% of referrals. Detractors are responsible for 80% to 90% of negative-word-of-mouth comments, which tend to be shared widely and can be very detrimental.

Consider the following thought experiment. You move to a new town and are planning to visit a particular dentist for the first time. The first person you speak to provides negative comments about that dentist. How many positive word-of-mouth commentaries will you need to counteract the initial negative comments? Probably at least ten.

The fact that a dozen of the most successful and highly regarded companies use the NPS system is not, *per se*, hard evidence of its effectiveness. The *Ultimate Question 2.0* presents some hard evidence from an in-depth study of Philips, headquartered in the Netherlands. Founded in 1891, in 2010 Philips had sales of $36 billion, employed more than 125,000 people, and did business in more than 60 countries. Across 30 product groups, the NPS of Philips was compared to the average score of competitors in each product group. When the NPS of Philips was greater than the average NPS of their competitors, annual sales growth was 8% on average; when the NPS of Philips was lower than that of competitors, sales growth was *minus* 5% on average.

Perhaps the most unique application of the NPS protocol was its application by an entire town: Steamboat Springs, Colo. When Tom Kern, CEO of the Chamber Resort Association, found out in 2013 that the NPS for small businesses in Steamboat Springs was 68, he swung into action. Mr. Kern and a group of business owners decided to give the whole town customer service training. The owner of McKnights Irish Pub & Loft stated that "we're trying to exceed expectations a little bit in each interaction." Employees were instructed as to how to have a warm conversation that improves the shopping experience. A bartender at McKnights commented, "It's fun. It's more like socializing than work. ... We find that people are a lot happier in this atmosphere. I've seen a big difference in my tips, and in myself, too."[13]

The biggest payoff from implementing the NPS metric is the possibility of taking corrective action. If the customer is willing to take a one-question survey by an independent organization—and about 90% of customers are—an organization can identify the problem through follow-up questions such as, "What is the primary reason for your less than complete satisfaction?" This information allows corrective action by a branch or team. By facilitating closed-loop learning, NPS metrics can increase over time. Companies have also used branch or departmental NPS data as a basis for employee recognition.

Additionally, calculating NPS facilitates investment in customer loyalty and making estimates of the anticipated return for each incremental improvement in NPS. Increased customer loyalty will lead to increased profits, which can facilitate additional loyalty-enhancing investments.

Reichheld and Markey identify five major problems with traditional customer satisfaction surveys:

(1) They are too long and unnecessarily complex
(2) They seem designed for research, not to fix problems
(3) Results are not provided to frontline personnel on a close-to-real-time basis
(4) Anonymous surveys virtually eliminate the possibility of closing the loop
(5) Because of their length and complexity, response rates tend to be low, which reduces the reliability of data collected[14]

When customers who provide low evaluations are asked if they would be willing to speak briefly with the branch manager, approximately 90% agree to being called. According to data collected at Apple Retail, a total of one hour of conversations by a store manager with detractors generates more than $1,000 in incremental revenues, or about $25 million a year.

The developers of the NPS system have provided a five-point loyalty-enhancing checklist.

(1) Have you reached a consensus on your business's five most critical "moments of truth" with customers?
(2) Do employees and managers get customer feedback routinely, on a daily or weekly basis?
(3) Do you let customers know the impact their feedback had on improving your processes?
(4) Do you know the percentage of detractors your operations now convert into promoters through service recovery processes?
(5) Can you put a dollar value on turning a detractor into a promoter?[15]

In-Depth Analyses

Techniques that tend to obtain more in-depth analyses than satisfaction surveys include focus groups, which may be comprised of prospective or actual customers; opt-in databases where customers provide identifying information and permit the collection of additional information; online behavioral analyses; proprietary commercial data bases; and various Internet-based analytic tools.

More than 70% of companies collect and use live customer data in service environments.[16] Lester Wunderman (who, incidentally, has been credited with creating the term "direct marketing"), predicted this trend in 1967: a computer can know and remember as much marketing detail about 200,000,000 consumers as did the owner of a crossroads general store

> about his handful of customers. "I can know and select such personal details as who prefers strong coffee, imported beer, new fashions, bright colors. ... Those marketers who ignore the implications of our new individualized information society will be left behind."[17]

Four Seasons Hotels keeps detailed records as to the preferences of patrons at all of its properties. They know if a client prefers Coke or Pepsi, and the preferred color of flower arrangements, etc. The relatively small retail clothing company Mitchells, introduced in Chapter 3, identified 3,000 customers who had not made a purchase during the prior two years. As related in the book *Hug Your Customers*, Mitchells invited all 3,000 to a special promotion, and 438 came in and made a purchase.[18]

Although it is easier to conduct surveys than focus groups, and the former are useful for identifying overall trends, the latter are more useful in uncovering the "whys" of a particular marketing issue. Focus groups, though, have a mixed record in terms of predicting customer reactions to a new product or service. One criticism is that individuals may be reluctant to express ideas that vary from the evident consensus.[19] Another problem, with which readers who have participated in focus groups might be familiar, is that overly dominant participants can skew the conclusions drawn in a group "discussion."

The focus group approach went seriously awry for Coca-Cola in the 1980s. Extensive and costly focus group testing led the company to replace the classic Coca-Cola recipe with "New Coke." Big mistake—possibly the biggest blunder in marketing history.[20]

Procter & Gamble (P&G) anticipated a big market in China for its inexpensive disposable diaper, priced at ten cents. Yet the product was not well received. Were the diapers too rough, or too flimsy, too expensive? A P&G marketing executive listened in on a focus group discussion with a translator. As the moderator went through the standard protocol of questions, one woman's answer caused hearty laughter from the group, including the translator.

As related by Clayton Christensen and colleagues in *Competing Against Luck*, the woman said that "the highlight of her week was renewed intimacy with her husband—three times in one week. How did this relate to the diaper? Because the baby slept through the night! The moderator then asked her what her husband thought about the diaper. 'That was the best ten cents he ever spent ...' More laughter." Consequently, P&G conducted research in China and found that babies with Pampers fell asleep 30% faster and slept an extra 30 minutes a night. Needless to say, P&G refocused their advertising to reflect a different product feature.[21]

Focus groups do not always accurately discover what the customer does or does not want. For example, during the design process for a new laptop computer, many focus group participants said they wanted a larger screen. One manufacturer adopted this suggestion. But few customers wanted the laptop because it was too big to carry around. Later the manufacturer found out that what the customers actually wanted was a clearer image, i.e., higher resolution, which can be achieved with a screen the same size or smaller.[22]

The founder of the American Girl doll company, Pleasant Rowland, employed a focus group after her first director of marketing insisted that she had to have one. Ms. Rowland watched behind a one-way mirror as mothers of preteens soundly and visibly rejected the idea that girls of ages seven to 12 would be interested in dolls with life stories. It was virtually unanimous that "my daughter would never like anything like that, based on a doll's history. And all those accessories would just get caught in the vacuum cleaner." However, Rowland was confident that young girls wanted more than a doll—they wanted an experience. Thirteen years after its founding, the company was sold to Mattel for $700 million.[23]

Another example of why focus groups have fallen out of favor: Unilever PLC asked moms which of the company's food products they liked most. The moms always responded that they most often fed their children Unilever's most healthful offerings, when, in fact, the best sellers were high-calorie snack foods.[24]

Perhaps Steve Jobs was correct when he claimed that "a lot of times people don't know what they want until you show it to them."[25] It is doubtful that a focus group or a survey would have predicted that people wanted to sleep in other peoples' homes (Airbnb) or share rides in other people's cars (Uber, Lyft).

A voluntary opt-in self-profiling process can also provide valuable data. Such information can be used to attract prospects, convert prospects to customers, retain customers, and increase sales. Ernan Ronan, in his book *Voice-of-the-Customer*, provides useful guidelines for establishing a trusting and respectful relationship between prospects/customers and the company. He recommends that the company create a meaningful value exchange. This might entail first access to products/services, a price reduction, free or expedited shipping, and so forth. The opt-in process can be used to obtain information about new products or services. This information facilitates targeted marketing which can be multichannel at some point.[26]

Caesar's Entertainment successfully used an opt-in program for two decades. Their dogged data-gathering methods were so successful that as of 2010 they were the world's largest casino operator, despite having many outdated properties.[27] After a customer joined the Total Rewards loyalty program and received a membership card, Caesar's could obtain a remarkable amount of information. Caesar's knew the games the customer preferred, the amount gambled, the food liked, the preferred type of evening entertainment (e.g., stand-up comedy, 80s rock concerts, etc.), and the time of year the person tended to visit. If a member lost more money than usual, Caesar's might immediately offer a free room and $1,000 in free play, and/or free air travel. If a customer had a bad day, Caesar's would know this on a real-time basis and perhaps offer expedited seating for a free upscale dinner.[28] In 2010, Caesar's sent out 750 million offers a year to its 42 million Total Rewards members. (Eighty-five% of gambling revenues came from Total Rewards members.) In 2010, the second-largest casino operator, MGM, sent out a mere 500 million offers a year. Because all casinos essentially provide the same experience, the ability to offer personally desired offers, including some on a real-time basis, provided a competitive advantage to Caesar's Entertainment.[29]

Online behavioral analyses can also be derived from anonymous observations of data provided by Internet sites visited. Such data are obtained from a universe of more than more than 100 million web pages. One company, Dstillery, has data-sharing arrangements with some ten million websites. Dstillery claims that it can reliably track about half of the U.S. population that uses a computer by viewing installed cookies for an average of 90 days. Dstillery sells this information to potential advertisers on a real-time basis. Advertisers competitively place bids within fractions of a second. Advertisers include Facebook, eBay, HP, American Airlines, the Vanguard Group, Microsoft, GE, Target, Pfizer, Yahoo, and the New York Yankees. Even the Internal Revenue Service employs such tracking.[30] A relatively recent trend, employed by major online advertising sellers such as Facebook and Google, goes even further. Based on the companies' knowledge of users' social networks, and the web behavior of users' friends and family, they can target personalized ads that anticipate a person's needs based on their social interactions. For example, when a close friend searches online for a new couch, a user can get served with ads for furniture stores. When two friends discuss the fact that the first friend is looking for a new couch, the second might suggest the retailer whose ad she just saw.

Data brokers have no compunction about preserving the identity of users. Epsilon Data Management (now part of Alliance data) has annual revenues of more than $1 billion. Epsilon has data-sharing agreements with retail organizations that share data about clients to a data cooperative. This allows participants to obtain information about prospective new clients. The company has information on 250 million Americans and sends out more than 40 billion emails annually. Another data broker, Acxiom, has data about nearly all U.S. consumers, and has revenues in excess of $1 billion—with clients including almost half of the Fortune 100 list of America's largest corporations.[31]

Several data analytic tools allow companies to gain vast amounts of information. Google Analytics enables companies to see the path taken by each purchaser and where they left off. Using this technology, such information is available from any internet-connected third party, and it is possible to filter data to obtain segmented reports. At a more granular level, Mixpanel claims to provide the most advanced mobile analytics in the world; Amplitude claims to provide real-time dashboards; and Kissmetrics provides email automation on its behavioral analytics platform.[32]

Via the live chat tool Olark, an organization can monitor qualitative data on a real-time basis, and have this information accessible to all employees. Livechat and Intercom provide related data; Fullstory and Inspectlet provide video recordings of customer behavior.[33]

By 2012, 90% of the world's data had been created in the prior two years. Thus, the world's data have been growing at about 40% a year.[34] With just three pieces of information—a person's date of birth, gender, and zip code—one can identify about 87% of the U.S. population.[35] Walmart collects an immense amount of data every hour from its customer transactions (details below).[36]

Automated analysis of online product reviews provides valuable information from the voice of the customer. Text-mining can detect the relevance of various product attributes, and evaluate a brand's position relative to its peers. Automated analysis of brand reviews can supplement, rather than supplant, marketing decisions. One research team's algorithm is in the public domain and has been fully described.[37]

Two companies, Affectiva and Emotient, have recently developed and commercialized facial recognition technology. Affectiva was founded by Rana el Kaliouby, an emotion measuring pioneer, and seeks to become an emotion economy platform.[38] Emotient, a San Diego based company, was bought by Apple, and uses facial tracking to identify peoples' feelings. Both firms have developed algorithms to decode facial expressions. To develop their algorithms, they recorded millions of expressions, noting tiny musculature movements, then sorted them by emotions, including anger, disgust, joy, boredom, and surprise. Large consumer product companies such as Honda Motor and Proctor & Gamble have licensed the technology to ascertain how people are reacting to their products. Large advertisers such as Unilever, Kellogg, and Mars have used webcams to watch consumers while they are viewing ads.[39] A U.S. start-up founded by Rana June, called

Lightpath, has developed a technology to sense and analyze consumers' mental states via custom-built wristbands that send real-time biometric data. Lightpath's clients include Google, Pepsi, 20th Century Fox, and Jaguar.

An informative (and intrusive) form of facial recognition is an app commercialized and launched by Russian developers. Called FaceFind, it can identify a person in a crowd with 70% certainty, by matches with KVontakte, Russia's version of Facebook. Thus, a café can ping a database and find out about recent conversations. It might turn out that a focal person likes chocolate ice cream. The person would hear a beep and read "Chris, the Infinity Café has fresh chocolate ice cream waiting for you. Show your screen and receive a second scoop free." Arguably, a horrific invasion of privacy, yet consider that all the information was self-reported on public forums.[40]

Along these lines, Clorox, based in Oakland, California, uses eye tracking technology that pinpoints which packaging designs attract consumers' attention. P&G likewise uses eye tracking technology, both in retail stores throughout the country and in controlled environments.[41]

"Mystery shoppers"—agents who pose as customers to grade operations—are still a popular low-tech option for data gathering. More than 450 companies provide that service, and many belong to the Mystery Shoppers Provider Association (MSPA). These companies claim to be able to monitor interactions online, on-site, and on the phone. They can provide periodic reports that include examination of the intangible elements of customer service; the identification of employees who may be driving customers away; whether staff members are actually promoting added services they were asked to offer; and benchmarking of services against those offered by competitors.[42] Unfortunately, there is little systematic evidence as to the efficacy of retaining a mystery shopping firm.[43] However, high-performing businesses go to extraordinary lengths to get an in-depth understanding of their customers. It has been reported that P&G even sends researchers to live with customers to observe how they use products and to identify unmet needs.[44]

Finally, a relatively new, albeit infrequently used, approach to getting feedback is from models—called product specialists—at auto shows. The product show specialists (often aspiring fashion models) need to have detailed and extensive knowledge of vehicle specs and pricing. Car companies now want to elicit comments from potential purchasers, and the specialists are expected to ask and keep a record of reactions. "Is the car's color sufficiently bright?" "What do you think of the trunk?" Years ago, one auto show attendee provided extensive negative comments on Nissan Infinity's trunk. Nissan executives quickly ordered a design change.[45]

Consistent High Quality

Approaches to the delivery of consistently high quality products/services include formal policies or established procedures that enhance customer satisfaction and loyalty. The existence of reliably high quality is integral to the development of a brand.

The development of a climate of expected excellence is often associated with a successful brand. The establishment of a personal relationship between employees and customers fosters satisfaction and loyalty on behalf of the customer. The total package of products/services is still another way to conceptualize quality.

In 1832, Moses Taylor built his food distribution business by placing a premium on quality in its purchases of food products. Agents inspected each and every carton, and went to farms to make sure the shipping crates were not decayed. They inspected ships for security. They examined every shipping manifest for accuracy. In the words of Moses Taylor, "a really superior product defies competition."[46]

To ensure consistent customer satisfaction, Marriott Hotels has established standard operating procedures (SOPs) for virtually all repetitive tasks. For instance, Marriott identified the 66 separate steps necessary to properly clean a hotel room in less than 30 minutes. They prepared recipe cards for cooking specific dishes, with specific procedures (e.g. hash brown potatoes should only be turned once on the grill). Encyclopedic SOP manuals promoted consistent quality across a system where Marriott owned only about 1% of its hotels.[47]

To promote quality service among sales associates, Sam Walton made them take a pledge.

> Now I want you to raise your right hand—and remember what we say at Walmart, that a promise we make is a promise we keep—and I want you to repeat after me: from this day forward I solemnly promise and declare that every time a customer comes within ten feet of me, I will smile, look the person in the eye and greet him (or her) So help me Sam.

Sam Walton prefaced his pledge by acknowledging that some associates "are naturally shy, and maybe don't want to bother folks. But if you'll go along with me on this … it will help you become a leader."[48]

A customer came into a Walmart's hardware department seeking a specific type of paint. The sales associate knew that Walmart did not carry that brand, so she sent the customer to a nearby paint store that did have it. Walmart expects that sales associates will be gracious and helpful when asked where a product is in the store. They might even walk with the customer to show the location. Walmart will not abide the associate who, not even looking up, grunts while pointing in some direction.[49]

Along the lines of Sam Walton's ten-foot rule, Nick Sarillo, founder of Nick's Pizza and Pub, says, "Smile and greet a customer whenever you come within five steps of one." For the process of opening and closing the kitchen, Nick uses laminated "ops cards" for each task involved. Each card is in a separate slot with red at the top and green at the bottom. In the morning all cards have the red side showing. When a task is completed, the corresponding ops card is turned so that the green side is showing.[50]

To assist new salespeople in making a presentation to a potential customer, the owner of one company developed a detailed checklist entitled "New Business Briefcase." The checklist has 12 categories, each with extensive details. For example, the laptop category lists the following steps to be checked: decks saved on desktop; rename with date/deck name; power cord, attached; mouse, mouse pad; check memory available; check new desktop icon for use; portable laptop speakers and mouse (with extra batteries; additional extension cord; etc.). To the extent that success depends on mastering details, this checklist has that issue covered.[51] Whoever said "retail is detail" is 100% right.[52]

A recent customer at Disney World reported that while he and his party were riding a Disney Transportation bus, the driver asked if they liked their rooms. One member of the party mentioned to the bus driver that his bar sink had a continual drip that he feared would keep him awake all night, but said that he didn't have time to call maintenance. The driver immediately replied, "Sir, I'll take care of it for you."

On returning from dinner late that evening, the man discovered that his bar sink was perfectly dry.[53]

Also indicative of the quality of service at Disney World is the immaculate cleanliness of the property. It has been claimed by some that the "average lifespan of a piece of trash" on the grounds at Disney World is four seconds. The authors of *Delivering Quality Service* are skeptical of this figure and estimate the lifetime to be closer to 30 seconds.[54]

The staff members (they are actually called the "cast") at Disney World are not just meticulous with regard to the property. They are courteous, friendly, and extraordinarily gracious, even after being repeatedly being asked "What time is the 3 p.m. parade?"[55]

At the initial location of Stew Leonard's supermarket, a three-ton granite block at the store's entrance states the company's philosophy. Rule 1: The customer is always right. Rule 2: If the customer is ever wrong, reread Rule 1.[56] In 1986, the store in Norwalk, Conn. was the most profitable retail store of its kind, according to the *Guinness Book of World Records*. The 100,000 square foot store achieved gross revenue, that year, of $100 million.[57]

A certain customer once went out of his way to purchase his dinner at a Stew Leonard's store. He was told that the store was out of chicken breasts, and so at 6 p.m. he placed a note in the suggestion box: "I'm upset. I made a special stop on my way home to buy chicken breasts for dinner, but you're sold out and now I'll eat a TV dinner instead." Just after the note was discovered, a Purdue chicken truck backed into the loading dock to make a delivery. The store manager arrived at the customer's home at 6:20 p.m. As Ron Zemke wrote: "You can imagine the smile on the customer's face when he answered the door and found [the store manager] with a complimentary two-pound package of fresh Perdue chicken breasts."[58]

Dunkin' Donuts has a 23-page booklet that specifies what it requires in a coffee bean. But purchasing high quality coffee beans is just the beginning. They must be used within ten days of delivery; if not, they must be returned on the next supply truck. Once the coffee is brewed (between 196 and 198 degrees Fahrenheit, exactly), it can be served for only 18 minutes; after that, it must be thrown out.[59]

Stockouts have a dramatic, non-linear, negative effect in online retailing. A firm can improve fulfillment rates through a focused small investment in inventory.[60]

A 2010 cover story in *HR Magazine*, "Questing for Quality," stated that HR is a catalyst for developing work processes and career opportunities that result in high levels of employee engagement. As Rita Zeidner put it, for high performing organizations, "good enough" is not good enough.[61]

In *Hug Your Customer*, Jack Mitchell relates how, at a retail conference, the keynote speaker asked if any of the attendees knew their top 100 customers. Jack Mitchell was the only person to raise his hand. He commented that he and his sales team members actually know the names of at least 250 customers, and they usually know a good deal more about their customers. According to Mitchell, despite the growth of Internet shopping,

> it's clear to me that customers are thirsting for relationship-driven companies. They want to be coddled. They like it when they are smiled at. They appreciate thank-you notes. And great sellers want to work for relationship-driven companies. Those companies are more successful because relationship selling inevitably leads to high productivity and high profitability. In a relationship-driven company it's a lot more fun to go to work in the morning. And we want to have fun.[62]

In *The Service Profit Chain*, the authors note that although financially it may make sense for a company to shift frontline personnel from one store to another, it often comes at the cost of breaking the continuity of a customer-employee relationship.[63] The customer-server relationship may be valued so highly that customers are willing to follow a server, even to a different company. Hair stylists, for example, may have a cult following of clients who will loyally travel almost anywhere their stylist goes.

A study of 362 buyer-salesperson dyads that included measures of customers' loyalty to the selling firm found that only customer loyalty to the *salesperson* affected tangible financial results. The higher the level of "salesperson-owned loyalty," the greater the growth in sales and selling effectiveness (i.e., sales volume and variety). "Firms must be cognizant of the risks that salesperson-owned loyalty poses for the seller ... and this is particularly problematic if the salesperson defects to a competitor."[64]

In broader terms, retail employee job performance (both in-role and extra-role, i.e., job performance and organizational citizenship behaviors) was found in three matched samples to affect customer evaluations of the retailer. Indicators of customer attitudes included satisfaction, purchase intention, loyalty, and word-of-mouth comments. The data base consisted of 1,615 retail employees, 57,656 customers, and 306 stores of a single retail chain.[65]

Sometimes customer service employees encounter customers who are rude and verbally aggressive (yelling, blaming, interrupting). Employees tend to respond to such verbal aggression by experiencing a depletion of emotional and self-regulatory resources, leading to an increase in employee incivility.[66] Employees should be trained to not respond in kind, which escalates hostility.

The establishment of personal, long-term relationships is what keeps the dwindling number of independent pharmacies in business. These retailers do not have the pricing power of large chains (CVS, Rite Aid, Walgreens), nor the space to stock many non-prescription products. Mail-order providers such as Express Scripts and CVS's mail-order service often have lower prices. However, local independent pharmacies rely on established relationships, which provide a comfort zone for customers. These often go beyond an in-depth knowledge of a patient's medications. They may include formulating specific ointments for unique skin conditions. One pharmacist likened this to a recipe where the cooking is very specific to the patient. Other specialized services include compounding a formulation for a child, which requires creating and flavoring small dosages, or providing adherence packaging that breaks down exactly when a patient should take drugs each day. These pharmacists even make house calls.[67]

Target Stores (formerly Dayton Hudson) specifically mandates that its commitment to quality customer service includes the following attributes:[68]

1. No-hassle merchandise returns
2. Fast, accurate checkout
3. Assistance when you need it
4. Merchandise you want when you want it
5. Sparkling clean stores
6. Clean restrooms
7. Quick check and credit approval
8. Shopper friendly store layout
9. Helpful product information
10. Carry-out service on request
11. Friendly employees
12. And so much more!

Nordstrom's bundle of benefits includes stocking a broad variety of styles and sizes of merchandise; piano players to enhance the atmosphere in stores; a very generous return policy (an unconditional guarantee); a real-time inventory system to locate products in other stores; billings that are always accurate, timely, and attractive; store designs that give the feeling of small boutiques while simultaneously offering the benefits of one-stop shopping that comes with large department stores.[69]

Nordstrom also takes special pride in its displays, and its return policy. Displays are set up so that the customer can not only see a skirt and blouse, but a whole ensemble (shoes, accessories, sweaters, etc.). This saves customers the trouble of visiting various product departments to create an ensemble.

As for returns, the story goes that a new Nordstrom store was located where a tire supply store was previously housed. When a customer showed up to return two tires that he had purchased in the tire store, the salesperson issued the customer a credit! More details about Nordstrom appear in Chapter 9.

Chip Bell, in *Managing Knock Your Socks Off Service*, relates how upon entering his room at the Plaza Club of the Radisson Plaza Hotel, he found a personal handwritten note on the dresser. His name was already inserted in the laundry bags in the closet and appeared on matches in the ashtrays (truly archaic). On check-in, the frontline service person called ahead to have fresh ice put in the ice bucket. They even put a bookmark for the present date in the *TV Guide*. One week later, he received by mail another handwritten personal note. Bell's second stay was even more memorable as it was obvious to him that the hotel really wanted him back.[70]

At Four Seasons, management keeps records of guest preferences—so that a guest might have a refrigerator stocked with diet Pepsis and yellow flowers on the table. (More details on the customer-directed practices at Four Seasons hotels appear in Chapter 9.) At Ritz-Carlton, the halls feature fabulous side furniture and artwork, and a frequent visitor will get a monogrammed pillowcase.[71]

At AchieveGlobal, a company with 150 years of customer experience, Sharon Daniels, the president and CEO, says, "Associates who work with customers must understand emotions, express empathy, be good listeners, and above all, show genuine respect and care." When an associate answers a question, offers options, or tries to resolve a problem, these are all "defining moments" in customers' eyes, and they add up to a big impression.[72] Andy Fromm, CEO of Service Management Group (now SMG) reported that his firm surveys more than 20 million customers annually. In Fromm's words "a good employee or a good sales associate might be worth five to 10 times an average one. We've seen that. It's unreal."[73]

Two primary customer service strategies are problem-focused behaviors, and emotion-focused behaviors. The former focuses on removing obstacles to ease the customers' experiences. The latter approach emphasizes modulating customer emotions via empathetic behaviors. Problem-focused strategies increase the intensity of customers' positive emotions, whereas emotion-focused strategies decrease the intensity of negative customer emotions.[74]

The fame of an endorser may prod consumers toward a more positive view of their own future financial situation. This effect is stronger if the consumer can identify with the endorser. So, it is not mere coincidence that famous athletes are retained to promote luxury brands (such as Rolex or Lexus).[75]

If a would-be persuasive message mentions only the good points of a product or service, skeptical shoppers may seek out references from detractors as well as advocates. If the persuader merely indicates that potential negatives have also been considered, prospective consumers tend to have a more positive reaction to the message. Indeed, if positive testimonials are merely accompanied by comments of people who found little to dislike, this somewhat sly fashioning of two-sidedness will increase receptivity.[76]

The name given to a product/service can affect consumer preferences as well. The first author of an academic article begins by recounting a dinner at a high-end restaurant with her husband:

As we sat deliberating over the menu, the server asked if we

> had made any selections. My husband looked up at the server in anguish and said that he felt like a steak, but he wasn't all that hungry. The server suggested that my husband select the smaller of the two steaks on the menu. My husband admitted that he had considered that option, but did not want to be perceived to 'be a lady.' Sure enough, I looked at the menu and saw that the smaller steak had been given the name 'ladies' cut.' Although my husband managed to overcome the negative associations of the ladies' cut and ended up choosing the smaller steak (only after ensuring that the server understood he was not a lady).[77]

The importance of a name and implied experience of a label was succinctly displayed in a whimsical cartoon in *Barron's*. A boy, about six years old, is sitting at his lemonade stand with his sign, "Lemonade, 25¢," and he has no customers. Nearby a girl, about six years old, has a long line of potential buyers. Her sign: "Lemonade Solutions, $1."[78]

A sarcastically demotivating poster by Customer Disservice–Despair, Inc. offers this motto: "Because we're not satisfied until you're not satisfied."[79]

Among the more esoteric factors that can affect the attractiveness of a brand or product category is the appropriateness of the font used to describe the brand. This can convey a congruous or incongruous meaning. An example of a highly congruent typeface or font would be the use of snowdrift (a font with the appearance of icicles atop each letter) in describing a frozen food or ice cream. Other typefaces similarly bear connotative meaning that might be considered appropriate for a given product.[80] Apple, a company famous for its uncompromising design decisions, is nearly as dedicated to its use of the clean, simple Helvetica Neue font as it is for creating minimalist and sleek consumer electronic products.

The anticipated "durability" of the product/service experience—how long an anticipated purchase will continue to provide pleasure—often influences a customer's purchase decisions. One way to strengthen the durability of a purchase (e.g., a cruise ship vacation) is to invoke the notion of a "lifetime of memories." Disney and De Beers (the diamond merchant) emphasize the enduring value of their offerings.[81] The watchmaker Patek Philippe advises, "You never actually own a Patek Philippe. You merely look after it for the next generation."[82]

Hagtvedt and Patrick have provided experimental evidence to support the idea that visual art—as De Beers uses in its ads—can be used to enhance and extend a brand. The art "confers an impression of luxury, prestige, and high class on the brands with which it is associated"[83]

Frequent exposure to perceived or conceptually related cues can enhance product evaluations and customer choices. Consumer behavior is strongly influenced by subtle environmental cues.[84] At the extreme, an automobile dealership in Minnesota might consider linking itself to cold weather or mittens; a restaurant in Arizona may want to consider linkages to the dry and hot climate.[85]

Still another factor worth considering is a product's physical or positional location in a display of multiple products. Evidence from five experimental studies indicates a "center-stage" effect. Evidently, people assign meaning to the location of an item shown among many. Products placed in the center are seen as more popular, and are chosen more often than chance would dictate. This has implications for shelf layouts in a store and Internet presentations.[86]

The appearance of scarcity (which is reflective of popularity) can influence the perceived desirability of a product. Van Herpen, Pieters, and Zeelenberg question what might go through a consumer's mind if a particular type of Bordeaux is almost, but not completely, sold out. There may be lots of bottles of other Bordeaux wines, but one particular bottle "stands on a nearly empty shelf, because consumers before you have apparently bought this particular wine today." The authors' three experiments indicate that scarcity can heighten demand. The scarcity effect has managerial implications. A nearly emptied shelf space (for just one of several products) may not represent a lost opportunity compared to a fully stocked shelf, but rather increase demand due to a scarcity effect.[87]

Is it advantageous to present options sequentially (one at a time) or simultaneously (all at the same time)? A recent study found that the latter approach produced more satisfaction with the purchased item. The researchers conjectured that when items are presented sequentially, the chooser has the persisting hope that a better option will come along. This hope undermines the evaluation of the selected item.[88] Building on the scarcity effect, a product might be tied to the day of week, or to a limited promotion period, or small production runs. Perhaps the most famous example of product unavailability is McDonald's regular but infrequent recycling of the McRib in and out of its menu for 30 years.[89]

A business can enhance consumer quality inferences by visibly toning down its marketing efforts—which the authors label (de)marketing. (De)marketing will likely reduce sales in the short run, but increase perceived high quality among knowledgeable consumers, who often attribute a product's performance in the marketplace to product quality, rather than marketing efforts.[90]

Whether the creation of more product categories tends to enhance customer satisfaction is still not certain. This appears to be the case among less experienced customers.[91] A study in *Marketing Science* found that when the time cost is considered, the optimal number of options is five or six. When the cost of searching is high, three or four options are optimal.[92] In contrast, the question as to whether there can be too many options was examined in a meta-analysis of 50 studies. The net result, overall, is that there are essentially no negative effects from increased options.[93] In Internet selling, many companies now turn to a user-generated category approach, in which user experience (where consumers sort products into clusters of products they feel are similar) is used to determine product categories. Similarly, product categories can be created dynamically through empirical analysis of consumer behavior. For example, Netflix offers online movie watchers categories based on their own (and others') watching of related movies, resulting in descriptive categories such as "Witty TV Comedies Featuring a Strong Female Lead," "Politically Incorrect Stand-Up Comedy," or "Buddy Sitcoms."

Enterprise-Rent-A Car®'s motto "we'll pick you up," makes the company's service offering practically irresistible. Enterprise provides multiple service facets to promote consistent quality. The company screens new hires carefully, and expects frontline personnel to learn and use the customer's name and offer unsolicited help.[94]

Consumers are creatures of habit. They often ignore product innovations by different brands because they do not want to spend the mental energy needed to choose among products. In their *Harvard Business Review* article on habits, Lafley and Martin recommend that consumers' habits be strengthened by innovations being rolled out as progressions of a brand, rather than a break from the past.[95]

A great deal of attention has been devoted to how organizations should deal with product/service lapses in quality and in the complaint process. Bottom line: an organization must have a protocol for rapid recovery in case a product or service lapses.

Only about 5% of customers complain about poor products/services, and between 10 and 30% of non-complaining customers will do business again with the organization. In contrast, about 70% of customers will do business again if they are satisfied with the way their complaint was handled; and 95% of complaining customers will do business again if their complaints are resolved instantly.[96]

Nauman and Giel, in *Customer Satisfaction Measurement and Management*, state that a good customer complaint system should enable easy access; rapid responsiveness; no hassles (it should not be an endurance test for the customer); employees who are trained and empowered to make accommodations (in the case of Lexus dealers, "doing whatever it takes" to satisfy a Lexus owner); and creating a customer database to document past complaints.[97] Other steps include apologizing, listening with empathy, owning the problem, focusing on fixing the problem rather than assigning blame, keeping promises, and following up.[98]

Because of the importance of eliciting feedback regarding problems or complaints, managers should not simply accept a customer's denial of a problem after a problem has been brought up. Kristin Anderson observed,

> Just because you don't think it's a big deal doesn't mean your customer doesn't think it's a big deal. When your customer *says* it's a big deal, it's a

big deal. And when your customer says, 'It's no big deal,' it's *still* a big deal. Otherwise, why would they bring it up?[99]

Feargal Quinn, CEO of the Irish supermarket chain Superquinn, describes his company's attempt to forestall and/or immediately mitigate complaints. He relates:

> We had just opened one of our newest stores. I was visiting to see how things were getting on when I was approached by the new store's manager. "Oh, Mr. Quinn, Mr. Quinn, this is a terrible situation!" he complained. "What do you mean?" I asked. "Well," said he, "the store's layout is all wrong! They've placed my office right over there, smack in the middle of the store, where all of our customers can see me. I can't get anything done. I've spent the last two days doing nothing but talking to customers, answering their questions, listening to their complaints!" I looked him straight in the eyes and said, "Ahh, but that's the point, exactly."[100]

In the final analysis companies do not change because of data. They change because of the vivid complaints of distraught customers. Complaints that are raised on social media sites are an especially big deal. Frank Eliason, whom *Business Week* has called the most famous customer service manager in America, was hired as Comcast's director of digital care. One month after Eliason joined Comcast, someone started a website called I HATE COMCAST. Although senior management took the matter seriously, the rants did not disappear. Eliason concluded that in order to make the case for change, he had to have a story to tell top management.

The story that prompted the complaint had to do with a customer wanting to modify a Comcast NBA League Pass, after the NBA season had started. The customer was told it was too late. The I HATE COMCAST site started to swell with other negative comments. After some Twitter exchanges, Eliason privately messaged the initial complainant: Don't worry about it; we are crediting $170 to your account. This led to the latter person stating privately that he was now a "happy Comcast customer."[101]

In a comprehensive study to ascertain best-practice complaint management, research was carried out in collaboration with the Customer Service Network in the U.K. Twelve suggestions were advanced, including speed of response and establishing a no blame culture. Data from both for-profit and nonprofit organizations found a correlation between the strength of complaint-management process and business performance.[102]

Knox and van Oest, in the *Journal of Marketing*, examined the effects of complaints and the effectiveness of recovery with regard to 20,000 customers over a period of two and a half years. They found that the probability of a customer ending a business relationship after a negative customer service experience depends on prior experiences. Positive prior experiences mitigate the effects, and unless there is a second failure shortly after the first, the customer relationship quickly returns to normal. However, when there were prior complaints the drop off is long-lasting.[103]

David Segal, the *New York Times* columnist who focuses on solving customer complaints (aka "The Haggler"), put Quicken Loans to a test. He posted an anonymous message on Quicken Loans' Twitter account. The message stated: "I am not happy with Quicken Loans! And you can tell because I used an exclamation point." Bianca Mutti, part of the team that monitors the Twittersphere, responded within hours. She wrote "Please send me an e-mail," and provided her email address. The Haggler responded using his Haggler email account, stating, "That tweet was a test. And you passed." Emily Mutti responded "Thanks for solving this mystery for us! I mean it, and you can tell because I used an exclamation point."[104]

Related to the issue of product/service recovery is how a firm handles returns. Return systems affect customer loyalty intentions. Dimensions of a good return system include its responsiveness, possible compensation, site ease of use, and minimal customer effort expenditure.[105]

Worse than a product/service lapse that affects a limited number of customers is a product-harm situation that requires a full recall of the product. A study of 60 product recalls, 36 which took place in the United Kingdom and 24 in the Netherlands, involved Cadbury chocolate, Basset's candy, Morrison's soup, Olvarit's baby food, and many more companies and brands. Key factors affecting recovery were the extent to which blame was attributable to the company (e.g., a bottler may have attached an incorrect label) and the amount of publicity generated. The evidence suggested that in most cases (except for where blame must be acknowledged and publicity is low), the company should increase advertising for both the brand and the category.[106]

Signet Jewelers (the owner of Jared, Kay Jewelers, and Zales) was accused in multiple instances of swapping fake diamonds for real ones when jewelry was brought in for repairs. On Kay Jeweler's Facebook page a mother claimed that the diamond ring she purchased for her daughter's high school graduation might be a fake. Although the company strongly "objected" to the allegations on social media, the company did not categorically deny them. The stock price declined 29% in six months.[107]

A service quality debacle occurred in 2017, when United Airlines forcibly "re-located" a seated passenger with a ticket. Evidently the flight attendants were only authorized to offer up to $800 for passengers to voluntarily give up a seat. When one passenger was dragged out of the plane by airport police, he was badly harmed (broken nose, two teeth knocked out). United apologized for the incident, but that was only after several feeble comments. The publicity was so ubiquitous that the incident was the number one trending topic on Chinese media.[108] A few days later, United declared a new policy: no one gets bumped if already on board.[109]

Adopting Best Practices

Unquestionably, the most passionate advocate for identifying and adopting best practices was Sam Walton, founder of Walmart. Sam was famous for constantly checking out competitors, looking for good practices to incorporate. He would question customers and sales associates. (He would do this even when he was on vacation with his family in a new place.) His observation of stores' displays and merchandising practices led Walmart to adopt the use of metal fixtures to hold shelves, instead of wood.

In his words, "I was in [Kmart's] stores constantly because they were the laboratory and they were better than we were. I spent a heck of a lot of time walking through their stores talking to their people and trying to figure out how they did things."[110] Walton claimed that Walmart wouldn't be as good as it is without Kmart, which made Walmart a better retailer.

In the early years, Walmart stores were placed in small towns, away from big cities—to avoid going head-to-head with Kmart and other sizable discount retailers such as Target. When Walmart was small, this helped Walton get access to a lot of information. He would say "Hi, I'm Sam Walton from Bentonville, Arkansas. We've got a few stores out there and I'd like to visit with [the head of the company] about his business." "As often as not, they'd let me in, maybe out of curiosity," he recalled, "and I'd ask lots of questions about pricing and distribution, whatever. I learned a lot that way."[111]

Marriott Corporation experimented with several new ventures which were deemed failures: a travel agency, a cruise line, theme parks, and home security. So when Marriott decided to initiate a hotel that was intended to attract business people—a little less upscale than the traditional Marriott facility—the company was very deliberate. Three years of planning included visits to competitors' hotels at the same price point. In addition to finding practices to adopt, Marriott conducted focus groups and surveys. It was via a survey that Marriott selected the name Courtyard.[112]

For decades, an organization called Best-in-Class Clearinghouse has had many corporate participants and formally merged with the American Productivity and Quality Center (APQC)—a member-based nonprofit organization. APQC, which had more than 500 corporate and nonprofit members as of 2016, claims to be the world's foremost online authority in benchmarking, best practices, process and performance improvement, measures and metrics. Founder Jack Grayson explained, "Productivity and quality improvement is a race without a finish line. Your organization's future will be determined by how well and how quickly you learn, adapt, and improve."[113]

Research reports published by APQC include numerous case studies. With respect to the Elevations Credit Union, the implementation of the APQC process classification framework provided the "ability to get real in-process metrics [which] was a fundamental change in how we operated." Process changes resulted in a 60% reduction in the time to make vehicle loans; a 50% reduction in the time to make home equity loans; and a 37% increase in consumer loans per month.[114]

As noted above, Sam Walton would constantly visit Kmart stores, because they were well-run and a source of good information. Jim Sinegal, CEO of Costco, when asked to compare his chain with Walmart, said,

> You're not going to get me to fall for that one. Listen, Sam's is a very formidable competitor. They're part of Walmart, the biggest corporation ever in terms of sales volume, and continuing to grow. They've made significant improvements to their Sam's operations. We watch them like a hawk. Hardly a week goes by that I'm not in a Sam's.

Sinegal also purchases items at Sam's to compare them with Costco's competing products.[115]

Customer Satisfaction Drives Operations

Companies can enhance customer satisfaction via well-designed service delivery systems; by using closed-loop information systems to correct problems; by extending the use of successful practices; or by simply going the extra mile to please individual customers.

According to Ken Dagler, president of the Australian Customer Service Association, the four most important words in providing service quality are "measure, measure, measure, and measure."[116] That dictum captures the practices of companies like UPS and Southwest Airlines. In complex service delivery settings, success depends on countless standards and measurement systems. (We describe the attention to detail and extensive measurement of efficiency at UPS in Chapter 2.)

Delivery systems can be improved by breaking large shipments into customer-specified sizes rather than the take it or leave it standardized lot sizes; timing shipments to arrive when customers want them, not simply when it is convenient for the company; and modifying billing forms to meet customer information system requirements. Organizations can also make service/product modifications to meet particular customer needs, and provide special discounts for long-term pre-orders.[117]

Disney World devotes considerable attention to developing systems that enhance the customer experience. For example, when guests board a tram, drivers repeat the pickup point three times so that visitors have a better chance of remembering where they parked. Employees cruise parking lots in golf carts looking for cars with lights on and engines running. (Seventy% of visitors arrive by car, many after a several-hundred-mile drive.) When a car is found still running, attendants leave a note that says, "Don't worry, we have your keys." Disney World has a full-service automobile repair shop on-premises; the charge to the customer is zero.[118]

Poorly designed service systems can often be detected by employee comments such as the following:

- "Just wait a couple of more days. I'm sure it will show up soon."
- "My computer is down, can you call back later?"
- "Oh, that's a sales floor (or warehouse, or accounting, or field service) problem. I'm in customer service … No, I don't have that telephone number."
- Customer: "Can I ask you a question?" Service rep: "Make it quick, I've got a meeting to go to."[119]

According to *The Ultimate Question 2.0*, the NPS process will be ineffective if organizations fail to close the loop between information and action. NPS is not just another way to gauge customer satisfaction; ultimately it is a business philosophy, a series of operational practices, and a leadership commitment. The logic behind NPS is so simple and intuitive that executives may be lulled into thinking that implementation will be simple. Think again.[120]

First, executives must be convinced that it is a worthwhile investment to increase promoters and decrease detractors. However, conventional budgeting, resource allocation processes, rewards, and bonuses militate against adoption of the NPS methodology. Given daily pressures to meet financial targets, many executives and managers may be skeptical about investing in the NPS system. The commitment of management is essential.

Second, traditional marketing researchers have not been uniformly positive about the use of NPS, a competitive approach to measurement. In this regard Reichheld and Markey quote Upton Sinclair: "It is difficult to get a man to understand something when his salary depends upon his not understanding it.[121]

When a company is making profits (temporarily) despite having poor customer service, Reichheld and Markey refer to this phenomenon as "bad profits." Bad profits extract value from customers—by providing a poor product/service and/or by using complex pricing systems that make it difficult for a customer to get out—rather than creating real value. AOL grew from 350,000 users in 1993 to about four million by the end of 1995. But the quality of service left customers feeling shortchanged, and the annual churn rate rose to 72%. The company's membership still continued to grow, and in January 2000, AOL merged with Time Warner in a deal that initially valued AOL at more than $190 billion. But the company began to stumble and the culture became concentrated on "trapping" customers who wished to leave, according to a *New York Times* article in late 2005.[122] In 2009, Time Warner finally gave up on the AOL brand, ridding itself of AOL at a valuation of $3.2 billion, yielding a loss of roughly $187 billion in just nine years. The pursuit of bad profits not only harms investors; it also alienates customers and employees.

Companies that earn "good profits," such as Enterprise Rent-A-Car, Jet Blue, and Southwest Airlines, gain market share because of their overarching vision of providing great results for customers and an inspiring mission for employees. Reichheld and Markey note the history of US Airways, which dominated traffic from the Baltimore-Washington International Airport despite providing mediocre service. In 1993, US Airways market share at BWI was 41%. Then Southwest Airlines entered the market with lower fares and superior service. By 2010, Southwest Airline had a 53% market share while US Airways' share dropped to 6%.

NPS, the proportion of promoters minus detractors, is one way to detect good versus bad profits—provided that line managers own the process. When an independent survey organization provides data, managers can track overall trends. When data are collected internally, managers can spot departments and even individuals who are having problems. This enables building customer feedback into daily operations and closing the loop by talking to customers and taking appropriate actions. Reichheld notes that customer feedback has a lot more "wallop" when conveyed to employees by an actual recording of the customer's voice, rather than by a summary of statistics.[123]

Leading NPS practitioners such as Schwab and Apple Retail work hard to contact every detractor, and they usually accomplish this within 24 hours. American Express has tried to raise its NPS by taking its customer care representatives off the clock. The company stopped measuring average call time. Instead, it allowed customers to decide how long they wanted to talk. For NPS methodology to be successfully implemented, CEOs must view increasing promoters and decreasing detractors as mission-critical.

In *Hug Your Customers*, Jack Mitchell describes several examples of how his small chain of retail stores has gone the extra mile. A customer needed a blue cashmere topcoat in size 42. There were none in stock, but Mitchell lent his size 42 topcoat to the customer. A woman brought in a dress purchased at Bergdorf's that needed alterations in a hurry. "We did it for her. That's a hug." And on occasion the store has been opened after hours on a Sunday, solely to allow one customer to pick up alterations.[124]

A spontaneous value-added benefit can create a memorable experience. A wedding reception was booked in the Taj Mahal hotel in Atlantic City. Because the reception took place on a slow night, the desk clerk took the liberty of upgrading the newlyweds to a luxurious suite. Perhaps the hotel anticipated that the couple would return on future anniversaries.[125]

J. W. Marriott, Jr., in *The Spirit to Serve,* recalled that an engaged couple booked a week at a Marriott Caribbean resort for their honeymoon. When the groom was found to have terminal brain cancer, the couple wanted to move their honeymoon date forward to allow for chemotherapy. But the only available seven-day stretch fell during a blackout period. When told of this couple's situation, the GM upgraded their accommodations and charged no fee.[126]

A cardholder called the American Express service center, distressed because she had lost her card and her mother had died. Normally, the fastest American Express can distribute a new card is overnight. But the caller had to make funeral arrangements immediately. A customer care professional and her team arranged to get a replacement card the same day using the shipping firm Sonic Delivery. The cost was about $500, paid for by American Express.[127]

Part of the remarkable success of Priceline is its focus on service. The new CEO makes sure that the customer service phone number appears on every web page. The impact on loyalty more than compensates for the extra cost. Every Priceline customer service agent is fluent in English and must speak at least one other language. Many speak three or four, particularly in Europe. Altogether, Priceline offers service in 42 languages and is looking to add more.[128]

Lance Bettencourt and colleagues have emphasized the value of a service lens (rather than the traditional marketing approach of a goods-dominant logic). Marketing creates value through the service lens by discovering customer wants and concerns, and facilitating customers' participation in the service interaction. Customers seek tech support, for example, which is provided by Best Buy's Geek Squad and Apple's genius experts. Having product features that go unused diminishes the potential value to customers.[129]

Price Consciousness

Sol Price started Fed-Mart in 1955, initiating the "discount store" concept. By 1976, more than 100 discount store chains existed, of which more than three-quarters disappeared by 1990. However, the idea appealed to both customers and retailers.[130]

Walmart limited markups of purchased products to no more than 30 to 40%. If an item sold at the suggested retail price of $1.95, and Walmart purchased the item for 70 cents, it could sell the product at $1.25, gaining an operating profit of 55 cents per item sold. If Walmart would only charge 95 cents—a markup of about 35 percent—and sold three times as many units at that price as they did at $1.25, the profit would be greater: 75 cents versus 55 cents.[131]

The successful implementation of this low-price formula led the present Walmart to become the world's largest corporation in terms of revenues in 2016 ($482 billion), with 2,300,000 associates worldwide.[132]

Walmart's scale enables it to obtain low prices from suppliers. Sam Walton wanted aggressive buyers. He explained that they were not obtaining great prices for Walmart, but for customers. Walmart insists on never being undersold. When Walmart reached the stage of being able to compete head-on with its initial biggest rival, Kmart, Walmart would sell a tube of Crest toothpaste for six cents if that was what Kmart charged.

To put their low-price philosophy into practice, Walmart established an exceptionally efficient distribution system. By 2016 the company had 42 regional distribution centers in the U.S., with 50.1 million square feet of storage space.[133]

Each distribution center could service 16 trucks simultaneously, operating 24/7 and servicing a U.S. fleet of more than 6,000 trucks.

Walmart installed its own dedicated satellite communication system in 1987, enabling the company to make real-time decisions pertinent to the optimal allocation and location of inventory—and reducing the cost of communications by dispensing with third-party information platforms.

Walmart's low prices caused many "mom and pop" stores to go out of business. Walton addressed that complaint by pointing out that because Walmart was traditionally only located in small towns, its presence enabled those towns to remain viable. Additionally, 75% of all store managers started as hourly associates, so Walmart spawned many successful careers. Further, Walton noted that small retail companies can compete successfully if they operate in a niche with good merchandising, along with knowledgeable and helpful sales associates. There was no way Walmart could offer the extensive selections and customer assistance of dedicated hardware stores, or other specialty retailers.

Nonetheless, price consciousness has become a major concern especially for brick and mortar stores—even if they possess a sizable Internet footprint. In 2016, Staples had the third-largest Internet site for commercial purposes, yet the company as a whole was struggling.[134] Even Target, a very successful chain, declared in 2017—after reporting sales and profit declines—that the company would invest billions of dollars to lower prices and remodel hundreds of stores. Trendy merchandise was not enough to attract shoppers.[135]

Costco recently developed and sold a golf ball that was reviewed favorably in comparison to the best-selling ball on the market, the Titleist ProVI. The Costco golf ball sold for $1.25—far below the Titleist ProVI price of around $4 per ball. The ball quickly sold out. The owner of the Titleist brand, which has more than 2,500 patents, threatened a lawsuit and the Costco ball was taken off the market until the legal issues were resolved.[136]

A dramatic demonstration of the importance of price was demonstrated on April 2, 1993, when Marlboro announced a permanent price cut of 20% throughout the U.S. The results were generally positive for Philip Morris, with increased brand-switching to Marlboro and away from discount brands.[137] But a rise in price can lead to disaster. At the other extreme, the company then called Citibank infuriated its customers, and caused a revolt, by announcing that it would charge a fee for the use of its ATMs, whereas previously the use of ATMs had been free.[138]

More important than the price charged for a service or product is the organization's price image, i.e., the general perception of a company's price-competitiveness. Having a low price image (a good thing for a seller) is akin to a good brand image. It should be noted that although average prices are central to price image, there are also non-price signals. These include the size of the store, absence of fancy amenities, a large parking lot, and location in a large shopping center. Hamilton and Chernev in "Low Prices Are Just the Beginning," propose a thought experiment. Consider a consumer shopping for a television set at Best Buy. Rather than call over a sales associate, she will check the price online. Now imagine the same consumer at Walmart, where she knows in advance that she will find the identical television (as offered online) at exactly the same price, if not lower. Would she be equally likely to pull out her phone to check prices at Walmart as at Best Buy?[139]

Extensions and spin-offs can affect price image, as when J. C. Penney added the Sephora line of beauty products or when Burger King in the U.K. added an £85 Kobe beef and *foie gras* hamburger. Going in the other direction, Whole Foods began promoting low-priced vertical extensions in its plan to lower its price image. According to data from five studies, the effects of a line extension depend on whether consumers have the intent of browsing versus buying. In the former case, a vertical extension has the predicted effect on price image. However, when consumers are focused on a purchase, the effects are counter-intuitive. An upscale extension can have a negative effect on price image, and a downscale extension can have a positive effect on price image.[140]

Price discounts (rebates, coupons, one-time price reductions) can positively affect consumers' perceptions of a product or brand. Consumer "involvement" may increase if they perceive products/services as linked to personally relevant goals and values.[141] These effects are enhanced if presented at the place of purchase (e.g., through an in-store discount), rather than at a time or place disconnected from the purchase occasion, such as by mailed coupons or newspaper inserts.[142]

According to Dan Cathy, president of Chick-fil-A, Tiffany Holland "had the wacky idea of inviting the first 100 customers who came in when we opened a new store to eat at Chick-fil-A free for a year. Her idea meant giving away about $28,000 worth of food at every new store." But the promotion created many millions of dollars' worth of publicity for Chick-fil-A.[143]

Reward programs can also boost short-term revenues and customer loyalty. However, there is an order effect with respect to rewards. It's best to start with a small reward, followed by a larger one for subsequent purchases. This has been found to yield increased satisfaction.

A pattern of diminishing gifts is demotivating and disliked.[144]

With regard to specific types of food purchases, consumers have varying preferences for either a bonus pack (extra items) or a price discount, depending on the product. In connection with food purchase items seen as healthful, e.g., a low-fat blueberry muffin, consumers prefer a bulk pack to a price discount. However, if the food purchase is for a relatively unhealthful item, e.g., chocolate chip cookies, customers prefer a price discount. The logic is unassailable. If the purchase is a form of "vice," it is better to buy a smaller quantity.[145]

Hamilton and Srivastava have written that 2 + 2 is not the same as 1 + 3. When retailers partition prices, consumers prefer that the low-benefit component has a lower price and the high-benefit component a higher price.[146] A related but distinct phenomenon appears when customers engage in trading in an older item and purchasing a newer one, such as an automobile or golf clubs. The evidence indicates that broadly speaking, customers prefer a good deal on the selling side (payment to them for their item), rather than on the buying side (for a new item).[147] However, the ratio of the price of the old item to the new item is crucial. The preference for the selling price only holds up when the ratio of the two prices is low. When the ratio is high, the preference for selling at a good price is reversed, and the desire for a good deal on the selling side (when the total economic value is held constant) diminishes.[148]

Retailers' use of private labels generally provide customers with a lower-price alternative. Respondents from 23 countries indicated their willingness to pay a higher price for a national brand compared to a private label brand—perceived higher quality being the primary determinant. Objective tests, though, have found little if any difference in quality between private labels and national brands. The perceived gap in quality is small and diminishing over time. National brand managers can increase perceived quality differences via advertisements that focus on quality and the amount of knowledge that goes into producing high-quality goods. Heavy price promotions of national brands make consumers more price-conscious and diminish the perceived quality gap.[149]

The presentation order in which items are displayed also affects customer choices. Based on five studies, Suk, Lee, and Lichtenstein conclude, "It is most profitable to present prices to consumers in descending order."[150] Related to price presentation order is whether it is desirable to first present a product display, followed by the price, or vice versa. Imagine that upon walking into a department store, a sweater catches your eye. When you look at the tag you find that the price is $49.99. Alternatively, the customer might see racks of clothes clearly marked at $49.99. The authors found that functional magnetic resonance imaging (fMRI) provides a useful tool in tracking the neural correlates of key decision components without disrupting the process. The early exposure to price, or "price primacy," actually was found to alter patterns in the medial prefrontal cortex of the consumer. The authors' conclusion is that price primacy can increase the purchase of bargain-priced products when their worth is easily recognized.[151] The conclusion is reasonable, but the use of neuroimaging is a practice that many—including the present author—would find troubling.

Based on a review of scanner-obtained data from 18 major grocery chains in the Netherlands, along with customer price images, the authors were able to identify "lighthouse" products that signal low prices, but which make up a small portion of store spending and do not seriously affect revenue. At traditional supermarkets, breakfast products and hair cosmetics were "lighthouse" products; at discount stores, laundry detergents, rice, and pasta were most influential.[152]

Closings of brick and mortar stores continue to accelerate. Credit Suisse forecasted that almost 9,000 stores would close in the U.S. in 2017. Numerous prominent chains are substantially cutting back on their stores, such as RadioShack, Sears, Kmart, and Macy's. Internet sales, although representing less than 20% of the retail marketplace, are growing rapidly, while margins for offline retailers have consistently shrunk.[153]

Best Buy has become the last major U.S. electronics retailer by promising to match any other merchant's price—whether online or offline. The technical capabilities of their Geek Squad add to the attractiveness of Best Buy's product offerings.[154]

Walmart has been buying small, niche, and "hip" Internet sites. With the acquisition of ModCloth, ShoeBuys, and Moosejaw, Walmart is seen as finally taking on Amazon in expanding its reach.[155,156] Walmart has also been using technology to reduce costs (and prices). For example, in the fall of 2016, Walmart planned to use drones to identify when product stocks were running low or misplaced—a process that could be accomplished in one day: far faster, and with a lower risk of accidents, than doing the job manually. (Previously, it took employees a month to complete the process.) As of the fall of 2016, every manager had the smartphone app "My Productivity" to request restocking of items and to check sales trends while roaming the aisles and assisting customers. Previously, managers spent thousands of hours annually in the back rooms of their stores.[157]

Mickey Drexler, who redefined Gap Inc. and built other recognizable brands including Old Navy, Banana Republic, and Madewell, also transformed J. Crew using higher quality to allow the company to charge a premium for its casual, preppy styles. This happened in 2010. But recent financial results have been dismal, with ten straight quarters of declining sales among established stores, and profits dropping over the past six years from approximately $120 million to a loss of $25 million in 2016. Although J. Crew derives nearly 50% of its revenues online, and has only 460 stores, the financial results indicate that customers are less willing to pay a premium for J. Crew's quality. Drexler defended the role of brick and mortar stores in this manner: "you go into a store—I love this, I love this, I love this. You go online and you just don't get the same sense and feel of the goods because you are looking at a picture." Online, the quality of goods can get lost in a sea of options. Prices drive decisions and social media accelerate fashion changes.[158]

Although more than a dozen retailers went bankrupt in the first five months of 2017, the feature story in *Barron's* was that some traditional retailers can thrive in an e-commerce world. For example, as noted above, Best Buy matches the prices of Amazon and big-box retailers, and competes on service.[159]

Brick and mortar stores can enhance their chance of survival by going beyond price matching. An important practice is to arrange for the exclusivity of a known brand, as Macy's has done with Tommy Hilfiger. T. K. Maxx has tried a less powerful form of exclusivity through the creation of store brands.[160]

Stores like Home Depot and Lowe's are somewhat cushioned against competitors by specializing in products that are difficult to ship—such as lumber, enamel flooring, large appliances, carpets—notwithstanding Amazon's free shipping service.[161] Also, retailers that are quick to react to (and/or shape) customers' needs have a strong position, as is the case with Inditex, which operates Zara and Zara Home. As was noted in Chapter 2, Zara's speed to market is extraordinary.[162] Nimble, high-quality brands, such as Calvin Klein, Tommy Hilfiger, Victoria's Secret, and Coach, can also compete without having the lowest prices.[163]

Sears Roebuck was once the leading department store in the U.S. In its present formation as Sears Holding Co., according to retail analyst Brian Suzzi, "There's no reason to go to Sears. It offers a depressing shopping experience and uncompetitive prices."[164] Raymond Keating observed that if Sears Holding is going to survive, "it must make the necessary investments in customer choice and service, while also competing on price."[165] Based on the company's 2018 bankruptcy filing, it appears Sears was unable to heed this advice.

When the son of the founder of the Great Atlantic & Pacific Company (A&P) opened a tiny store in Jersey City, N.J., it offered the lowest prices of any existing grocery store. Soon A&P was opening one, then two, and then three stores, a day. By 1920 it became the largest retailer in the world; by 1929 it was the first retailer to have sales of $1 billion. Plenty of opposition came from state and federal government administrators, one calling A&P "a giant bloodsucker." A&P ceased operations in November 2015, after 156 years of business.[166]

Kaleb Harrel, cofounder of Hawkers Asian Street Fare, recommends giving away samples and discount cards at events with a thousand attendees. "As a result of the free samples and discount cards, 10 to 15 percent of attendees will visit us, and at least 25 percent of them will be new customers. We spend around $2,000 but we get 25 new customers, each generating about $1,500 of value over two years."[167]

A remarkable development in the brick-and-mortar retail world is the rise of the "extreme value retailer," Ollie's Bargain Outlet. Using an opportunistic purchasing strategy, Ollie's has been able to sell brand-name merchandise for up to 70% less than department stores and specialty stores, and up to 50% less than Walmart and Target. Products come from closeouts, liquidations, or bankruptcies. Market-watchers predict Ollie's will grow from 200 outlets to 900 in a decade.[168]

Artificial Intelligence (AI) algorithms are being used to determine prices. Whereas older software relied on matching the prices that competitors charged ("dynamic pricing"), new systems crunch mountains of historical and real-time data to predict customer and competitor behavior under different scenarios. An experiment comparing earlier software to AI algorithms found that the latter yielded 5% higher margins.[169] Of course, Big Data and customer-tracking also mean that AI algorithms can take individual consumers' behavior into account, offering different prices or promotions to different customers online.

A gas station owner recently complained that his AI software was malfunctioning. A competitor across the street had slashed prices, but his station's algorithm responded by *raising* prices.

There wasn't a bug. Instead, the software was monitoring the real-time data and saw an influx of customers, presumably because of the long wait across the street. It [the AI software] could tell that no matter how it increased prices, people kept coming in.[170]

As Andy Kessler has noted, it is no coincidence that nearly every important technology development during the past 20 years also saves time (in contrast to waiting in line): print-at-home boarding passes, automatic hotel checkout, ATMs, taxis available on demand (e.g., Uber), EZ Pass and similar state-specific systems in several U.S. states. Some time-saving options entail extra fees, such as Fast Pass at Disney World, early boarding on several airlines, and Task Rabbit employees who will wait in line or assemble furniture for a fee.[171]

For price-based appeal to work, reaching a critical mass is essential. LinkedIn (now owned by Microsoft) has far more appeal than competitors' offerings of professional networking. The same advantages of scale apply to Facebook and Twitter. For a while, Microsoft subsidized the cost of the console that played Xbox games. Uber evidently is trying to rapidly gain a critical mass in many markets.[172]

Customer Satisfaction Drives Rewards

According to a study by researchers at the University of Michigan, a 1% increase in customer satisfaction associates with a 2.37% increase in a firm's ROI.[173] Several companies have tied employee compensation to customer satisfaction ratings— such as FedEx Customer Critical, a premier unit of FedEx. FedEx as a whole grew very rapidly from 1988 to 2001, with revenues increasing four-fold—a compound annual growth rate of 14%.

FedEx's Customer Critical unit tied customer assistance teams' quarterly bonuses to customer satisfaction ratings. Further, all division employees participated in a bonus plan and profit sharing based on customer satisfaction ratings.[174]

Taco Bell collected satisfaction data from 800,000 customers and found that stores in the top category with respect to customer satisfaction ratings outperformed the other stores on all measures. As a result of this finding, Taco Bell revised its employee selection process, improved training, and increased latitude for employee decision making on the job.[175]

Non-financial rewards can also be effective in motivating improved performance. Charles Schwab commented that he has never encountered anyone, no matter how exalted their station, "who did not do better work and put forth greater effort under a spirit of approval than under a spirit of criticism."[176]

Commenting on his company's NPS system, Peter McCabe, chief quality officer at GE's healthcare division, explained, "It was a 'Texas hold em' kind of thing. We went all in." Twenty percent of managers' bonuses were tied to the NPS metrics achieved.[177]

At First Interstate Bank in California, individuals with consistently outstanding customer service were awarded a "five-star badge," an award restricted to only 10% of employees. Recognition was also contingently based at the branch level, based on customer satisfaction at that branch.[178] Motorola has installed individual recognition programs based on customer satisfaction.[179] American Express distributed monthly bonuses of up to 35% of base pay, largely on the basis of customer responses to The Ultimate Question ("would you recommend…").[180]

Although many companies recognize frontline workers for improving customer service—some reward behaviors that are antithetical to providing good service. Schneider and Bowen, in *Winning the Service Game*, describe an unnamed organization where customer service representatives were encouraged to exhibit warmth and friendliness in their telephone conversations with customers. However, the reward system was based on the duration of "talk time." Employees whose telephone conversations exceeded three minutes were chastised. One unintended result was a high incidence of "mysterious disconnects" that occurred when telephone calls were running too long.[181]

Employee Latitude

As Schneider and Bowen note, granting employees broad authority to make decisions is both enterprise-directed and customer-directed. The practice is consistent with increasing internal work motivation, and is a core job characteristic in the Job Characteristics Model.[182]

Nordstrom is arguably the best exemplar of granting employees wide latitude to make decisions that affect customers. (See Chapter 9.) The employee policy manual at Nordstrom is printed on a pocket-sized plastic card. It consists of two rules: (1) Use good judgment in all situations; (2) There will be no other rules.

In broad terms, Schneider and Bowen claim that "the people make the place."[183] Through good selection, training, and empowering management practices, employees provide excellent customer service. *Service Profit Chain* shows that five factors accounted for 80% of the total variance in customer satisfaction:[184]

Practice	Explanatory Power
1. Latitude to meet customer needs	37%
2. Authority to serve customers	19%
3. Knowledge and skills to serve customer	13%
4. Rewards provided to employees for serving customers well	7%
5. Customer satisfaction is a high priority of management	4%

Summarizing the evidence, employee latitude accounted for more than 55% of the variance in customer satisfaction.

Four Seasons Hotels employees are encouraged to make real-time decisions that enhance the customer experience—such as the receptionist who remained on the telephone for more than 30 minutes to help guide a guest to make an important meeting under difficult driving conditions.[185] See Chapter 9 for more examples.

Innovation Is Encouraged

Sam Walton knew as early as 1960 that the discount retail model represented the future. Along the way, he introduced a number of innovative customer-directed practices. A band, a small circus, and a carnival atmosphere would accompany a new store opening—plus exceptionally low prices on some loss leaders. At established stores, Walmart introduced "shopping cart bingo." Each cart had a number, and the shopper whose number was called would receive a discount on the contents of the cart, having won bingo. In April 1983, Walmart opened its first Sam's Club store with a membership fee of $25.[186] (About five months later the first Costco Wholesale opened.) Walmart also pioneered in the use of a dedicated satellite transmission system, enabling the company to track sales data for every item in every region and store. Walmart collects 2.5 *petabytes* of customer transaction data per hour. One petabyte is one quadrillion bits of data, or the equivalent of 20 million file cabinets of data.[187]

As noted above, Marriott Hotels introduced a number of unsuccessful businesses, including theme parks ("Great American Theme Parks"), but they had a hit when they introduced a business-focused mid-priced chain, Courtyard by Marriott. Another huge success was their acquisition of the Ritz-Carlton Hotel chain in 1995. Marriott pioneered in providing in-room checkout in the early 1980s, and instituted a check-in protocol ("first ten") avoided lengthy check-in lines. The Marriott Rewards program encompassed all affiliated properties (e.g., Courtyard, Marriott, Residence Inns, and Ritz Carlton).[188]

Jet Blue was the first airline to offer in-flight TV and leather seats. Leather seats are twice as expensive as the cloth seats most airlines use, but they last twice as long and are easier to clean, allowing crews to turn a plane around sooner. Jet Blue uses its color for marketing—everything being blue including potato chips. The sign in one airport departure lounge reads "CAUTION: NEXT MEAL 2,500 MILES." The crew members' dark blue uniforms were created by a fashion designer, which cost a bit more but produced a distinctive image.[189] Other airlines have copied several of these approaches, among them Delta Airlines, whose new uniforms (in 2018) were designed by renowned fashion designer Zac Posen.

Four Seasons was the first hotel to have armoire-enclosed televisions in rooms, and lighted mirrors in bathrooms. It was the first national chain to introduce concierge service. Four Seasons pioneered in on-premises four-star restaurants (with celebrity chefs), high-end fitness centers, spas, and golf courses.[190]

For decades, new products have been introduced with unique features. Pledge not only lifted dust from your furniture: it also polished and waxed wood. Quaker Oats' oatmeal did not have to be soaked overnight; you could cook it in minutes.[191] V8 Vegetable Juice is more than 80 years old, and still provides a popular combination of vegetables (tomato, beet, carrot, celery, lettuce, watercress, parsley, and spinach). As Christensen et al. note in *Competing Against Luck,* V8 does not compete against sodas or coffees, but against vegetables. "V8 wins hands down against peeling carrots, boiling spinach, and flossing celery strings out of your teeth."[192]

In 1903, King Gillette made his first sale and shipped his initial batch of 168 safety razors. In 1904, Gillette sold more than 12 million razors. In 1946, Aaron Lapin first developed what would be named Reddi-wip; in 1963, Douglas Engelbert invented the computer mouse; in 1974, Art Fry developed the Post-it Note. Henry Petroski uses those products to argue that necessity is not the mother of invention. Rather, successful inventors are constantly on the lookout for what we don't need.[193]

Christensen and colleagues claim that successful products and services perform "a Job to Be Done." Notable examples of companies that have helped people solve a problem include Uber, Airbnb, IKEA, and Open Table. A less well known innovation is Sargento's prepackaged ultrathin cheese slices. This product was a huge success, with $50 million of revenues in year one and $150 million in year two. Christensen and colleagues ask: "Why did this product thrive, when the vast majority of the other 3,400 consumer packaged goods launched in the same year didn't even survive their first twelve months in the market?" Ultrathin sliced cheese solved a problem consumers were struggling with. They wanted to enjoy the delicious cheese experience of their daily sandwich without the calories, fat, and guilt that came with it.[194]

Attention-getting, breakthrough innovations are scarce. Nielsen tracked more than 20,000 new products launched between 2012 and 2016. Just 92 sold more than $50 million in year one and sustained that sales level in year two. That works out to a success rate of less than one-half of 1%.[195]

A study by Bain & Company of the world's major companies found that between 1999 and 2009 only 9% achieved sustainable growth—defined as an average annual increase in profits and revenues of 5.5% over that period.[196]

It remains to be seen whether the innovative luxury appliance retailer, Pirch, will attain sustainable growth. Its publicly displayed motto is "live joyfully"; its sales associates greet customers warmly. The company wants customers to view its stores as a sort of playground where they can have fun trying out various products—while sampling complimentary chef-prepared snacks and beverages. Pirch even encourages customers to bring bathing suits to try out $20,000 granite tubs and a steam room.[197] Pirch has the fourth highest level of sales per square foot in the U.S. (after Apple, Murphy USA, and Tiffany.)[198] A less dramatic but analogous example: at selected Maytag stores, customers can bring dirty laundry to test different models of washers.[199]

Samsung's Chef Collection refrigerator dispenses both still and sparkling water. It also has five cooling zones, including a second freezer compartment. The company's Flex Duo oven permits cooking in two places at different temperatures. Its WaterWall dishwasher has a linear system which, according to Samsung, cleans better than a rotary spray, especially in hard-to-reach corners.[200]

Virtual fit software programs took off as a marketing tool in 2017. The program, based on customers' descriptions of their body dimensions and hair color, creates a virtual model, enabling customers to see how they would look in different outfits. Gallino and Moreno, in a field experiment, found that use of the virtual fitting model increased average profitability by approximately $425 per customer—mostly due to a higher conversion rate, but about one-third due to larger orders and reduced fulfillment costs arising from returns (due to customers ordering several sizes).[201] More recently, Amazon has introduced an Internet-connected camera device intended to capitalize on the same idea. The Echo Look "Style Assistant" asks consumers to take pictures of their outfits, learns their preferences and style, and provides suggestions of items the user might want to purchase from home.

An innovative five-year-old French fashion rental company, Le Tote, charges as little as $39 a month for customers to receive a customized selection of clothing and accessories from established high-fashion brands such as French Connection, Vince Camuto, and Joie. Customers can wear items a few times, then return them or purchase them. Because it solicits customer comments, Le Tote has a vast amount of information as to a particular customer's preferences, along with the fit and quality of items it sells.[202]

Taco Bell spent four years to develop and roll out a Dorito-flavored taco during which time Taco Bell and Dorito experimented with more than 40 recipes. Due to the differing textures (chips versus shells), it took teams of engineers to develop a proprietary seasoning. The company sold 100 million Doritos Locos Tacos in the first ten weeks. Taco Bell's same-store sales increased by double digits, a rare phenomenon in the fast food business.[203]

Panera Bread, the 2,000-unit bakery chain, worked for a decade to eliminate artificial additives (often preservatives). In 2015 they announced a "no no" list of 96 ingredients that they would never use. As of 2017, Panera attained a completely "clean," menu, eliminating 122 ingredients: zero artificial flavors, preservatives, sweeteners, or colors. This required recipe changes. For instance, the very popular broccoli cheddar soup required 60 revisions to preserve the taste and texture without artificial ingredients. The numerous changes in ingredients also resulted in extensive changes in Panera Bread's supply chain and employee training programs.[204]

Jet Blue's "nap pods," introduced at Kennedy Airport in 2016, consist of futuristic-looking blue and white pods where passengers may snooze for free. For privacy, a large visor pulls down, and built-in speakers provide soothing sounds. A timer gently wakes users so that they don't miss their flights.[205] The success of this innovation remains to be seen.

Shyp, a relatively new start-up, allows customers to avoid returning a product at a package delivery store such as UPS or FedEx. After the customer sends a photo of the product, a courier should arrive within 20 minutes to whisk the item away. With the tag line "we'll take it from here," Shyp charges just $5 for the pickup service. Shyp has been described as the Uber for packages. Sales in 2016 were growing by 20% a month.[206]

Zara is a highly innovative and fast-moving fashion company. Based on input from store managers about current trends, it can complete a coat design in one day. Pattern makers create prototypes during the first week. By the 13th day, 8,000 coats go out to stores. Zara, a division of Inditex SA, has more than 7,000 stores in 92 countries.[207]

Economists often reference the "invisible hand" that magically connects buyers and sellers and which figures out how much goods or services are worth. However, in Uber's case, the magic is analytics. Uber's customers can find out before they book a ride how many vehicles are in the area and how long it will take before one gets to them. Uber drivers know whether it's worth their while to get into their car, because they know how many customers are out there, where they are, and how much they are willing to pay.[208]

Finally, Calvary Hospital, in Bronx County, N.Y., has introduced the Bodkin Rule. An elderly Jewish patient (Mr. Bodkin) fell out of bed and was told he would need gentle restraining straps going forward. Due to Mr. Bodkin's prior experience in a concentration camp, he refused any restraints, saying "If I fall out of bed again, let me die on the floor. But don't you tie me up." Calvary discontinued belts and straps throughout the hospital, replacing them with human arms. The extra cost in terms of nursing time, and developing a staff of volunteers, was $1.3 million but it no doubt generated many contributions.[209]

Multiple Ways to Reach Customers

Big Data is probably the most sophisticated new approach to reaching customers. Big Data interventions typically are based on patterns of behavior among anonymous individuals. In contrast, targeted marketing, which is based on purchases or clicks, can identify customer tastes and make recommendations or offer coupons. Push notifications provide a potentially enormous set of contacts. Social media have played an important role in creating brand awareness. And several formulations of multichannel marketing remain useful, including one of the oldest: direct mail campaigns.

Big Data: what is it, anyway? Big Data is generally defined as data sources that are massive in terms of volume, velocity, and variety, but nobody has established cut points to distinguish Big Data from big data, so to speak. Certainly, the volume and velocity of data collected by Walmart would fall into the range of Big Data. Implementations of Big Data analyses have enabled the use of evidence-based decision making rather than "HIPPO"—the highest-paid person's opinion. Voluminous data regarding airline flights (weather, traffic, historical patterns, etc.) have been used to improve the accuracy of ETAs (Estimated Time of Arrivals). A correction that improves accuracy by six minutes can save airlines a great deal of money in labor costs, and facilitate more rapid aircraft takeoffs and turnarounds. According to a *Harvard Business Review* article, "Big Data: The Management Revolution," a single airline that knows exactly when its planes will land (and acts accordingly) can save several million dollars a year at *each airport* it operates out of.[210]

In 2012, Kroger Supermarkets employed a system called QueVision, with the goal of ensuring that when a customer arrived at the checkout line, no more than one person would stand ahead of him or her. Data sources included the number of customers entering a store; the number waiting at checkout lines (obtained by infrared cameras); store layout and size; and historical transaction logs for each of its 2,400 stores. One byproduct of the use of QueVision was the discovery that many customers made small purchases in the morning and at lunchtime. This led to the introduction of 2,000 express checkout lines.[211]

Use of QueVision reportedly reduced the average checkout time from four minutes to less than 30 seconds. Although an examination of "before" and "after" data cannot unequivocally establish causal relationships, customer satisfaction scores increased by 24% from 2012 to 2013 according to *Information Week*. Financial results were even more impressive. In the first fiscal quarter of 2013, Kroger had profits of $462 million versus a loss of $307 million for the comparable quarter in 2012, which reflected a 13% increase in sales to $24 billion.[212]

A survey by consultants NewVantage Partners found that in 2012, 5% of U.S. firms were using Big Data; in 2015, 63% were—a more than ten-fold increase. The title of chief data officer, a title that has only recently emerged, is now found in 54% of companies surveyed. Michael Malone, the author of the piece, stated:

> The commercial impact of this revolution can be found everywhere from products and services that can predict the unique needs of individual customers, to improved credit precision, to stores that adapt (through special discounts and deals that pop up on your smartphone) to each customer who walks through the door.[213]

Evidence of the growth of big data comes from an examination of three recent Society for Industrial and Organizational Psychology (SIOP) conference programs. In 2013, SIOP held four separate sessions with the terms "Big Data" or "Analytics" in the title. That number jumped to 11 in 2014, and to 15 in 2015.[214]

Randomized field trials (RFT) have been increasingly applied in e-commerce. The most successful Internet companies according to Jim Manzi, the founder and chairman of Applied Predictive Technologies, are "relentless experimenters." Google ran about 12,000 RFTs in 2009, with about 10% of the trials leading to a change. A commonly cited example is an experiment in which Google tested the optimal color shade of advertising links that would increase clicks and thus ad revenue. Capital One bank in 2012 did thousands of randomized field experiments every month.[215]

Rich Fairbank and Nigel Morris, two experts in conducting RFT, identified a small regional bank (OakStone Financial) that in 1994 was willing to collaborate with them. They wondered whether a credit card solicitation would have better success if mailed in a blue, as compared to a white, envelope. Rather than debate, they simply mailed 50,000 randomly selected households the blue envelope and 50,000 randomly selected households the white one. In the year 2000 the regional bank (subsequently called Capital One) conducted 60,000 RFTs annually. By 2011, Capital One was a Fortune 500 company with a worth of $50 billion.[216]

As Manzi put it:

> A company can earn a lot of money by making experiments a central element of how it makes decisions…"All else equal a company that does field experiments will have a material advantage over those that do not.[217]

A fascinating use of big data is related to the purchase of used cars at auction. Nobody wants to buy a used car sight unseen, so purchasers often wind up dealing with pushy used car salespeople. Carvana, an online car auctioneer launched in 2013, contacted Kaggle, an online community of data scientists that had solved problems for Merck and Facebook. Carvana offered a prize of $10,000 for the best solution to predict whether a car offered at auction would be a "lemon." Carvana found that it could avoid lemons and buy better cars for $500 less than what similar cars would sell for. This allowed them to offer their customers an average $1,500 discount from market prices. Carvana also used extensive data analytics (including full credit reports from multiple companies, LexisNexis, and news databases) to reduce the risk of a default.[218]

Push Notifications: the widespread use of smartphones has created the possibility of contacting an enormous number of people. "It's hard to over-hype the power of mobile push notifications," remarked entrepreneur Ariel Seidman. "Yet, without certain precautions, there is a high likelihood that the mobile user will hit uninstall. If push notifications are accompanied by a vibrate signal, the uninstall rate immediately skyrockets."

Noah Weiss, an executive at Slack, emphasizes the importance of obtaining permission from users. Weiss, who has conducted more than 100 experiments with push notifications, recommends that companies start with a small sample, say 5% of contacts, and that the initial contact should be positive with a brief narrative.[219]

Targeted, customized offerings: can include coupons provided by opt-in loyalty programs that can be either distributed in person or via the Internet. Internet companies can also obtain data without opt-in provisions, and data brokers can provide enormous amounts of detailed information about potential prospects.

Online opt-in programs provide the fundamental building block of Ronan's Voice of the Customer marketing system. The user must provide something of value, to obtain participation of prospects or customers.[220] Online retailers can track not just what customers purchase, but what they have looked at, and how they navigate through a site. Algorithms can predict what individual customers will read or wear next. Retailers can experiment by varying promotions, page formatting, and customer reviews.[221]

Customer purchase data can be used to create customized brochures for mail promotions. Target received a good deal of unwanted notoriety in connection with the statistical "pregnancy prediction score" it developed based on the purchase of 25 items. The purchase of unscented lotions and supplements such as calcium, magnesium, and zinc are indicative of a woman in the second trimester. With enough data, Target can predict with 87% accuracy what month a woman will give birth. Target will try to "hook parents-to-be at the critical moment before they turn rampant—and loyal—buyers of all things pastel, plastic, and miniature."[222] In a memorable article, "How Target Figured Out a Teen Girl Was Pregnant before Her Father Did," the facts can be summarized thus: an angry man storms into a Target store outside of Minneapolis demanding to speak to the manager. "My daughter got this in the mail ... she's still in high school and you're sending her coupons for baby clothes and cribs?" The store manager apologizes profusely, and then calls the man a few days later to apologize again. The father somewhat abashed, says that he owes the manager an apology.[223]

Target has a team of statisticians dedicated to studying consumer habits. They note age, income, job history, and credit cards used for purchases in stores and online. Then they can send a precisely timed coupon or reminder. If, for example, someone purchased a lot of cereal at Target but no milk that must mean the customer is buying milk elsewhere. Target will provide irresistible offers for milk.[224]

Netflix has ways of observing what people watch and figuring out what each viewer might want next. According to Laura Martin, a financial analyst at Needham & Company, "no company on earth has better predictive algorithms about how consumers watch TV and films on digital platforms."[225]

Data analytics were used to build an algorithm to set the optimal prices for Rue La La, a company offering designer apparel and accessories at a deep discount for a limited time (what is often referred to as "flash sales"). Numerous variables, entered into a software tool, make demand predictions. A field experiment to test the impact of the algorithm saw a 10% increase in revenues in the test group.[226]

Customization can be conducted at three levels of granularity: mass market, segment- specific, and individual-specific. Using optimization procedures, which can take into account 300 variables or more, a company can achieve substantial improvements over traditional promotions. However, the optimization process is largely empirical, i.e., inductive, rather than deductive. The overall effects of all three types of customization promotions, though, have minimal impacts in offline stores.[227]

Kashmir Hill, the author of the article on Target's pregnancy predictions, wrote, "it creeped people out that the company knew about their pregnancies in advance." Consequently, Target has learned to be far more subtle in the design of promotional coupon booklets. There will be coupons for detergents as well as diapers.[228] Nonetheless, Kashmir Gill notes that the mining of purchase data and the statistical analysis of patterns may have contributed to the growth of Target from $44 billion to $67 billion in eight years.[229]

According to Chris Anderson's *The Long Tail: Why the Future of Business is Selling Less of More*, the Internet has enabled retailers to create modifications of products that can easily be located online. Online channels change the shape of the demand curve because consumers often value niche products geared to their particular interests. Anderson argues that niche products can be highly profitable.[230]

Ronan, in *Voice-of-the-Customer Marketing*, recommends multichannel marketing. His analyses support the use of old-fashioned, direct mail promotions. The Internet provides the least expensive way to contact prospective customers, but he bases his argument on four hypothesized parameters. In one scenario he first assumes a finite universe of 50,000 prospects, and a profit per unit sold of $200. Second, Internet contacts cost five cents, considering costs associated with creative, administrative, and overhead expenses. Third, a traditional direct mail piece, which must include a personalized letter, an attractive outgoing envelope (not a label), and a real postage stamp, would cost $1.50 per mailing. However, a direct mail package that was elegant could cost $5 (100 times more per piece than an email). The fourth parameter is the assumed sales (or "hit") rate per contact. Ronan assumes hit rates of 0.0013 for email; 0.02 for traditional direct mail; and (perhaps unrealistically) 0.10 for the elegant package. The arithmetic plays out with email contacts leading to 65 units sold; gross revenue of $13,000 and a net profit of $10,500. The traditional direct mail yields sales of 1,000 units, revenues of $200,000, and a net profit of $125,000. A luxurious package would produce sales of 5,000 units, revenues of $1,000,000, and a net profit of $750,000.[231]

In the final analysis, the accuracy of Ronan's hypothesized parameters is an empirical question. But even if the estimated hit rate for the luxurious package was one-tenth of what Ronan assumed, it would still be more than seven times as profitable as Internet-based targeting. Of greater consequence is the claim that effective marketing should use multiple channels, including emails, direct mail contacts, an Internet presence, and the constructive involvement of social media.[232]

Internet websites have advantages over traditional methods insofar as costs are significantly lower and message delivery a lot faster. Companies can use a variety of Internet strategies, including achieving a presence in social media and blogging communities. A key ingredient, in converting website visitors to buyers, is trust. Organizations can enhance trust by investing in sophisticated technologies as well as visual design—and by conveying and demonstrating their concern for customer privacy and security.[233] One study found that the effects of word-of-mouth referrals produce substantially longer carryover effects and substantially less price sensitivity.[234] Word-of-mouth marketing can also entail one-to-one responses to influence narratives on social networking sites or blogs.[235]

Word of mouth (WOM): has never lost importance; indeed, it was estimated in 2008 that social talk generated more than 3.3 billion brand impressions across industries daily—and the growth of that number, some 12 years later, is unimaginable. Based on both field and laboratory investigations, giving a product away increases WOM comments by about 20%. Giving away non-product extras (such as hats or recipes) generates about a 15% increase in WOM metrics. However, neither a portion of the product (a sample) nor a coupon or rebate was linked to increases in WOM. The financial consequences regarding whether a product gift is financially beneficial depends in part on the empirical association between conversations that would not otherwise occur and purchases per conversation, and partly on costs such as mailing.[236]

Social media presence: is crucial to current customer-directed practices. Guy Kawasaki and Peg Fitzpatrick offer 123 sets of specific and detailed suggestions in their book, *The Art of Social Media*.[237] They also offer advice and information about advanced opportunities for multiple platforms, including Facebook, Google+, Instagram, LinkedIn, Pinterest, SlideShare, Twitter, and YouTube. Their book culminates in a template for a new enterprise seeking to establish a social media presence. They group their suggestions into three categories. In connection with step one, "build the foundation," the authors suggest that all profiles, avatars, and email signatures be refreshed and matched. The organization must create an uncluttered and not fully symmetrical website, and activate the LinkedIn long-form posting feature. Step two is to "amass your digital assets." These should include multiple short (three- to four-second) intro and outro clips to use with all videos, and establishing a blog. The third step, "go to market," advises adding two curated (as opposed to created) posts daily to each platform, and two 500-word original posts each week. A 1,000-word post should accompany the website's launch. Two-minute videos should be shared at the rate of two per week. Graphics with testimonials should be posted at the rate of two per day.

In 2009, to reintroduce the Fiesta, Ford decided to lend 100 Fiestas for six months to recipients who agreed to discuss their experiences. Ford chose candidates with large social media followings, and required them to post three messages daily. Within six months, 60,000 posts had garnered millions of clicks, including more than 4.3 million YouTube views. The $5 million campaign generated 50,000 sales to new customers—a result that would have cost tens of millions of dollars using a traditional promotional campaign.[238]

A telescreen outside the office of Clorox Company's CEO, Bennor Dorer, flashes statistics on how often the company's Brita water filters are mentioned on social media; it also shows samples of consumers' comments and photos.[239]

Consultant Libby Dubick stresses the importance of increasing an organization's presence on social media. This might entail "friending" or following someone on a platform such as Facebook and others so that the organization's posts (containing useful information and an attractive look, of course) will be visible to that friend's connections.[240] Entrepreneur Ilya Pozin has compiled a list of 20 companies with great social media presence. He says, "potential customers and consumers are looking for social media accounts that are smart and funny; they want accounts that are good conversationalists but will also actually listen to their needs."[241] Most target audiences seek a social channel that provides value to their lives in some way. Examples of stellar social media sites include Space X's Facebook and Twitter streams, which include live broadcasts of rocket launches and pictures from space; TED Talks, which provide expert speakers on a wide range of subjects, as well as their Twitter account, which has more than two million followers; Pizza Hut (which takes an off-beat approach); Old Spice (funny commercials); Charmin (with its funny and playful tone); and Oreo "[which] isn't just quirky, its social media is also incredibly intelligent when it comes to jumping on live pop culture events."[242]

To summarize, this chapter has provided ten categories of customer-directed practices.

It is argued that the extent to which organizations enact high levels of such practices, they should achieve higher levels of organizational performance. The next two chapters provide systematic evidence pertinent to the effects of enterprise-, employee-, and customer-directed practices on organizational performance. Chapter 5 presents results from five survey studies conducted with respondents from four countries. Results are consistently positive, providing substantial support for the validity of the Cube One framework. Chapter 6 presents results of practices as related to market capitalization data from Fortune's list of America's Most Admired Companies. The results are generally supportive, but lack the statistical power associated with the results in Chapter 5.

Customer-Directed Practices: A Short Ten-Item Survey

Actual Practices

The purpose of this section is to ascertain the *actual practices* (as distinct from stated or printed policies) in the organization where you work (or most recently worked). If you work in a subsidiary of a larger organization, focus on the local organization where you work (or worked). Please use the following scale to record your responses to the ten statements that follow:

1 = Never or Almost Never (or Not Applicable)
2 = Infrequently
3 = Occasionally or Sometimes
4 = Frequently
5 = Always or Almost Always

(1) **Customers Are Surveyed.** Customers are regularly surveyed using an effective format such as "Would you recommend?" to ascertain delight, not mere satisfaction_____

(2) **In-Depth Analyses Are Conducted.** Practices such as focus groups, and/ or opt-in data bases are used to gain a fuller understanding of customer preferences. _____

(3) **Consistent High Quality.** The quality of products/services is consistently of high quality, yielding a trusted brand, and lapses are responded to effectively. _____

(4) **Adopting Best Practices.** The best practices of competitors are studied and adopted, or improved upon, where possible (i.e., benchmarking). _____

(5) **Customer Satisfaction Drives Operations.** The goal of customer satisfaction importantly influences operational decisions at all organization levels. _____

(6) **Price Consciousness.** Prices of goods/services are continually reviewed to improve the organization's competitive position. _____

(7) **Customer Satisfaction Drives Rewards.** Customer satisfaction is an important factor in determining pay increases and other rewards of individuals or departments. _____

(8) **Employee Latitude.** Employees are granted wide latitude to use their own judgment in order to satisfy customers. _____

(9) **Innovation Is Encouraged.** New products/services are introduced. _____

(10) **Multiple Ways Used to Reach Customers.** Big Data; the use of targeted, individualized offerings; social media programs; multichannel marketing. _____

Notes

1 Keiningham, T., and Vavra, T. (2001). *The customer delight principle: Exceeding customers' expectations for bottom-line success*. New York, NY: McGraw-Hill.
2 Reichheld, F., with Markey, R. (2011). *The ultimate question 2.0: How net promoter companies thrive in a customer-driven world*. Boston, MA: Harvard Business Review Press.
3 Keiningham and Vavra, op. cit.
4 Ibid. Consistent with this assertion is the conclusion of Reichheld and Markey (op. cit., p. 48) that "there is only a tenuous connection between satisfaction rates and actual customer behavior and between satisfaction rates and a company's growth."
5 See Keiningham and Vavra (op. cit., pp. 12–15). Notwithstanding the questionable connection between customer satisfaction scores and financial performance, large companies' ASCI scores evidently relate to company market value. See Fornell, C., Mithas, S., Morgeson III, F.V., and Krishnan, M. S. (January, 2006). "Customer satisfaction and stock prices: High returns, low risk." *Journal of Marketing*, 70, 3–14.
6 Deming, W. E. (1986). *Out of the crisis*. Cambridge, MA: MIT Center for Advanced Engineering Studies.
7 Keiningham and Vavra, op. cit.
8 Chandrashekaran, M., Rotte, K., Tax, S. S., and Grewal, R. (February, 2007). "Satisfaction strength and customer loyalty." *Journal of Marketing Research*, 44, 153–163.
9 Adigüzel F., and Wedel, M. (October, 2008). "Split questionnaire design for massive surveys." *Journal of Marketing Research*, 45, 608–617.

10 Borle, S., Dholakia, U. M., Singh, S. S., and Westbrook, R. A. (September–October, 2007). "The impact of survey participation on subsequent customer behavior: An empirical investigation." *Marketing Science*, 26(5), 711–726. Another Demonstration that correlation does not equate to causality.

11 HBR Idea Watch. (January–February, 2017). "The power of positive surveying: Nudging customers to reflect on good experiences gooses sales." *Harvard Business Review*, 95(1), 22–24.

12 Reichheld with Markey, op. cit. This is the source of the information on the NPS system.

13 Mount, I. (October 16, 2014). "A whole town in Colorado pushes to improve its customer service." *New York Times*, p. B8. The initial results were mixed. The proportion of visitors giving the friendliness of store personnel rose a perfect score of 10 rose from 53%in 2014 from 47% in 2013. However, the score for the entire town dropped a point to 67. Mr. Kern said it was too early to draw conclusions.

14 Reichheld with Markey, op cit. Still another concern with traditional customer satisfaction surveys is their use in international contexts. It has been found that when respondents complete a questionnaire in what is their second (i.e., not native) language, this systematically results in the reporting of more intense emotions. See de Langhe, B., Puntoni, S., Fernandes, D., and van Osselaer, S. M. J. (April, 2011). "The anchor contraction effect in international marketing research." *Journal of Marketing Research*, 48, 366–380.

15 Markey, R., Reichheld, F., and Dullweber, A. (December, 2009). "Closing the customer feedback loop." *Harvard Business Review*, 87(12), 43–47.

16 Yang, K. (2008). *Voice of the customer: Capture and analysis*. New York, NY McGraw-Hill.

17 Tanner, A. (2014). *What stays in Vegas*. New York, NY: Perseus Book Group, p. 238. Copyright © 2014. Quotation reprinted with permission of PublicAffairs, an imprint of Perseus Books LLC, a subsidiary of Hachette Book Group, Inc.

18 Mitchell, J. (2015). *Hug your customers*. New York, NY: Hachette Books. It might be noted that the average purchase was slightly under $700.

19 Roman, E. (2011). *Voice-of-the-customer marketing*. New York, NY: McGraw-Hill.

20 Terlep, S. (September 18, 2016). "Focus groups fall out of favor: Technology-driven tools do a better job of explaining consumer behavior today." *Wall Street Journal*. Retrieved at www.wsj.com/articles/focus-groups-fall-out-of-favor-1474250702

21 Christensen, C. M., Hall, T., Dillon, K, and Duncan, D, S. (2016). *Competing against luck*. New York, NY: Harper Business, p. 88. Quoted material used with permission of HarperCollins Publishers. Copyright © 2016.

22 Yang, op. cit. It is not clear whether focus groups were involved in the redesign process along with surveys.

23 Christensen et al., op. cit., pp. 95–97. To boost sales, in February, 2017, American Girl added a boy to their collection, Logan, a drummer on the Nashville music scene. See *Newsday*, February 16, 2017, p. 40.

24 Terlep, S. (September 18, 2016). Focus groups fall out of favor: Technology-driven tools do a better job of explaining consumer behavior today. *Wall Street Journal*. Retrieved at www.wsj.com/articles/focus-groups-fall-out-of-favor-1474250702

25 Mui, C. (October 17, 2011). Five dangerous lessons to learn from Steve Jobs. *Forbes*. Retrieved at http://www.forbes.com/sites/chunkamui/2011/10/17/five-dangerous-lessons-to-learn-from-steve-jobs/#5e4de7e160da

26 Ronan, op. cit.

27 By 2015, Caesar's had dropped to become the third-largest U.S-headquartered casino. Retrieved at https://www.statista.com/statistics/257531/leading-casino-companies-worldwide-by-revenue/. In 2015 Las Vegas Sands was the largest in large part due to its expansion to Singapore in and, especially, Macau. MGM was second-largest, reflective of its expansion into Portugal, Australia, South Africa, and Macau.

28 Tanner, op. cit.

29 Ibid. For two decades Caesar's refrained from supplementing its data with information from external outside data brokers. But evidently, for the past decade even Caesar's has opted to purchase additional data (e.g., magazine subscriptions, favorite baseball team, etc.)

30 Ibid. Tanner notes, however, that sophisticated nonhuman bots have been found to fraudulently insert click data that add about 20% imprecision. Dstillery could reduce this by obtaining identifying information about Internet users, but refuses to do this for ethical reasons.

31 Ibid. Tanner also provides information on several other data brokers such as InfoUSA and Database USA which had more than 102 million cell phone numbers as of 2012.

32 *First Round Review*. (February 23, 2016). "The tools early-stage startups actually need to understand their customers." Retrieved at http://firstround.com/review/the-to ols-early-stage-startups-actually-need-to-understand-their-customers/

33 Ibid.

34 Yang, op. cit.

35 Tanner, op. cit.

36 McAfee, A., and Brynjolfsson, E. (2012). "Big data: The management revolution." *Harvard Business Review*, 90(10), 60–68.

37 Lee, T. Y., and Bradlow, E. T. (October, 2011). "Automated marketing research using online customer reviews." *Journal of Marketing Research*, 48, 881–894.

38 Foster, T. (July/August, 2016). "The mind readers. These entrepreneurs are racing to claim a new tech frontier: Your emotions." *Inc.*, 76–83.

39 Bartlett, M., and el Kaliouby, R. (May 24, 2016). "Facial-recognition technology is judging us." *Wired*, p. 64.

40 Webb, A. (September, 2016). "Knowing customers before they know you: The technology that lets you identify them—literally—is here." *Inc.*, 128.

41 Terlep, op. cit.

42 A U.K.-based mystery shopping firm provides a long list of claimed advantages. See http://www.mystery-shoppers.co.uk/how_mystery_shopping_helps.htm. Jennifer Steinhauer in the *New York Times* provided an early write-up. See http://www.nyti mes.com/1998/02/04/business/the-undercover-shoppers-posing-as-customers-pai d-agents-grade-the-stores.html

43 One empirical study using mystery shoppers was conducted in libraries in New Zeeland. Results were mixed. See http://www.emeraldinsight.com/doi/abs/10.1108 /00242530510574138?journalCode=lr

44 Bolgar, C. (June 9, 2011). "How companies can stay ahead of the S-curve." *Wall Street Journal*, p. A10.

45 Stoll, J. D., and Steele, A. (January 15, 2015). "The auto-show model is now studying you. Today's product specialists can get $1,000 a day to show off autos, gather customer intelligence." *Wall Street Journal*, p. B1.

46 Smith, S. S. (March 4, 2014). "Moses Taylor rode rails, banks, telegraph to top." *Investor's Business Daily*, p. A3.

47 Marriott, J. W. Jr., with Brown, K. A. (1997). *The spirit to serve*. New York, NY: HarperCollins.

48 Walton, S., with Huey, J. (1992). *Sam Walton: Made in America*. New York, NY: Doubleday. Copyright © 1992 by Estate of Samuel Moore Walton. Quoted material reproduced with permission of Doubleday, an imprint of the Knopf Doubleday Publishing Group, a division of Penguin Random House LLC. All rights reserved.

49 With regard to the name Wal-Mart, as of 2009 the name was changed to Walmart, so for consistency the newer name is used hereafter.

50 Burlingham, B. (February, 2010). "Lessons from a blue-collar millionaire." *Inc.*, 32(1), 56–63.

51 Anonymous, (2006), exhibit from a graduate student organizational analysis report.
52 Walton, op. cit.
53 Capodagli, B., and Jackson, L. (2001). *The Disney way fieldbook*. New York, NY: McGraw-Hill.Vignette abstracted with permission of McGraw-Hill Global Education Holdings, LLC. Copyright © 2001 by the McGraw-Hill Companies, Inc.
54 Zeithaml, V. A., Parasuraman, A., and Berry, L. L. (1990). *Delivering quality service*. New York, NY: The Free Press.
55 Ford, R. C., Brown, S. W., and Heaton, C. P. (2001). "Delivering excellent service: Lessons from the best firms." *California Management Review*, 44, 39–56.
56 Ibid.
57 Zemke, R. (January, 1988). "Empowerment: Helping people take charge." *Training*, 25(1), 63–64.
58 Ibid.
59 Zeithaml et al., op. cit.
60 Jing, X., and Lewis, M. (April, 2011). "Stockouts in online retailing." *Journal of Marketing Research*, 48, 342–354.
61 Zeidner, R. (July, 2010). "Questing for quality: For high-performing organizations, 'good enough' is not good enough." *HR Magazine*, 55(7), 24-28.
62 Mitchell, J. (2015). *Hug your customers*. New York, NY: Hachette Books. The quote is on p. 8. Regarding learning the names of 250 customers, Mitchell comments that this is no big deal. After all, to learn Chinese a youngster around the age of six needs to know 214 radicals just to be able to look up a word in a dictionary.
63 Heskett, J. L., Sasser, W. E., and Schlesinger, L. A. (1997). *The service profit chain*. New York, NY: Free Press.
64 Palmatier, R. W., Scheer, L. K., and Steenkampf, J-B. E. M. (May, 2007). "Customer loyalty to whom? Managing the benefits and risks of salesperson-owned loyalty." *Journal of Marketing Research*, 44, 185–199.
65 Maxham, J. G., III, Netemcyer, R. G., and Lichtenstein, D. R. (March–April 2008). "The retail value chain: Linking employee perceptions to employee performance, customer evaluations and store performance." *Marketing Science*, 27(2), 147–167.
66 Walker, D. D., van Jaarsveld, D. D., and Skarlicki, D. P. (2017). "Sticks and stones can break my bones but words can also hurt me: The relationship between customer verbal aggression and employee incivility." *Journal of Applied Psychology*, 102(2), 163–179.
67 Reich-Hale, D. (March 5, 2017). "Rx for survival: How independent pharmacies are focusing on the personal touch." *Newsday*, pp. 33–35
68 Bell, C. R., and Zemke, R. (1992). *Managing knock your socks off service*. New York, NY: AMACOM.
69 Schneider, B., and Bowen, D. E. (1995). *Winning the service game*. Boston, MA: Harvard Business School Press.
70 Bell and Zemke, op cit., p. 198.
71 Sucher, S. J., and McManus, S. E. (September 30, 2005). "The Ritz-Carlton Hotel Company." *Harvard Business Review*, case distributed by the European Case Clearing House (ECCH). Along these lines, Hotel 1000 in Seattle (part of the Preferred Hotel Group) was able to win the loyalty of Leslie Ciminello by making sure that she knew that on arrival there would be lactose-free milk in her refrigerator along with gluten-free cereal. See Edleson, H. (October 8, 2013). "The extra mile for repeat customers." *New York Times*, p. B8.
72 Daniels, S., (2013). "Developing customer centric employees to enrich your customers' experience." *Workforce Management*, 92(3), S3. (The notion of a "defining moment" resembles a "teachable moment" in education.) There is evidence that the strength of an associate's smile is positively associated with customer satisfaction with the service received. So "service with a smile" seems to have positive effects due to emotional contagion and mimicry. The researchers caution that too much management pressure

for smiling may decrease perceived authenticity. See, Barger, P. B., and Grandey, A. A. (2006). "Service with a smile and encounter satisfaction: Emotional contagion and appraisal mechanisms." *Academy of Management Journal*, 49(6), 1229–1238.

73 Chittum, R. (October 30, 2006). "Price points: Good customer service costs money." *Wall Street Journal*, p. R7.

74 Little, L. M., Kluemper, D., Nelson, D. L, and Ward, A. (2013). "More than happy to help? Customer-focused emotion management strategies." *Personnel Psychology*, 66, 261–286. Relatedly, a meta-analysis of 22 studies has found that employee job satisfaction is modestly/moderately associated with customer satisfaction. However, the entire association is completely "explained" by customer-perceived quality of service. See Brown, S. P., and Lam, S. K. (2008). "A meta-analysis of relationships linking employee satisfaction to customer responses." *Journal of Retailing*, 84(3), 243–255.

75 Mandel, N., Petrova, P. K., and Cialdini, R. B. (2006). "Images of success and the preference for luxury brands." *Journal of Consumer Psychology*, 16(1), 57–69.

76 Rucker, D. D., Petty, R. E., and Briñol, P. (2008). "What's in a frame anyway? A meta-cognitive analysis of the impact of one versus two sided message framing on attitude certainty." *Journal of Consumer Psychology*, 18(2), 137–149.

77 White, K., and Dahl, D. W. (2006). "To be or *not* be? The influence of dissociative reference groups on consumer preferences." *Journal of Consumer Psychology*, 16(4), 404–414. Quoted material reproduced with permission from Wiley.

78 Byrnes, P. (May 23, 2016). Cartoon in *Barron's*, p. M10.

79 See the website https://despair.com/products/customer-disservice

80 Doyle, J. R., and Bottomley, P. A. (2006). "Dressed for the occasion: Font-product congruity in the perception of logotype." *Journal of Consumer Psychology*, 16(2), 112–123.

81 Wood, S. L., and Bettman, J. R. (2007). "Predicting happiness: How normative feeling rules influence (and even reverse) durability bias." *Journal of Consumer Psychology*, 17(3), 188–201.

82 https://www.bing.com/search?q=patek+philippe+slogan&src=IE-SearchBox& FORM=IESR3A&pc=EUPP_

83 Hagtvedt, H., and Patrick, V. M. (2008). "Art and the brand: The role of visual art in enhancing brand extendibility." *Journal of Consumer Psychology*, 18, 212–222. Hagtvedt and Patrick caution, however, that luxury brands should be very careful as to the cues provided by price information. Indeed, they note that Tiffany managed to triple sales by adopting a new marketing approach—"affordable luxury." But by doing so, Tiffany rapidly eroded its image as a luxury brand. It took dramatic increases in prices, store renovations, and about a decade for the Tiffany brand to regain its luster. See "The broad embrace of luxury: Hedonic potential as a driver of brand extendibility." *Journal of Consumer Psychology*, 17(3), 188–201. A separate threat to luxury brands is potential for satiation; people tiring of a luxury over time. Research has found that it is helpful to create subcategories of luxuries, e.g., different spa treatments or cruises. See Redden, J. P. (February, 2008). "Reducing satiation: The role of categorization level." *Journal of Consumer Research*, 54, 624–634.

84 Dijksterhuis, A., Smith, P. K., van Baaren, R., B., and Wigboldus, D. H. J. (2005). "The unconscious consumer: Effects of environment on consumer behavior." *Journal of Consumer Psychology*, 15(3), 193.

85 Berger, J., and Fitzsimons, G. (February, 2008). "Dogs on the street, pumas on your feet: How cues in the environment influence product evaluation and choice." *Journal of Marketing Research*, 45, 1–14.

86 Valenzuela, A., and Raghubir, P. (2009). "Position-based beliefs: The center-stage effect." *Journal of Consumer Psychology*, 19, 185–196. (A similar evaluation used to be made by scrutinizing the physical proximity of Soviet leaders to the prime minister.)

87 Van Herpen, E., Pieters, R., and Zeelenberg, M. (2009). "When demand accelerates demand: Trailing the bandwagon." *Journal of Consumer Psychology*, 19, 302–312.

88 Mogilner, C., Shiv, B., and Iyengar, S. S. (April, 2013). "Eternal quest for the best: Sequential (vs. simultaneous) option presentation undermines choice commitment." *Journal of Consumer Research*, 39, 1300–1312.

89 Sevilla, J., and Redden, J. P. (April, 2014). "Limited availability reduces the rate of satiation." *Journal of Marketing Research*, 51, 205–217.

90 Miklôs-Thal, J, and Zhang, J. (February, 2013.). "(De)marketing to manage consumer quality inferences." *Journal of Marketing Research*, 50, 55–69. (The authors provide evidence that there are conditions under which (de)marketing will be financially successful.)

91 Mogilner, C., Rudnick, T., and Iyengar, S. S. (August, 2008). "The mere categorization effect: How the presence of categories increases choosers' perceptions of assortment variety and outcome satisfaction." *Journal of Consumer Research*, 35, 202–215. Botti, S., and McGill, A. L. (April, 2011) note that the choices must be more than merely offering three ways of preparing one type of meat: rare, medium, or well done. See "The locus of choice: Personal causality and satisfaction with hedonic and utilitarian decisions." *Journal of Consumer Research*, 37, 1(6), 1065-1078.

92 Kuksov, D., and Villas-Boas, J. M. (May–June 2010). "When more alternatives lead to less choice." *Marketing Science*, 29(3), 507–524.

93 Scheibehenne, B., Greifeneder, R., and Todd, P. M. (October, 2010). "Can there ever be too many options? A meta-analytic review of choice overload." *Journal of Consumer Research*, 37, 409–425. Yet, as the number of options increases, consumers find that assortment size can increase the difficulty of making a decision. This prompts customers to choose "more justifiable options," i.e., practical, utilitarian products versus less justifiable hedonic indulgences. See Sela, A., Berger, J., and Liu, W. (April, 2009). "Variety, vice and virtues: How assortment size influences option choice." *Journal of Consumer Research*, 35, 941–951. Assortment size can have a detrimental effect on customers' views of a retailer when the attractiveness of the set of offerings is enhanced. So, increased assortment is helpful in cases of great variability in the quality/attractiveness of items offered. See Chernev, A., and Hamilton, R. (June, 2009). "Assortment size and option attractiveness in consumer choice among retailers." *Journal of Marketing Research*, 46, 410–420.

94 Smith, S. S. (January 25, 2012). "The Enterprise in Taylor: The CEO steers his car-rental firm ahead of the pack." *Investor's Business Daily*, pp. A3–A4.

95 Lafley, A. G., and Martin, R. L. (January–February 2017). "Customer loyalty is overrated: Focus on habit instead." *Harvard Business Review*, 95(1), 47–53.

96 Ronan, op. cit.

97 Naumann, E., and Giel, K. (1995). *Customer satisfaction measurement and management.* Cincinnati, OH: Thompson Executive Press.

98 Mitchell, op. cit.; Ronan, op. cit.; Schneider and Bowen, op cit.

99 Bell and Zemke, op. cit., p. 49. Quoted material reproduced with permission of HarperCollins Leadership. www.harpercollinsleadersip.com

100 Keiningham and Vavra, op cit., p. 174. Copyright © 2001 Keiningham and Vavra. Quoted material reproduced with permission of copyright holders.

101 Ronan, op. cit., pp. 218–221. As an aside, Reichheld and Markey in *The ultimate question 2.0* have found that Net Promoter scores in the cable and satellite TV industry "are embarrassingly low, averaging negative three percent." They assert that customers are rarely enthusiastic when they have limited choice, and when prices keep ratcheting up while providing mediocre service (p. 82).

102 Johnston, R., and Mehra, S. (2002). "Best-practice complaint management." *Academy of Management Executive*, 16(4), 145–154. Customers often use social media to trash the reputation of a company. The popular "mommy blogger" Heather Armstrong was so angry over her Maytag washer and the company's ensuing service problems that she told her million followers on Twitter to never buy a Maytag. See Bernoff, J., and

Schadler, T. (July–August 2010). "Empowered: In a world where one angry tweet can torpedo a brand, corporations need to unleash their employees to fight back." *Harvard Business Review*, 88(7–8), 95–101.

103 Knox, G., and van Oest, R. (2014). "Customer complaints and recovery effectiveness: A customer base approach." *Journal of Marketing*, 78(5), 42–57. Dougherty, D., and Murthy, A. in their (September, 2009) *Harvard Business Review* article, "What service customers really want" recommend that agents have the leeway, knowledge, and authority to solve a problem in the first contact, p. 22. (Perhaps the process can be summarized and one and done.)

104 Segal, D. (June 8, 2013). "An oasis in a desert of customer service." *New York Times*, p. B3.

105 Mollenkopf, D. A., Rabinovich, E., Laseter, T. M., and Boyer, K. K. (May, 2007). "Managing internet product returns: A focus on effective service operations." *Decision Sciences*, 38(2) 215–250.

106 Cleeren, K., van Heerde, H. J., and Dekimpe, M. G. (March, 2013). "Rising for the ashes: How brands and categories can overcome product-harm crises." *Journal of Marketing*, 77, 58–77.

107 Fickenscher, L. (June 4, 2016). "Customers' moan about fake stones." *New York Post*, p. 21.

108 https://www.bloomberg.com/view/articles/2017-04-13/lessons-from-the-united-airlines-debacle

109 *The Washington Post*. (April 17, 2017). "United: No bump if already on board." *Newsday*, p. A31.

110 Walton, S., with Huey, J. (1992). *Sam Walton: Made in America*. New York, NY: Doubleday, p. 190.

111 Ibid., p. 81. Wal-Mart dropped the hyphen (and then the short-lived star) and became just Walmart in 2009. http://www.cnbc.com/id/32403443

112 Marriot, op cit.

113 The American Productivity and Quality Center website: https://www.apqc.org/APQC-knowledge-base. Also see https://www.apqc.org/apqc-current-members

114 Wolfe, C. (February 12, 2014). "Elevations credit union case study." *APQC*, pp. 10, 13.

115 Chu, J., and Rockwood, K. (November, 2008). "Thinking outside the big box." *Fast Company*, 128–132. Wal-Mart studied Kmart, and Costco studied Wal-Mart.

116 Bell and Zemke, op. cit.

117 Ibid.

118 Ibid.

119 Ibid., pp. 90–91. Quoted material reproduced with permission of HarperCollins Leadership. www.harpercollinsleadersip.com

120 Reichheld, op cit. The authors also note that the daily pressures for managers to make their numbers can operate as a negative force against the use of the NPS methodology. They compare the situation to gravity, a hidden force that is always at work, pulling things down. It takes a lot of hard work to make NPS part of the organization's way of operating.

121 Ibid., p. 16

122 Stross, R. (September 25, 2005). "Why Time Warner has fallen in love with AOL again." *New York Times*. p. 3.

123 Reichheld, op. cit. Note that although the internal collection of customer feedback is of greater value in improving customer satisfaction and loyalty than anonymous data obtained by third parties, the internal collection of data creates the potential for frontline personnel to game the system. When customers seem pleased the service provider can urge the customer to provide a positive feedback score (a perfect 10), and can indicate where the customer should call or email this rating. If the interaction is not favorable, the service provider might make a mistake in recording the customer's name and/or telephone number when reporting the contact.

124 Mitchell, op. cit.

125 Bell and Zemke, op. cit.

126 Marriott, op. cit.

127 Frauenheim, E. (August, 2010). "Making the call for themselves." *Workforce Management*, 89(8), 16–20.

128 Huston, D. (April, 2016). "How I did it…Priceline's CEO on creating an in-house multilingual service operation." *Harvard Business Review*, 94(3), 37–40.

129 Bettencourt, L. A., Lusch, R. F., and Vargo, S. L. (Fall, 2014). "A service lens on value creation: Marketing's role in achieving strategic advantage." *California Management Review*, 57(1), 544–66.

130 Walton, op. cit.

131 Ibid. In fact, given the hypothesized cost and selling price numbers, sales need be only two-and-a-half times greater, not three times.

132 Among the Fortune 500 companies in 2016, the next three largest companies were in China (State Grid, China National Petroleum, and Sinopec Group). The next four largest were Royal Dutch Shell, Exxon Mobile, Volkswagen, and Toyota. See https://www.google.com/?gws_rd=ssl#q=world's+largest+companies+by+revenue+2016

133 The 42 regional distribution centers in the U.S. were a small part of the more than 150 regional merchandise distribution centers worldwide. See http://corporate.wal mart.com/our-story/our-business

134 http://investorplace.com/2016/05/spls-staples-stock-office-depot-ftc/

135 Safdar, K. (March 1, 2017). "Target gets a lesson that low prices matter." *Wall Street Journal*, pp. 1–2.

136 Costa, B. (March 21, 2017). "A big battle over little golf balls." *Wall Street Journal*, p. A18.

137 Chen, T., Sun, B., and Singh, V. (July–August, 2009). "An empirical investigation of the dynamic effect of Marlboro's permanent pricing shift." *Marketing Science*, 28(4), 740–758. Although Philip Morris experienced a slight overall decline in revenues, the losses incurred by competitors were significantly higher.

138 Schneider, B., and Bowen, D. E. (1995). *Winning the service game*. Boston, MA: Harvard Business School Press.

139 Hamilton, R., and Chernev, A. (2013). "Low prices are just the beginning: Price image in retail management." *Journal of Marketing*, 77(6), 1–20.

140 Hamilton, R., and Chernev, A. (February, 2010). "The impact of product line extensions and consumer goals on the formation of price image." *Journal of Marketing Research*, 47, 51–62.

141 Suh, J-C., and Yi, Y. (2006). "When brand attitudes affect the customer-satisfaction-loyalty relation: The moderating role of product involvement." *Journal of Consumer Psychology*, 16(2), 145–155.

142 Naylor, R. W., Raghunathan, R., and Ramanathan, S. (2006). "Promotions spontaneously induce a positive evaluative response." *Journal of Consumer Psychology*, 16(3), 295–305. Complicating matters, there is evidence that subsequent to a spontaneous positive evaluation, consumers may incorporate additional evidence to form more deliberate and less positive opinion. See Honea, H., Morales, A. C., and Fitzisimons, G. J. (2006). "1 = 2: When a singular experience leads to dissociated evaluations." *Journal of Consumer Psychology*, 16(2), 124–134.

143 Bingham, T., and Galagan, P. interviewed Dan Cathy. (March, 2010). Be more innovative. *T+D*, 64(3), 36–41.

144 Haisly, E., and Loewenstein, G. (February, 2011). "It's not what you get but when you get it: The effect of gift sequence on deposit balances and customer sentiment in a commercial bank." *Journal of Marketing Research*, 48, 103–115. Sometimes, though, a customer does not so much see value in the product or service, but rather in the deal. Some goods are purchased because they are especially good deals, and they will

remain unworn in a closet. See Moyer, D. (November, 2006). "Homo uneconomicus." *Harvard Business Review*, 84(11), 160.

145 Mishra, A., and Mishra, H. (February, 2011). "The influence of price discount versus bonus pack on preference for virtue and vice foods." *Journal of Marketing Research*, 48, 196–206.

146 Hamilton, R., and Srivastava, J. (August, 2008). "When 2 = 2 is not the same as 1 + 3: Variations in price sensitivity across components of partitioned prices." *Journal of Marketing Research*, 45, 450–461.

147 Zhu, R., Chen, X., and Dasgupta, S. (April, 2008). "Can trade-ins hurt you? Exploring the effect of a trade-in on consumers' willingness to pay for a new product." *Journal of Marketing Research*, 45, 159–170. Also see Srivastava, J., and Chakravarti, D. (October, 2011). "Price presentation effects in purchases involving trade-ins." *Journal of Marketing Research*, 48, 910–919.

148 Kim, J., Rao, R. S., Kim, K, and Rao, A R. (February, 2011). "More or less: A model and empirical evidence on preferences for under-and overpayment in trade-in transactions." *Journal of Marketing Research*, 48, 157–171.

149 Steenkamp, J-B, E. M., van Heerde, H. J., and Geyskens, I. (December, 2010). "What makes consumers willing to pay a price premium for national brands over private labels?" *Journal of Marketing Research*, 47, 1011–1024.

150 Suk, K., Lee, J., and Lichtenstein, D. R. (October, 2012). "The influence of price presentation order on consumer choice." *Journal of Marketing Research*, 49, 708–717.

151 Karmarkarm U. R., Shiv, B., and Knutson, B. (August, 2015). "Cost conscious? The neural and behavioral impact of price primacy on decision making." *Journal of Marketing Research*, 52, 467–481.

152 Lourenço, C. J. S., Gijsbrechts, and Pappe, R. (April, 2015). "The impact of category prices on store price image formation: An empirical examination." *Journal of Marketing Research*, 52, 200–216.

153 Kapner, S. (April 22–23, 2017). "Store closings accelerate: Pace of shutting retail locations has doubled this year; internet erases pricing power." *Wall Street Journal*, pp. B1–B2. Pertinent to the relative success of online versus traditional off-line businesses, are the data on market capitalizations. In a short piece in *Inc.* (May, 2017, p. 3), entitled "Retail Darwinism," market capitalizations are reported for 2007 and 2007, respectively: Target $51billion, $31billion; Sears $22 billion, $1 billion; Macy's $21 billion, $9 billion; JC Penney $18 billion, $2 billion. In contrast, the data for Amazon were astonishing: $17 billion and $418 billion.

154 Edwards, C. (December 21, 2009.) "Why tech bows to Best Buy." *Bloomberg Businessweek*, pp. 50–56. Best Buy has demanded that product manufacturers modify their software, and even provide Best Buy with exclusive items. Best Buy was the first merchant to offer a motorcycle that ran solely on electricity.

155 https://www.wsj.com/articles/with-niche-sites-wal-mart-tries-selling-to-hipsters-1490347802?mod=djem_jiewr_ES_domainid

156 Wal-Mart spent $3.3 billion in 2016 to acquire Jet.com, primarily to transform Wal-Mart's web operations via a fresh team of e-commerce executives. It also is in talks to acquire Bonobos Inc., a company that started as an online-only retailer, but is now adding brick-and-mortar stores. See the Bloomberg story, "Walmart in talks to buy Bonobos." (April 18, 2017), *Newsday*, p. A35.

157 Graham, J. (October 17, 2016). "Innovation: The secret behind Wal-Mart's smile." *Investor's Business Daily*, pp. A1, A10.

158 Safdar, K. (May 24, 2017). "J. Crew's big miss: How technology transformed retail." *Wall Street Journal*. Retrieved at https://www.wsj.com/articles/j-crews-big-miss-how-technology-transformed-retail-1495636817

159 Racanelli, V. J. (May 22, 2017). "Life after Amazon: Best Buy, Wal-Mart, Home Depot and others are thriving on retail's disruption." *Barron's*, pp. 12–13.

160 Kumar, S. (April 5, 2016). "Competitive strategies for brick-and-mortar stores to counter 'showrooming'." Paper presented at the Omega Seminar at Baruch College.

161 Ibid.

162 Norton, L. P. (May 22, 2017). "Brick-and-Mortar retail in the age of Amazon." *Barron's*, pp. 14–15.

163 Ibid.

164 Keating, R. J. (Jan. 6–12, 2012). "Lessons from Sears' past success and current troubles." *Long Island Business News*, p. 15A.

165 Ibid. It was also noted that retail stores generally spend between $6 and $8 per square foot annually on updating their stores. Sears spent between $1.50 and $2.

166 Levinson, M. (October 11, 2013). "When creative destruction visited the mom-and-pops." *Wall Street Journal*. Retrieved at https://www.wsj.com/articles/when-creative-destruction-visited-the-momandpopswhen-creative-destruction-visited-the-momandpops-1381528068?mg=prod/accounts-wsj

167 Inc. 5000 Insights. (December, 2016/January, 2017). You need to grow your customer base by 10 percent. What's the cheapest way to do it? p. 26

168 Much, M. (March 8, 2016). "'Extreme value retailer' is this company's claim to fame." *Investor's Business Daily*, p. A5.

169 Schechner, S. (May 9, 2017). "To set prices, stores turn to algorithms." *Wall Street Journal*, pp. A1, A10. What makes the AI algorithms particularly powerful is that they constantly update tactics after learning from experience.

170 Ibid., p. 10.

171 Kessler, A. (February 18, 2014). "Don't tread on me—or make me stand in line." *Wall Street Journal*, p. A11. (Task Rabbit was purchased by IKEA in 2017.)

172 Philips, J. G. (May 19, 2016). "Why Facebook's imitators failed." *Wall Street Journal*, p. A11.

173 Keiningham and Vavra, op. cit.

174 Ibid. Similarly, it was reporter in *Bloomberg Businessweek* that C-suite executives had their compensation pegged to customer service scores, August 9–15, 2010, p. 75.

175 Heskett et al., op. cit.

176 Naumann, E., and Giel, K. (1995). *Customer satisfaction measurement and management*. Cincinnati, OH: Thompson Executive Press.

177 McGregor, J. (January, 30, 2006). "Would you recommend us? That simple query to customers is shaking up planning and executive pay." *BusinessWeek*, pp. 94–95.

178 Bell and Zemke, p. 184.

179 Naumann, E., and Giel, K. (1995). *Customer satisfaction, measurement, and management*. Cincinnati, OH: Thomson Executive Press.

180 Frauenheim, E. (August, 2010). "Making the call for themselves." *Workforce Management*, 89(8), 16–20

181 Naumann, E., and Giel, K. (1995). *Customer satisfaction measurement and management*. Cincinnati, OH: Thompson Executive Press.

182 Schneider and Bowen, op. cit., p. 157.

183 The specific reference is Schneider, B. (1987). "The people make the place." *Personnel Psychology*, 40, 437–453.

184 Heskett et al., op. cit.

185 Sharp. I. (2009). *Four Seasons: The story of a business philosophy*. New York, NY: Portfolio.

186 Walton, op. cit.

187 McAfee, A., and Brynjolfsson, E. (October, 2012). "Big data: The management revolution." *Harvard Business Review*, 90(10), 60–68

188 Marriott, op. cit.

189 Newman, M. (Winter, 2001). Onward and upward. *GMJ* (*Gallup Management Journal*), 18–22. Its founder, David Neeleman, was fully dedicated to Jet Blue's success. When a flight was 20 minutes late, Neeleman helped vacuum the plane, then joined the

baggage handlers loading the cargo hold. When the plane was ready to take off he used the plane's P.A. system to apologize to customers for the delay.

190 Sharp, op. cit.

191 Moseley, L. W. (1972). *Customer service: The road to greater profits.* New York, NY: Chain Store Age Books.

192 Christensen et al., op. cit., p. 180.

193 Petroski, H. (July 26, 1999). "Invention is the adopted child of necessity." *Wall Street Journal*, p. A22.

194 Ibid., p. 57.

195 Ibid., p. 57–58.

196 Reichheld et al., op. cit., p. 29.

197 Gustafson, K. (June 18, 2015). "Pirch lets you take a shower, cook a meal in its stores." Retrieved at http://www.cnbc.com/2015/06/18/pirch-lets-you-take-a-shower-cook-a-meal-in-its-stores.html

198 http://fortune.com/2015/12/30/pirch-kitchen-bath-store-sales/

199 Hamilton, R. W., and Thompson, D. V. (December, 2007). "Is there a substitute for direct experience? Comparing consumers' preferences after direct and indirect product experiences." *Journal of Consumer Research*, 34, 546–555.

200 Grobart, S. (January 13–19, 2004). "My fridge is smarter than yours: Samsung aims to dominate the appliance business by 2015." *Bloomberg BusinessWeek*, pp. 32–33.

201 Gallino, S., and Moreno, A. (April 6, 2017). "The values of fit information in online retail: Evidence from a randomized field experiment." Paper presented at a Baruch College research colloquium.

202 McBride, S. (February 13, 2017). "Survival of the fitted." *Bloomberg Businessweek*, pp. 31–32.

203 Carr, A. (July/August, 2013). "The hard sell at Taco Bell: Inside the years long experiment—created with a handshake deal—that led to fast food's biggest new thing." *Fast Company*, 36–38.

204 Jargon, J. (February 21, 2017). "What Panera had to do to go 'clean'." *Wall Street Journal*, p. R4.

205 Rudd, C. (April 24, 2016). "Flights to dreamland." *Newsday*, p. A12. It is unclear whether nap pods will "take off."

206 McCracken, H. (March 2016). "For eliminating the hassle of sending packages." *Fast Company*, 98–101.

207 Kowsmann, P. (December 7, 2016). "A model for fast fashion: Zara's parent identifies trends and quickly moves garments from sketch pads to stores." *Wall Street Journal*, pp. B 1–2

208 Garrett, G. (Winter, 2016). "Applying Uber's business analytics lesson." *Wharton Magazine*, 22(1), 5.

209 Brescia, M. J. (May 29, 2010). The Bodkin rule and you. Email fundraising letter received from Calvaryfundlife@calvaryhospital.org.

210 Ibid.

211 Hurst, B. (April 10, 2014). "Speedy checkout wins the retail technology of the year." Retrieved at https://www.retailcustomerexperience.com/articles/speedy-checkout-wins-retail-technology-of-the-year/

212 Jargon, J. (May 1, 2013). "Retailers wage war against long lines: Infrared vision helps Kroger reduce wait times to 26 seconds." Retrieved at https://www.wsj.com/articles/SB10001424127887323798104578453293807869744

213 Malone, M. S. (February 23, 2016). "The Big-Data future has arrived." *Wall Street Journal*, p. A17. Quotation reproduced with permission of Dow Jones and Company, Inc. © 2016 Dow Jones and Company, Inc.

214 Guzzo, R. A., Fink, A., King, E., Tonidandel, S., and Landis, Ron. (2015). Big data recommendations for Industrial-Organizational psychology. Unpublished manuscript. 24 pp.

215 Manzi, J. (2012). *Uncontrolled: The surprising payoff of trial-and-error for business, politics, and society*. New York, NY: Basic.

216 Ibid. Note that randomization is crucial, as this provides a way to hold approximately equal all the factors which might bias one group versus another.

217 Op. cit., p. 144.

218 Kelleher, D. (July/August, 2014). "Big data small budget. So you think Big Data is just for the giants? So did these companies—once." *Inc.*, 72.

219 First Round Review article, What you must know to build savvy push notifications. Retrieved at http://firstround.com/review/what-you-must-know-to-build-savvy-push-notifications/

220 Although online retailers need not obtain opt-in authorization in the U.S., matters have been complicated in recent years by the European Union's General Data Protection Regulation—EU GDPR—which applies to all companies doing business with individuals based in the EU).

221 Ronan, op. cit.

222 Hill, K. (February 16, 2012). "How Target figured out a teen girl was pregnant before her dad did." Retrieved from https://www.forbes.com/sites/kashmirhill/2012/02/16/how-target-figured-out-a-teen-girl-was-pregnant-before-her-father-did/2/#7b6810c647e8

223 Ibid.

224 Rosenwald, M. (March 19–26, 2012). "Bound by habit. Understanding and tweaking routines and lead to big, big profits." *Bloomberg Businessweek*, pp. 106–107.

225 Tiernan, R. (July 11, 2016). "Netflix shares could fall 40% or more as excitement slows." *Barron's*, p. 23. It might be noted that the author of the article on Netflix anticipated a drop of 40% or more. Twelve months later, Netflix stock rose more than 50%.

226 Hanna, J. (March, 2006). "Price check: Assistant professor Kris Ferreira on machine learning and optimization in online retail." *HBS Alumni Bulletin*, 28–29. Along these lines, Debbie Davidman, chief information officer of an accounting firm indicated that data analytics, based on a wealth of client data, can be used to figure out how to market more services to clients. See Starzee, B. (January 6–12, 2017). "Big data days ahead: CPA firms becoming more focused on analytics." *Long Island Business News*, p. 30.

227 Zhang, J., and Wedel, M. (April, 2009). "The effectiveness of customized promotions in online and offline stores." *Journal of Marketing Research*, 46, 190–206.

228 Ibid.

229 First Round Review article, What you must know to build savvy push notifications. Retrieved at http://firstround.com/review/what-you-must-know-to-build-savvy-push-notifications/

230 Elberse, A. (July–August, 2008). "Should you invest in the long tail?" *Harvard Business Review*, 86(7–8), 88–96.

231 Ronan, op. cit.

232 Ibid.

233 Schlosser, A. E., Whitte, T. B., and Lloyd, S. M. (April, 2006). "Converting web site visitors into buyers: How web site investment increases consumer trusting beliefs and online purchase intentions." *Journal of Marketing*, 70, 133–148.

234 Trusov, M, Bucklin, R. E., and Pauweis, K. (September, 2009). "Effects of word-of-mouth versus traditional marketing: Findings from an internet social networking site." *Journal of Marketing*, 73, 90–102.

235 Kozinets, R. V., de Valck, K., Wojnicki, A. C., and Wilner, S. J. S. (March, 2010). "Networked narratives: Understanding word-of-mouth marketing in online communities." *Journal of Marketing*, 74, 71–89. A long queue could have value to sellers, insofar as consumers (1) tend to see a queue as indicative of a good value, and (2)

count the number of people behind them: the more the merrier. Some consultants recommend that companies use one long line that feeds multiple cashiers, and that service providers who have consumers waiting on the telephone should emphasize the number of people behind them in the queue, rather than the number ahead of them. See Joo, M., and Fishbach, A. (August, 2010). "A silver lining of standing in line: Queuing increases value of products." *Journal of Marketing Research*, 47, 713–724.

236 Berger, J., and Schwartz, E. M. (October, 2011). "What drives immediate and ongoing word of mouth?" *Journal of Marketing Research*, 48, 869–880. Data on word of mouth indicates that good experiences lead on average customers sharing their good experience with nine people; and negative experiences get shared, on average, with 16 people. See Shafer, A., (November, 2011). Crunching the numbers. *Inc.*, 24.

237 Kawasaki, G., and Fitzpatrick, P. (2014). *The art of social media: Power tips for power users.* New York, NY: Portfolio/Penguin.

238 Wilson, H. J., Guinan, P. J., Parise, S., and Weinberg, B. D. (July–August, 2011). "What's your social media strategy?" *Harvard Business Review*, 89(7/8), 23–25.

239 Rerlep, S. (September 18, 2016). "Focus groups fall out of favor; Technology-driven tools do a better job of explaining consumer behavior today." *Wall Street Journal.* Retrieved at www.wsj.com/articles/focus-groups-fall-out-of-favor-1474250702

240 Dubick, L. J. (January 16, 2017). "7 steps to using social media effectively." *Barron's*, p. 31.

241 Pozin, I. (March 6, 2014). "20 companies you should be following on social media." *Forbes.* Retrieved at https://www.forbes.com/sites/ilyapozin/2014/03/06/20-companies-you-should-be-following-on-social-media/#6f76be8e64f2

242 Ibid.

PART II

5

VALIDITY EVIDENCE

Survey Research

Notwithstanding the evidence cited in Chapters 2 to 4 that successful organizations enact high levels of enterprise-, employee-, and customer-directed practices,
the obvious and crucial question remains: is the Cube One framework valid?
Three types of evidence have accumulated over the past decade: survey research,
market capitalization analyses, and in-depth case studies. In broad terms, survey
research examines a limited number of variables and their associations across many
organizations. The goal is to account for (or find strong associations with) a small
number of independent variables. In scientific jargon, this approach is called the
nomothetic approach.[1] Chapters 7 to 10 examine organizations in great depth,
including subtle nuances of practices—called the ideographic approach.[2]

Organizations that enact high levels of all three sets of practices (enterprise-,
employee-, and customer-directed), i.e., High, High, High, are classified in Cube
One. Organizations that enact low levels of the three practices, i.e., Low, Low, Low,
are in Cube 27. Obviously, the validity of the Cube One framework requires a sizable difference in rated performance between organizations in Cube One versus
Cube 27. This is clearly the most consequential comparison.

A copy of the schematic provided in Chapter 1 appears as Figure 5.1. (Figure
5.1 is identical to Figure 1.1 and is repeated for convenience.) Note that Cube 2
is comprised of High enterprise- and customer-directed practices, and a Middle
level of employee-directed practices. As will be seen in Chapter 10, Mayo Clinic
is best characterized as in Cube 2.

The most crucial comparison in terms of organizational performance is
between the organizations classified in Cube One versus those in Cube 27. The
difference in organizational performance (between Cubes One and 27) in the
U.S. sample exceeded 14 standard deviations, at 14.2 sigma (σ). The classic definition of a statistically significant difference is approximately 2σ (a probability less
than 0.05). The widely acclaimed definition of a virtually error-free process is 6σ

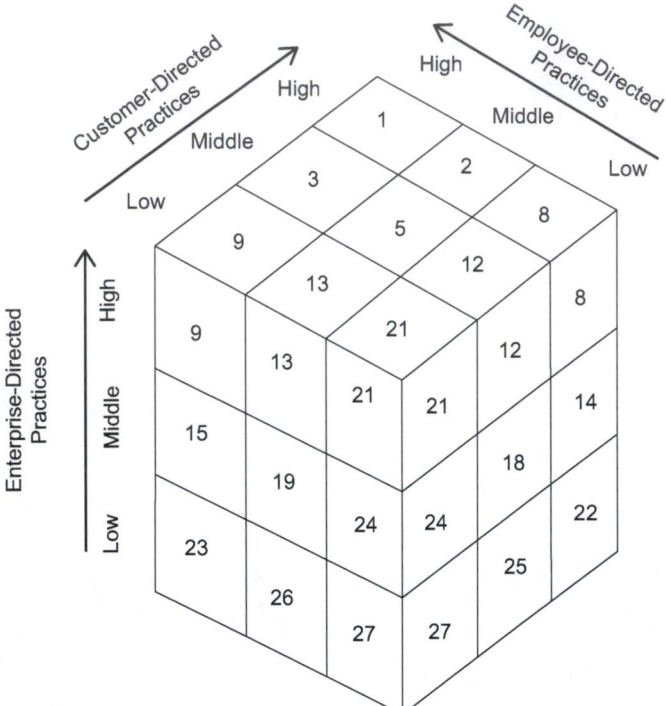

FIGURE 5.1 Schematic Representation of the Cube One Framework

(approximately 3.4 errors in one million observations (a probability of 0.000034). A difference of 14.2σ adds seven zeros to the 6σ probability: a probability that the correlations are spurious being less than one in 100 billion).[3]

In four survey studies the same three ten-item scales of practices and the same three-item performance measure were used in the U.S., Singapore, and Brazil (translated), and among a sample of managers from South Korea. The key components of the instrument are provided at the end of this chapter as Appendix 5.1. In the survey, the first ten items (in Part Three of the survey) pertain to enterprise-directed practices. Each respondent's scores, added up, create a sum of enterprise-directed practices (abbreviated in tables as EntSum).

In keeping with conventional notation, measures that are analyzed empirically are capitalized. Items 11–20 (also in Part Three of the survey) pertain to customer-directed practices, and the sum was calculated for each respondent (CSum). The ten items (in Part Four) capture employee-directed practices, which were summed for each respondent (ESum).

A key challenge in conducting research on organizations is to find a defensible measure of organizational performance. Although objective indicators of organizational performance are often seen as more desirable than perceptual indicators (such as ratings), the use of objective measures can be problematic in four regards.

First, they usually capture only one aspect of performance—for example, return on assets. (In this sense, psychometricians would say they are deficient, not capturing all relevant components.)

Second, financial metrics reflect varying assumptions. Some firms, for example, may capitalize R&D expenditures as an asset; others may show R&D as an expense that offsets revenues.

Third, objective metrics are usually only relevant to the for-profit sector (and often just one industry, e.g., in retailing, sales per square foot). Financial metrics are far less applicable in terms of assessing and comparing performance of non-profit and government organizations. Fourth, respondents are unlikely to have detailed knowledge of financial metrics.

Reflective of the first two problems, accounting, and financial measures have generally been uncorrelated.[4] Meyer and O'Shaughnessy call this phenomenon the "performance paradox." They write, "While performance measures and measurement activity have proliferated over time, performance measures tend to be very weakly correlated with one another."[5]

Because the Cube One framework is relevant, conceptually, to all work organizations, our measure of performance is applicable to organizations in all three sectors. Specifically, we asked respondents to evaluate their focal organization in terms of three criteria: success in accomplishing its mission; performance compared to similar or competing organizations; and the level of performance attained relative to maximum potential. The specific items appear in Part Five of Appendix 5.1.[6]

We collected data from individuals employed full-time and attending graduate programs at two universities in a large metropolitan area, and from individuals recently employed and attending a full-time MBA program. Participation was voluntary and all responses were anonymous. Respondents described the organization where they currently or recently (within the past year) worked. Because the items related to organizational practices and organizational performance, participants had little reason to inflate scores for a self-enhancing purpose.[7]

To test for common method bias, the questionnaire included two items conceptually unrelated to either organizational practices or organizational performance. Items 3 and 4 in Part One of the survey (see Appendix 5.1) relate to self-efficacy and benign world view, respectively. The absence of a relationship between these items and the central variables indicates that associations among the central variables are not artifactual, i.e., results are not due to a response-set bias (some people consistently responding with high scores; others providing consistently low scores.)[8]

Comparing Performance across Cubes: The Taxonomy

As noted above, organizations that are high on all the sets of practices are in Cube One; those low on all three are in Cube 27. To facilitate examination of results across the intermediate 25 cubes, we created three Mega cubes. Mega cube A is comprised of organizations in cubes 2 to 10 (2H and 1M, or 2H and 1L).

TABLE 5.1 Average Organizational Performance among Five Levels of Practices and Standardized Mean Differences between Groups

Levels of Practices	N	Mean Organizational Performance	SD	d between Adjacent Levels
I. (Cube 1)	82	23.28	3.31	
				0.20
II. (Cubes 2–10 = Mega cube A)	205	22.55	3.80	
				0.570
III. (Cubes 11–17 = Mega cube B)	133	20.29	4.37	
				0.46
IV. (Cubes 18–26 = Mega cube C)	186	18.25	4.61	
				0.93
V. (Cube 27)	73	13.86	5.07	

Note: The ANOVA F $(4, 674)$ = 78.60, $p < 0.001$, two-tailed. The average d statistic between adjacent groups = 0.54. The d statistic for the difference in performance between Cube One and Cube 27 was 2.22.[9]

Mega cube B is comprised of organizations classified in cubes 11 to 17 (1H, 1M, and 1L, or 3M); and Mega cube C is comprised of organizations in cubes 18–26 (2M and 1L, or 1H and 2L, or 1M and 2L).

Because the three items comprising the measure of organizational performance are scored on a ten-point scale, the maximum performance score is 30. Support is provided by a consistent *pattern* of relationships between levels of organizational performance and the five major categories of sets of practices: Cube 1, Mega cube A, Mega cube B, Mega cube C, and Cube 27. See Table 5.1.

Correlational Analyses

Another way to test the validity of the Cube One framework is to examine the separate correlations between each set of practices and organizational performance. See Table 5.2.

The magnitudes of correlations (also referred to as effect sizes) can be defined using the cut points provided by Cohen in his classic article in *Psychological Bulletin*. In connection with most social science research, Cohen labeled a correlational effect size as small if it is $r \geq 0.15$ but < 0.30. A medium effect size was associated with $r \geq 0.30$ to $r = 0.49$; and a large effect size was achieved at $r \geq 0.50$.

As shown in Table 5.2, the relationship between enterprise-directed practices and organizational performance was almost large ($r = 0.49$). The correlation between employee-directed practices and organizational performance was large at $r = 0.52$.

TABLE 5.2 Basic Statistics and Correlations[10]

Variable	M	SD	N	Correlations wwith Org. Perf.
Enterprise-Directed Practices	31.04	6.90	692	0.49
Customer-Directed Practices	28.25	7.92	685	0.42
Employee-Directed Practices	31.41	7.80	688	0.52
Organizational Performance	20.11	5.06	691	1.00
Self-Efficacy	3.78	1.04	667	0.07
Benign World View	3.35	1.09	668	−0.01

The association between customer-directed practices and organizational performance ($r = 0.42$) fell in the medium range.[11]

Campbell and Fiske noted many years ago that the validity of a measure is called into question if it correlates highly with conceptually unrelated variables—that is, if it lacks discriminant validity.[12] As noted above, the two measures examined that are conceptually unrelated to management practices or organizational performance are self-efficacy and Benign World View. Self-efficacy was assessed by responses to the statement "In general, a person can accomplish whatever he/she sets out to accomplish." The measure of Benign World View was "In the long run, those people who work the hardest achieve the most." Correlations were computed between the four central variables (enterprise-, customer-, and employee-directed practices along with organizational performance) and the conceptually unrelated measure of self-efficacy. The four correlations ranged from $r = 0.02$ to $r = 0.07$. Similar results were found with regard to the four central variables and the conceptually unrelated variable of Benign World View. The correlations ranged from $r = −0.06$ to $r = −0.00$. These low correlations provide a solid basis to reject the conjecture that the sizable main results are a spurious artifact of common method bias.

Correlations between the three sets of practices and organizational performance were similar in nonprofit/government organizations when compared to for-profit organizations (see Table 5.3). Correlations between enterprise-, customer-, and employee-directed practices among for-profit organizations were $r = 0.49, 0.43$, and 0.48, respectively. The corresponding correlations among respondents in nonprofit/government organizations were consistently higher ($r = 0.56, 0.44$, and 0.59, respectively). Thus, the present evidence indicates that the Cube One framework is equally valid in the nonprofit/government sector as compared to the for-profit sector—even though for-profit organizations were more likely to enact enterprise- and customer-directed practices compared to organizations in the nonprofit/government sector.

As shown in Table 5.4, the study found similar results among small (500 or fewer employees) and large (more than 500 employees) organizations, although large organizations were more likely to enact all three sets of practices.

TABLE 5.3 Basic Statistics and Correlations: For-Profit and Nonprofit/Government Subsamples

	Variable	*For-Profit*			*Nonprofit/Govt.*			*t-Value*	*1*	*2*	*3*	*4*
		M	*SD*	*N*	*M*	*SD*	*N*					
1.	Enterprise-Directed Practices (EntSum)	31.92	7.00	467	29.10	6.28	217	5.07	—	0.53	0.65	0.56
2.	Customer-Directed Practices (CSum)	29.07	7.75	463	26.44	8.04	214	4.01	0.67	—	0.52	0.44
3.	Employee-Directed Practices (ESum)	31.44	7.78	464	31.24	7.91	216	0.03	0.60	0.53	—	0.59
4.	Organizational Performance	20.01	5.06	466	20.26	5.09	217	−0.61	0.49	0.43	0.48	—

Note: Correlations for for-profit organizations appear below the diagonal and for nonprofit/government organizations appear on the upper right quadrant. All correlations significant at $p < 0.001$, two-tailed. T-values which are > 4.00 are significant at $p < 0.001$, two-tailed.

TABLE 5.4 Basic Statistics and Correlations: Large and Small Organizations

| Variable | Large | | | Small | | | t-Value | 1 | 2 | 3 | 4 |
	M	SD	N	M	SD	N					
1. Enterprise-directed Practices (EntSum)	31.86	7.06	224	29.27	6.96	142	3.43	—	0.63	0.64	0.49
2. Customer-directed Practices (CSum)	29.68	7.55	219	25.08	7.25	140	5.73	0.62	—	0.50	0.44
3. Employee-directed Practices (ESum)	32.85	7.36	220	30.39	8.46	142	2.93	0.64	0.53	—	0.54
4. Organizational Performance	21.49	4.26	224	19.83	5.40	142	3.27	0.52	0.38	0.48	—

Note: Large organizations have ≥ 500 employees and small organizations < 500 employees. Correlations for large organizations appear below the diagonal and for small organizations above the diagonal. All correlations were statistically significant at $p < 0.001$.

Although not a central focus in testing the validity of the Cube One framework, we also examined correlations among the three sets of practices. The median correlations among for-profit and nonprofit/governmental organizations were $r = 0.60$ and 0.53, respectively—see Table 5.3. If the Cube One framework is valid, then it is reasonable to expect that well-run organizations would be attentive to the interests of the three central stakeholders: the enterprise itself, employees, and customers. And conversely, poorly run organizations would be likely to enact lower levels of the three sets of practices. Because correlations are calculated across organizations (the organization being the unit of analysis), intercorrelations among practices are entirely consonant with the Cube One framework.

Multinational Correlational Analyses

Responses to the identical 30-item surveys of enterprise-, customer-, and employee-directed practices come from samples of respondents in the U.S., Singapore, Brazil (with translation to Portuguese), and South Korea.[13] The mean ages of respondents in the four countries were 31 in the U.S., 28 in Brazil, 29 in Singapore, and 28 in South Korea.[14] Because the Brazilian data were collected most recently, we included a second measure of organizational performance: a five-item behavior-based scale that is an abbreviated version of that developed by Griffin, Neal, and Parker.[15]

Research and writing on national cultures have often asserted that management practices must align with those cultures. Hofstede, a prominent author and researcher on cross-national research, notes "cultural constraints in management theories … not only practices but also the validity of theories may stop at national borders."[16] In a later publication, Hofstede advised: "For best results a multinational's management practices should fit the local culture."[17]

However, over the past five years, research has found that a fit between management practices and national culture is not essential. A meta-analytic review, published in 2014, of 156 studies involving more than 35,000 companies and enterprises in 29 countries, revealed startling results. The authors found that the higher the fit between High Performance Work Practices and national culture (according to widely accepted national culture perspectives), the *lower* the level of business performance. Moreover, "although we found moderating effects of national culture, these effects were mostly the opposite of those hypothesized using standard national culture-based logic."[18] Differences in national culture notwithstanding, high performance work practices related positively to business performance in all 29 countries. Results were statistically significant in 26 out of 29 countries.

Hartnell and colleagues in 2016 found that organizational performance is highest when task-oriented leadership style is at odds with organizational culture. Organizational performance was lower when leader task orientation matched that of the organizational culture (i.e., high–high or low–low).[19]

As mentioned in Chapter 2, Bloom and colleagues in 2012 reported on a study that entailed measuring management practices in 10,000 organizations in 20 countries. Three practices were consistently, and positively, associated with three dependent variables: productivity, profits, and revenue growth. The three practices were goal setting, performance measurement, and incentives—three of the five components of GMFAC (for explication, see Chapter 2). Sizable correlations were found both within and across countries. The authors concluded that management practices explained "the astonishing differences in performance across firms and countries."[20]

The present author is agnostic regarding the impact of differences in national culture on the validity of the Cube One framework. That is, the validity of the framework across cultures is ultimately an empirical question. The multinational data described next appear in Table 5.5.

The correlations between enterprise-directed practices and Organizational performance in the U.S., Brazil, Singapore, and South Korea were $r = 0.49, 0.39,$ $0.27,$ and $0.47,$ respectively—all statistically significant. When the five-item behavior-based measure of performance was examined in the Brazilian sample, the correlation rose from 0.39 to 0.46. With regard to customer-directed practices, the correlations were $r = 0.42, 0.36, 0.43,$ and $0.53,$ respectively. The behavior-based performance measure in the Brazilian sample increased the correlation from 0.36 to 0.44. In connection with employee-directed practices the correlations were $r = 0.52, 0.42, 0.43,$ and $0.20,$ respectively. The five-item behavior-based Organizational performance measure increased the correlation in the Brazilian sample from 0.42 to 0.53.

Discriminant validity evidence was obtained in the Singapore and Brazil samples with regard to self-efficacy. In the Brazilian sample, the correlation of self-efficacy with the three-item performance measure was $r = 0.02;$ and with the five-item behavior-based performance measure it was $r = 0.05.$ Looking at the mean correlation in the Brazilian sample of self-efficacy with the three sets of practices and the two organizational performance measures the result was $r = 0.02.$[21] In the sample from Singapore, the correlations between the two conceptually unrelated variables and organizational performance were: self-efficacy, $r = 0.20$ (not statistically significant) and benign world view, $r = 0.11.$ In the South Korean sample, self-efficacy and benign world view correlated with organizational performance at $r = -0.17$ and $r = 0.06,$ respectively.[22] The median correlation was $r = 0.05;$ seven of the correlations between conceptually unrelated variables and organizational performance can be characterized as less than small; none of the correlations were statistically significant.

Perhaps the most salient finding pertains to the multiple regression coefficient (R) between all three practice measures (enterprise-, customer-, and employee-directed) when examined together to predict organizational performance. The results were sizable in all four national cultures. More specifically, the associations in the samples from the U.S., Brazil, Singapore, and South Korea were $R = 0.54,$

TABLE 5.5 Correlations between Three Types of Practices and Organizational Performance by Country

Variables	Enterprise-Directed US[1]	Enterprise-Directed Brazil[2]	Enterprise-Directed Singapore[3]	Enterprise-Directed SK[4]	Customer-Directed US	Customer-Directed Brazil	Customer-Directed Singapore	Customer-Directed SK	Employee-Directed US	Employee-Directed Brazil	Employee-Directed Singapore	Employee-Directed SK
1. Org. Perf.1	0.49***	0.37***	0.27*	0.47**	0.42***	0.36***	0.43**	0.55**	0.52***	0.42***	43***	0.20
2. Org. Perf.2	n/a	0.46***	n/a	n/a	n/a	0.44***	n/a	n/a	n/a	0.53***	n/a	n/a

Note: [1] n = 695–702; [2] n = 129; [3] n = 60; [4n] = 34. When all three sets of practices were entered together in a regression equation on Org. Perf.1, Rs were: U.S. 57, Brazil 0.48, and Singapore 0.54. When regressed on Org. Perf. 2: Brazil 0.58.

*$p < 0.05$, two–tailed; **$p < 0.01$, two–tailed; ***$p < 0.001$, two–tailed

0.48, 0.54, and 0.55 respectively. Using the behavior-based measure of organizational performance in Brazil, the multiple regression rose from $R = 0.48$ to $R = 0.58$. Additional multinational data appear in an article published in 2017 in *International Management Review*.[23]

Additional Survey Research

Research initiated by Elizabeth Letzler (and coauthored by the present author) examined what might be described as the full-blown conceptual causal model.[24] We obtained data for enterprise-, customer-, and employee-directed practices and also for the corresponding intermediate variables: enterprise capability, customer capability, and employee capability. The three capability measures were seen as assets to the enterprise which in turn would influence organizational performance. We defined enterprise capability in terms of efficiency, effectiveness, and adaptability compared to other organizations. We measured customer capability in terms of the level of satisfaction, likelihood of repeat purchases, and willingness to recommend the organization to others, the latter item being similar to what Reichheld calls "the ultimate question."[25] We measured employee capability by the level of employee satisfaction, comparison of the employing organization to others as a place to work, and likelihood of the participant to be working for the current employer in five years. The capabilities were seen as influencing (or at least related to) organizational performance. See Figure 5.2 for the complete conceptual causal model. (Figure 5.2 is identical to Figure 1.2 and is repeated for convenience.)

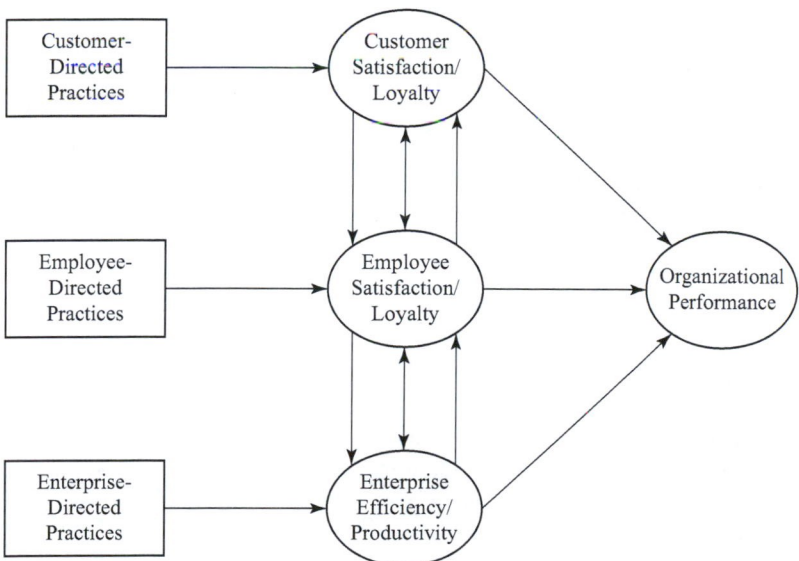

FIGURE 5.2   Schematic of the Cube One Quasi-Causal Model

We derived the basis for operationalizing the three sets of practices by reviewing 394 books and non-academic articles, plus 1,748 articles published in the most prominent academic journals (e.g., *Journal of Applied Psychology*, *Academy of Management Journal*). In total, we gleaned 1,637 practice statements from the literature review and sorted them into three sets of practices. In the final analysis, 78 items were used in the research: 26 for each set of practices. Exploratory and confirmatory factor analyses showed three distinct capabilities and organizational performance.

Elizabeth Letzler (who was in a booth in the main conference area) invited participants at management training seminars offered by a large training organization in New York City to voluntarily and anonymously complete a questionnaire. She obtained 1,156 questionnaires, of which 993 were usable. Participants included employees from all three sectors. The typical for-profit organization had revenues of $960 million and 937 employees working at the local worksite.

As predicted, the three sets of practices (enterprise-, customer-, and employee-directed were correlated to their corresponding capabilities, with $r = 0.62, 0.29$, and 0.63, respectively. The correlations between enterprise- and employee-directed practices were sizably associated with organizational performance. (As noted above, correlations over 0.50 have been designated as large.) However, the association between customer-directed practices and customer capability only approached a medium size. All correlations were significant at $p < 0.01$. The correlations of enterprise-, customer-, and employee-directed practices with organizational performance were similar to the results in prior correlational analyses, with $r = 0.52, 0.48$, and 0.54, respectively.[26] When practices and capabilities were analyzed simultaneously in a multiple regression model, the result was very large, $R = 0.77$, which means that 59% of variance in organizational performance (the square of R) was "explained" by or attributable to the six variables in the quasi-causal analysis.[27]

Summary of Survey Research

This chapter has reviewed the results of several independent research efforts, all of which provided strong support for the validity of the Cube One framework. Analyses of levels of organizational performance across the 27 cubes yielded a difference of 14.2σ between Cube One and Cube 27. The comparison of means across five categories—Cube One, Cube 27, plus the three Mega cubes—yielded a significant result with $p < 0.001$.

Correlational results in the initial U.S. sample were sizable, and the results were generalizable—being applicable to large and small organizations and as well as those in all sectors. Correlations were consistently larger in the nonprofit/government sector than in the for-profit sector. Hence, the Cube One framework is applicable to all work organizations. Evidence of discriminant validity is clearly present. Absent this evidence, common method bias would pose a competing alternative explanation for the findings.

Correlational analyses conducted with respondents in three countries other than the U.S. were also consistently supportive. The behavior-based measure of performance was consistently superior to the three-item measure (achieving goals, comparison to other organizations, and degree of potential achieved).

Elizabeth Letzler used structural equation modeling to allow examination of three layers of management decisions: practices selected and enacted by management; posited connections between practices and competencies; relationships between competencies and organizational performance.[28] That 59% of variance was explained by the three sets of practices and three capabilities is remarkable—more than twice the level associated with a large effect size. A large effect size in terms of correlations is $r \geq 0.50$, which corresponds to a threshold of 25% of explained variance ($\sqrt{.50}$).

Customer-directed practices (although consistently significant with medium effect sizes) had a somewhat lower association with organizational performance than the other two sets of practices. In prior publications it was conjectured that respondents (who served in the role of organizational employees) would likely have more knowledge of enterprise- and employee-directed practices than of customer-directed practices. For instance, employees might be unaware of whether customer satisfaction surveys had been distributed, or focus groups conducted. Having customer-directed practices reported by customers would, presumably, partly mitigate this limitation.

Another plausible reason why customer-directed practices yielded slightly lower correlations is that several important marketing techniques were not included in the original ten-item and even the 26-item scales. It would have been better to reference satisfaction as captured by Net Promoter Score; to conduct in-depth analyses of customer preferences, such as by opt-in or Voice of the Customer programs, which can enable customization; and to include more current marketing techniques, such as push notifications, the application of A/B experiments, or the use of Big Data.

Likewise, we noted in Chapter 2 that a broader coverage of enterprise-directed practices would likely improve validity results in that regard. Supply chain management, and various operational techniques, along with financial considerations, should be included in future research and in the use of surveys for diagnostic and intervention purposes.

When it comes to explaining organizational performance we have encountered no "silver bullets" or perpetually enduring sets of practices that will provide *the* prescription for generating excellent organizational performance.[29] Given the assumption of substitutability, what matters is that multiple demonstrably effective practices be enacted with high levels of frequency and be carried out in a skillful manner. We will show, in Chapter 11, how survey data can be used for diagnostic and implementation purposes, i.e., to achieve improved performance based on a systematic analysis of diagnostic data.

Another issue relates to causality. To be sure, medium or large effect sizes were found in several survey research endeavors. But the direction of causality has not been indisputably established. Perhaps high levels of organizational performance provide the wherewithal to enact more enterprise-, customer-, and employee-directed practices.

Other than by conducting experimental research, which is infeasible when it comes to testing the results of multiple practices (and employing random assignment of practices to provide a plausible claim of *ceteris paribas*), the next-best alternative is an examination of longitudinal waves of data. We employ this approach in the next chapter, where we examine management practices and financial metrics at two points of time.[30]

Appendix 5.1

Survey of Attitudes and Organization Practices

This voluntary exercise is designed to record—on a group basis—various views and attitudes pertinent to organizational behavior and human resource management. Please do *not* put your name on this survey.

Part One: Attitudes and Opinions

For each of the 4 statements that follow, please respond using the following scale:

5 = Strongly Agree
4 = Inclined to Agree
3 = Neither Agree nor Disagree
2 = Inclined to Disagree
1 = Strongly Disagree

(1) Most employees cannot be trusted; therefore, they must be closely supervised to ensure effective job performance.   1._____

(2) Most employees are capable of self-management. That is, employees can determine for themselves what they should be doing, when, where, and how.   2._____

(3) In general, a person can accomplish whatever he/she sets out to accomplish.   3._____

(4) In the long run, those people who work the hardest achieve the most success in life.   4._____

Part Two: Background Data

(1) Age Category (check one): 20–24 _____ 25–29 _____ 30–34 _____ 35–39 _____ 40–44 _____ ≥ 45_____

(2) Sex: Female _____ Male _____

(3) Undergraduate Grade Point Average (e.g., A = 4.00, B = 3.00, C = 2.00, etc.) GPA = __.___

Part Three: Actual Company Practices

The purpose of this section is to ascertain the *actual practices* (as distinct from stated or printed policies) in the organization for which you currently work (or most recently worked). If you work in a subsidiary of a larger organization, focus on the local organization where you work (or worked). Please use the following scale to record your responses to the 20 statements that follow:

1 = Never or Almost Never (or Not Applicable)
2 = Infrequently
3 = Occasionally or Sometimes
4 = Frequently
5 = Always or Almost Always

(1) Individuals are held accountable for accomplishing specific (quantifiable) goals.　　　　　　　　　　　　　　　　　　1._____

(2) Individuals receive specific performance feedback that is useful for improving their performance.　　　　　　　　　　2._____

(3) Where possible, the performance of individuals and groups is quantifiably measured and monitored over time.　　　3._____

(4) Salary increases (e.g., raises, bonuses) are proportionate to an individual's job performance.　　　　　　　　　　4._____

(5) Promotions are based almost entirely on job performance.　5._____

(6) Individuals are selected for employment based on objective criteria (e.g., written tests, performance tests, work samples, etc.)　6._____

(7) Training is provided for employees who need to upgrade their knowledge and skills.　　　　　　　　　　　　　　7._____

(8) Organizational performance improvement is financially rewarded by a group incentive plan (e.g., gainsharing, profit-sharing, etc.)　　　　　　　　　　　　　　　　　8._____

(9) Management encourages the delegation of decision-making authority to lower-level employees (i.e., real empowerment).　9._____

(10) Individuals are encouraged to perform a wide variety of tasks whenever possible.　　　　　　　　　　　　　　10 _____

(11) Customers are regularly surveyed via questionnaire regarding their satisfaction with products and/or services.　　11._____

(12) Focus groups (i.e., in-depth interviews) are regularly held with customers to gain a fuller understanding of wants and/or needs.   12._____

(13) Products and/or services are continually upgraded as part of an ongoing program of quality improvement.   13._____

(14) The best practices of competitors are studied and adopted, or improved upon, where possible (i.e., benchmarking).   14._____

(15) The goal of customer satisfaction importantly influences operational decisions at all organization levels.   15._____

(16) Prices of goods/services are continually reviewed to improve the organization's competitive position.   16._____

(17) The quality of products/services is regularly assessed by an independent organization as part of a continuing audit.   17._____

(18) Customer satisfaction is an important factor in determining pay increases of individuals or departments.   18._____

(19) Employees are granted wide latitude to use their own judgment in order to satisfy customers.   19._____

(20) Product or service innovations are regularly sought and budgeted for on a continuing basis.   20._____

Part Four: Actual Company Practices Continued

Once again, the focus is on the *actual practices* (as distinct from stated or printed policies) in the organization for which you currently work (or most recently worked). If you work in a subsidiary of a larger organization, focus on the local organization where you work (or worked). Please use the following scale to record your responses to the ten statements that follow:

1= Never or Almost Never (or Not Applicable)
2= Infrequently
3= Occasionally or Sometimes
4= Frequently
5= Always or Almost Always

(1) Open, two-way communication is employed. All employees are informed about new developments and encouraged to express their ideas and complaints.   1._____

(2) Distinctions between hierarchical ranks are minimized. Management downplays status symbols (e.g., executive dining rooms and other perks).   2._____

(3) Employee layoffs are avoided where possible, by first attempting to place employees in other jobs within the organization.   3._____

(4) Employee growth is encouraged by providing in-house training and/or reimbursements for outside training/educational
programs.   4._____

(5) Work-family conflicts are minimized by adopting such policies as flexible work hours, day care assistance, and encouraging managerial tolerance.   5._____

(6) The organization responds to employee concerns by taking
appropriate actions, not just by words.   6._____

(7) Managerial integrity is demonstrated in dealing with employees. All employees are given the same information; promises
are kept.   7._____

(8) Employees are treated with respect and as mature adults.
Communications are straight-forward, not condescending or
patronizing.   8._____

(9) Employees know they can make (a few) mistakes. Management
attempts to minimize the role of punishment and fear.   9._____

(10) Management encourages employees to feel that they are part
of a team.   10._____

Part Five: Organizational Performance

The purpose of this section is to obtain information about the performance of
the organization for which you work(ed). Please circle the number which most
closely describes your response to the following three questions:

(1) Overall, how successful is the organization in accomplishing its mission and
goals?

1	2	3	4	5	6	7	8	9	10
Completely				Moderately					Completely
unsuccessful				successful					successful

(2) Overall, how does the organization's performance compare to the performance of similar, or competitive, organizations?

1		2	3	4	5		6	7	8	9	10
Extremely poor											Exceptionally outstanding
Lower performance					Average						Higher performance
than all others											than all others

(3) Overall, at what % of maximum potential performance (the maximum being 100%) is the organization now achieving?

1		2	3	4	5		6	7	8	9	10
0 to 10%					About 50%						90 to 100%
Vast improvement potential					Some room for improvement						Potential is now virtually Fulfilled

Notes

1 Babbie, E. (1995). *The practice of social research*, 7th ed. Belmont, CA: Wadsworth Publishing Company.

2 Ibid.

3 The probability is 0.00000000000256, thus an additional seven zeroes compared to 6σ. For a detailed description of these results, see Kopelman. R. E., and Prottas, D. J. (2012). "Rationale and validity evidence for the Cube One framework." *Journal of Managerial Issues*, 24(1), 27–46.

4 Murray, A. I. (Summer 1989). "Top management heterogeneity and firm performance." *Strategic Management Journal*, 10, 125–141.

5 Meyer, R., and O'Shaughnessy, K. (1993). "Organization design and the performance paradox." In R. Swenberg, ed. *Explorations in economic sociology*, New York: Russell Sage Foundation.

6 Considerable evidence indicates that subjective measures of organizational performance can be valid and equivalent to objective measures. See, Wall, T. D., Michie, J., Patterson, M., Wood, S. D., Sheehan, M., Clegg, C. W., and West, M. (2004), "On the validity of subjective measures of company performance." *Personnel Psychology*, 57, 95–118.

7 Podsakoff, P. M., MacKenzie, S. B., Lee, J-Y., and Podsakoff, N. P. (2003). "Common method biases in behavioral research: A critical review of the literature and recommended remedies." *Journal of Applied Psychology*, 88(5), 879–903.

8 Ibid.

9 The *d* statistic represents the number of standard deviations between two independent samples. This difference reflects what is called effect size. It is generally agreed that a *d* up to 0.20 is small; 0.3–0.5 is medium; 0.60 to 0.80 is large. So, the *d* statistic between Cube One and Cube 27 of 2.22 might be characterized as immense. See Cohen, J. (1992). "A power primer." *Psychological Bulletin*, 112(1), 155–159.

10 Further data is provided in Kopelman and Prottas, op. cit.

11 In fact all correlations where *r* was ≥ 0.19 were statistically significant at a probability of less than one in a thousand ($p < 0.001$). The multiple associations between all three sets of practices examined in concert with organizational performance yielded a result of R = 0.58. The reason the combined association was not appreciably greater than the three sets of practices when examined individually is due to "multicollinearity." What this means is that there were high correlations within organizations of levels of enactment of the sets of practices. As would be expected, well-run (and high-performing) organizations are more likely to enact high levels of all the three sets of practices than poorly run organizations. Note that this pattern has no bearing on the use of the Cube One framework for diagnostic purposes. We discuss and demonstrate this in Chapter 11.

12 Campbell, D. T., and Fiske, D. W. (March 1959). "Convergent and discriminant validation by the multitrait-multimethod matrix." *Psychological Bulletin*, 56(2), 81–105. In the present research there were multiple measures of constructs (traits) and multiple methods, in that item formats changed in predictor and dependent variables.

13 An independent validation of the accuracy of the initial translation was conducted by having a second bilingual person perform the same translation, assessing accuracy by the proportion of words identically translated. There was agreement on 389 of the 396 words in the survey, or slightly over 98%. Thus, the first translation was used with confidence in its accuracy.

14 Mean age was obtained using midpoints of age categories.

15 Griffin, M. A. , Neal, A., and Parker, S. K. (2007). "A new model of work role performance: Positive behavior in uncertain and interdependent contexts." *Academy of Management Journal*, 50(2), 327–347. (We recommend incorporating the abbreviated five-item behavior-based measure of organizational performance in future research, along with the three-item measure.)

16 Hofstede, G. (1993). "Cultural constraints in management theories." *Academy of Management Executive*, 7(1), 81–94.

17 Hofstede, G. (1993). *Culture's consequences*, 2nd ed. Thousand Oaks, CA: Sage. Similarly, Adler emphasizes that cultural differences constrain or even dictate whether management practices will be effective in different cultures. See, Adler, N. J. (2008). *International dimensions of organizational behavior*, 5th ed. Mason, OH: Thompson/South-Western.

18 Rabl, T., Jayasinghe, M., Gerhart, B., and Kuhlmann, T. M. (2014). "A meta-analysis of country differences in the high-performance work system-business performance relationship: The roles of national culture and managerial discretion." *Journal of Applied Psychology*, 99(6) 1011–1041. The quote appears on page 1020.

19 Hartnell, C. A., Kinicki, A. J., Lambert, L. S., Fugate, M., and Corner, P. S. (2016). "Do similarities or differences between CEO leadership and organizational culture have a more positive effect on firm performance? A test of competing predictions." *Journal of Applied Psychology*, 101(6), 846–861.

20 Bloom, N. Genekas, C., Sadn, R, and Van Reenen, J. (2012). "Management practices across firms and countries." *Academy of Management Perspectives*, 26(1), 12–33.

21 In the Brazilian sample only a small proportion of respondents completed the benign world view items, so the results are not reported.

22 About two-thirds of the sample from South Korea completed the two conceptually unrelated measures.

23 Kopelman, R. E., and Prottas, D. J. (2017). "A multinational examination of the validity of the Cube One framework: Comparison of results in the U.S., Brazil, and Singapore." *International Management Review*, 13(1), 5–9.

24 Letzler, E. A., and Kopelman, R. E. (July 2008). "An integrated model of organizational performance." *Advances in Management*, 1(4), 5–15. An earlier version was presented at the 60th Annual Meeting of the Academy of Management (Atlanta), 2006. (Letzler and Kopelman claim that capabilities should be managed as assets, as is recognized in the marketing, HRM, and management literatures.

25 Reichheld, F. (with Markey, R.). (2011). *The ultimate question 2.0.* Boston, MA: Harvard Business Review Press.

26 Letzler, E. A., Kopelman, R. E., and Prottas, D. J. (2012). "The three faces of the Cube One framework." *The Journal of Business Inquiry*, 11(1), 13–32. An earlier version of this article was presented at the 2012 Annual Meeting of the Southern Management Association, and included in the Proceedings, pp. 1912–1917.

27 Letzler and Kopelman, (2008) includes detailed results of Structural Equation Modelling (SEM) analyses, examining five models—including interaction effects and indirect effects. The mediating role of capabilities was supported; the direct role of customer capability was not.

28 Structural equation modeling examines independent, mediating, and dependent variables, which resembles a longitudinal design, but all data were collected simultaneously. A longitudinal design (employed in Chapter 6), would permit causal inferences to be made with more confidence.

29 Jim Collins noted in *Good to great* (2005). New York, NY: Collins, that greatness does not emanate from a "killer application" or a miracle moment.
30 The author recognizes that this chapter on survey-based evidence is fairly technical, and probably not as interesting or memorable as good anecdotes or case studies. We present case studies in Chapters 7 to 10. In Chapter 6, we review evidence based on financial performance.

6

VALIDITY EVIDENCE

Financial Metrics

In the prior chapter, we presented results of five survey research studies pertinent to examining the validity of the Cube One framework. Two of the studies involved large U.S. samples. Survey respondents from Brazil, Singapore, and South Korea comprised the other three. The median correlations between the three predictors (Enterprise-, Customer-, and Employee-directed practices) and Organizational Performance in the five studies were $r = 0.49, 0.62, 0.46, 0.43,$ and 0.47, respectively.[1] Examining the composite association of the three sets of practices and Organizational Performance yielded multiple regression coefficients of $R = 0.54, 0.77, 0.48, 0.54$ and 0.55, respectively. In brief, all the correlational and regression results were medium to large in terms of effect sizes. (R in the second U.S sample included capabilities.)

Correlation is not proof of causality.[2] In the five prior survey studies the three sets of enacted practices may have been more the *result* of organizational performance than the *cause*. Of course, in some situations, correlations would seemingly have only one causal interpretation. For example, there is a consistently large correlation between the number of fire trucks at the scene of a fire and the size of the fire. Logically, it is implausible to argue that the more fire trucks that show up at a fire scene, the greater the subsequent damage.

Over the past two decades, much research has been done on multiple human resource management practices (i.e., HPWP) that relate to organizational performance. But virtually all of the research has been cross-sectional, with both variables measured concurrently. However, longitudinal organizational performance data have been collected among a small number of publicly traded companies. For instance, Wright and his colleagues examined multiple HR practices and autonomous business units within the same company and explored the relationships between HR practices and past, concurrent, and subsequent measures of operational and financial performance and organizational performance. They concluded that the relationships reflect reciprocal influence.[3]

In 1964, Pelz and Andrews advocated the collection of longitudinal panel data—"panel" meaning that the same information sources provide data over time. In their words regarding causal inferences, "If in fact A determines B rather than the reverse, the correlation A1B2 should exceed B1A2."[4] The use of cross-lagged correlational analysis can identify the relative strengths of correlations in terms of the effects of variable A on B, and vice versa. Indeed, several researchers have viewed the use of cross-lagged correlational analyses as a superior approach to making valid causal inferences, compared to (the far more commonplace static analysis.[5] As Kenny has noted: "The strength of cross-lagged analysis lies in its narrowness; it has been developed for and adapted to panel data analysis."[6] If the cross-lagged differential (A1B2 versus B2A1) is not zero, this may indicate a causal effect of A on B. Evidence for causality has been found in connection with: (1) intentions to purchase a car and purchase of a car;[7] (2) employee expectancy beliefs regarding possible rewards and individual job performance.[8]

The ideal research design to establish causality is the experiment (either in a lab or in the field). Experiments require random assignment of participants to conditions, and it is recommended that participants be unaware (or "blind") as to whether they are in the treatment or control group. Random assignment is a good way to control for other variables, and achieve *ceteris paribus*. For example, more than 100 experiments have established that specific goals yield higher individual task performance than vague goals.

However, conducting experimental field research to test the validity of the Cube One framework requires a high level of commitment. Organizations (or divisions) would need to be randomly assigned to treatment and control groups. The treatment would entail introducing change(s) at one group of companies (or corporate divisions), but not others. More specifically, assessing the utility of the Cube One framework would entail changing (presumably increasing) the level of enterprise-, customer-, or employee-directed practices in some unit(s) but not others. Then the organization would need to track performance in both conditions to ascertain if the treatment condition "worked." This later facet of experimental research is actually a reasonably cautious way to introduce change. Rather than metaphorically "jumping in with both feet," if the treatment condition proves worthwhile, the organization might modify (or "roll out") similar changes in other units. However, the use of random assignment and having participants unaware of the intervention (i.e., being "blind" to the situation) would be difficult to justify in practice.

A close approximation, or a precursor, to an experimental design is the use of a cross-lagged correlational analysis with panel data, a technique that has been classified as a pre-experimental design.[9] Massimino and Kopelman used the cross-lagged panel analysis methodology in their research on eight management/marketing practices and market capitalization.[10] A schematic of the cross-lagged panel analysis is provided in Figure 6.1. Details as to method follow. The focus should be on Correlations 5 and 6 viz.: are POP (perceived organizational practices) in 2003 more related to MC (market capitalization) in 2006, or vice versa?[11]

POP were measured by 10,000 executives, directors, and security analysts regarding the ten largest companies (based on revenues) in each industry. The ratings of attributes used 11-point scales, with endpoints of zero (worst) and 10 (best). The eight attributes, which were summed for each company, were as follows:

1. Wise use of corporate assets
2. Quality of products or services
3. People management: ability to attract and retain talented people
4. Social responsibility to the community and the environment
5. Innovativeness
6. Quality of management
7. Financial soundness
8. Long-term investment value

The first three dimensions/attributes correspond to what the Cube One framework would classify as enterprise-, customer-, and employee-directed practices, respectively. (The first three attribute ratings were subsequently used in two other studies—described below—that focus on the Cube One framework.)[12]

The Massimino and Kopelman (2012) research examined data on rated attributes (or factors that presumably would affect organizational performance) in 2002–2003 (called '03) and again in 2005–2006 (called '06). Likewise, relative

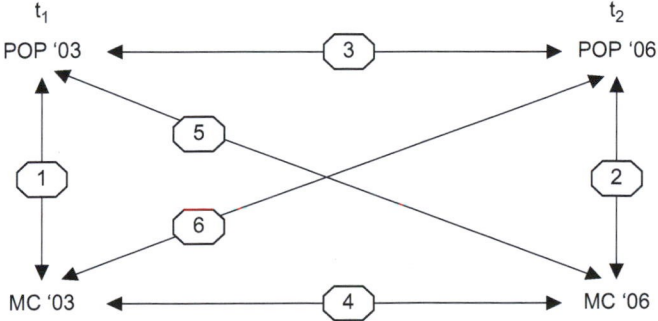

FIGURE 6.1   Correlations Comprising the Cross-Lagged Panel Analysis

MC data consisted of the market value of each company in a specified industry. Companies that did not remain as publicly traded entities throughout the period from 2002 to 2006 were dropped from the analysis. (Some companies went out of business; others were acquired or taken private.) Consequently, the number of companies dropped from 577 in the 2002 *Fortune Magazine* list of America's Most Admired Companies (AMAC) to 219 companies in 2006. Because eight companies were in industries where data existed for only two companies, the final sample consisted of 211 companies in 44 industries (down from 48 industries in 2002–2003). All six correlations (per Figure 6.1) were computed using the type of statistic most appropriate for analyzing ranked data, the Spearman rank-order correlation.[13]

The industry was the unit of analysis, with 44 different industry classifications. Correlations were examined for industries with three or four companies; those with five or six; and those with seven or eight companies. An analysis was also performed, collectively, for all 44 industries. The research focused on the relationship between management practices as assessed via attribute ratings, and organizational performance as assessed by relative MC. Results are shown in Table 6.1.

All correlations were positive, and most were statistically significant. The key comparison is between Correlations 5 and 6—i.e., was POP'03 more associated with MC'06, or was MC'03 more associated with POP'06? For industries with three or four companies, the correlations were $r_s = 0.664$ and 0.245, respectively. The difference is consistent with the idea that perceived corporate attributes have more effect on MC than vice versa. Correlation 5 explained 44% of the variance (0.664 squared). In comparison, Correlation 6 explained merely 6% of variance (0.245 squared): a greater than seven-fold difference. Because these correlations were computed for only 21 industries, the difference in correlations was barely statistically significant. Across all 41 industries, the corresponding key correlations were 0.62 and 0.38, the difference being almost statistically significant at $p = 0.07$.

Small sample size can impede finding clear-cut evidence of causal priority with cross-lagged panel analyses. As Kenny observed, "It is very difficult to obtain statistically significant differences between cross-lagged correlations even when the sample size is moderate (75 to 300)."[14] The sample size in the Massimino and Kopelman study was only 41, not even close to the lower bound of a moderate size sample (75–300). Yet the differences in the key cross-lagged correlations were sizable, if not uniformly statistically significant.

Unlike the survey research studies in Chapter 5, the measure of performance can be seen as highly objective, i.e., "hard data," which provides an alternate approach to assessing the validity of the Cube One framework. It is noteworthy, as well, that the data were obtained from two different sources, which mitigates the possible threat of common method bias.

TABLE 6.1 Correlations for Cross–Lagged Panel Analysis

Number of Companies in Industry	Number of Industries (k) in Category	1 POP '03 MC '03	2 POP '06 MC '06	3 POP '03 POP '06	4 MC '03 MC '06	5 POP '03 MC '06	6 POP '06 MC '03
3 to 4	21	0.74***	0.67***	0.79***	0.96***	0.66***	0.25
5 to 6	14	0.56*	0.62**	0.52*	0.96***	0.52*	0.39
7 to 8	9	0.77**	0.50	0.66*	0.93***	0.67*	0.64*
All Industries	44	0.70***	0.62***	0.69***	0.96***	0.62***	0.38*

Notes: POP = perceived organizational practices; MC = market capitalization;
k = number of industries in category, * $p < 0.05$; ** $p < 0.01$; *** $p < 0.001$ (one-tailed).

Cube One Market Capitalization Studies

Two additional studies used nearly the same design as described above. Data from *Fortune's* lists of America's Most Admired Companies provided experts' judgments (perceptions) regarding the relative performance of 621 companies in terms of eight attributes. As noted above, the first three attributes correspond to the three sets of practices deemed essential to successful organizational performance per the Cube One framework. The attributes (1) *Quality of products and services*, (2) *People management: Ability to attract, develop, and keep talented people*, and (3) *Use of corporate assets* are pertinent to the implementation of customer-, employee-, and enterprise-directed practices, respectively.

The *Fortune* methodology for producing the 2008 ratings entailed examining, in late 2007, attribute ratings of 3,721 experts who were highly knowledgeable about the 621 companies in 64 industries.[15] The Hay Group, which has administered the Most Admired ratings since 2001, queried "up to 10 top executives and 7 outside board members of the [eligible pool] of *Fortune 1000* companies."[16] Ratings used the above-described 11-point scale.

For each of the three focal attributes, the highest-, middle-, and lowest-ranked thirds of companies in each industry group were assigned to three categories (High, Middle, and Low) and the categories were converted into scores of 3, 2, and 1. Because the Cube One framework posits that all three sets of practices are necessary for organizational success, the three scores were combined multiplicatively. The POP scores were obtained at two points in time based on attribute ratings published in 2006 and 2008, reflective of judgments made in late 2005 and 2007, respectively.

The criterion variable was the capitalized market value of each company. Although many factors affect this metric, including the amount of debt and financial leverage, it is indisputably an objective indicator, reflecting the judgments of investors as to company value. MCs for each company were measured by calculating the mean capitalization for every trading day in 2005 and 2006, and for 2007 and 2008. The initial sample included 291 companies in 55 industries. Three of the industries were omitted because data existed for only two of the companies; thus, the final sample was 285 companies in 52 industries. The unit of analysis was the industry, and Spearman rank-order correlations were computed for the key correlations.[17]

For each industry, two correlations were compared: (1) between POP in 2006 and MC in 2008 and (2) MC in 2006 and POP in 2008. Results are shown in Table 6.2.[18]

As expected, POP in 2006 was positively correlated with MC levels in 2006; the same was found for POP and MC in 2008. The correlations were 0.61 ($p <$ 0.01) and 0.65 ($p <$ 0.001), respectively.

Based on the assumption that POP should have more effect on MC than vice versa, cross-lagged correlations were examined. In industries where only three or four companies were available for analytical purposes, the POP1MC2 correlation was significant: $r_s = 0.62, p < 0.01$. The MC1POP2 correlation was 0.40 (and not

TABLE 6.2 Mean Correlations between Perceived Organizational Practices and Market Capitalizations: Concurrent and Cross-Lagged Results

Number of Companies in Industry	Number of Industries (k)	1 POP '06 MC '06	2 POP '08 MC '08	3 POP '06 MC '08	4 POP '08 MC '06
3 to 4	17	0.64**	0.85***	0.62*	0.40
5 to 6	20	0.58**	0.64**	0.71**	0.54*
7 to 9	15	0.56*	0.53*	0.39	0.55*
All Industries	52	0.61***	0.65***	0.60***	0.50***

Notes: POP = perceived organizational practices; MC = market capitalization; k = number of industries in category, * $p < .05$; ** $p < .01$; *** $p < .001$ (one-tailed).

significant). The difference did not reach conventional levels of statistical significance due to the small sample size (k = 17).

We found similar results for industries with data from five or six companies. The corresponding correlations were $r_x = 0.71$, $p < 0.01$ versus $r_s = 0.54$, $p < 0.05$. Again the difference was not statistically significant due to the small number of observations (k = 20). In industries with data from seven to nine companies, the relative magnitudes of correlations were in the opposite direction to our expectation. Examining cross-lagged data for the entire sample of 52 industries, results went in the predicted direction ($r_s = 0.60$ $p < 0.001$ versus $r_s = 0.50$ $p < 0.001$) but the difference was not statistically significant ($p = 0.24$).[19]

Overall, the findings were supportive—POP being more predictive of MC than MC of POP—but the small sample sizes virtually precluded reaching statistical significance. Because the correlation between POP in 2006 and 2008 was very high, at $r = 0.84$, the limited variance in the theorized predictor served as a ceiling on results. The two-year inter-measurement interval was probably too short a time period for the effects of the posited independent variables to affect the predicted dependent variable.

Consequently, we performed a second test of the Cube One framework using the same methodology with a four-year interval between measurements, collecting essentially identical types of data for 2006 and 2010. Again we deduced that if management practices (as captured by the POP measure) relate causally to organizational performance (as measured by relative MC levels), then the correlation between POP1MC2 should exceed the MC1POP2 correlation. Results with the four-year inter-measurement interval are shown in Table 6.3.[20]

As expected, the POP1MC2 correlation exceeded the MC1POP2 correlation across all 36 cases with $r_s = 0.65$ $p < 0.001$ versus $r_s = 0.50$ $p < 0.01$.[21] But once again, the small sample size (k = 36) made it unlikely that the differential predictions would be statistically significant. The exact statistical significance of the difference was $p = 0.24$.[22]

TABLE 6.3 Mean Correlations between Perceived Organizational Practices and Market Capitalizations: Concurrent and Cross-Lagged Results

Number of Companies in Industry	Number of Companies in Industry (k)	1 POP '06 MC '06	2 POP '10 MC '10	3 POP '06 MC '10	4 POP '10 MC '06
3 to 4	14	0.43	0.85***	0.74**	0.48*
5 to 6	14	0.57*	0.8111 pt	0.64**	0.51*
7 to 8	8	0.48	0.72*	0.48	0.51
All Industries	36	0.49**	0.81***	0.6511 pt	0.50**

Notes: POP = perceived organizational practices; MC = market capitalization; k = number of industries in category, * p < .05; ** p < .01; *** p < .001 (one-tailed).

To attempt to compensate for the small sample sizes, we conducted a *post hoc* analysis whereby we converted each company's industry ratings to parallel those of an eight-company industry. Thus a company ranked third out of four would have a ranking of six out of eight, and so forth. On an across-company basis the correlation POP1MC2 was r_s = 0.46 and MC1POP2 was r_s = 0.34. The differential was a little smaller, but with the larger sample it more closely approached statistical significance with p = 0.13.

All in all, the differential in the second Cube One MC study (with a four-year inter-measurement interval) of 0.15 was greater than the differential in the two-year inter-measurement interval, which was 0.10. However, the sample size was reduced due to the passage of time. The magnitude of the differential in the Massimino and Kopelman study was 0.24, which, in part, may have reflected a measure of POP based on eight attributes versus three.

Results in the three MC studies can also be analyzed with a less rigorous, nonparametric statistical test, the binomial distribution. In seven out of nine independent cases, POP1MC2 was greater than MC1POP2. Assuming each correlation was equally likely to occur, the probability of seven out of nine findings being in the predicted direction is p = 0.07. If the composite results are included (even though they are not independent of the industry size data), there were ten out of 12 positive results, p = 0.016.

Statistical significance is not equivalent to practical significance. Statistical significance means that differences in group metrics are *not* likely to be the result of sampling error. One problem is that statistical significance can be found even with small differences if the sample size is large enough. Effect size is a more pertinent measure of practical significance. In the three studies described in this chapter, the POP1MC2 correlations were consistently large, at 0.62, 0.65, and 0.65; and they were larger than the MC1POP2 correlations which were. 0.38, 0.50, and 0.50.

The next four chapters present in-depth case studies and use the Cube One framework as a lens to explain organizational performance. The fourth case, on the Mayo Clinic, also presents statistical data that support the Cube One framework.

Notes

1 The median correlation between practices and Organizational Performance in Brazil was based on the use of the behavior-based measure.

2 Simon, H. A. (1954). "Spurious correlations: A causal interpretation." *Journal of the American Statistical Association*, 49(267), 467–479.

3 Wright, P. M., Gardner, T. M., Moynihan, L. M., and Allen, M. R. (2005). "The relationship between HR practices and firm performance: Examining causal order." *Personnel Psychology*, 58, 409–446.

4 Pelz, D. C., and Andrews, F. M. (1964). "Detecting causal priorities in panel study data." *American Sociological Review*, 29, 836–848. Quote is on page 848.

5 For instance, see Campbell, D. T., and Stanley, J. C. (1963). *Experimental and quasi-experimental designs for research*. Chicago: Rand-McNally.

6 Kenny, D. A. (1975). "Cross-lagged correlations: Practice and promise." *Psychological Bulletin*, 82, 887–903. The quote appears on page 891.

7 Pelz and Andrews, op. cit.

8 Lawler, Edward E., III. (1968). "A correlational-causal analysis of the relationship between expectancy attitudes and job performance." *Journal of Applied Psychology*, 52(6), 462–468. However, Schneider, B., Hanges, P. J., Smith, D. B., Salvaggio, A. N. (2003). in their research seemingly found "reverse causation." In their article, "Which comes first: Employee attitudes or organizational financial and market performance?" *Journal of Applied Psychology*, 88(5), 836–851, they seemingly found an opposite result compared to Lawler. In their most vivid situation, organizational financial performance was more predictive of employee satisfaction with job security than vice versa. Schneider and colleagues did not measure managerial practices, but various forms of employee satisfaction. It is logical that organizational financial performance would be more associated with subsequent satisfaction with employee job security satisfaction than that employee job security satisfaction would lead to financial performance.

9 Campbell and Stanley, op. cit.

10 Massimino, P. M., and Kopelman, R. E. (2012). "Management practices and organizational performance: A longitudinal analysis using cross-lagged data." *The Journal of Global Business Management*, 8(2), 58–65.

11 The article by Feldman, J. (1975). "Considerations in the use of causal-correlational techniques in applied psychology." *Journal of Applied Psychology*, 60(6), 663–670 points out that no correlational analysis can ever unambiguously demonstrate causality. As a methodological purist, Feldman also notes that many assumptions inhere in the use of cross-lagged correlations. These include linearity; a clearly defined causal system; a high degree of measurement reliability and validity; use of an interval scale; homoscedasticity. Technically speaking, analyzing multiple (three or more) waves of data using latent growth analysis is likely to provide a closer approximation to causality than a cross-lagged analysis. See Ployhart, R. E. and Vandenberg, R. J. (2010). "Longitudinal research: The theory, design, and analysis of change." *Journal of Management*, 36(1), 94–120.

12 The listing of the five attributes not examined is provided simply for completeness in reporting.

13 Because correlation coefficients are necessarily constrained (between −1 and 1), mean correlational results were computed after performing *r* to *z* transformations.

14 Kenny, D. A. (1975). Cross-lagged correlations: Practice and promise. *Psychological Bulletin*, 82, 887–903. The quote appears on page 894.

15 Fortune Datastore. (2008). Fortune corporate reputation industry reports. Retrieved at http://www.timeinc.net/fortune/datastore/reputation/index/html

16 Haygroup. (2008). Fortune's most admired companies. Retrieved at http://www.haygroup.com/ww/Best_Companies/Index.aspx?ID 1582

17 Reflecting the aforementioned *r* to *z* transformations.

18 Kopelman, R. E. (2010). "Validity evidence for the cube one framework: Examination of objective data." *The Journal of Global Business Management*, 6(1), 22–28.
19 The difference between correlations would have reached the conventional level of significance ($p < 0.05$) had the number of industries (k) been approximately 100 instead of 52. This number of observations would be on the low side of what Kenny, op. cit. defined as a moderate number of cases (75 to 300).
20 Kopelman, R. E. (2012). "Validity evidence for the Cube One framework: A cross-lagged panel analysis of objective data." *The Journal of Business Inquiry*, 11(1), 1–12.
21 Where the number of companies was small (three or four) once again the correlation between POP1MC2 was sizably greater than MC1POP2 at $r = 0.74$ ($p < 0.01$) versus at $r = 0.48$ ($p = 0.08$). The magnitudes of explained variance were respectively 55 versus 23%. However, given the small number of cases ($k = 14$), the differential was not significant, with $p = 0.23$.
22 In this instance the difference would have been statistically significant (one-tailed) if there had been approximately 80 industries instead of 36.

PART III

7

THE REMARKABLE TURNAROUND AT CONTINENTAL AIRLINES AS EXAMINED THROUGH THE LENS OF THE CUBE ONE FRAMEWORK

Thus far, the evidentiary support for the Cube One framework has been comprised of survey research conducted with five samples, and two studies examining financial metrics. All survey research effect were Medium to Large. This book next examines four case studies that provide additional support for the Cube One framework. With regard to proof, there is the apocryphal story of the practitioner who tired hearing about empirical studies, and asked for some real-life evidence.

As noted previously, case studies are reflective of the idiographic approach to studying a subject matter. Instead of seeking to find the few variables that provide a parsimonious explanation of variance, case studies permit a detailed and nuanced examination of a phenomenon.

A case study that tracks changes in management practices and examines subsequent longitudinal evidence of effects, parallels a quasi-experimental research design, but without the scientific rigor of cross-lagged correlational studies.[1] Often case studies lack a control or comparison group, so it is difficult to ascertain the magnitude of results, or the validity of a theory being invoked to explain findings.

In the case of Continental Airlines, results can be compared to industry outcomes with regard to four indicators of service performance: on-time percentage, mishandled baggage, denied boardings, and customer complaints. Data are examined for the ten major airlines over a ten-year period, including the longitudinal record of Continental's results. The data cover the five-year period before the intervention, and the five-year period after the intervention.

It is recognized that the four case studies in Chapters 7 to 10 are to some extent "dated." This is acknowledged. However, the recency of the facts of a case is not critical to assessing the validity of a model used to explain the observed phenomena. In terms of recency, the next chapter compares Google to another early Internet search company. The quest to remain up-to-date with Google would be akin to running after a moving train that is accelerating.

Continental Airlines Case

The remarkable turnaround at Continental Airlines during the 1990s provides a vehicle for using the Cube One framework to explain the results achieved. Although Gordon Bethune and Greg Brenneman did not frame their initiatives in terms of management practices that were enterprise-, customer-, and employee-directed, they nonetheless "touched all the bases."

Evidence of organizational performance is provided by comparing results during the five-year period before Bethune and his team arrived (1990–1994) with the five-year period afterward (1995–1999). Bethune and his team framed their actions in terms of their "Go Forward" plan, which included "Fly to Win." Clearly, these concepts are not pertinent to most organizations. How does a bakery fly to win?

Published versions of the Continental Airlines case have examined results from several perspectives, including corporate finance, leadership, and business management. The airline's executives have told the story of their achievements using the concepts they adopted to conceptualize and guide their actions. Their intervention, however, can be more clearly interpreted through the Cube One framework, which also extends the applicability of the Continental experience to other settings.

Continental Airlines: The Initial Situation

On October 24, 1994, Gordon Bethune was appointed interim CEO—for merely a ten-day period. After ten days Continental's board of directors would decide his future with the company. Bethune and Greg Brenneman, a turnaround consultant on retainer from Bain and Company, spent the ten days developing a plan for presentation to the board. Bethune successfully sold the plan to the board and was appointed CEO going forward; Brenneman became president. The improvement plan was implemented, and is examined through the lens of the Cube One framework.[2]

In November, the Board approved hiring Gordon Bethune. When he took command of Continental Airlines late in 1994, the company had gone through two bankruptcies (in 1983 and 1990) and had had ten chief executives in as many years. For the full year 1994, Continental lost $613 million (versus a loss of $199 million in 1993), and late in 1994 it appeared that the company was headed for its third bankruptcy. Continental was losing $55 million a month, had $40 million in cash, and would probably be unable to pay its 40,000 employees as of January 17, 1995.

These dismal financial results were not accidental; they were a reflection of Continental's poor service quality as measured by the U.S. Department of Transportation (DOT). For 1994, Continental ranked lowest of ten major airlines (the lowest being scored tenth out of ten) on three of the four key metrics: percentage of on-time arrivals; reports of mishandled baggage; and number of complaints to the DOT, with Continental having three times the number of complaints as the industry average. The carrier also was among the lowest on the fourth key metric: passengers with tickets who were denied boarding. As Bethune put it in his book, *From Worst to First*, "We weren't just the worst big airline. *We lapped the field.*"[3]

Employee morale was abysmal. Employees had suffered numerous layoffs, pay cuts, and pay freezes; and the promised wage "snap backs" and profit-sharing distributions never materialized. On-the-job injuries, turnover, and sick time were also very high and employees were not proud of where they worked. While visiting a Continental baggage ramp in Houston, Brenneman noted that almost all employees had torn the company's logo off their shirts. When one mechanic was asked why, he explained, "When I go to Wal-Mart tonight, I don't want anyone to know that I work for Continental."[4]

Pre-Bethune Management Practices at Continental

Enterprise-Directed Practices

As it existed in 1994, Continental Airlines was the result of numerous mergers and acquisitions, including the original Continental Airlines, Pioneer Airlines, Texas Air, People Express, New York Air, and Eastern Airlines. As a consequence, Continental flew 13 different types of airplanes. This made maintenance expensive, since numerous parts were required in multiple locations and mechanics had to be trained in different fleet types. Inefficiencies in matching aircraft to market size were common, with 120-seat passenger planes often flying with only 30 passengers. Capacity and demand were out of alignment. For example, six flights flew daily from Greensboro, N.C. to Greenville, S.C. and Brenneman dryly asked the scheduling team, "Why are we flying that route six times a day when both customers who want to fly that route are on the first flight?"[5] All told, 18% of all flights were cash-negative—especially the low-priced flights in the CALite division, the company's low-cost airline-within-an-airline that unsuccessfully tried to mimic the economies attained at Southwest Airlines.

According to Brenneman, the CALite division created several "doom loops." By focusing only on costs, Continental had created a product few travelers wanted to buy; this in turn created losses, which increased the costs of borrowing, which led the company to reduce wages, which reduced morale, and so forth. Further, the poor service quality that customers experienced on CALite flights spilled over so that travelers avoided choosing Continental for full-fare flights.[6]

Continental tried to reduce costs by rewarding pilots for saving fuel. Consequently, pilots slowed down their planes and turned off the air conditioning. "So the pilots were up front thinking they were doing great, while customers in the back were hot and late—not a good combination if you want to keep your customers happy."[7] This is another demonstration of a self-inflicted doom loop.

Customer-Directed Practices

According to Bethune, in 1994 Continental was a company "where everything went wrong, a place investors, employees, and most of all customers agreed they wanted nothing to do with"[8] As noted above, the quality of customer service per DOT metrics was the lowest of any major airline. Table 7.1 provides data summarizing annual DOT metrics for Continental Airlines during the focal periods of this case study: from 1990 to 1994 and from 1995 to 1999.

Before Bethune's arrival, Continental's award-winning frequent-flier program, OnePass, had been discontinued in another cost-saving effort, and business-class seating and food on many flights had been eliminated as well. But as Bethune noted, lowering costs and prices cannot succeed if the product is not something people want. It would be akin to making a really inexpensive pizza by leaving off the cheese. In his words (emphasis in original): "*I don't know of any successful company that doesn't have a good product.*"[9] Research has found that decreased customer satisfaction—which is what happened at Continental in the 1990s—has a greater impact on profitability than an equivalent increase would have had.[10]

Employee-Directed Practices

By 1994, after years of layoffs, wage freezes, wage cuts, and broken promises, the culture at Continental, according to Bethune,

> was one of backbiting, mistrust, fear, and loathing. People, to put it mildly, were not happy to come to work. They were surly to customers, surly toward each other, and ashamed of their company. And you can't have a good product without people who like coming to work. It just can't be done.[11]

Before Bethune took over Continental, the prevailing corporate approach to communication was to share only the information that legally was required to be shared. Employees typically learned about changes affecting the company from newspaper reports—after the fact. Consequently, wild rumors were common. Meanwhile, the exhaustive company manual of rules displayed management's lack of trust in its employees. The manual even included instructions on how to fold particular paper forms, and listed the penalties for failure to comply.

TABLE 7.1 Service Quality at Continental Airlines: 1990–1999

	1990	1991	1992	1993	1994	1995	1996	1997	1998	1999
On-Time	12/12	9/12	10/10	8/10	10/10	4/10	2/10	5/10	6/10	5/10
Mishandled Baggage	N/A	N/A	N/A	9/10	10/10	2/10	2/10	2/10	2/10	3/10
Denied Boardings	N/A	N/A	N/A	7/9	7/9	4/10	1/10	1/10	1/10	2/10
Complaints	N/A	N/A	N/A	8/9	9/9	9/10	3/10	4/10	5/10	4/10
Mean	12/12	9/12	10/10	8/9.5	9/9.5	4.75/10	2/10	3/10	3.5/10	3.5/10

Sources: Bureau of Transportation Statistics database. On-Time Performance Data 1990, 1991, 1992, made available online at http://www.transtats.bts.gov/Fields.asp?Table_ID=236 by Research and Innovative Technology Administration (RITA), Washington, DC; Air Travel Consumer Report 1993, 1994, 1995, 1996, 1997, 1998, 1999, published and made available online at http://airconsumer.dot.gov/reports/index.htm by Office of Aviation Enforcement and Proceedings, Washington, DC
Five-year average ranking 1990–1994 = 9.6 out of 10.6.
Five-year average ranking 1995–1999 = 3.35 out of 10.0.
Because Continental was in bankruptcy 1990–1992, only on-time performance data could be obtained for those years.

One of the employee perks for working for an airline is free passes when seats are available. But before Bethune, flight privileges generally were ignored, as they generated no cash flow. The poor predictability of flight arrivals increased employee stress. If a flight attendant's plane was scheduled to land at 3 p.m., she couldn't promise to be home for a 7 p.m. school recital.

Bethune's Summary of the Before Situation

Continental before Bethune was (in Bethune's words) a "crummy" place to work, with "very unhappy employees, a rotten product, no money on hand (and not much coming in) and a backbreaking debt structure." Moreover, he noted, the company "flew the wrong planes to the wrong cities for the wrong prices, and they were usually late to boot."[12] With their turnaround program, Bethune and his colleagues did virtually all the right things, taking Continental from Cube 27— the lowest in Cube One's three-dimensional taxonomy—to Cube One.

If one is in search of ways to mismanage an organization, the practices enacted by Continental pre-Bethune can serve as a template. For an organization that adopts the enterprise-, customer-, and employee-directed practices of Continental before Bethune (i.e., being in Cube 27), failure is virtually assured.

Post-Bethune Management Practices at Continental

Enterprise-Directed Practices

Bethune had had no choice but to furlough many employees during the first year of the turnaround. Inaction in reducing expenses would have cost the jobs of the remaining 30,000 other employees. But to mitigate the pain of the staff reductions, Continental moved as many employees as it could to alternate locations, and paid their relocation costs, if a facility had to close. In other cases, terminated employees were kept on the payroll for a month and given help in finding other work.

Beginning in 1995, Bethune implemented numerous enterprise-directed practices. The company closed a major hub and associated maintenance facilities, furloughing 7,000 employees. Fifty of the 61 vice-presidents were replaced by about 20 people. Continental reduced its 13 types of aircraft to five, with plans to further reduce to four, thereby saving millions of dollars in training and maintenance. Continental made better matches of aircraft with market demand, and canceled many unprofitable routes and destinations—which Bethune characterized as flying to places people did not want to go.

Continental began phasing out the money-losing CALite operation. In 19 cities where Continental flew only a few flights a day, the company determined that contracting out ramp work (baggage handling, plane cleaning, etc.) would save money. Employees were shown the books so they could see the costs, along with competing bids from contractors. In 17 of the 19 cities, Continental workers submitted and won competitive bids, finding creative ways to lower costs. In New

Orleans, for example, workers eliminated the distinction between gate and ramp personnel, with employees working upstairs on some days and downstairs on others. Everyone kept their job.

Continental adopted a profit-sharing plan to motivate employees to help improve corporate performance. The plan distributed 15% of all pre-tax profits to employees in February, around Valentine's Day. Bethune recalls,

> On a recent flight I took, the cabin was full and, as usual, the passengers had plenty of questions and problems that kept the flight attendants hopping. … I stepped into the galley and saw one flight attendant take a breath and let out a sigh of frustration. 'It's hard work,' I said, 'but don't forget—these full flights mean more in your profit-sharing check come February.' She gave me a smile. 'I know,' she said. 'Believe me. I know.'[13]

Customer-Directed Practices

In 1995, Continental began focusing on improved service quality. On-time arrival had consistently been found to be the most important factor in determining customer satisfaction (per J. D. Power surveys), so Continental monitored and rewarded that metric. In January 1995, the company announced that all employees (except managers) would receive a $65 monthly bonus if Continental was among the top half of large airlines in on-time arrivals.

Whereas in January 1994, only 61% of Continental flights had been on time, In January 1995, 71% were on time (good enough for seventh place out of ten large airlines). Within a month after announcing the potential bonus (in February 1995), 80% of flights landed on time, good enough for fourth place, and Continental distributed $2.5 million worth of bonus checks (deliberately kept separate from paychecks). This practice continued on a monthly basis—with the individual bonus amount later raised to $100 if Continental was in the top three in both on-time arrivals and baggage handling.

Continental posted monthly DOT metrics in 600 common areas, enabling employees to track performance. As Table 7.1 shows, service quality improved rapidly and dramatically.

Continental restored the popular OnePass program, along with business-class seats and meals on most flights. The failed CALite experiment was terminated.

Because Continental was the "residue" (Bethune's term) of the merger of six airlines, its planes bore different insignias. Bethune had all aircraft freshly painted with the same logo in 1995.

Employee-Directed Practices

As employees' initial skepticism faded, their attitudes improved dramatically. For six years in a row, from 1997 through 2002, Continental was listed among *Fortune's* top 100 places to work. Continental employees became known for their "high commitment behavior," such as the gate agent who boarded a passenger at the last minute, and then ran downstairs to help load bags onto the aircraft.

Before Bethune, employees had to follow detailed rules to the letter, with no exceptions permitted—even if the rules did not seem to make sense. For instance, if two passengers were flying together, one at full price but the other at a discount, and their plane was taken out of service or delayed, policy called for putting the full-fare passenger on the next competitor's flight and requiring the accompanying discounted-fare passenger to wait for the next Continental flight. This so angered passengers and gate agents that Bethune literally burned the manuals in a public ceremony, and employees were empowered to do what made the most sense for customers and the company in any given situation.

Flight attendants were given discretion in solving problems. If, for example, the caterer brought five too few meals, instead of waiting for the caterer to return to the kitchen for five meals—causing a flight delay—flight attendants could trade drinks for meals, and achieve on-time departure. Thanks to the countless ways Continental employees used their discretion to improve customer satisfaction for the 100,000 passengers on its 2,100 daily flights, complaints about Continental to the DOT declined from a monthly average of 68 in 1994 to 26 in April 1995.

Improved communication was central to the turnaround. Bethune instructed top managers to tell groups of employees in person about impending changes, and give workers a chance to offer their opinions—which initially were quite bitter and skeptical. Bethune noted that it is more important to share bad news than good news. When wage "snap backs" were not going to occur immediately after the company became profitable—as had been promised in the 1993 bankruptcy resolution agreement—employees were notified in advance. The company opened its financial books and explained to employees why they would have to wait longer.

Because employees might be reluctant to voice their views in public meetings, Bethune established an 800 telephone number that only he answered. The company also monitored, on a flight-by-flight basis, the number of employees who sought flight passes and the number of empty seats at takeoff. With these data in hand, the company figured out how to provide more free flights for employees.

How Bethune and Brenneman Characterized Their Intervention

Bethune and Brenneman shared their comprehensive turnaround plan with employees in January 1995. Their "Go Forward" plan consisted of four components, which included practices directed at productivity, customers, and employees. All of them were implemented simultaneously.

- The "Fly to Win" facet combined actions that improved cost-effectiveness, such as closing a hub and letting 7,000 employees go, and expanded the customer base to include more first-class and business-class travelers, as opposed to the low-cost travelers known as "backpacks and flip-flops." It also enhanced market presence by restoring OnePass, the popular frequent flier plan that had been discontinued as a cost-reduction measure.

- The "Fund the Future" component also focused on improving efficiency and finances. Continental sold aircraft, and matched craft size to market size. They reduced the number of types of aircraft from 13 to five.
- The "Make Reliability a Reality" portion of the turnaround focused on measuring, improving, and rewarding service in terms of DOT quality metrics. Every non-managerial employee received a monthly bonus if Continental achieved above-average performance in on-time arrivals. Later, Continental included baggage handling as a bonus criterion, and instituted profit sharing.
- "Working Together" included expanding employee discretion, improving flight schedule reliability, improving communication with employees, and encouraging respect and trust.

As can be seen, Bethune and Brenneman conceptualized a four-point plan in terms that are not easily generalizable to other contexts. The names given to the categories or dimensions also do not make clear the specific practices to be implemented; viz, "fly to win," "working together." Nonetheless, as seen above, Bethune and Brenneman implemented practices that were enterprise-, customer-, and employee-directed. A schematic showing specific examples of Continental's enterprise-, customer-, and employee-directed practices embedded in the Cube One framework is provided in Figure 7.1.

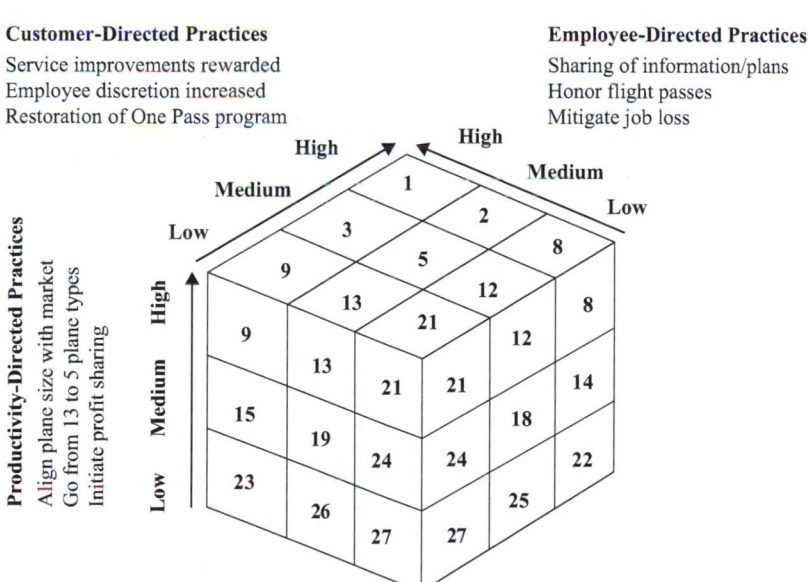

Customer-Directed Practices
Service improvements rewarded
Employee discretion increased
Restoration of One Pass program

Employee-Directed Practices
Sharing of information/plans
Honor flight passes
Mitigate job loss

Productivity-Directed Practices
Align plane size with market
Go from 13 to 5 plane types
Initiate profit sharing

FIGURE 7.1 Schematic Representation of Continental Airlines' Practices Within the Cube One Framework

Viewing Continental's practices through the lens of the Cube One framework, a generalizable explanation as to why Bethune and Brenneman's intervention was successful is provided. Bethune and Brenneman took Continental from Cube 27 to Cube One.

Gauging the Impact of the Changes

In terms of quality of service provided, the data in Table 7.1 are quite compelling. During the first five-year period, mean service rankings were 9.6 out of 10.6; i.e., on average Continental was roughly in tenth place out of 11 airlines. For the second five-year period, mean rankings rose to 3.35 out of 10. In 1996 and 1997, J. D. Power rated Continental the best airline with flights of 500 miles or more—in essence, the best large commercial airline in the U.S.

Many investors agreed that Continental's performance and prospects had improved. The stock price soared from $3.25 before Bethune to more than $50 in 1997. Market capitalization data, provided in Table 7.2, permit comparison of Continental to the other large airlines. Continental's market capitalization went up by a multiple of 5.6 from the first to the second five-year interval. In contrast, market capitalizations of the other large airlines increased by a multiple of 2.6.

The turnaround at Continental has been widely viewed as remarkable. It has even been described as "incredible," and "nothing short of astronomical." These last descriptors are from Nitin Nohria (currently the Dean of Harvard Business School), and colleagues.[14]

Nonetheless, Continental was far from a perfect airline even after the first five years under Bethune. According to Continental's chief technology officer, by 2002 the company still had a clunky mainframe-based IT system that was inflexible and not designed for customer service.[15] Before Bethune retired in 2004, though, Continental launched another improvement program, "First to Favorite," which began consolidating disparate IT and customer relationship management systems to create integrated, cross-enterprise systems.

The before-and-after case study research design is pre-experimental and is perforce subject to methodological limitations. The evidence cannot confirm unequivocally the validity of any theory, as the independent variables (practices) outnumber the data points, yielding zero degrees of freedom. Nor can we establish the validity of a theory by adducing supportive evidence. Science is most successful when competing hypotheses are tested, and one of the hypotheses can be falsified.[16] Thus, finding data supportive or consistent with a theory cannot unequivocally establish its validity.

Yet, it is hard to attribute the success of Continental to other causes than the management intervention by Bethune and Brenneman. Was it mere coincidence that service quality went roughly from tenth out of ten to third out of ten; the stock price went up more than 15-fold, and the market capitalization rose at approximately two and a half times the industry average.

TABLE 7.2 Year-End Market Capitalizations of Major Airlines: 1990–1999

	1990	1991	1992	1993	1994	1995	1996	1997	1998	1999
CAL	0	0	0	512,964	247,346	1,193,342	1,579,961	2,818,929	2,008,217	3,070,124
AMR	3,014,004	4,817,053	5,088,352	5,075,250	4,040,343	5,669,136	8,013,646	11,715,473	10,826,615	9,921,561
DAL	2,362,127	3,267,434	2,528,436	2,742,448	2,555,603	3,766,434	5,292,803	8,806,933	7,425,132	6,618,387
NWAC	0	0	0	0	1,328,244	4,658,646	3,818,756	4,968,515	2,077,285	1,879,457
LUV	737,572	1,440,484	2,726,183	5,199,909	2,398,281	3,310,436	3,188,152	5,435,205	7,631,167	8,134,030
UAL	2,408,874	3,462,582	3,056,765	3,570,430	1,085,983	2,261,059	3,662,437	5,437,427	3,170,958	4,151,455
U	711,144	559,762	600,882	761,672	257,371	827,754	1,500,207	5,705,250	4,545,320	2,291,154

Source: The Center for Research in Security Prices online database accessed via Wharton Research Data Services at http://wrds.wharton.upenn.edu/.
Note: CAL (Continental Airlines), AMR (American Airlines), DAL (Delta), NWAC (Northwest Airlines), LUV (Southwest Airlines), UAL (United Airlines), U (US Airways). TWA not listed because of bankruptcy status.

The Cube One framework is complex, in that some enacted practices do not lie on just one plane in the three-dimensional model shown in Figure 7.1. For instance, measuring on-time arrivals and rewarding employees for improvements in service quality likely affected all three dimensions. Productivity, customer satisfaction, and employee satisfaction all increased. However, many practices can clearly be classified as primarily directed toward one of the three dimensions.

All in all, the Cube One framework provides a systematic way to think about the key determinants of organizational performance, and a way to interpret instances of organizational success and failure. Such a framework is especially valuable in today's increasingly competitive global environment, and is consistent with the call for ways to integrate theoretical research and practical application.

Brief Epilogue: Meeting the Challenges of a New Century

How has Continental fared in the decade after Bethune's retirement in 2004? Two of the key practices implemented under Bethune and his team—monthly bonuses and profit sharing—continued after Bethune's retirement. Evidently some of the momentum also continued, as *Fortune* magazine ranked Continental the most admired airline in the U.S. for the years 2004 to 2008. Quality of service performance did drift down, though, from the mean ranking of 3.35 out of 10 during the years 1995–1999. Between 2000 and 2004, Continental's mean service ranking was barely above average at 6.5 out of 13.5, and during the subsequent five years the ranking was essentially unchanged—at 10.65 out of 19.75. With regard to market capitalization data, only three large airlines had shares that traded continuously during the ten-year period of 2000 to 2009: Continental, American, and Southwest. The mean market value of Continental Airlines shares increased 71% in the period 2005–2009, compared to 2000–2004. In contrast, the market valuation at American increased by 37%, and the value decreased by 27% at Southwest. (The Southwest decline may reflect reversion to the mean. The valuation was very high during 2000 to 2004, the amount being nearly twice that of Continental and American combined.)

In 2010, Continental merged with United Airlines. Continental announced the merger by taking out full-page print ads with the droll caption: "With this wing I thee wed." On January 1, 2011, the newly formed company announced that employees had the opportunity to earn $100 a month and a chance to earn a "13th month" bonus if on-time performance for the year reached 80% or greater. How well United/Continental continues to address the needs of its investors, customers, and employees will, no doubt, determine its performance in the decade ahead.

Notes

1 Campbell, D. T., and Stanley, J. C. (1963). *Experimental and quasi-experimental designs for research*. Chicago: Rand-McNally. Case studies are classified as pre-experimental.
2 An earlier version of the Continental Airlines case was published in a professional journal and used with permission by Wiley. The citation is: Kopelman, R. E., and Chiou, A.

Y. (2011). "Getting organizational improvement off the ground: Using the Cube One framework to learn from the turnaround at Continental Airlines." *Global Business and Organizational Excellence*, 30(4), 29–39.

3 Bethune, G. (1998). *From worst to first: Behind the scenes of Continental's remarkable comeback.* New York: John Wiley & Sons. The quote is on p. 4, emphasis in original. Additional interpretations of the Continental story include D'Agostino, D. (2006). "Case study: Continental airline's tech strategy takes off." Retrieved at http://www.cioinsigh t.com/c/a/CasStudies/CaseStudy-Continental-Airlines-Tech-Strategy-Takes-Off/. Accessed on November 5, 2010. Also see Sutherland, M. 2000. "Continental airlines." Case published by the Stanford Business School (revised July 05). (This case focuses on finance issues at Continental.)

4 Brenneman, G. (1998). "Right away and all at once: How we saved Continental." *Harvard Business Review*. (HBR Reprint 4193, 2000). The quote appears on p. 10.

5 Op. cit., p. 5.

6 Ibid.

7 Nohria, N. Mayo, A. J., and Benson, M. (2006/2009). "Gordon Bethune at Continental Airlines." Harvard Business School Case 406-073 (revised 16 June, 2009 case 9-406-073). The quote appears on p. 12.

8 Bethune, op. cit., p. 9.

9 Bethune, op. cit., p. 101.

10 Keiningham, T., and Vavra, T. (2001). *The customer delight principle: Exceeding customers' expectations for bottom-line success.* New York, NY: McGraw-Hill.

11 Bethune, op. cit., p. 14. Quotation reproduced with permission of Wiley. Copyright © 1998 by John Wiley & Sons.

12 Bethune, op. cit., p. 75.

13 Bethune, op. cit., pp. 243–244. Quotation reproduced with permission of Wiley. Copyright © 1998 by John Wiley & Sons.

14 Mayo, A. J., Nohria, N., and Rennella, M. (2009). *Entrepreneurs, managers, and leaders: What the airline industry can teach us about leadership.* New York, NY: Palgrave Macmillan.

15 D'Agostino, D. (2006). "Case study: Continental airline's tech strategy takes off." Retrieved at http://www.cioinsight.com/c/a/Case-Studies/Case-Study-Continental -Airlines-Tech-Strategy-Takes-Off/.

16 Platt, J. R. (1964). "Strong inference." *Science*, 146, 348–353.

8

GOOGLE AND ALTAVISTA

Two Pioneers in Internet Searches

In the prior chapter, the Continental Airlines case examined before-and-after data. The changes implemented by Gordon Bethune and Greg Brenneman, were entirely consonant with the Cube One framework; and were perfectly synchronized with the subsequent improvements in operating performance. The changes resulted in (or at least were closely followed by) positive outcomes—the most encompassing being the increase in the stock price within two years, from $3.25 to more than $50 per share. Viewing the changes through the lens of the Cube One framework provides support for the validity of the model.[1]

Rather than employing a before-and-after design, this chapter examines two companies in the same industry: one that became extraordinarily successful; the other extinct.[2] Both AltaVista and Google were pioneers in Internet searches. In fact, the former had the "first mover" advantage, accompanied by a cadre of devoted and loyal users. We can explain the different outcomes by examining the enterprise-, customer-, and employee-directed practices the two companies enacted.

The initial case study covers the period through 2010. We describe subsequent events in an epilogue, and examine them through the lens of the Cube One framework. This framework need only be valid at explaining phenomena during the focal time frame (from December, 1995, when AltaVista was founded up until 2010); however, it is also pertinent to the period from 2011 to 2017.

Google

Founded on September 7, 1998, Google rose from relative obscurity to become a seemingly overnight miracle. Indeed, Google is one of the greatest successes in business history. Stories about Google's main complex in Mountain View, Calif.

carry a legendary aura, and the company's placement at the top of *Fortune* magazine's Top 100 Best Companies to Work For has cemented its position as an excellent employer.

Google's service offerings alone, while outstanding, would hardly be enough to warrant the company's extraordinary accolades. The main search engine is impressive, but Google's other services face stiff competition. Gmail, Google's email service, provides a clean, sleek interface, but it is not the only company to offer unlimited email storage space. (Yahoo! was the first to do so.) Google Talk, Google's instant messaging service, is also clean and bare-bones, but still fights for users among industry giants such as Skype (which Google acquired in 2011), AOL Instant Messenger, and Microsoft's Windows Live Messenger. Google's web browser, Chrome, has also received less than enthusiastic responses from Internet users accustomed to the features of more mature offerings such as Mozilla Firefox and Microsoft Internet Explorer. However, in 2006, Google acquired a prime Internet property, YouTube, and a few years later created considerable excitement about two forthcoming products: Google Wave, which would allow users to share photos simply by dragging and dropping; and Google's remote GPS, which would speak travel directions and provide traffic information.

As a company to emulate, Google differs from traditional companies in that it offers almost no direct contact with its end users. Google has neither sales representatives nor service providers (such as greeters or flight attendants) to provide a more personal touch. Still, Google manages to attract an almost fanatical following. Its corporate culture is widely perceived as spontaneous and fun-loving, but Google's success was not accidental. The company has introduced various practices that helped it attain its current position. These practices come to the fore when the company's performance is analyzed through the lens of the Cube One framework.

Enterprise-Directed Practices

There are an almost unlimited number of enterprise-directed practices that could be cited in connection with any company. Below are practices that seem particularly pertinent to Google's success.

Google Conducts Its Business in a Planned and Cost-Effective Manner

Despite Google's freewheeling and casual image, the company develops new projects cautiously and is driven by two primary concerns: user interest and profit-and-loss calculations.[3] When either profitability or user interest is lacking, Google will terminate the project and either reassign or lay off the programmers. One such example is Google's Lively project. Originally designed as a "network of avatars and virtual rooms created and decorated by its users"[4] (*Lively—3D Avatars and Rooms*) much akin to Linden Lab's *Second Life*, the project existed for a mere four months. After accumulating only 10,000 visits in a seven-day period Google pulled the plug on January 1, 2009.[5]

Google Hires Employees in a Systematic Fashion

Google's hiring processes are legendarily complex. Applicants face numerous rounds of interviews, often stretched over a period of months—and sometimes they are assigned "homework" to turn in.[6] Applicants also face challenges such as estimating the number of trees in New York City's Central Park, or solving complex mathematical equations. During Google's formative years (until 2000) a hiring committee, comprised almost entirely of employees, made all the hiring decisions. They interviewed every applicant, and often discussed and debated potential hires for hours. Google's founders, Larry Page and Sergey Brin, insisted on this method of grilling applicants to avoid Silicon Valley's infamous "hiring spiral," in which each successive wave of employees hires employees who are less capable and therefore less threatening to themselves.[7]

Google's hiring criteria are demanding and objective. The first requirement is a very high Grade Point Average (GPA) from an elite university.[8] The Internet abounds with examples of applicants who were not hired for GPA-related reasons—for example, because of a "C" grade during sophomore year.[9] Although the conventional corporate wisdom is that GPAs do not matter as much as experience, Google's stringent hiring practices have yielded an exceptionally capable workforce. In an effort to expedite the hiring process, Google has started to examine data on nearly 300 variables—including number of languages spoken, age when first using a computer, and number of patents held.[10]

Employees Are Cross-Trained and Empowered

At Google, almost no employee is a specialist in the traditional sense. Google's engineers are not trained for specific tasks. They work on multiple projects. Engineers are allowed—indeed encouraged—to mingle with their colleagues and participate in the projects that capture their interests. One of the methods by which Google accomplishes this is by sharing prodigious amounts of data internally. Project details are not kept secret from the rest of the company.

The Organization Continuously Seeks to Improve Productivity

Apart from offering employees sabbaticals and new career opportunities, Google seeks to expand its employee experiences via external means. For example, in November, 2008, Google began job swaps with Proctor and Gamble.[11] Google employees working at P&G are able to see how a preeminent consumer product company executes its marketing campaigns, including the details and planning.

Beyond developing Google employees, this experience no doubt enhances Google's ability to absorb new management and marketing practices, both being necessary for continued rapid growth.

Organization Infrastructure Is Continuously Improved

An example of an economical infrastructure improvement is Google's use of "White Box" servers constructed out of industry-standard parts. This enabled the company to obtain the performance of an $800,000 IBM server at a cost of $250,000.[12] Moreover, whereas a typical company's server resides on one computer, and is usually hard to update, Google's approach allows updating almost at will. By spreading data and work processes across many computers, Google can wait until one cluster of servers is completely dead before replacing it entirely with up-to-date machines without so much as a slowdown in service. This allows Google to keep pace with new developments in computer hardware and software, instead of relying on outdated computers.

Employee-Directed Practices

Management Facilitates Two-Way Communication with Employees

All employees are required to write five lines each week on Google's internal company website about what they did the previous week. These reports are open for all to see. Google also has an "ideas mailing list" that circulates new product ideas among employees. Many of Google's innovative products have resulted from these company-wide brainstorming activities, including Gmail and Google's plan to digitize books.[13]

Departments Collaborate and Solve Problems Together

Believing that the collective is far greater than the sum of its parts, Google prides itself on its group-based work environment. Projects are developed by small groups that are formed and dissolved as needed. As Google CEO Eric Schmidt has put it, "there is much greater progress if you have many small teams going out at once."[14]

The flexible team approach was not implemented from Google's inception. In 2001, Google used a traditional approach to team management. Employees were organized into teams that reported to managers, who reported to Page and Brin.[15] But the two founders felt the company had become sluggish, so they decided on a more flexible approach: cutting out middle management and having hundreds of small groups of employees work on projects simultaneously while reporting directly to them.[16]

Google does not expect every project to succeed. Successful projects are quickly developed into more mature offerings, while groups working on projects headed nowhere are disbanded and reformed into new project groups.[17] In an interview with University of Washington students, Schmidt explained, "We try to keep it small. You just don't get productivity out of large groups."[18] Further, to foster collaboration, Google eschews private offices. Employees often are crammed into close quarters in order to get things done.[19]

Customer-Directed Practices

Google Has a Customer-Centric Philosophy

Google provides many products that enable customers to interact with their environment, such as search, Gmail, and YouTube. However, the company does not have customer service personnel who interact with users in a traditional sense. Individuals who contact Google regarding search or advertisement concerns are usually greeted with automated responses. Google strives to earn customer trust in other ways. Indeed, its success rests heavily on the trust its users have in the company and its offerings; and Google's motto, "Don't be evil," captures the foundation of this effort. Still, many Internet users question the virtue of some of Google's actions, such as a search algorithm that exposes a great deal of the searcher's personal information, or Google Maps, which provide photographs of residential buildings. Consequently, Google strives to convince users that the company is mindful of their privacy concerns.

Google Seeks Customer Feedback for Product Improvement

User feedback is an important contributor to Google's product development. Most telling is Google's eagerness to accept user feedback in the form of blogs. While the company maintains a main blog site, every project under development at Google also has its own blog site where project progress is continuously monitored and users are encouraged to share their thoughts in an effort to improve the final product.[20]

Product/Services Are Continuously Improved

"Beta" status software, a term traditionally used to denote an initial test version not ready for public consumption, has frequently been used by Google almost as a tag line on its projects. In fact, so many of Google's projects are known for having a seemingly eternal "beta" status that even the official company blog acknowledges this with good humor.[21] This policy stems from Google's quest for perfection and the belief that perpetual refinement of a product is the basis for future success.[22] This practice of ongoing refinement facilitates bringing excellent products to users while maintaining the flexibility to update them as desired.[23]

A Wide Range of Products/Services Is Available

Although its origins are rooted in the Google search engine, the company has since branched out to become a complete online services provider. Gmail offers email services to regular users, and provides a solutions package for organizations and corporate customers (*Google Communicate*). Gmail is included as part of Google Apps, which encompasses not only email, but also Google Calendar, an agenda management solution; Google Docs, an online-based office suite; Google Sites for setting up web pages; and Google Video for customers to host and share their videos. As of 2010, more than two million businesses ran Google Apps, and this just scratches the surface of what Google provides its users. Google Maps not only provides basic street maps all over the world, but includes a built-in directory to search for businesses and services, and can be coupled with either real-time traffic information or mass-transit schedules to provide users the quickest route to their destination. Furthermore, all of Google's popular services are accessible via mobile phones.

Google also has made advances offline. The G1 phone was a potential competitor to the well-established Apple iPhone; likewise, in 2008, Google's Chrome Internet browser started to compete directly with Microsoft. One year later, Google unveiled Chrome OS, an operating system even more squarely aimed at Microsoft.[24]

Product/Service Lapses Are Followed by Quick and Effective Recoveries

In September of 2009, Google's popular online office service, Apps, suffered a major service outage that also affected Gmail. Because many enterprises and educational organizations relied on Apps and Gmail for their internal email usage, this service outage had wide-ranging negative effects.[25] During the recovery process which took 90 minutes, by no means a quick and immediate recovery, Google continuously updated users as to the status of the recovery via its Apps Status Dashboard website. An almost play-by-play report of what Google was doing to restore service, and an estimated time when full service would be restored, was provided on this website.[26] This transparency and real-time communication about the restoration of service went far to alleviate customer concerns.

Employee-Directed Practices

Google Grants Employees Considerable Autonomy

The most famous—and probably most beloved—example of the autonomy that Google grants its employees is the "20 percent rule." Employees are encouraged to spend 20% of their working hours (either spread out or batched) pursuing projects that interest them, with the understanding that these side projects may be adopted by the company as part of Google's products and services lineup. These projects have ranged from improving existing services to saving the planet. When a software engineer is reassigned or recruited into a new team, the project team leader is expected to allow the engineer to continue to work on the 20% side project(s) with no interference.

Although the sanctity of the 20 percent rule has caused some griping among team leaders who feel that they have to compete for the attention of software engineers, Google has gained many unexpected synergies out of side projects—such as Gmail and Google News, which are now some of the most popular services.[27] Side projects need not be geared toward external users; employees may also focus on internal projects. (The Google shuttle, described below, was born out of a 20 percent time project.) Another example of a successful outgrowth is the development of the "Testing grouplet" to detect flaws in software code while a project is still in the early stages of development.

Google Provides a Comfortable, Amenity-Laden Work Environment

Google's renowned perks enable employees to focus on their work more effectively, free from worries about mundane details of life. Employees have on-premises access to laundry services, haircuts, daycare, physicians, and more. One of the most often noted perks is the exceptionally high-quality food offered at Google's Mountain View campus, ranging from Irish oatmeal with fresh berries to roasted quail—all at no cost to employees. In an interview with ZDNet, Google's chief culture officer, Stacy Sullivan, stated that food was the most appreciated perk.[28] According to Sullivan, every Google field office offers food service, with cafeterias and hired chefs available whenever space permits. Google cofounders Page and Brin believe that "no employee should be more than 150 feet from a food source."[29]

Another distinctive characteristic of the work environment—one that may be seen as unfavorable by some employees—is the relative scarcity of private offices. A recent article noted that employees "[give] up their big space to be crammed in this [conference] room to get things done" (Lashinsky, 2007). Presumably, employees with a high need for intellectual stimulation see this feature as not being a big negative.[30]

Retaining the best employees is perhaps even more crucial than recruiting the best candidates. Thus, Google CEO Schmidt stated, Google has "no intention of getting rid of these really important aspects of culture."[31] Purportedly, the rationale for the founders having shares with a 10-to-1 voting ratio compared to regular shares was to prevent shareholders from voting to cut what Page and Brin saw as important Google perks.[32]

Google Keeps Employees Informed

By sharing prodigious amounts of data internally with its employees, Google's managers not only achieve a high level of employee productivity and creativity, but also enhance employee satisfaction and loyalty. The implicit but clear message is that employees can be trusted with highly sensitive information.

Google Encourages Employees to Balance Work Life and Private Life

A perk that rivals the food service in popularity among Google employees is the company's shuttle service—also provided free of charge.[33] Google operates 32 shuttle buses at its Mountain View campus, which serve more than 1,200 employees, or one-quarter of the Google workforce in Silicon Valley.[34] The shuttles operate on two shifts, and have leather seats and wireless Internet access. The shuttles also allow pets and bikes, but do not allow loud personal cell-phone calls—all told, "an unparalleled transit network."[35] The main purpose of Google's shuttle service is to free employees from the burdens of navigating rush-hour traffic, thereby reducing stress, and possibly gaining extra hours of work.[36]

Employees who choose to drive instead of taking the shuttle receive a $5,000 subsidy toward the purchase of a hybrid car. Google also provides a $500 subsidy that covers food costs for employees with newborns, helping them through the hectic first four weeks.[37]

Google Satisfies Employees' Developmental Goals

Although the perks are outstanding and pay levels are high at Google (for example, in 2006, employees earned up to $130,000 *plus* stock grants and stock options) compensation is not the primary motivation for many employees; personal development is. Career development and growth opportunities include working on challenging technical, managerial, and financial problems; having the opportunity to work and network with high-achieving individuals; and building human capital by participating in the job-swapping program. Google has also initiated a sabbatical program to allow employees to recharge their intellectual energies.

Conclusion

It is clear that during its first dozen years, Google adopted management, marketing, and human resource practices that resulted in exceptional levels of productivity and creativity, excellent customer satisfaction, and high levels of employee satisfaction and loyalty. Per the Cube One framework, it is reasonable to classify Google in Cube One (High, High, High).

Once again, it should be noted that some practices affect more than one dimension of the Cube One framework. For example, Google's provision of excellent transit and food service not only had employee-directed, but also enterprise-directed effects. Employees could think about work-related matters while commuting and did not need to stop working to get food. Because practices can have the effect of inhabiting three-dimensional space, it is not appropriate to count the number of practices primarily directed to the enterprise, customers, and employees.

AltaVista

Today, some users of the Internet (those with decades of experience) will recall that AltaVista was the first true search engine. During its time, AltaVista was the first website to facilitate rapid search results (instead of the "crawl" associated with browsing via pre-written programs). AltaVista's primacy, however, lasted only until it was acquired in 1998 by Compaq—a mini-computer company—after which it was rapidly overtaken by Google. Google and AltaVista shared several characteristics. Both companies were originally dedicated to search, and both informed the public that Internet information was available to regular users. The disparity in their eventual development, however, has led many commentators to speculate about what went wrong at AltaVista.

Originally launched by Digital Equipment Corporation (DEC), AltaVista gained acclaim not only from the press, but also from users.[38] In 1995, people marveled at the possibility of using key words to search the Internet,[39] and Lewis reported that AltaVista offered the "fastest and most precise information agent on the Web."[40] Some commentators feared that AltaVista's indexing capabilities might overwhelm the Internet, an idea that seems quaintly implausible today. Books were published to help users make the most out of AltaVista search engine commands.[41] Although the AltaVista engine quickly gained users, there were signs that all was not well in the kingdom of DEC.

Customer-Directed Practices

Customer-Directed Practices That Partly Missed the Mark

With regard to the Cube One framework, a review of some of the practices that AltaVista implemented to foster customer satisfaction shows that the company was only partially on track to succeed.

Conflicted Goals Hampered Product and Service Offerings

Rather than emphasizing AltaVista's search capabilities, the company's vice president of corporate research emphasized the ability of DEC's Alpha computers to run the AltaVista search engine.[42] In 1996, DEC planned to spin off AltaVista into a separate company with the goal of receiving "recognition for developing a cutting-edge Internet technology [that would] boost sales of Digital computers."[43] But, based on interviews with DEC employees, John Battelle, author of *The Search* (a 2005 book about Google and its rivals) concluded that the initial plan was to utilize AltaVista solely to showcase DEC's Alpha computers—there being no long-term plan for growing the AltaVista search business.[44] As a result, AltaVista received neither sufficient funding nor the staff needed for rapid product development and market expansion in the crucial early months of growth.[45] The reticence about making a commitment to AltaVista apparently reflected a pervasive cultural problem at DEC, which Edgar Schein, author *of DEC is Dead, Long Live DEC: The Lasting Legacy of Digital Equipment Corporation*, characterized as resulting from an academic approach to business. In his in-depth study of the culture at DEC, Schein found constant foot-dragging with projects being "reviewed to death."[46]

AltaVista Made a Wide Range of Products/ Services, but Lacked Focus

Even during the dark times, innovation at AltaVista brought glimmers of hope. Early in 1998, the company unveiled a service that permitted translation of entire web pages between English and various other languages. Named Babel Fish, the service quickly caught on as many used free translation services for email and chatting.[47] AltaVista Discovery—a free desktop search program also launched in 1998, that enabled users to search through files on their own computers—similarly garnered positive reviews from various sources.[48] Around this same time, AltaVista also began providing free email services, along with user home pages, instant messaging, shopping capabilities, and a range of branded content.[49] With this bustle of activity, AltaVista continued to enjoy a reputation for strong technology—but with hazy prospects for making money, it also invited the question, "What is their business?"[50]

Enterprise-Directed Practices

By 1996, AltaVista's lack of solid revenues became apparent, as AltaVista under DEC did not sell ads, but rather, sought to license its search technology to organizations for internal corporate use.[51] By the end of 1996, AltaVista's hoped-for initial public offering (IPO) was nowhere in sight, and DEC started to allow the sale of ads to boost its business prospects. This change apparently led to confusion among dedicated users, who had grown accustomed to ad-free searches.[52]

Greatly hampered by limited resources and staffing, AltaVista eventually failed to keep pace with technological change in the realities of search, according to Louis Monier, the founder and primary engineer who designed the AltaVista search engine algorithm.[53] Monier revealed that AltaVista's search engine was built around calculating the number of links that pointed to a single page, and this ultimately had disastrous consequences.[54]

AltaVista was never a stand-alone company, but rather a division of what was then a "mini"—versus a mainframe or a "micro"—computer company. Because DEC had no plans for making money from searches, AltaVista's technical capability and service quality turned from "superb in 1995 to virtually gone in 1997 and to an embarrassment in 1998."[55] Indeed, Monier orally confirmed (to this writer) that the conclusions offered in published reports were correct. With declining technical superiority, not only did customer satisfaction and loyalty disappear, so too did key employees, and the lack of a coherent business model led to scattered results.

By mid-1997, DEC decided against spinning off AltaVista, but decided to keep the search engine as part of its attempt to provide Internet business solutions.[56] Battelle's interviews reveal that during this time most of the original management team, including AltaVista's CEO, Ilene Lang, resigned, and engineers behind AltaVista's technology were dispersed. These significant personnel changes reduced the company's ability to upgrade its service offerings.[57]

In 1998 Compaq (another "mini" computer company) acquired DEC, along with the AltaVista search engine. Compaq's plan for AltaVista was to turn it into a portal site that would compete with Yahoo! To accomplish this, Compaq wanted AltaVista to add portal features so that it could participate in what management considered the "astounding growth" of portal companies.[58] In hindsight, it is clear that this plan was doomed, but during the late 1990s, portals were seen as the way to garner Internet revenues.[59] Despite Compaq's stated support for AltaVista's development, by the late 1990s most industry analysts doubted whether Compaq could provide the resources and staff needed to develop competitive products and services.[60] During this time, AltaVista lost what was left of its original DEC engineering team, with the departure of the lead engineer and more than 30 software engineers.[61] Thus, neither the quality nor the scope of the company's products or services could remain competitive.

In June 1999, Compaq sold AltaVista to CMGI, an Internet investment company. In an Internet business world enamored with the concept of Internet portals, doubt grew as to whether CMGI could turn AltaVista around. *Forbes* magazine lamented AltaVista's "arcane" search capabilities and the lack of rich features provided by competitors such as Yahoo and Lycos.[62] Concomitantly, Internet users at IT-enthusiast sites such as Slashdot decried AltaVista's move toward portal features and the lack of focus on search.[63]

Organization Infrastructure Was Not Continuously Improved

In 1999, CMGI announced another Initial Public Offering (IPO) attempt for AltaVista. This drew renewed criticisms from IT users, as Google began drawing more attention with its singular focus on search and simple user interface.[64] *Wired* magazine also reported on AltaVista's inability to properly update its search capabilities without causing service issues.[65]

Departments Did Not Collaborate to Solve Problems

Aside from a lack of proper funding and manpower needed for growth, AltaVista further faced disagreements among its leaders. AltaVista's first CEO, Ilene Lang, envisioned the company as an Internet software solution company, providing services such as security, search, and email. AltaVista's primary engineer, Louis Monier, believed search should be AltaVista's focus.[66] This long-standing disagreement among top management, coupled with DEC's inconsistent view of AltaVista's future, plagued the company for years. According to C. Gordon Bell, who spent 23 years at DEC as vice president of R&D,[67] DEC did not understand that customers wanted solutions to problems, which is what software provides. Customers did not want to purchase the capability for processing data, which is what hardware provides.[68]

Business Was Not Conducted in a Focused and Cost-Effective Manner

In 1999, CMGI announced its IPO attempt for AltaVista, and revealed its intention to provide free Internet access. The press hailed this move as forward-looking, but users lamented the perceived lack of focus.[69] By 2000, even the popular press had become aware of AltaVista's lack of a coherent business model. An article in *Forbes* magazine indicated that AltaVista was perhaps unwisely attempting to serve two distinct (non-synergistic) functions: as both a search engine and a feature-rich Internet portal.[70] Later in 2000 AltaVista lost its second CEO, Rod Schrock, and Internet news sites increasingly speculated whether AltaVista could survive without a viable business model.[71]

In 2003, after four years under CMGI, AltaVista was once again sold, this time to Overture, an Internet advertising company. The selling price was about 5% of what CMGI had paid for AltaVista. By this time, AltaVista's once-vaunted technical expertise had dissipated. Google was far in the lead in Internet search. In July 2003, a mere three months after AltaVista's sale to Overture, Overture was in turn purchased by Yahoo! By 2004, AltaVista's existence as an independent search engine was effectively terminated as many Internet blogs and news sites reported that AltaVista had abandoned its own search database in favor of Yahoo!'s.[72]

Employee-Directed Practices Fell Short

In some respects, AltaVista's employee-directed practices were initially good. But their efficacy declined over time.

Challenging Work Opportunities Dwindled

Employees, at first, performed state-of-the-art information technology, engineering, and marketing work, creating opportunities for growth. These intrinsic benefits slowly vanished as the product went, in the founder's words, from "superb" to an "embarrassment."

Employees Were Not Kept Informed

Few employees knew of DEC's plans for AltaVista. As noted earlier, AltaVista was a small software division (product, actually), in a large hardware company, and DEC was unwilling to make a commitment to growth.

Work Teams Were Dissolved

In an attempt to cut costs, engineers who had worked together were dispersed throughout DEC. This undoubtedly had a negative effect on morale and loyalty. Many of the engineers who were not relocated resigned.

Conclusion

AltaVista had the basis for good customer satisfaction because of its high technical capabilities, and the range of product and service offerings. But lack of a coherent business strategy and misapplied resources prevented the development of a successful search engine or a competitive portal site. Since AltaVista had assembled a talented team of engineers, employee-directed practices probably were good at the outset. But as these practices diminished, the technical talent continued to leave.

Overall, AltaVista can reasonably be classified as Middle level on customer- and employee-directed practices (at least initially), but consistently Low on enterprise-directed practices. In terms of the Cube One framework these conditions would place AltaVista initially around Cubes 21–23 (M, M, L).

The fates of Google and AltaVista were clearly not a matter of luck. The markedly different business outcomes reflected the management, human resource, and marketing practices employed. These two cases cannot prove the validity of the Cube One framework, but they are supportive.

The Cube One framework provides a basis for analysis and diagnosis of organizational performance: especially valuable in today's competitive environment.

Epilogue: Google 2010–2017

In 2009, 720 million Google users conducted 2.5 billion searches daily.[73] By 2017, 1.17 billion users conducted 4.97 billion searches daily.[74] Google's revenue growth slowed from 29% in 2011 to 13% in 2015—as might be expected of such a big company.[75] However, in 2016 Google revenue growth increased to 20%.[76]

From 2010 to 2017, Google continued to enact high levels of Enterprise-, Customer-, and Employee-directed practices. In 2015, Google hired a new chief financial officer, Ruth Porat, to bring costs under control. Porat slowed hiring growth and for the first time in the company's history required justification and approval of expenses such as travel, supplies, and events. She combined several companies: YouTube Red with Google Play Music; Chrome OS and Android (two mobile operating systems); GV and Capital G (two venture capital operations); and X and ATAP (two advanced research labs). Porat earned the sobriquet "Ruthless Ruth."[77]

Prior to the new CFO, Google had continued its practice of cutting unsuccessful ventures promptly. Google Glass was terminated in 2003, less than two years after its debut in 2002.[78] The robotics division, which was comprised of 11 companies, was terminated and liquidated, probably because the major unit, Boston Dynamics, was going to take too long to be profitable. Google's X division, which seeks "to do things never done before," kills more than 100 concepts annually.[79]

The hiring process was streamlined. Previously, candidates were interviewed 15 to 25 times each, a process that consumed 250 hours of employee time. The number of interviews was cut to about five.[80]

Emblematic of Google's search for extraordinary new products is the roll-out and development of Google Maps software. Its most formidable initial competitors were MapQuest and Yahoo Yellow Pages. Although the initial roll-out of Google Maps occurred before 2010, the history of its development highlights Google's desire to make things that haven't previously existed. Their first two "Beta" versions were deemed unsatisfactory, but the third version met their minimum criterion of being at least "10 times" better than the entrenched competition.

Google Maps was not only able to provide directions to a specific location; it could look up places by user-selected categories, such as a French restaurant in Boca Raton. Then Google Maps provided reviews, videos, and other data, before ultimately providing driving directions that allowed for traffic conditions. Users could not only read information; they could see and hear numerous details (such as menus and the appearance of multiple venues).

However, Bret Taylor, the leader of the team that developed Google maps, recognized the formidable task of overcoming inertia and the power of entrenched brands. A "better mousetrap" was not a sufficient condition for success.[81] In his words: "I don't think it is particularly arrogant of me to state that Google Maps was about two million times better than MapQuest when we launched."[82] Still, it took three years for Google's product to overtake MapQuest. Potential users thought "MapQuest doesn't get you lost; why switch?"[83]

Innovation has been a fundamental basis for Google's customer-directed practices. The philosophy of Larry Page, founder and CEO, is that the future is shaped by big bets, not incremental improvements.[84] *Barron's* list of the World's Best CEOs quotes Page as saying, "we should be building things that don't exist."[85]

Since 1999, one of Google's major projects has been self-driving cars. The project now is a stand-alone company called Waymo.[86] Ultimately, Google sees autonomous fleets of these cars as being available on an immediate-lease basis. As noted in *Bloomberg Businessweek*: "Forget about investing in an expensive and depreciating asset that sits idle 97 percent of every day."[87]

Google has also established several independent entities under the Alphabet umbrella (more on this below). Project Loon is dedicated to bringing wireless access to four to five billion people by 2020 via hundreds of satellites and helium-filled balloons.[88] Other ventures include Calico, a joint-venture established to extend the human life span; Verily, the home of health-minded contact lenses (that can monitor glucose levels); Neat, a smart-home innovator; DeepMind, which is dedicated to Artificial Intelligence; Cardboard, which focuses on virtual reality (VR) headsets; and Access, dedicated to the next generation in broadband access.[89]

In light of the above-noted new ventures, it is not surprising that in 2017, *FastCompany* rated Google the second-most innovative company in the world,[90] and ranked five of Google's apps as among the seven most popular in the U.S.: YouTube at number two, and Google search, Play, Maps, and Gmail in slots four to seven.[91] In 2013, one hundred hours of content were uploaded to YouTube every minute. In 2015, *Bloomberg Businessweek* rated Google the top company in the world in Internet media.[92]

Notwithstanding the increased scrutiny of expenses, Google has remained aggressive in retaining its employees. At times this has entailed giving employees more equity.[93] The extensive list of day-to-day employee perks was even expanded to include a 15-minute chair massage, video games, yurts, and pianos.[94] Company premises include numerous micro-kitchens and 25 restaurants.

One way to capture the effects of Google's employee-directed practices is to examine the results of a survey of 50,000 undergraduates and MBAs that appeared as a special supplement to the *Wall Street Journal*. The students, from 320 universities, were surveyed to create a list of the Top 100 Ideal Employers. Among students in Business and Computer Sciences, and among MBA candidates, Google was rated number one.

Among students of the Humanities, Google was rated number two (Walt Disney was first). Among Engineering students, Google was rated number three (after Boeing and NASA). The sixth set of students, those in Natural Sciences, rated Google as number six.[95]

The Restructuring of Google

In August, 2015, Google was restructured as the primary division of a new entity, Alphabet. The April, 2016, issue of *FastCompany* featured on its cover page the focal article with the (cute) title, "Will Google's Alpha Bet Pay Off?" Founder and CEO Larry Page provided several rationales for the restructuring.

1. A company of companies can innovate faster than a single large company.
2. By separating financial results for companies like Moonshots or Other Bets, Google can report more accurate bottom lines for its main businesses.
3. The "fantastical [Moonshot] ideas create a glowing halo around the company, fostering the impression that Alphabet is a place where magic happens."

4. The new structure will get more ambitious enterprises under way, in part by empowering great entrepreneurs.
5. A higher level of focus will accelerate the profitability of the other non-Google divisions.

These rationales, viewed through the focus of the Cube One framework, touch all the focal key bases. The second and fifth rationales are primarily enterprise-directed; the first and fourth primarily relate to innovation and customer-directed outcomes; and the third rationale can be seen as primarily employee-directed.

The Status of Google/Alphabet in 2017

In December, 2017, the *Wall Street Journal* published the inaugural issue of the Management Top 250. The piece was entitled, "The Most Effectively Managed U.S. companies—and How They Got That Way." The components of the ratings included innovation, a satisfied workforce, and financial results. The overall rankings were as follows:

1. Amazon.com Inc.
2. Apple Inc.
3. Alphabet Inc.

Other overall data include the report that in 2017 Alphabet's Google became the most valuable brand in the world, assessed at a worth of $109 billion by Brand Finance.[96] In May, 2016, Alphabet became the company with the largest market capitalization at $499 billion, slightly edging out Apple which had a capitalization of $496 billion.[97]

Notes

1 Scientific purists might argue that causal precedence is insufficient to establish causality. It is true that a before-after design cannot rule out alternative explanations, but if the alternative explanations had an effect on the performance of other airlines, such (exogenous) effects were not evident—as the rest of the industry did not experience dramatic improvements in various operating metrics.
2 The two case analyses reported here are based on an academic paper and an article coauthored with Andy Chiou. The work was initially presented at the 2010 meeting of the Eastern Academy of Management, and subsequently published in a practitioner journal published by Wiley. See Kopelman, R. E. and Chiou A.Y. (2010). "Examining the performance of Google and AltaVista through the lens of the Cube One framework." *Global Business and Organizational Excellence*, 29(6), 38–49.
3 Goel, V. (2009). "How Google decides to pull the plug." *The New York Times*. Retrieved at http://www.nytimes.com/2009/02/15/business/worldbusiness/15iht-15?_r=1, Accessed on August 21, 2009.
4 *Lively—3D avatars and rooms.* (n.d.). Retrieved at http://www.lively.com/goodbye.html. Accessed on November 1, 2009.

5 Goel, op. cit.
6 Delaney, K. J. (2006). "Google adjusts hiring process as needs grow." *The Wall Street Journal*. Retrieved at http://online.wsj.com/public/article/SB1161562967299004 33-aeEgtH. Accessed on October 4, 2008.
7 Battelle, J. (2005). *The search: How Google and its rivals rewrote the rules of business and transformed our culture*. New York, NY: Portfolio.
8 Delaney, K. J. (2006). "Google adjusts hiring process as needs grow." *The Wall Street Journal*. Retrieved at http://online.wsj.com/public/article/SB1161562967299004 33-aeEgtH. Accessed on October 4, 2008.
9 Phillysays. (2007). "Hiring at Google, the process that doesn't involve marrying one of the founders." *The Empirical Skeptic*. Retrieved at http://eskeptic.wordpress.com/ 2007/05/31/introducing-the-part-of-the-google-hiring-process-that-doesnt-involve -marrying-one-of-the-founders/. Accessed on November 14, 2008.
10 Delaney, op. cit.
11 Byron, E. (2008). "A new odd couple: Google, P&G Swap Workers to Spur Innovation." *The Wall Street Journal*. Retrieved at http://online.wsj.com/article/SB1227057879174 39625.html. Accessed on November 1, 2009.
12 Jacobs, A. (2001). "Google's secrets." *Network World Web Acceleration Newsletter*. Networkworld.Retrieved at http://www.networkworld.com/newsletters/accel/2001 /00991542.html. Accessed on January 31, 2009. Also see Vise, D. and Malseed, M. (2005). *The Google story*. New York: Delacorte Press.
13 Hardy, Q. (2005). "Google thinks small: It has huge sales, prodigious profits and a bid to log all the information in the world—one tiny project at a time." *Forbes*. Accessed on September 25, 2008. Also see global/2005/1114/054A.html#47c4efdc530b
14 Delaney, K. J. (2006). "Google adjusts hiring process as needs grow." *The Wall Street Journal*. Retrieved at http://online.wsj.com/public/article/SB1161562967299004 33-aeEgtH. Accessed on October 4, 2008.
15 Battelle, J. (2005). *The search: How Google and its rivals rewrote the rules of business and transformed our culture*. New York, NY: Portfolio.
16 Ibid.
17 Hardy, op. cit.
18 Vise, D. and Malseed, M. (2005). *The Google story*. New York, NY: Delacorte Press.
19 Lashinsky, A. (2007). "Google is no. 1: Search and enjoy." *CNN Money.com*. Retrieved at http://cnnmoney.printthis.clickability.com/pt/cpt?action=cpt&title=Go. Accessed on October 4, 2008.
20 Goel, op. cit.
21 Glotzbach, M. (2009). "Google Apps is out of beta (yes, really)." *The Official Google Blog*. Retrieved at http://googleblog.blogspot.com/2009/07/google-apps-is-out-of -beta-ye. Accessed on August 21, 2009.
22 Aslay, M. (2008). "Is Google's perpetual beta a winning strategy?" *CNET News*. Retrieved at http://news.cnet.com/8301-13505_3-10054293-16.html. Accessed on August 21, 2009.
23 Chitu, A. (2007). "Perpetual Beta." *Google Operating System*. Retrieved at http://goo glesystem.blogspot.com/2007/05/perpetual-beta.html. Accessed on August 21, 2009.
24 Claburn, T. (2009). "Google chrome OS: Vaporware or victory?" *Information Week*. Retrieved at http://www.informationweek.com/shared/printableArticleSrc.jhtml;j sessionid=QP0FHES3SNQOBQE1GHRSKHWATMY32JVN. Accessed on August 21, 2009.
25 Slashdot. (March 25, 2009). "How Google routes around outages." Retrieved at https ://tech.slashdot.org/story/09/03/25/1933254/how-google-routes-around-outages. Accessed on December 2, 2017.
26 *Google Apps Status Dashboard*. (n.d.). Retrieved at http://www.google.com/appsstatus. Accessed on September 1, 2009.

27 Goel, V. (2009). "How Google decides to pull the plug." *The New York Times.* Retrieved at http://www.nytimes.com/2009/02/15/business/worldbusiness/15iht-15?_r=1. Accessed on August 21, 2009.

28 Mills, E. (2007). "Meet Google's culture czar." *ZDNet Australia.* Retrieved at http://www.zdnet.com.au/insight/software/soa/Meet-Google-s-culture-czar/0,139023 769,339275147,00.htm. Accessed on October 4, 2008. for a more recent account, see Khosla, V. (October 11, 2016). Retrieved at https://tech.economictimes.indiatim es.com/news/people/google-is-globally-stressing-on-employee-freedom-so-that-it-c an-compete-with-talent-from-startups-/54789557. Accessed on December 2, 2017.

29 Lashinsky, A. (2007). "Google is no. 1: Search and enjoy." *CNN Money.com.* Retrieved at http://cnnmoney.printthis.clickability.com/pt/cpt?action=cpt&title=Go. Accessed on October 4, 2008.

30 Ibid.

31 Heft, M. (2008). "Google at 10: Searching its own soul." *The New York Times.* Retrieved at http://www.nytimes.com/2007/03/10/technology/10google.html?page. Accessed on October 4, 2008.

32 Battelle, J. (2005). *The search: How Google and its rivals rewrote the rules of business and transformed our culture.* New York, NY: Portfolio.

33 Lashinsky, op. cit.

34 Heft, M. (March 10, 2007). "Google's buses help its workers beat the rush." *The New York Times.* Retrieved at http://www.nytimes.com/2007/03/10/technology/10goo gle.html

35 Ibid.

36 Ibid.

37 Lashinsky, op. cit.

38 Battelle, J. (2005). *The search: How Google and its rivals rewrote the rules of business and transformed our culture.* New York, NY: Portfolio.

39 Kim, J. (December 15 1995). "DEC helps untangle the Web—for free." *USA Today,* p. 5B.

40 Lewis, P. H. (1995). "Digital equipment offers web browsers its 'Super Spider'." *The New York Times.* Retrieved at http://www.nytimes.com/1995/12/18/business/digital -equipment-offers-web-browsers-its-super-spider.html. Accessed on October 11, 2009.

41 Ray, E. J., Ray, D. S., and Seltzer, R. (1998). *AltaVista search revolution.* New York, NY: Osborne Publishing.

42 Lewis, P. H. (1995). "Digital equipment offers web browsers its 'Super Spider'." *The New York Times.* Retrieved at http://www.nytimes.com/1995/12/18/business/digital -equipment-offers-web-browsers-its-super-spider.html. Accessed on October 11, 2009.

43 Zuckerman, L. (1996). Digital faces tough market for AltaVista. *The New York Times.* Retrieved at http://www.nytimes.com/1996/09/03/business/digital-faces-tough-ma rket-for-altavista.html. Accessed on October 12, 2009.

44 Battelle, J. (2005). *The search: How Google and its rivals rewrote the rules of business and transformed our culture.* New York, NY: Portfolio.

45 Ibid.

46 Schein, E. H. (2003). *DEC is dead, long live DEC: The lasting legacy of digital equipment corporation.* San Francisco, CA: Berrett-Koehler.

47 Zajac, A. (1998). "Alta Vista breaks the language barrier: Translation software speeds Internet communications." *SFGate.com.* Retrieved at http://www.sfgate.com/cgi-bin/ article.cgi?f=/e/a/1998/02/08/BUSINESS3473.dtl&type=printable. Accessed on October 12, 2009.

48 Krigel, B. L. (1998). "AltaVista debuts Discovery search app." *CNET News.* Retrieved at http://news.cnet.com/AltaVista-debuts-Discovery-search-app/2100-1023. Accessed on

October 12, 2009; also see Slashdot. (2001). "Replacements for AltaVista Discovery?" *Slashdot: News for nerds, stuff that matters.* Retrieved at http://ask.slashdot.org/articl e.pl?sid=01/06/12/1849233. Accessed on October 12, 2009; also Agarwal, A. (2008). "Organise your web research." *The Financial Express.* Retrieved at http://www.financial express.com/news/organise-your-web-research/274270/0. Accessed on October 12, 2009.

49 Lazarus, A., Leuning, E., and Festa, P. (1998). "AltaVista unveils free email." *CNET News.* Retrieved at http://news.cnet.com/2100-1023-208001.html. Accessed on October 12, 2009.

50 Zajac, op. cit.

51 Zuckerman, op. cit.

52 MacDonald, C. (1996). "AltaVista searches for profits." *CNET News.* Retrieved at http://news.cnet.com/AltaVista-searches-for-profits/2100-1001_3-255980.html. Accessed on October 12, 2009.

53 Monier, L. (November 18, 2009). Personal communication.

54 Because AltaVista trusted the content of pages, not taking into consideration the source of the links, spammers directed users to various types of unwanted sites. The result was that AltaVista's search went, in Monier's words, from "superb in 1995 to virtually gone in 1997 and to an embarrassment in 1998." Meanwhile, Google had solved the spam problem by detecting the source of web pages.

55 (Monier, November, 2009). Personal communications. It might be noted that Louis Monier's opinions should be seen as highly credible not only because he was the engineer primarily responsible for designing the AltaVista search engine algorithm, but also because he subsequently held high-level positions at two very successful IT companies: eBay and Google.

56 Muller, J. (25 June, 1997). "In about-face, Digital drops AltaVista IPO says it now makes sense to keep unit." *The Boston Globe,* p. C3.

57 Battelle, J. (2005). *The search: How Google and its rivals rewrote the rules of business and transformed our culture.* New York, NY: Portfolio.

58 Hu, J. (1999). "Compaq's AltaVista strategy emerges." *CNET News.* Retrieved at http://news.cnet.com/2100-1023-220032.html. Accessed on October 12, 2009.

59 Reflective of this mindset, in 1998 *Business Week* wrote a special report on Internet portals. See Green, H., and Jaffe, S. (1998). "Poking around in the portals." *Business Week.* Retrieved at http://www.businessweek.com/1998/36/b3594017.htm. Accessed on October 12, 2009.

60 Hu, op. cit.

61 Battelle, J. (2005). *The search: How Google and its rivals rewrote the rules of business and transformed our culture.* New York, NY: Portfolio.

62 Patsuris, P. (1999). "Can anything save AltaVista?" *Forbes.com.* Retrieved at http://www .forbes.com/1999/06/29/mu8.html. Accessed on October 12, 2009.

63 Slashdot. (1999a). "AltaVista redesign is more 'portal-like'." *Slashdot: News for nerds, stuff that matters.* Retrieved at http://slashdot.org/article.pl?sid=99/10/24/0151223. Accessed on October 12, 2009.

64 Slashdot. (1999b). "Altavista to go for the IPO." *Slashdot: News for nerds, stuff that matters.* Retrieved at http://slashdot.org/article.pl?sid=99/12/01/0939233. Accessed on October 12, 2009.

65 Oakes, C. (1999). "AltaVista de-indexes web search." *Wired.com.* Retrieved at http://www.wired.com/print/science/discoveries/news/1999/11/32246. Accessed on October 12, 2009.

66 Battelle, J. (2005). *The search: How Google and its rivals rewrote the rules of business and transformed our culture.* New York, NY: Portfolio.

67 Background on C. Gordon Bell is provided at http://www.computerhistory.org/trus tee/c-gordon-bell

68 Battelle, op. cit.

69 Stein, T. (1999). "AltaVista offering free internet access." *SFGate.com*. Retrieved at http://www.sfgate.com/cgi-bin/article.cgi?file=/chronicle/archive/1999/08/1 3/BU45381.DTL. Accessed on October 12, 2009; also see Goodley, S. (2003). "Connected comment: Simon Goodley on the fall and sale of Altavista." *Telegraph. co.uk*. Retrieved at http://www.telegraph.co.uk/technology/3305773/Connected -comment.html. Accessed on October 12, 2009.

70 Doan, A. (2000). "AltaVista searches for new identity." *Forbes.com*. Retrieved at http:// www.forbes.com/2000/08/02/mu1.html. Accessed on October 12, 2009.

71 Mannes, G. (2000). "AltaVista exec departs: What hath Rod Schrock wrought?" *TheStreet.com*. Retrieved at http://www.thestreet.com/print/story/1134755.html. Accessed on October 12, 2009.

72 Baker, L. (2004). "Lycos search engine now using Inktomi results." *Search Engine Journal*. Retrieved at http://www.searchenginejournal.com/lycos-search-engine-now-using-inktomi-results/440/. Accessed on October 12, 2009; also WebmasterWorld. (2004). "When will Yahoo power AltaVista?" *WebmasterWorld.com*.

73 Trugman, J. M. (November 8, 2015). "Jobs grow where DC regs don't." *New York Post*, p. 57. Also see Barr, A. (July 14, 2015). "Google takes a stricter approach to costs." *Wall Street Journal*, pp. B1, B5.

74 Retrieved at https://www.statista.com/statistics/265796/us-search-engines-ranked-by -number-of-core-searches/ Indicative of the power of Google search, Encyclopedia Britannica did a study that found that the average user looked at the encyclopedia only once a year. Why? According to Clive Thompson it is "Because it's a pain in the butt." See the piece by Lenore Skenazy. (January 9, 2014). "A hearty breakfast of Google and YouTube." *Wall Street Journal*, p. A13.

75 Barr, A. (July 14, 2015). "Google takes a stricter approach to costs." *Wall Street Journal*, pp. B1, B5.

76 Retrieved at https://www.smartinsights.com/search-engine-marketing/search-engi ne-statistics/

77 Ibid.

78 Friedman, J. (March 23, 2015). "How Google innovates: Hide secrets and spend big." *Investor's Business Daily*, p. A7.

79 Ibid.

80 Rafter, M.V. (April, 2015). "Just Google him, (a profile of Laszlo Bock.)" *Workforce*, pp. 40–43 and 49–?? It also might be noted that with fewer interviews, the time to hire was cut to 47 days from around five months.

81 *First Round Review*. (January 22, 2016). "Take on your competition with these lessons from Google Maps." Retrieved at http://firstround.com/review/take-on-your-com petition-with-these-lessons-from-google-maps/

82 Ibid.

83 Ibid.

84 "Google shoots for the moon: Larry Page sets out to prove that the future is shaped by big bets." *FastCompany*, (December 2015/January 2016). Issue 201, p. 72.

85 Bary, A. (March 24, 2014). "World's best CEOs." *Barron's* special edition, pp. S1–S43.

86 The name Waymo is meant to be shorthand for a new way forward for mobility. See the Associated Press article. (December 19, 2016). "Google's driverless project gets an identity of its own," *Newsday*, p. A34.

87 Naughton, K. (October 29, 2015). "Inside GM's fight to get to the future first." *Bloomberg Businessweek*, cover page and pp. 51–53.

88 Stone, B. (March 9–15, 2015). "Google and Facebook build a new internet." *Bloomberg Businessweek*, pp. 42–43.

89 Ibid.

90 The 10th annual survey can be retrieved at https://www.fastcompany.com/most-in novative-companies/201. For the record, Amazon was rated #1 and Uber #3.

91 Carr, A., Lidsky, D., McCorvey, J. J., McCracken, H., and Wilson, M. (April, 2016). "Search for the future." *FastCompany*, pp. 60–68. The cover of the issue had the cute tittle, "Will Google's alpha bet pay off?" Regarding slots 1 and 3, they were held by Facebook and Facebook Media.

92 *Bloomberg Businessweek* special issue of the 500 top companies in 50 industries. (January 6, 2015). pp. 141–166.

93 Barr, op. cit.

94 Lidsky, D. (May 2010). "Who's Next: Interview with Minnie Ingersoll." *FastCompany*, pp. 37–38. Also see Glader, P. (August 25–31, 2014). "Google comes to Pittsburgh." *Bloomberg Businessweek*, pp. 49–50.

95 Universum, (2014). "The top employers in the U.S." Special supplement to the *Wall Street Journal*, see pages 3–7.

96 Blumenthal, R., and Salzman, A. (April 10, 2017). "Calculating brand magic." *Barron's*, p. 15.

97 Largest companies by Market Cap Today. (May 14, 2016). Retrieved at http://dogsofth edow.com/largest-companies-by-market-cap.htm.

9

THREE REMARKABLY SUCCESSFUL CUSTOMER-CENTRIC COMPANIES

Zappos.com, Four Seasons, and Nordstrom

The prior two chapters incorporated differing methodological designs with respect to case analysis. The Continental Airlines case examined before and after data along with industry comparisons; the Google and AltaVista cases examined a highly successful and an unsuccessful company in the same industry. In both chapters, the Cube One framework served as the basis for explanation and interpretation. The current chapter presents an analysis of three exceptionally successful customer-centric companies. The argument is made that customer-centricity is but one-third of the job.[1]

Comparisons are made between each of the three focal companies and comparable organizations in their industries: online shoe sales, five-star hotels, and clothing-based department stores.[2] For example, Four Seasons is compared to Ritz-Carlton. This approach parallels the classic research design of Collins and Porras in *Built to Last*.[3]

However, there is an important difference. The research by Collins and Porras was essentially an inductive inquiry (i.e., the research question being "What observed differences can be induced to explain why the visionary companies are superior to the comparison companies?")[4] In contrast, interpretations of case study (and survey) results in this book are deductively based. In the current chapter, enterprise-, customer-, and employee-directed practices and their effects are examined for three focal and comparison companies. This is partly accomplished by utilizing the vast amount of information made available by current information technology. Independent Internet-based data are examined with respect to focal and comparison companies. These data permit statistical inferences on both a within- and across-company basis.

The three focal companies were chosen because of their widely acclaimed excellence in customer service. Indeed, each of the three companies has made customer service its distinctive strategic competitive advantage—the basis for their self-described "brand." The main objective of this chapter is to demonstrate that although the focal companies are indisputably and remarkably dedicated to customer satisfaction, they also enact practices highly promotive of employee satisfaction and enterprise-related criteria. In essence, customer satisfaction is seen as a necessary, but insufficient, condition for organizational success. This claim is supported by prior research on *exclusively* customer-driven companies; they consistently achieved below-average financial returns.[5]

What follows are in-depth (yet relatively brief) case studies of the three focal companies each using the same five-part format. After a brief history of the company, evidence of success is provided based on examining the financial results of focal and comparison companies. Then customer-directed practices are reviewed, along with evidence of customer satisfaction using Internet databases (ResellerRatings.com and TripAdvisor.com) as well as traditional independent sources, such as the American Customer Satisfaction Index ratings.

Next, for each focal company a sampling of employee-directed practices is reviewed, along with Internet-based evidence of employee satisfaction from Glassdoor.com. Lastly, enterprise-directed practices are described and evidence pertinent to the efficient use of resources is examined.

Zappos.com

History

The initial pitch that the aspiring online shoe entrepreneur made to potential investor, Tony Hsieh, in 1999, was underwhelming. Hsieh, upon selling his start-up, Link Exchange, to Microsoft, co-founded a venture capital firm (Venture Frogs) to make first-round investments in start-ups. But he was quite skeptical about the prospects for an online shoe company; he wondered who would want to purchase shoes online without the opportunity to try them on?[6]

But the passion of Nick Swinmurn, the originator of the idea, was infectious, and soon Hsieh and his Venture Frogs investment fund were meeting with Swinmurn to explore the potential viability of an online shoe company. Venture Frogs became an angel investor, taking a hands-off approach, and hoping that the start-up would attract the attention of larger investment companies.[7]

But the initial investment that Angel Frogs made in the company (later named Zappos) did not pan out as planned; there was no interest among large investment companies. Yet Hsieh increasingly shared Swinmurn's enthusiasm, and became hands-on regarding the daily functioning of the company. In 2000 he took on the role of CEO and by 2002, Hsieh was "all in," investing almost all his personal assets in Zappos.[8]

Despite Hsieh's direct involvement, the company made some serious mistakes—most notably, the outsourcing of the order fulfillment function—and for several years was perilously close to extinction. Gradually the company developed a viable strategy and gained loyal customers, enthusiastic employees, and positive cash flow.

Evidence of Success

Between 2000 and 2008 revenues at Zappos rose from $1.6 million to more than $1 billion, an annualized compounded rate of increase of approximately 125 percent. Zappos was sold to Amazon early in 2009 (after the stock market had collapsed), with the price at the transaction's closing of $1.2 billion. By comparison, in 2000, revenues of Shoebuy.com, another online shoe seller, were $1.8 million, and rose to approximately $90 million in 2006, when the company was purchased for $60 million. That same year, in 2006, sales at Zappos topped $500 million.[9]

As the details that follow clearly demonstrate, Zappos is a customer-centric organization. It is also highly concerned about employee satisfaction and productivity. Hence, Zappos can be classified in Cube One.

Customer-Directed Practices at Zappos

Zappos' employees identified the firm's most fundamental core value as "Deliver WOW through service." Hsieh defines WOW service in terms of doing "something that's above and beyond what's expected … and [which has] an emotional impact on the receiver. We are not an average company, our service is not average, and we don't want our people to be average. We expect every employee to deliver WOW."[10]

Customer satisfaction is the ultimate goal of Zappos. Indeed, CEO Tony Hsieh states that the goal of Zappos is to provide the best customer service possible. Zappos describes this philosophy as "branding through customer service."[11] Therefore, Zappos does not shy away from contact with customers, but actively encourages customers to reach out to it. Zappos' customer-service hotline appears on the top of every Zappos webpage, proclaiming 24/7 customer service via telephone; in contrast many online vendors list their customer service number at the bottom of a single page or bury it in difficult-to-find locations. Zappos' 365-day return policy is also among the best in the retail industry, far superior to Piperlime.com's 45-day, and Shoebuy.com's 60-day return policies. Both of Zappos' primary selling points, 24/7 customer service, and a 365-day return policy, are emblazoned on the company's packaging, reminding customers that at Zappos customer service is always available. A key facet of the free shipment and return policy is that it allows a shopper to purchase and try on, say, six pairs of shoes at his/her home along with various outfits, and return four pairs of shoes at no cost. The outfits need not be brought to the store, nor must the unwanted shoes be physically returned to a store.

Other customer-directed practices include free shipping on both sent and returned items; *not* measuring customer service call times so reps are not pressured to get off the phone; encouraging reps to satisfy customers, even if it means directing a customer to a competitor. Perhaps the most illustrious customer-directed practice is the offer Zappos makes to all newly trained employees after five weeks; Zappos offers to pay $2,000, plus wages earned, if the newly trained employee quits on the spot—the premise being that Zappos only wants to retain employees who are loyal and confident.[12]

Clearly, Zappos is dedicated toward the ideal of superb customer service—or as Hsieh has put it, delivering happiness. Table 9.1 shows customer satisfaction ratings provided by users of Zappos and Shoebuy.com. The data clearly show that Zappos provides superior customer service.[13]

Employee-Directed Practices

Open communication channels are an important component of the Zappos culture. One example is the monthly newsletter, *Ask Anything*, in which employees' anonymous questions are compiled and answered in an email, sent throughout the entire company. Questionnaires also are frequently administered to assess employee attitudes. And when there is important news to be shared, CEO Hsieh communicates directly to all employees via email.[14]

With regard to employee growth and development, Zappos has a vision of providing training and mentorship that will permit an entry-level employee to achieve a senior leadership position within five to seven years. In this regard, Zappos offers an extensive curriculum of more than 30 courses, such as Leadership Essentials and Science of Happiness 101.[15]

Although starting salaries are generally not above market, Zappos does provide full health insurance coverage and profit sharing programs.[16] Occasionally, Zappos surprises employees, such as when the company gave a 10% cash bonus to all employees in 2008, after having a good year in 2007.

TABLE 9.1 Customer Satisfaction Ratings at ResellerRatings.com: Comparison of Scores for Zappos.com and Shoebuy.com

Dimension	Zappos.com	Shoebuy.com
Product and Service Pricing	6.98	5.37
Shipping and Packaging	6.88	3.14
Customer Service	8.27	0.76
Return/Replacement Policy	8.19	1.15
Chance of Future Purchase	7.23	2.11
Lifetime Rating	9.29	3.87

Perhaps the most unique employee-directed practice is the encouragement of employees to have fun on the job. Zappos core values specifically include:

- Create fun and a little weirdness.
- Be adventurous, creative, and open-minded.
- Build a positive team and family experience.

In keeping with these values, hiring practices include asking such questions as "If you had magic powers, what would they be?" Zappos also seeks to hire people who would enjoy "hanging out" after work with their colleagues.[17] Zappos' unorthodox methods carry dual objectives: that employees fit with their jobs, as well as the company's culture.[18]

Consistent with the desire to hire people-oriented individuals, Zappos encourages employees to respond spontaneously and warmly to customers. Employees are encouraged to form a Personal Emotional Connection (PEC) with them. For example, one Zappos employee sent flowers to the funeral of a customer's husband, an action that was taken without first checking with a supervisor. This gesture purportedly earned Zappos 30 lifetime customers.[19]

Employee satisfaction ratings on the Internet site Glassdoor.com are much higher for Zappos than they are for Shoebuy.com and Onlineshoes.com. But due to the small numbers of ratings for the two other Internet shoe companies, employee satisfaction scores are compared to those at Footlocker—see Table 9.2.[20]

Enterprise-Directed Practices

Notwithstanding its fun-loving culture, Zappos has also enacted practices that increase productivity. For instance, during the company's difficult formative years Zappos laid off about 50% of employees and required those who remained to

TABLE 9.2 Employee Satisfaction Using Data from GlassDoor.com Comparison of Zappos and Footlocker on Eight Dimensions

Dimension	Zappos	Foot Locker	p value
Career Opportunities	3.89	2.80	$p < 0.001$
Communication	4.14	3.10	$p < 0.001$
Compensation and Benefits	3.98	2.97	$p < 0.001$
Employee Morale	4.52	3.09	$p < 0.001$
Fairness and Respect	4.07	2.90	$p < 0.001$
Recognition and Feedback	4.07	3.41	$p = 0.014$
Senior Leadership	4.31	3.22	$p < 0.001$
Work/Life Balance	4.17	3.01	$p < 0.001$
Composite Score (8 items above)	33.14	24.49	$p < 0.001$
Overall Rating (separate item)	4.19	3.07	$p < 0.001$

either take significant pay cuts or work for free in exchange for stock. Again in 2008 (only a few months after giving all employees bonuses for a good 2007), Zappos laid off 8% of the staff because growth had slowed.

Early on, Zappos initiated a very creative way to achieve efficiencies. Because the company's buyers were only able to handle about 50 brands each, and Zappos could not afford to hire the number of buyers needed to address the more than one thousand brands, a novel approach to achieving efficiencies was implemented. Zappos let vendors have total access to all inventory, sales, and profitability data. Provided with complete visibility of the business, vendors were able to write suggested orders for buyers to approve. A side benefit associated with the demonstrated level of trust was that vendors helped Zappos obtain inventory of hot-selling items, an outcome that increased profits and productivity.[21]

Zappos' inventory management system itself is another driving force behind the company's success. Eschewing the usual brick-and-mortar shoe systems of stacking shoes with the same brand close to each other—a practice that requires time and effort to sort through shoes, and prevents optimal utilization of warehouse shelf space—Zappos tracks the location of every pair of shoes, thus permitting random storage within its warehouse.[22] The rationale behind this system is that it does not matter where shoes are physically placed; the inventory control system can instantaneously locate all shoes in the warehouse. This smooth, digitized inventory system allows Zappos to fulfill orders expeditiously.

Four Seasons

History

Isadore Sharp, a Canadian architect and builder, was working for his contractor father in 1960 when he designed a motel for a family friend. This experience inspired him to design, build, and operate the Four Seasons Motor Hotel in 1961 as a destination for business travelers. Over the next decade, Sharp opened three Four Seasons hotels. Opening a luxury facility in London in 1970 proved to be a key moment for the company. This property pioneered in providing many quintessentially Four Season luxury services, setting the stage for its future direction. By the end of the 1970s, Four Seasons owned ten hotels across Canada, had management contracts in San Francisco and Chicago, and owned its own branded hotel in Washington, DC.[23] The company began shifting its business model to focus solely on hotel management, as opposed to owning land and buildings.

The 1980s brought significant expansion of Four Seasons, led by the opening of flagship hotels in a dozen U.S. cities. The company went public in 1986, and by the end of the decade, was established as a North American leader in hospitality. In 2007, Four Seasons returned to private ownership with three owners: Bill Gates of Microsoft, Prince Al-Waleed bin Talal of Saudi Arabia, and Isadore Sharp and his family.

Evidence of Success

One way to gauge the success of a company is to look at its market capitalization in relation to revenues. When Four Seasons was taken private in 2007, the acquisition price was $3.8 billion—almost 15 times its 2006 revenues of $253 million. In 2006, Marriot Hotels (which owned Ritz-Carlton) had revenues of $12.2 billion and a capitalized market value of $17.7 billion, or 1.46 times revenues. Arguably, the price paid for Four Seasons was too high, but the more than tenfold difference in market capitalization to revenues speaks to the success of the organization.

As the analysis that follows explains, Four Seasons is an extraordinarily customer-centric company. Yet, it is also very concerned about the way employees are treated because, as has often been noted with regard to service businesses, a company cannot realistically expect employees to treat customers better than they are being treated. Finally, because Four Seasons is committed to achieving a high return on its properties, it has been highly productive with regard to all resources. As will be demonstrated below, Four Seasons can clearly be classified in Cube One.

Customer-Directed Practices at Four Seasons

The corporate strategy of Four Seasons rests on four pillars:[24]

1. Operate only midsize hotels of exceptional quality—that is, the best in their location.
2. Make uncompromising service the distinguishing and most significant competitive edge.
3. Create a culture of respect and trust that grants employees the discretion to solve problems.
4. Create a brand name synonymous with exceptional quality.

Sharp has put it as follows: "We are going to win on quality. Quality is far and away the chief factor in competitiveness."[25]

Property and Other Tangibles

Four Seasons has properties that are physically appealing, if not breathtaking. For example, in its Maui resort the driveway has lush landscaping leading to a broad lobby with a panoramic view of the beach and the mountains. The internal features are world-class and distinctive.

Room Features and Amenities

Four Seasons has long sought to distinguish itself through room features and amenities. Initially, this meant providing rooms that were uniformly spacious and quiet, and having beds outfitted with the most comfortable mattresses and the finest linens. Over time, many of Four Seasons' pioneering offerings have become standard practices in the luxury segment of the hotel industry, such as lighted bathroom mirrors and armoire-enclosed televisions.

Hotel Offerings

Four Seasons continuously upgrades its service offerings. For instance, the company was the first to provide concierge service nationwide in the U.S., which enabled securing for guests hard-to-get restaurant reservations, tickets for show and sporting events, and even meetings with local dignitaries. Further, Four Seasons was the first hotel to offer four-star restaurants replete with celebrity chefs and healthful food options, and it pioneered in providing on-site high-end fitness clubs, spas, and golf courses.

Service by Staff

According to Sharp, the unifying goal of Four Seasons is to provide service superior to that of any competitor, surpassing the highest expectations of the most discerning customers. To this end, the company has implemented specific service standards for all operations. For instance, at check-in, the receptionist is required to:

1. actively greet the guest, smile, make eye contact, and speak clearly and in a friendly manner,
2. use the guest's name and offer a "welcome back' to returning guests, and
3. complete the check-in within four minutes.[26]

Standards like these govern employee behavior in a variety of contexts and provide a customer service road map.

For Four Seasons, exceptional service means attending to the smallest details regarding the customer experience. An important tool is a companywide guest history database. Four Season notes highly detailed guest preferences, such as the direction of windows, or whether soft drinks should be in bottles or cans. When the vice president of a national organization checked into a room at the Four Seasons Ottawa, for example, she was greeted by a flower arrangement in her favorite colors.

Four Seasons has protocols not only for the provision of customer service, but also for dealing with service lapses. There is a daily "Glitch Report" that is discussed among hotel employees every morning. During this meeting customer service mistakes from the previous day are discussed and necessary corrections can be made.[27] This meeting also serves as a forum for discussing the special needs and preferences of newly arriving guests.

Four Seasons employees are encouraged to take the initiative in making real-time decisions that enhance the customer experience. In one legendary case, a Four Seasons employee scrambled to track down a tuxedo on very short notice for a guest attending a black-tie-only event, lending the guest an employee's tuxedo. In another instance, a Four Seasons receptionist remained on the telephone for more than 30 minutes to insure that a guest could make it to an important meeting under difficult driving conditions.[28]

Hiring and Training for Service

Recruitment, training, and termination practices support customer service. Believing that skills can be trained, but not attitudes, Four Seasons uses behavior-based interviews to identify individuals who are comfortable serving others and have a positive attitude. All new employees must go through a highly formalized training program that lasts 12 weeks. The program includes 30 hours of classroom training followed by formal testing, as well as experiential activities run by senior Four Seasons managers. The company quickly parts ways with employees, and managers in particular, who are disrespectful to guests or coworkers.

Data on customer satisfaction at 16 Four Season and 16 Ritz-Carlton hotels have been analyzed using the customer satisfaction ratings provided by more than 8,000 hotel guests on Tripadvisor.com. The findings are presented in Table 9.3. Although the differences in ratings may not seem sizable (with 5 being the maximum score), they are statistically significant in three out of four regions. Across all four regions, customer ratings exceeded those at Ritz-Carlton with a significance level of $p < 0.001$.[29]

Employee-Directed Practices

Four Seasons aims to treat employees in a respectful and supportive manner, in keeping with its written code of values, labeled the "Golden Rule." Beyond mere platitudes, the company's code of values is backed by concrete actions.

TABLE 9.3 Comparison of Customer Satisfaction Ratings of Four Seasons and Ritz-Carlton: Data from TripAdviser.com

Region	Four Seasons	Ritz-Carlton	p value
East[1]	4.38	4.26	< 0.05
South[2]	4.43	4.11	< 0.001
Mid-West[3]	4.50	4.47	ns
West[4]	4.64	4.18	< 0.001
Overall Ratings	4.58	4.19	< 0.001

Note: Footnotes are explained in the Notes section.

Four Seasons Is Concerned with Employee Comfort

When the company takes over the management of a hotel, it usually starts by upgrading employee facilities. For example, when Four Seasons took over management of a four-year-old Atlanta hotel in 1997, the company immediately painted and cleaned employee areas. In their first staff meeting, the Four Seasons GM promised employees, "As we clean and fix some guest areas, we'll continue to upgrade staff facilities as well." When employees at a Four Seasons hotel in London expressed dissatisfaction with work areas, the company promptly installed new floors, lockers, and showers. In yet another instance, in Singapore, Four Seasons upgraded the staff cafeteria to look and feel like a freestanding restaurant.

Four Seasons Goes to Great Lengths to Protect Jobs

Four Seasons has exhibited extreme reluctance to lay off employees during downturns. During the recessions of 1981–1982 and 1991–1992, the company initiated job sharing and flex time to enable all employees to keep their jobs. During the post-9/11 downturn, employees voted to work four days a week instead of five so that the company could preserve jobs. Further to prevent layoffs, some employees voluntarily took unpaid leaves of absences; others used accrued vacation time. In sum, Four Seasons management has a history of being flexible and creative to maintain employment during downturns.

Attractive Pay and Benefits

Four Seasons offers attractive pay and benefits packages, including an extensive stock option program and a generous health plan. In addition, employees receive free meals in the company cafeteria and six nights of free stays annually (after one year of employment) for themselves and their families at Four Seasons properties throughout the world.[30] Four Seasons automatically contributes 3% of an employee's salary to a 401(k) and another 3 to 5% in profit sharing. Salaries are between the 75th and 90th percentile, the magic level needed to attract the right people.[31] Moreover, the company offers flexible workweeks that include compressed schedules.

Two-Way Communication

Four Seasons regularly uses questionnaires to solicit feedback on ways to improve both the employee and customer experience. Top management communicates directly with all employees, particularly during times of crisis. So for example, after 9/11 CEO Sharp wrote two letters to employees outlining the company's response to the disaster and its evolving strategy.

A Minimum of Hierarchical Distinctions

The company has a flat organizational structure, and avoids practices that may be seen as divisive. There are no separate cafeterias based on title, and an open door policy provides access to executives. There is also a program for departments to elect a nonsupervisory representative to meet with the hotel general manager monthly. During these meetings, the participants discuss ideas on how the hotel might improve systems and respond more effectively to customer likes and dislikes.

In light of the way staff at Four Seasons are treated, it is not surprising that annual turnover among full-time employees is less than one-third of the industry average.[32] Table 9.4 presents comprehensive employee satisfaction data for Four Seasons and Ritz-Carlton.[33] None of the differences are significant, which suggests that Ritz-Carlton also treats its employees quite well. When compared to Hilton, however, Four Seasons has significantly higher employee satisfaction ratings on nearly all dimensions (see Table 9.5).[34] It should be noted, however, that Hilton properties are generally considered three- or four-star hotels, not five-star hotels like those managed by Four Seasons.

Given the generous pay practices at Four Seasons, it would be expected, *a priori*, that employee satisfaction ratings examined both on a within- and across-company basis should be high with regard to the dimension Compensation and Benefits. Across-company differences are partly supportive—see Tables 9.4 and 9.5—and on a within-company basis, Compensation and Benefits were rated higher than the other facets of employee satisfaction, $p = 0.02$.

Enterprise-Directed Practices

As concerned as Four Seasons is with providing guests with the utmost in luxury, it is also concerned with doing so in a highly profitable manner. The

TABLE 9.4 Employee Satisfaction Ratings at Glassdoor.com Comparison of Four Seasons and Ritz-Carlton

Dimension	Four Seasons	Ritz-Carlton
Career Opportunities	3.48	3.56
Communication	3.53	3.55
Compensation and Benefits	3.63	3.48
Employee Morale	3.71	3.86
Fairness and Respect	3.10	3.16
Recognition and Feedback	3.26	3.41
Senior Leadership	3.37	3.36
Work/Life Balance	3.00	3.16
Composite Score (8 items above)	27.09	27.55
Overall Rating (separate item)	3.60	3.57

TABLE 9.5 Employee Satisfaction Ratings at Glassdoor.com Comparison of Four Seasons and Hilton

Dimension	Four Seasons	Hilton	p value
Career Opportunities	3.48	2.89	$p < 0.05$
Communication	3.53	2.83	$p < 0.001$
Compensation and Benefits	3.63	2.95	$p < 0.001$
Employee Morale	3.71	3.10	$p < 0.01$
Fairness and Respect	3.10	2.61	$p < 0.05$
Recognition and Feedback	3.26	2.89	ns ($p = 0.064$)
Senior Leadership	3.37	2.67	$p < 0.01$
Work/Life Balance	3.00	3.32	ns ($p = 0.053$)
Composite Score	27.24	23.91	$p < 0.01$
Overall Rating	3.60	2.89	$p < 0.01$

company's strong financial results are a testament to this commitment. As a public company, its specific financial objectives included achieving an average return on capital that was 10 percentage points greater than the company's cost of capital, and achieving a compounded annual per share earnings growth of 20%.[35]

Improvements in operating margins are seen as a key driver of growth in earnings and returns. Margin improvements have been predicated on the practice of maintaining industry-high room rates and avoiding price discounts, even in the face of severe economic downturns, such as those experienced post-9/11. The company's pricing discipline has resulted in achieving industry-leading revenue per available room, which in 2005 for U.S. properties was more than 30% higher than that of Ritz-Carlton.[36]

Four Seasons achieves efficiency, in part, by being very mindful of staffing ratios. After acquiring the Regent hotel chain, Four Seasons trimmed the number of employees to get the employees-to-guest ratio in line with that of other Four Seasons properties.

From a broader perspective, it is notable that the Four Seasons business model yields a high return on invested capital. As primarily a management company, not a developer or an owner, Four Seasons minimizes its initial capital investment. The company's rule is to invest no more in a project than management fees will earn in the first five years.[37]

Also, the company's standard management contract runs for 30 years, with an option for another 30 years, thereby minimizing risk, aligning incentives, and ensuring a stable recurring revenue stream. In contrast, the average initial term of hotel management contracts is 13 years in the Americas, 12 in Asia Pacific, and 15 in Europe.[38]

Nordstrom

History

Arriving in Minnesota from Sweden in 1887 with five dollars in his pocket, John Nordstrom worked his way west to Alaska in 1897 in search of gold. Unlike countless others, Nordstrom succeeded in his quest and became $13,000 richer. In 1899, he invested all his money in a shoe store in Seattle with Carl Wallin, a shoemaker he had met in Alaska. Their store, Wallin, and Nordstrom, opened for business in 1901, marking the beginning of the retail legend of Nordstrom, Inc.

Nordstrom's business philosophy has always focused on unrivaled service, selection, quality, and value. The company successfully built a loyal customer base, and in 1923 a second Nordstrom store opened in Seattle. By 1960, the Seattle Flagship store, stocked with more than 100,000 pairs of shoes, was the largest shoe store in the United States; and Nordstrom was the largest independent shoe chain in the country.

The company went public in 1971 with sales passing the $100 million mark shortly thereafter. By the 1980s Nordstrom's sales topped $1 billion. By the year 2000, there were 77 full-line Nordstrom stores, and 38 Nordstrom Racks. From 2000 to 2010 Nordstrom's profits increased substantially, notwithstanding the economic turmoil between 2008 and 2010. In fact, throughout these years, Nordstrom kept all its stores open, and even opened new stores in 2009 while competitors' stores were closing. By the year 2011, there were 116 Nordstrom stores and 95 Nordstrom Rack stores.

Evidence of Success

Between 2001 and 2010 Nordstrom's profits increased nearly five-fold, with the company earning cumulative profits during this period of $4.3 billion. In comparison, between 2001 and 2010 another high-end department store chain, Saks Fifth Avenue, saw profits increase by 22%, and achieved cumulative profits during the period of $200 million. During the 2001–2010 period the change in market capitalizations of Nordstrom and Saks, were +188% and −32%, respectively.

Customer-Directed Practices at Nordstrom

In large measure, Nordstrom's success is attributable to the company's customer-driven philosophy. Over the years, Nordstrom's customer service has become legendary: sales clerks are known to pay shoppers' parking tickets, warm up customers' cars, lend money to cash-strapped customers, iron new purchases so that they could be worn the same day, and to send tailors to customers' homes.[39] Perhaps the most well-known Nordstrom folklore story concerns an employee who granted a full refund to a customer for returning a pair of car tires previously bought at the store's location before it was a Nordstrom.[40]

How does Nordstrom engineer such remarkable salesperson behaviors? One key component is the employee selection process: Nordstrom wants to hire only friendly people, striving to "hire the smile and train the skill."[41] Chairman Bruce Nordstrom asserts that it is not difficult to teach nice people how to sell, but it is almost impossible to teach salespeople how to be nice.

The selection process includes phone interviews, multiple one on one interviews, personality tests, background checks, and group interviews. In interviews a common task is to assemble an outfit for a specified situation.[42]

Another important component behind Nordstrom's excellent customer service is employee empowerment. Newly hired salespeople are given a card, entitled "the Nordstrom Rule Book," which contains only one rule:"Use your good judgment in all situations. There will be no additional rules."[43] Nordstrom empowers salespeople to make business decisions, and management backs these decisions.[44] In one instance, a salesperson gave $2,000 worth of replacement merchandize to a customer who had mishandled purchased garments without asking for anyone's permission because he knew that Nordstrom trusted his judgment.

The compensation system for sales people also fosters excellent customer service. Sales commissions average 6.75% of sales, and in some departments (such as lingerie) commission rates go up to 9%. Consequently, salespeople will show multiple sets of styles and colors of a particular set of items, even if they have the requested item in stock.

According to customer satisfaction data from the American Customer Satisfaction Index (ACSI), Nordstrom was the highest rated department store from 1995 to 2000 and in second place (1 point behind Target) in 2001. No measurements were taken of Nordstrom from 2002 through 2006; however when measurements resumed in 2007 Nordstrom was rated the highest in customer satisfaction and remained first from 2007 through 2010.

Employee-Directed Practices

Nordstrom offers extremely competitive pay, which includes profit sharing. In 2003, one of the company's most profitable years, each employee who worked at least 1,000 hours received a profit sharing bonus three times that of the previous year.[45] According to a 2007 U.S. Department of Labor Statistics study covering nearly 4.5 million retail salespersons, the average wage for retail salespeople was $11.79 per hour.[46] At Nordstrom, the average salesperson's pay in 2007 was above $18 per hour.[47]

To strengthen collegial relationships among employees, Nordstrom encourages all the salespeople to participate in its mentoring system. Besides having a mentor, new employees are encouraged to find their own sales techniques, because success at Nordstrom is defined as what works for each employee. Many top Nordstrom salespeople say that mentors are everywhere, and almost all top sales performers become mentors to new hires. The focus on growth and development also applies to managers. The company's New Manager Development Program helps new department managers transition from being individual contributors to team leaders.[48] Thus, the culture of mentoring and long-term learning encourages personal growth and engagement, contributing to employee satisfaction.

Glassdoor.com. provides employee satisfaction data for eight criteria: recognition and feedback, fairness and respect, compensation and benefits, communication, senior leadership, employee morale, work/life balance, and career opportunities. In light of the emphasis that Nordstrom has placed on internal promotions and generous incentive pay plans, it would be expected, *a priori*, that employees should report especially high satisfaction regarding these two domains. Mean satisfaction scores for each domain are provided in Table 9.6.[49] For comparison purposes, corresponding data are also provided for one of Nordstrom's strongest competitors, Dillard's. The difference in satisfaction with compensation and benefits was significant on an across-company basis ($p < 0.001$), but not on a within-company basis, (3.62 for compensation and benefits versus 3.46 on the other facets).

Enterprise-Directed Practices

Nordstrom's financial success reflects high levels of productivity. The company has consistently achieved the highest sales-per-square-foot in the industry, nearly twice that of other department stores.[50] Because a large portion of a salesperson's salary comes from commission, this motivates energetic work behaviors. Further, managers are usually promoted from within the ranks of salespeople, further enhancing the motivation to sell.

TABLE 9.6 Employee Satisfaction Ratings at GlassDoor.com Comparison of Nordstrom and Dillard's

Dimension	Nordstrom	Dillard's	Significance
Career Opportunities	3.48	2.43	$p < 0.001$
Communication	3.68	2.45	$p < 0.001$
Compensation and Benefits	3.62	2.89	$p < 0.001$
Employee Morale	3.83	2.50	$p < 0.001$
Fairness and Respect	3.17	2.22	$p < 0.001$
Recognition and Feedback	3.62	2.78	$p < 0.001$
Senior Leadership	3.25	2.52	$p = 0.002$
Work/Life Balance	3.22	2.76	$p = 0.052$
Composite Score (sum of 8 items)	27.87	20.56	$p < 0.001$
Overall Rating (single item)	3.57	2.42	$p < 0.001$

Another way that Nordstrom motivates employees is via publicly posted feedback on individual performance. Nordstrom posts a semi-monthly sales-per-hour chart in a back room of the store for everyone in the department to see.[51] Because everyone has access to the sales information of every other employee, salespeople are motivated not just by extrinsic rewards, but also by intrinsic feelings of achievement and social satisfaction (preferring to be at the top of the chart rather than the bottom).[52]

Top-performing salespeople at Nordstrom are given the title of "Pacesetters," which means that they meet or surpass an annual goal for net sales volume.[53] Pacesetters are given: a certificate of merit at an event held in their honor; special business cards decorated with the Pacesetter label; and a 33% merchandise discount credit card for one year. "When you have star salespeople, they ought to get paid like stars because they earn it," said Bruce Nordstrom.[54] Nordstrom also gives out All-Star and Customer Service All-Star awards at the recognition meeting. Because the All-Star Awards are a surprise, families are contacted ahead of time and invited to attend the award ceremony.[55]

Employees who regularly fail to exceed their draw receive personal training from their department manager. If it appears that a career in sales is not suited to that person, he or she is assigned to a non-sales job or is let go.[56] Thus, Nordstrom not only focuses on rewarding their star performers, but also monitors the performance of all employees, identifying potential performance problems, and addresses them. Nordstrom strives to keep the best salespeople and to motivate all to be better performers. Salespeople are proud to be called "Nordies."

Instead of simply dividing store space by brand or item category, Nordstrom differentiates itself from competitors by breaking store space into "lifestyle sections"—for instance, the "individualist" section displays mid-priced contemporary goods, while the "narrative" corner offers all kinds of classic styles from brands that are less costly.[57] This approach to merchandising space makes it easier for customers to find an ensemble of products that go well together, and customers are exposed to additional items that they might purchase. Nordstrom salespeople also have an electronic view of the chain's entire inventory, providing every salesperson access to the complete inventory at all times. This inventory system allows Nordstrom to minimize the incidence of stock outs.[58]

Conclusion: Customers, Employees, and Productivity Matter

The focal customer-centric companies all have achieved remarkable financial success. Zappos was purchased at a multiple of revenues that was twice that of Shoebuy.com, despite the fact that Zappos was purchased after the stock market "cratered" and Shoebuy.com was sold as the market reached its peak. Four Seasons was purchased at a multiple of revenues that was ten times the valuation of Marriott, which owned Ritz-Carlton. And Nordstrom, despite having lower revenues than Saks Fifth Avenues, achieved cumulative profits in the 2001–2010 decade that were 20 times the amount earned by Saks.

The focal companies consistently achieved higher levels of customer satisfaction than the comparison companies, and employee satisfaction was generally higher. Zappos and Nordstrom had higher levels of employee satisfaction than their respective comparison companies, but this was not the case with regard to Four Seasons and Ritz-Carlton which had comparable levels of employee satisfaction.

Patterns of employee satisfaction are consistent on a within-company basis with management practices. For instance, Four Seasons deliberately pays wages at 75 to 90%of the pay range, and satisfaction with compensation and benefits exceeded satisfaction with the other seven satisfaction facets ($p = 0.02$).[59] As would be expected given the nature of the hospitality business (open 24/7, including holidays), Four Seasons employees reported satisfaction with regard to work/family balance, which was significantly lower than their satisfaction with the other seven dimensions ($p = 0.012$).

As noted above, past research has found that an inordinately high customer-driven philosophy does not necessarily translate to financial results.[60] Rather, per the Cube One framework, customer-centricity is a necessary but insufficient condition for commercial success. Customer-directed practices constitute one-third of the job.

The review of practices at the three leading companies indicates that they devote considerable attention to achieving high levels of employee satisfaction and productivity. Internet-based evidence supports this interpretation. As noted previously, the Cube One framework entails examining practices that are usually not examined in concert; other approaches to analysis tend to be delimited by discipline. The multiple disciplines, conceptually, include human resource management, quality management, marketing, I/O psychology, and financial and operational productivity.

As in any research undertaking, there is usually no shortage of areas that might be improved. In this chapter, independent sources of information were obtained for all three focal companies, but descriptions of management practices rely partly on Hsieh's book about Zappos and Sharp's book on Four Seasons. Because these founders' accounts may emphasize intended policies as distinct from actual practices (that is the formal organization rather than the informal organization), there is the inherent risk of bias.

Beyond its ability to explain phenomena, it is argued that the Cube One framework can also be used for diagnostic and implementation purposes. Such practical issues are examined in Chapters 11 and 12. The next chapter, Chapter 10, focuses on the Mayo Clinic in comparison to other hospitals.

Notes

1 Analogously, in 1998, I authored a short article in the *National Productivity Review* entitled "Managing for productivity: One-third of the job," 17(3), 1–2.
2 The material in this chapter was first presented as a Professional Development Workshop at the 49th Annual Meeting of the Eastern Academy of Management in

2012 (Philadelphia). It also appeared in the *Proceedings,* pp. 1105–1128. The authors of the material were as follows: Andy Y. Chiou developed the content and analysis for Zappos.com; Louis J. Lipani, did the same for Four Seasons; and Zhu Zhu did likewise for Nordstrom. The present author was responsible for conceptualizing, editing, adding content, and providing oversight of the project. Subsequently, the material was published as an article in a professional journal published by Wiley. The full citation is as follows: Kopelman, R. E., Chiou, A.Y., Lipani. L. J., and Zhu, Z. (2012). "Interpreting the success of Zappos.com, Four Seasons, and Nordstrom: Customer centricity is but one-third of the job." *Global Business and Organizational Excellence,* 31(6), 63–78.

3 Collins, J. C., and Porras, J. I. (1994). *Built to last: Successful habits of visionary companies.* New York, NY: Harper Business.

4 In terms of the conduct of science, it is not considered appropriate to use the same set of data both to develop and test hypotheses. Statistically speaking after examining a data set to formulate hypotheses, there are no degrees of freedom left in the same data set to test hypotheses. Rather, after formulating hypotheses with one set of data, an independent set of data should be examined to replicate the results.

5 Basuki, W. A., and Henderson, S. (2003). "Whatever happened to the excellent marketers? A study of financial performance and excellent marketing." *Journal of General Management,* 29(2), 70–88.

6 Hsieh, T. (2010). *Delivering happiness: A path to profits, passion, and purpose.* New York, NY: Business Plus.

7 Ibid.

8 Ibid.

9 It might be noted that Zappos was purchased for 120% of annual revenues, Shoebuy. com for 67%.

10 Hsieh, op cit., p. 160.

11 Hsieh, op. cit., p. 142.

12 McFarland, K. 2008. "Why Zappos offers new hires $2,000 to quit." *Bloomberg Businessweek.* Retrieved at http://www.businessweek.com/smallbiz/content/sep20 08/sb20080916_288698.htm. Accessed on November 27, 2011.

13 Data were obtained from ResellerRatings.com, and accessed on September 11, 2011. The first five ratings pertain to the most recent six-month period; the lifetime ratings are for all reviews for Zappos, (n = 230) and Shoebuy.com (n = 175). The statistical significance of the differences in means cannot be ascertained because the distribution of scores is not provided, but mean differences are quite sizable, e.g., ratings of customer service of 8.27 versus 0.76 (out of 10).

14 Lennox, B., and Nie, W. (2011). "The case study: Creating a distinct corporate culture: How to embed a sense of passion." *Financial Times,* p. 14.

15 Chafkin, M. 2009. "The Zappos way of managing." *Inc.* Retrieved at http://www.inc. com/magazine/20090501/the-zappos-way-of-managing.htm. Accessed on September 5, 2011.

16 O'Brien, J. M. (February 2, 2009). "Zappos knows how to kick it." *Fortune,* 159(2), 54–60.

17 Perschel, A. (2010). "Work-life flow: How individuals, Zappos, and other innovative companies achieve high engagement." *Global Business and Organizational Excellence,* 29(5), 17–30.

18 Lennox and Nie, op. cit.

19 Chafkin, op. cit.

20 GlassDoor.com. Each dimension score is based on two items. For example, the Recognition and Feedback dimension consists of responses to: "Feedback you receive about your job performance" and "Recognition and praise you receive when you do a good job." The one-item overall rating was worded as follows: "Overall, how satisfied are you with (focal company as a place to work?"

21 Hsieh, op. cit.

22 Griffith, T. (2010). "Wow! From the Zappos fulfillment center. From the *Terri Griffith* web site." Retrieved at http://www.terrigriffith.com/node/205. Accessed on December 4, 2011.

23 Interestingly, Tom Peters and Robert Waterman in their classic book, *In search of excellence*, start their Introduction with their recent experience at the Four Season hotel in Washington, DC. While they had stayed at the Four Season once before, their meeting ran late; it was late at night and they had no reservation. Walking through the lobby they discussed how best to plead their case for a room, and they braced for the usual chilly shoulder accorded late-comers to a hotel. "To our astonishment the concierge looked up, smiled, and called us by name and asked how we were. She remembered our names! We knew in a flash why in the space of a brief year the Four Seasons had become 'the place to stay' in the District." p. xvii.

24 Christofferson, J. (January, 2007). "How Four Seasons creates a cycle of success." *Workspan*, 50(1), 24–27.

25 Sharp, I. (2009). *Four Seasons: The story of a business philosophy*. New York, NY: Portfolio.

26 Talbott, B. M. (September, 2006). "The power of personal service: Why it matters, what makes it possible, how it creates a competitive advantage." *CHR Industry Perspectives*, 1(1), 6-13. Ithaca: Cornell University.

27 Sharp, op. cit.

28 Talbott, op. cit. (Today with Google maps and Goggle's Daze, the need for driving assistance would be unlikely to be needed.)

29 Notes regarding the four regions: (1) Ratings of Four Seasons and Ritz-Carlton hotels in Boston, New York City, and Philadelphia, $n = 612$ and 1,174, respectively. (2) Ratings of Four Seasons and Ritz-Carlton hotels in Atlanta and Miami, $n = 397$ and 626, respectively. (3) Ratings of Four Seasons and Ritz-Carlton hotels in Chicago and St. Louis $n = 387$ and 420, respectively. (4) Ratings of Four Seasons and Ritz-Carlton hotels in Los Angeles, Austin, Dallas, and Hawaii, $n = 3,216$ and 1,739, respectively.

30 O'Brien, J. M. (January 18, 2008). What makes Four Seasons so special? Guests can check out anytime—but employees never want to leave. *Fortune*. Retrieved at http://money.cnn.com/2008/01/18/news/companies/fourseasons.fortune/index.htm

31 Ibid.

32 Christofferson, op. cit.

33 Each dimension score is based on two items. For example, the Career Opportunities dimension consists of responses to "Your opportunities for professional growth" and "Your opportunities for career advancement." The one-item overall rating was worded as follows: "Overall, how satisfied are you with [focal company] as a place to work?" Source: GlassDoor.com

34 Each dimension score is based on two items. For example, the Fairness and Respect dimension consists of responses to "Fairness in how promotions are given and people are treated" and "The level of respect shown by management toward employees." The one-item overall rating was worded as follows: "Overall, how satisfied are you with [focal company] as a place to work?" Source: GlassDoor.com.

35 Four Seasons Hotels and Resorts (2001). *Four seasons 2001 annual report*.

36 Talbott, op. cit.

37 Sharp, op. cit.

38 Jones Lang LaSalle Hotels, (June, 2005). *Focus on global hotel management agreement trends*. Ithaca, NY: Cornell University.

39 Spector, R., and McCarthy, P. D. (2005). *The Nordstrom way to customer service excellence; A handbook for implementing great service in your organization*. Hoboken, NJ: Wiley.

40 Mooney, A. C. (2008). "Nordstrom in 2003: Embarking on its second century of business." *Business Case Journal*, 15(2), 60–73.

41 Spector and McCarthy, op. cit.

42 Glassdoor.com.

43 Spector, R. (2001). *Lessons from the Nordstrom way*. Hoboken, NJ: Wiley.

44 Spector and McCarthy, op. cit.

45 Edler, B. 2006. "Employees first—A key to driving reputation, retention and results." *All Things Corporate*. Retrieved at http://atc.netcomsus.com/index.php/newsletters/newsletter_articles/36.html

46 U.S. Bureau of Labor Statistics, 2007. "Occupational employment and wages—retail salespersons." Retrieved at http://www.bls.gov/oes/home.htm

47 Lyman, A. (2009). "Nordstrom – Great service for over 100 years best company for 25 Years." *Great Place to Work® Institute, Inc.*, San Francisco.

48 Ibid.

49 Each dimension score is based on the mean response to two items (all with undefined five-point anchors). For example the Work/Life Balance dimension consists of responses to: "Management support in permitting time off when you think it's necessary" and "Employer support in balancing between work life and personal life." The one-item overall rating is worded as follows: "Overall, how satisfied are you with [focal company] as a place to work?"

50 Spector (2001), op. cit.

51 Spector and McCarthy, op. cit.

52 It should be noted that this feedback system has been characterized as objective feedback insofar as the metrics are factual and virtually incontrovertible. In a review of objective feedback interventions, data were examined regarding 30 laboratory studies and 42 field studies. Among the lab studies 26 out of 30 yielded positive results; among the field studies, 42 out of 42 yielded positive results. This does not mean that positive results were obtained for all metrics and all participants in a field study; rather what is referenced is overall effectiveness. See Kopelman, R. E. (1986) "Objective feedback" (chapter 7) in E. A. Locke (ed.) *Generalizing from laboratory to field settings*. Lexington, MA: Lexington Books. (pp. 119–146).

53 Spector and McCarthy, op. cit.

54 Spector and McCarthy, op. cit. p. 118.

55 Lyman, op. cit.

56 Spector and McCarthy, op. cit.

57 Timberlake, C. (August 1, 2011). "How Nordstrom bests its retail rivals." *Bloomberg BusinessWeek*, 103–106.

58 Ibid.

59 The employee satisfaction measures used by Glassdoor.com appear to have good psychometric properties. A sound measure of internal consistency reliability should reach α (Cronbach alpha) coefficient of 0.80; in the present research the reliability estimates for the focal companies ranged from 0.87 to 0.93, with a median coefficient of 0.92. Adding confidence to the validity of inferences based on the (one-item) composite satisfaction rating, the magnitudes of correlations with component facets were high, ranging from $r = 0.74$ to $r = 0.90$, the median being $r = 0.87$.

60 Basuki, W. A., and Henderson, H. (2003). "Whatever happened to the excellent marketers? A study of financial performance and excellent marketing." *Journal of General Management*, 29(2), 70–88.

10

THE MAYO CLINIC AND EXCELLENT HOSPITALS

The Mayo Clinic is an institution so eminent that it symbolizes the best of American medicine: "an important national institution, with the qualities of a cherished myth."[1] This case study employs a format similar to that used in the two prior chapters).[2] Although the reputation of the Mayo Clinic may be deserved, to determine whether the Mayo Clinic can be classified as Cube One entails a comparison of its practices and their effects relative to the most outstanding hospitals in the U.S. (i.e., those listed in the *U.S. News & World Report's* listing of the best U.S. hospitals.)[3]

History of the Mayo Clinic

According to Mayo Clinic History (2014), the Mayo Clinic developed gradually from the medical practice of a pioneer doctor, Dr. William Worrall Mayo, who in 1863 settled in Rochester, Minn. His dedication to medicine became a family tradition when his sons, Drs. William James Mayo and Charles Horace Mayo, joined his practice in 1883 and 1888, respectively. From the beginning, innovation was their hallmark and they shared a pioneering zeal for medicine. As the demand for their services increased, they asked other doctors and basic science researchers to join them in the world's first private integrated group practice. Although the Mayo doctors were initially seen as unconventional for practicing medicine through this team, the benefits of a private group practice were undeniable.[4]

Leonard Berry and Kent Seltman, the authors of *Management Lessons from the Mayo Clinic*, state that the Mayo Clinic's values emerged from collaborations. The first and most important was between the Drs. Mayo and the sisters of St. Francis of Assisi. Collaboration with the Franciscan community began in 1883 following a devastating and lethal tornado in Rochester, Minn. To help manage the seriously injured, Dr. W. W. Mayo requested help from the Franciscan sisters who operated a school in town. After the immediate crisis was over, Mother Alfred proposed that the sisters build a hospital in Rochester. Saint Marys Hospital opened in 1888.

At the outset, the Drs. Mayo found the sisters to be partners whose values overlapped with their own. Both the doctors and sisters focused on the needs of individuals.[5] Medical research and education have been important from the beginning, as Mayo has envisioned itself as a "three-shield organization." The central and largest shield in the Mayo Clinic logo represents patient care. But integrally linked to patient care are the complementary shields of medical research and medical education. William and Charles Mayo—who believed that they were better doctors because they had studied and observed other doctors on their "vacations" each year—defined that tripartite mission.[6] Mayo became a nonprofit organization in 1919. As noted by Berry and Seltman, the Mayos believed that, beyond decent financial security for themselves and their partners, surplus income should be dedicated to patient care. This policy paralleled the ethic lived every day at Saint Marys Hospital by the sisters of Saint Francis of Assisi, whose vows included one of poverty. The sisters worked without pay, 12 to 18 hours per day for six or seven days a week serving patients and supporting Mayo Clinic doctors.[7]

This partnership with the sisters of Saint Francis of Assisi also benefited Mayo indirectly. When the brothers came on the scene in the 1880s, surgical patient mortality primarily came from infections following "successful" surgeries. Although the brothers were technically gifted surgeons, much of the Mayo's success can be attributed to their early adoption of sterile surgical techniques and the complementary "cleanliness is next to Godliness" ethic of the Franciscan sisters.[8]

Innovations continued, and in the 1950s Mayo developed the first intensive care unit in the U.S. Mayo expanded geographically beyond Rochester, and presently the Mayo Clinic operates four hospitals. In addition to Saint Mary's Hospital, Mayo also operates Rochester Methodist Hospital, which dates from the 1950s, and the Mayo Clinic also built its own hospitals in Phoenix and Jacksonville, which opened in 1998 and 2008, respectively.[9] Over many decades, the mission of the Mayo Clinic has been constant: "to inspire hope and contribute to health and well-being by providing the best care to every patient through integrated clinical practice, education and research."[10] The formal mission, values, and core principles of the Mayo Clinic are presented in Table 10.1.

Patient-Directed Practices

Patient-directed practices are behaviors and procedures that engender patient comfort, satisfaction, and loyalty. Specifically, these practices focus on patients' physical well-being, their interactions with hospital staff, and the environment patients experience within the hospital. The Cube One framework posits that the

TABLE 10.1 Mayo Clinic Model of Care Mayo Foundation

Mission

Mayo will provide the best care to every patient every day through integrated clinical practice, education, and research.

Primary Value

The needs of the patient come first.

Core Principles

Practice

Practice medicine as an integrated team of compassionate, multi-disciplinary physicians, scientists, and allied-health professionals who are focused on the needs of patients from our communities, regions, the nation and the world.

Education

Educate physicians, scientists and allied-health professionals and be a dependable source of health information for our patients and the public.

Research

Conduct basic and clinical research programs to improve patient care and to benefit society.

Mutual respect

Treat everyone in our diverse community with respect and dignity.

Commitment to quality

Continuously improve all processes that support patient care, education and research.

Work atmosphere

Foster teamwork, personal responsibility, integrity, innovation, trust and communication within the context of a physician-led institution

Source: 2014 Mayo Foundation for Medical Education and Research http://www.mayo.edu/pmts/mc4200-mc4299/mc4270.pdf, p. 20.

frequency and quality of patient-directed practices contribute to overall hospital performance.

As noted above, the Mayo Clinic's fundamental espoused value is that "the needs of the patient come first."[11] This value has undergirded the organization's vision and climate from the start. Two of the vision statements at the Mayo Clinic best capture the organization's culture and enacted climate: (1) continually providing a primary and sincere concern for the care and welfare of each individual patient; and (2) continually pursuing excellence in everything that is done.[12]

The Mayo Clinic has codified its values, culture, and expectations in a document called the *Mayo Clinic Model of Care*. Below are some of the practices that reflect the Mayo Clinic's culture.

- Collegial, cooperative, staff teamwork with true multi-specialty integration
- An unhurried examination with time to listen to the patient
- Physicians taking personal responsibility for directing patient care over time in a partnership with the local physician

- Highest quality patient care provided with compassion and trust
- Respect for the patient, family, and the patient's local physician
- Comprehensive evaluation with timely, efficient assessment and treatment
- Availability of the most advanced, innovative diagnostic and therapeutic technology and techniques.[13]

The *Mayo Clinic Model of Care*, published in 2014, states, "At Mayo Clinic, we treat a whole person rather than an isolated disease entity. We recognize the additional time it takes to listen to patients and assess their needs in order to make sure that everything possible is done to provide quality care for our patients."[14] The Model of Care also states: "Patients report that the most significant difference between Mayo Clinic and other healthcare centers is that at Mayo Clinic everyone cares about them. Our patients see Mayo Clinic as a place of trust where they are treated with dignity and compassion."[15]

The essay by Jason Fried captures the Mayo experience from a patient's perspective. His health insurance plan permitted setting up appointments with a handful of doctors and specialists in a "tightly choreographed" one to three days. Jason Fried initially met with an internist who served as his primary care physician during the whole visit. Mr. Fried (Jason) and the internist had a 45-minute meeting. At the meeting Jason mentioned that he had a newborn son and that he and his wife were just getting over bad colds. In Jason's words, the doctor must have taken note of the family situation, "and must have entered it in the system, since over the next two days, every person that I met asked how my son was doing."[16]

Less anecdotally, Mayo around 2014 purchased two proton-beam radiation units, each costing $188 million. At that time some insurance companies and third-party payers refused to approve the much more expensive proton therapy. Furthermore, as of 2015, proton-beam technology was indisputably superior for only a limited number of types of cancers. Nonetheless, Mayo decided to underwrite the cost (placing one machine in Rochester, Minnesota, the other in Phoenix). Mayo was not alone in this decision. All of the top ten cancer centers in the U.S. then had, or were developing, proton therapy facilities.[17]

Appendix 10.1 contains three poignant examples of how Mayo manifests its values in patient-directed practices. We posit that the Mayo Clinic's patient-directed practices will stand out even among the best U.S. hospitals.

> *Conjecture 1: The level of patient-directed practices enacted at Mayo Clinic exceeds the average level of such practices at the best hospitals in the U.S.*

Employee-Directed Practices

Employee-directed practices are those policies, procedures, and managerial behaviors which engender employee satisfaction and loyalty, such as growth opportunities, work/life balance, and shared information. As noted previously, it is not reasonable to expect employees in a service setting to treat customers better than they (employees) see themselves as being treated.[18] Also reflective of a concern for employees, Mayo makes a strong effort to sufficiently train and internally promote employees.[19]

At the Mayo Clinic, for instance, employees are not pressured to rush the performance of their medical work. As one employee put it, "I could take an hour to do a dressing change carefully after pre-medicating the patient for pain and know that I would be able to complete the painful procedure without being interrupted." Or "I could spend an hour in a family conference or comfort a dying patient's family because that was not considered frivolous."[20]

Employee-directed practices are consonant with Mayo's primary value: taking care of the patients' needs.[21] The environment is designed to support employee performance as identified in the *Mayo Clinic's Model of Care*:

- Highest quality staff mentored in the culture of Mayo and valued for their contributions
- Valued professional allied-health staff with a strong work ethic, special expertise, and devotion to Mayo
- A scholarly environment of research and education
- Professional compensation that allows a focus on quality, not quantity
- Unique professional dress, decorum, and facilities[22]

There are only a handful of hospitals on *Fortune's* 2014 list of 100 Best Companies to Work For; and the Mayo Clinic has been on this list for 11 consecutive years.[23] Likewise, for the three years 2012–2014, DiversityInc (2014) has listed Mayo among the top ten with regard to diversity in the Hospitals and Health Systems Category. Mayo has a Diversity Council, tracks diversity statistics, and engages in formal succession planning and mentoring for women, blacks, Latinos, and Asians.[24]

From the beginning, Mayo found that patients' needs are best met via employee teamwork and empowered decision making. Berry and Seltman state,

> Empowerment is most important when any employee observes a patient in trouble, a patient whose medical condition appears to be deteriorating. … Plus-One refers to the expectation that any one person can consult an additional person up the chain of command to get what is needed for a patient.[25]

Also, "Teamwork cannot be sustained without mutual respect, for teamwork depends on trust, listening, inclusion, teammate contribution and fair treatment—the attributes of respect."[26] Additionally,

> The Clinic ardently searches for team players in its hiring and then facilitates their collaboration through substantial investments in communications

> technology and facilities design. … Further encouraging collaboration is an
> all-salary compensation system with no incentive payments based on the
> numbers of patients seen or procedures performed.[27]

Additional evidence of Mayo's employee-directed practices can be inferred from
the lists of ideal employer rankings. With respect to three types of college majors
and MBA students, Mayo is consistently among the top 80 ideal employers.[28]

In light of these practices, it is anticipated that the Mayo Clinic will be significantly above average compared to the best U.S. hospitals in terms of employee
satisfaction.

> *Conjecture 2: Employee satisfaction at the Mayo Clinic exceeds average levels of
> employee satisfaction at the best hospitals in the U.S.*

Enterprise-Directed Practices

Enterprise-directed practices encompass a wide variety of actions undertaken to
increase efficiency with regard to all resources. Such practices range from those
focused on improving employee motivation and ability, to those that emphasize
the more efficient use of capital and technology.

Berry and Seltman write as follows about the Mayo philosophy with regard
to technology:

> Technology designed strictly to save money usually results in an excessive
> waste of money and a mountain of heartache. All technology should solve
> real problems in the context of an organization's core values and strategy.
> Mayo Clinic has benefited enormously and durably from major technolog-
> ical investments. These investments have in common their direct link to the
> Clinic's core values and strategies. … Saving money through technology has
> frequently been the result, but rarely, if ever, the goal.[29]

At the Mayo Clinic a number of enterprise-directed practices simultaneously
enhance efficiency and better meet patient needs. Berry and Seltman cite numerous examples of employees undertaking evidence-based studies in their own
domains in order to improve internal benchmarks. Almost from the beginning,
Mayo has utilized what at the time was innovative information technology, from
creating integrated medical records and a mechanical system to transport them, to
implementing a centralized patient scheduling and appointment system.[30]

Working with supply chain managers, orthopedic surgeons turned a $2 mil-
lion annual loss on knee- and hip-joint replacements into a $6 million annual
profit in two years without compromising patient outcomes. At the administrative
level, Mayo follows a "one-bucket philosophy of resource allocation," by which
resources are allocated according to mission priorities: not by the revenue generated in each department.[31]

According to the *Mayo Clinic Model of Care,*

> One of Mayo Clinic's strengths is our simultaneous, efficient evaluation process. Although some patients' needs require that we address a single subspecialty problem, rather than have every medical problem addressed, we have the capability of bringing together a team of physicians and allied health staff to address different problems in the same patient during the same encounter. This capability, together with our highly efficient laboratory and radiology services, gives us the unique ability to complete an episode of care in a short period of time. In many cases, we can offer complex evaluation and testing followed by next-day surgery—a capability that is appreciated by patients who travel long distances to seek healthcare at Mayo Clinic.[32]

> What might be characterized as destination medicine entails creating an integrated system of comprehensive care that addresses the patient's medical problem(s) in an efficient manner. The practice of destination medicine enables patients and families who travel long distances to receive comprehensive and expeditious medical care.[33]

An article about vendor and supply chain management for hospital operating rooms notes that a vendor may be permanently barred from a Mayo facility if a problem is left unresolved—[and] "we will bar suppliers if we suspect their behavior or skills aren't in the best interest of our patients."[34]

In an article published in *The Joint Commission Journal on Quality and Patient Safety*, the authors state, "The Mayo Clinic Value Creation System is a coherent system engineering approach to delivering a single high-value practice to meet the needs of the patient. This methodology consists of four tightly linked phases—alignment, discovery, managed diffusion, and measurement."[35] The article also claims that Mayo's infrastructure and systems support are necessary to ensure that the "right thing to do" is the "easy thing to do."[36] In addition, as of 2013, "all Mayo Clinic sites had fully functional electronic medical records in place with the ability to readily share patient information. Current efforts are focused on expanding functionality, consolidating departmental systems, creating order sets, and developing rules/alerts to assist the practice."[37]

The *Joint Commission* article notes that in healthcare settings the metrics of success typically entail data which are assessed at multiple levels, such as the percentage of staff educated on the best practice; compliance with process measures where appropriate; and tracking outcomes to determine if the best practices are improving the ultimate care of patients. A Mayo representative asserts that "[we] have also found it beneficial to routinely track financial impacts to reinforce the finding that improved quality can in fact reduce costs."[38]

Reflective of the Mayo Clinic's concern for efficiency, when surgeons requested two additional operating rooms to meet the demand for open-heart surgery, the CEO, Dr. John Noseworthy, said no. In fact, he pushed the surgeons to cut costs by 20% (which was ultimately accomplished). Similarly, the CEO also pushed to "eliminate the white space" in surgeons' calendars. Consequently, surgeons accustomed to working every other day began working every day.[39] Improvements in technology have also improved patient satisfaction. As Berry and Seltman stated, "High levels of service satisfaction result in part from the strategic investment of millions of dollars each year in industrial engineering to create the processes and infrastructure that facilitate clinical quality and safety as well as the efficient delivery of care."[40]

> *Conjecture 3: Outcomes of enterprise-directed practices enacted at the Mayo Clinic exceed the average level of such practices at the best hospitals in the U.S.*
>
> *Conjecture 4: Combined levels of patient-directed, employee-directed, and enterprise-directed practices enacted at Mayo Clinic exceed the average levels of such composite practices at the best hospitals in the U.S.*

The next section examines evidence pertinent to these four conjectures. Because multiple sources of data are examined, the results are neither pure survey research (as per Chapter 5) nor purely an examination of financial metrics (Chapter 6).

Method

Procedure

The sample of hospitals was comprised of all hospitals listed in one or more of the 12 primary specialty areas in the *U.S. News & World Report Best Hospitals*, 2013. If a hospital was listed in more than one major specialty area, we computed the mean score. The 12 specialties are Cancer; Cardiology; Diabetes; Ear, Nose, and Throat; Gastroenterology; Geriatrics; Gynecology; Nephrology; Neurology; Orthopedics; Pulmonology; and Urology.

In total, the *U.S. News & World Report Best Hospitals* issue actually compiles data on 16 specialties; however, hospital rankings in four specialties are solely based on their reputation among specialists.[41] Due to the lack of any hard data in these specialty areas (e.g., survival rates, or safety), we excluded them from our analysis.

For analytical purposes, the summary *U.S. News* score is captured for each of the top 50 hospitals in each of the 12 major specialties. Mean scores were calculated for hospitals that were ranked in one or more specialties. As a result, the sample consists of 136 hospitals and the composite mean measure is the dependent variable for the study.

Measures

Independent variables. In terms of the Cube One framework, the independent variables are patient satisfaction (reflective of patient-directed practices); employee satisfaction (reflective of employee-directed practices); and financial and efficiency metrics (reflective of enterprise-directed practices).

Patient satisfaction data come from the U.S. Department of Health and Human Services' Centers for Medicare and Medicaid Services (CMS). According to the CMS website (www.cms.gov/medicare), the HCAHPS (Hospital Consumer Assessment of Healthcare Providers and Systems) Survey, also known as the CAHPS® Hospital Survey or Hospital CAHPS®, is a standardized survey instrument and data collection methodology that has been in use since 2006 to measure patients' perspectives of hospital care.

Hospital-level survey results for ten patient survey questions are publicly reported on the Hospital Compare website (http://www.hospitalcompare.hhs.gov). CMS also publishes national and state averages for these ten questions. The present study examined three measures. Two are questions from the study: (1) patients who gave their hospital a rating of nine or ten on a scale from 0 (lowest) to 10 (highest), and (2) patients who reported they would definitely recommend the hospital. This second metric corresponds closely to what Reichheld in *The Ultimate Question* found to be far and away the best predictor of customer loyalty, a question more predictive than customer satisfaction.[42]

In addition, we calculated a summary measure of the average of all ten published questions. This corresponds with Iga Rudawska's approach in her study on the dilemmas associated with measuring the quality of professional services. According to Rudawska, the starting point of such an analysis should be an "evaluation of the customer's satisfaction from the experienced service."[43] The overall sample size in our study for patient-directed variables is 127 hospitals.[44]

Employee satisfaction data obtained from Glassdoor.com are two-fold. First, respondents provided an overall rating on a five-point scale with endpoints of "very satisfied" and "very dissatisfied." Using Glassdoor.com's five-point scale, we generated an overall weighted average score for the best "non-Mayo" hospitals. Likewise, we obtained the percentage of employees who "would recommend this company to a friend" for each hospital.[45]

Dependent variable: Hospital performance. A review of the literature reveals both the considerable difficulty and lack of consensus regarding the definition and measurement of hospital performance. Analyses largely based on financial gauges are seen as too restrictive for organizations dedicated to helping people.[46] For example, Lemieux-Charles and colleagues have studied performance indicators in health care organizations in Canada and found that performance measures operate at different levels. "Institutional legitimacy is typically governed by different values (efficiency and cost containment) than technical/managerial legitimacy (quality of care and specialty training), and these differences can create tensions within an organization."[47]

Health care leaders themselves have identified the need for both financial and clinical measures in assessing hospital performance.[48] This conceptualization has, on a limited basis, been tested empirically.[49] Along these lines, when members of the World Health Organization European Regional Office developed a tool to assess hospital performance, they adopted a multidimensional approach, including clinical effectiveness, safety, patient centeredness, production efficiency, staff orientation, and responsive governance.[50]

Judgments of hospital performance seemingly differ based on perspective, as Miller and colleagues have noted: "Quality and safety of health care is a multidimensional construct depending on one's vantage point as a policy maker, purchaser, payer, researcher, or patient."[51]

Consistent with multidimensional conceptualizations of hospital performance, research has examined the relationship between hospital performance and numerous variables, including hospital characteristics—e.g., primary mission, whether for-profit or nonprofit;[52] top management culture;[53] patient satisfaction;[54] employee satisfaction;[55] productive efficiency;[56] HRM practices;[57] and regional variations in productivity.[58]

Adopting a broad perspective, Sparrow and Cooper have likewise noted that "organizational effectiveness requires the satisfaction of multiple constituencies— each having an influence on the priorities against which organizational performance should be judged."[59] Although numerous independent variables have been examined, almost indisputably the central criterion of hospital performance reflects their primary mission: the quality of health care provided; the patient cure rate; and patient survival, especially from curable diseases.[60]

In light of the central role of the quality of care, the present research found the ratings provided by *U.S. News & World Report* to be on target. Although their evaluation was comprised of several components, 70% of the composite score was based on three quality factors: survival score (32.5%), reputation as assessed by industry experts (32.5%), and patient safety (5%).[61] As noted above, ratings were provided for the top 50 U.S. hospitals in 12 primary medical specialties. For hospitals listed on more than one specialty, the average score was used.[62]

Analyses

To answer the fundamental question, "Is the reputation of the Mayo Clinic deserved?" Mayo Clinic scores were compared to scores from the sample of 134 non-Mayo best hospitals.[63] This analysis was performed for each of the four conjectures advanced above.[64]

Results

Patient Satisfaction

Based on a review of the patient-directed practices enacted at Mayo, we hypothesized that patient satisfaction scores at Mayo would be higher than those at the 134 non-Mayo Best Hospitals. For each of the three satisfaction metrics, scores were significantly higher at Mayo compared to the non–Mayo hospitals.[65] Details are provided in Table 10.2.

We also compared Mayo's results to a U.S. sample of 2,482 hospitals. Results were consistently significant and sizable.[66] With respect to the "Ultimate Question" item (whether the patient would definitely recommend), proportions for Mayo, the 134 non–Mayo Best, and the large U.S. sample were 86%, 78%, and 70%, respectively. With regard to the comparison between the Mayo and U.S. sample, the difference in proportions reached more than 12 sigma—an immense statistic. The proportion of patients who would assign an overall rating of nine or ten yielded a similar pattern of results: 84%, 72%, and 68%. Details are provided in Table 10.3.[67]

Employee Satisfaction

The difference between employee satisfaction scores for Mayo employees vs. all non–Mayo best hospital employees was not significant (mean satisfaction scores being 3.46 for Mayo employees and 3.42 for non–Mayo employees, respectively). The measure of whether the employee would recommend the company to a friend for Mayo vs. non–Mayo employees was also not significant (67.9% vs. 73.3%), and opposite to the predicted direction. Comparisons with the large U.S. sample were not available, due to an absence of Glassdoor.com ratings for the approximately 3,000 U.S. hospitals. Hence, it is reasonable to assert that overall, employee satisfaction at Mayo might be deemed average or Middle.[68] Treating

TABLE 10.2 Tests of Differences in Scores: The Mayo Clinic vs. best U.S. Hospitals

Variable	Mayo Hospitals	Best 134 Hospitals	
	Mean	Mean	Z-Score
Patient Satisfaction	0.77	0.70	5.12***
(Mean score on 10 items)			
Patient would definitely recommend	0.86	0.78	7.12***
Patient rating: 9 or 10	0.84	0.72	8.61***
Employee Satisfaction [a]	3.46	3.42	0.28[ns]
Employee would recommend	0.68	0.73	1.02[ns]
Profit Margin	0.07	0.03	1.38[ns]
Average occupancy rate	0.67	0.77	4.12***
Medicare ratio [b]	0.95	1.00	3.78***
Length of stay [c]	4.99	5.81	5.71***
Hospital Performance	89.31	69.27	7.26***

*** $p < 0.001$
[ns] = not significant

TABLE 10.3 Tests of Means: The Mayo Clinic vs. other U.S. Hospitals

Variable	Mayo Hospitals	U.S. Hospitals[a]	
	Mean	Mean	Z-Score
Patient Satisfaction (Mean score on 10 items)	0.77	0.71	5.07***
Patient would definitely recommend	0.86	0.70	12.29***
Patient rating: 9 or 10	0.84	0.68	11.52***
Employee Satisfaction	3.46	n/a	n/a
Employee would recommend	0.68	n/a	n/a
Profit Margin	0.07	n/a	n/a
Average occupancy rate	0.67	0.56	4.02***
Medicare ratio	0.95	1.00	n/a
Length of stay	4.99	5.43	3.44***
Hospital Performance	89.31	n/a	n/a

[a] 5,008 U.S. hospitals
[b] National averages came from the American Hospital Directory, a proprietary database.
*** $p < 0.001$; n/a = not available

employee satisfaction as indicative of employee-directed practices, this would place Mayo Clinic in Cube 2, High, Middle, and High.

Enterprise Operational Efficiency

General support was found for Conjecture 3. The difference in the profit margins at Mayo (6.77%) versus the non-Mayo best hospitals (2.89%) was sizable (more than twice as high). Yet given the relatively small sample sizes, the difference only approached statistical significance ($p < 0.08$).[69] It is notable that the hospital with the highest profit margin (14.8%) in the study is Mayo/Clinic/Saint Marys/Methodist Hospital.[70] Differences in the three other operational metrics were mostly positive. Measures of average occupancy rate, Mayo vs. non-Mayo (66.50% vs. 77.43%) was significant ($Z = 4.12$, $p < 0.001$), but in the opposite direction. Medicare expense ratios (for which a lower number is better) were for Mayo vs. non-Mayo (0.95 vs. 1.00), which was significant ($Z = 3.78$, $p < 0.001$). The average length of stay, for which the lower number is also better, was Mayo 4.99 days versus non-Mayo 5.81 days—another significant difference—in the predicted direction ($Z = 5.71$, $p < 0.001$).

Regarding national averages, differences in measures of average occupancy rate and average length of stay were significant. The average occupancy rate of Mayo vs. the national average (66.50% vs. 56.41%) was significant ($Z = 4.02$, $p < 0.001$). The Medicare ratio for Mayo vs. the national average did not permit a statistical comparison due to the lack of a national estimate of variance. However, the difference between the occupancy rate at Mayo (0.95) and the national average (which is by definition 1.00) entails comparison with an even larger sample (3,841 hospitals) than was the case using the 134 non-Mayo best hospitals. The average lengths of stay were 4.99 days at Mayo vs. the national average of 5.43 days were significantly different ($Z = 3.44, p < 0.001$).

Hospital Performance

Conjecture 4 posited that composite scores on independent variables would be higher at Mayo compared to the non-Mayo 134 best hospitals. Average hospital performance ratings were 89.31 for Mayo versus 69.27 for non-Mayo, an extraordinarily sizable and significant difference ($Z = 7.26, p < 0.001$).[71]

Discussion and Conclusion

As previously noted, the Cube One Causal framework posits that three sets of practices drive organizational performance: (1) customer-directed practices, which influence the satisfaction and loyalty of customers, who ultimately are the revenue providers; (2) employee-directed practices, which influence the satisfaction and loyalty of the organization's internal customers, employees, who convert inputs to outputs; and (3) enterprise-directed practices, which influence the ability of the organization to attract and retain capital and funding via the efficient use of resources, human and nonhuman. This is in line with Babic-Hodovic, and colleagues' assertion that the three core principles of quality management are employee management, process orientation, and customer orientation.[72]

Unlike past survey analyses, which obtained data from only one source, the present research examined data from four different sources. Obtaining data from multiple sources mitigates the threat of spurious results due to common method variance and associated problems.[73] Our study found relatively low levels of multicollinearity among the three independent variables. Multicollinearity—the phenomenon of one or more independent variables "picking up" the same variance as other variables—has been common when data are obtained from one source. In contrast, in the present research, mean intercorrelations among measures of the independent variables were quite low ($r = 0.23$). This reflects an important strength of the present analysis: the use of multiple independent sources of data.[74]

Hospitals are unique in the service industry because the nature of their business can have life or death consequences. Mistakes often cannot be undone. "Customers" requiring a "service" often feel vulnerable, frightened, in physical and emotional pain, and uncertain about their future. Hospitals must satisfy patients, the patient's families, employees, government agencies, suppliers, insurance companies, their administration, the board of trustees, and the community at large. In an environment such as this, management practices toward customers (patients), employees, and the organization itself are crucial to the success of hospitals and all who depend on them.

All three CMS measures of patient satisfaction significantly correlated with the *U.S. News & World Report Best Hospitals* average specialty score for hospital performance. The overall CMS score includes ratings on questions such as whether doctors and nurses communicated well with them, whether help was available when they needed it, and whether their room and bathroom were clean. The *U.S. News* hospital performance scores do not include patient satisfaction data in their ratings. However, because the *U.S. News* score is a composite of reputation, patient outcomes, patient safety, and structure, it is reasonable to deduce that patient-directed practices contribute to the *U.S. News* score on hospital performance.

In our multiple regression analysis, the single strongest predictor of hospital performance was the average score on employee satisfaction using the Glassdoor.com rating. In light of the service nature of hospitals, it is not surprising that employee-directed practices and consequent employee satisfaction would be the strongest performance predictor. However, Glassdoor.com data are not a random sample of employee opinions. Thus, sample bias is a possibility. But with regard to performance data, the significant associations with the *U.S. News & World Report Best Hospitals* performance ratings, indicates that results cannot be interpreted as artifactual, attributable to common method variance, or some other methodological flaw.

Glassdoor.com sample sizes were small. Only slightly more than one-fifth of the best hospitals met our requirement of a minimum of 40 ratings. In contrast to these Glassdoor.com data limitations, both the patient data and the enterprise data originated from government studies that sampled tens of thousands of patients, and thousands of hospitals, in a systematic, comprehensive manner.

The most "bottom line" indicator of efficiency—profit margin—was most strongly related to hospital performance. Productivity is improved by either increasing outputs using the same resources, or, by maintaining the same level of output while using fewer resources. Decreasing resources that lead to increased wait times—what might be characterized as "cost savings productivity"—will often decrease patient satisfaction. However, a decrease in resources resulting from process improvements—what might be labeled "client-focused productivity"—holds the potential for both enhanced efficiency and patient satisfaction. Hospitals that conserve resources while effectively serving patients may in the long run be more efficient than hospitals which cut back on patient care to save money.[75]

It is interesting to note, and somewhat surprising, that profit margin correlated significantly with all three measures of patient satisfaction. Of course, correlation does not imply causality, but does patient satisfaction lead to a higher demand for, and increased profitability among, certain hospitals? Or, alternatively, do more profitable hospitals possess the resources to initiate multiple processes—perhaps effecting shorter, less stressful hospital stays—that increase patient satisfaction? Research by Lemieux-Charles and colleagues supports the second premise as they found, "the availability of organizational resources affected HCO's [health-care organization] ability to implement staff and patient satisfaction recommendations, improve staff/patient ratios, improve the physical environment, or upgrade equipment."[76]

Performance measures have implications beyond individual hospitals or health care organizations. Castelli and colleagues conducted a study on the National Health Service in the United Kingdom and stated: "Measurement of output and productivity in non-market services is not just of interest to those working within the national accounts tradition but is also important for policy-makers charged with providing, funding and/or regulating these services."[77] Likewise, Medin and colleagues in an international study of hospital productivity in the Nordic countries stated:

> Therefore, the execution of systematic comparison of the provision of health care could be helpful for sharing experiences in solving comparable problems and identifying best practices. This type of information should provide evidence for policy makers in identifying optimal structures in the provision and reimbursement of health care.[78]

It is important to note that the present analysis of Mayo and other excellent hospitals has a built-in level of range restriction, given that the sample consisted of what might be arguably described as the top 2.8% of U.S. hospitals. It is likely that stronger results would be obtained with a sample more representative of the universe of U.S. hospitals.

Whether related to health care systems in the U.S.—which are a combination of government, for-profit, and nonprofit hospitals—or whether related to National Health Care Systems such as in England, the same factors govern their assessment: patient, employee, and efficiency dimensions critical to the mission of providing health care to society. Finding better ways to achieve optimal outcomes while preserving resources can enable more and better care. This has implications not only at the hospital level, but at all levels at which funding allocation decisions are made.

The Cube One framework advances a theory-based approach to assessing hospital performance that is not merely useful for gaining insights using empirical analyses. Rather, the fundamental purpose of the present inquiry has been to see whether a relatively new model, the Cube One framework, has relevance for explaining, diagnosing, and improving hospital performance. Our research finds that all three dimensions were significantly associated with hospital performance. Theoretically, when hospitals are classified as High, Middle, or Low in terms of those dimensions, a number of improvement-related inferences can be made.

Finally, regarding the Mayo Clinic analyses, Mayo had significantly higher scores for patient satisfaction, the efficiency measures of the Medicare ratio, and average length of stay. Mayo patients appear to cost less; stay in the hospital for a shorter time; yield a higher operating margin; and report higher satisfaction compared to patient averages of the other highest-rated hospitals. Although the research revealed no significant differences in employee satisfaction, this may be due to the measurement issues discussed previously with regard to the Glassdoor. com data as well as the comparison of Mayo with an elite sample of hospitals.

Is the reputation of Mayo Clinic deserved? We believe the correct answer is clearly yes. However, because Mayo Clinic rates High in terms of patient satisfaction, Medium in terms of employee satisfaction, and High in terms of efficiency-related outcomes, this would place Mayo in Cube 2. With regard to ratings of hospital performance, Mayo is significantly higher than the select set of best U.S. hospitals listed in *U.S. News & World Report*. Mayo is substantially above average in comparison to all U.S. hospitals. While in all regards, Mayo may not be indisputably the single best hospital in the U.S., it surely is among the very best.

Appendix 10.1: Examples of Patient-Directed Work Behaviors at the Mayo Clinic

Management Lessons from the Mayo Clinic

By Leonard L. Berry and Kent D. Seltman
McGraw-Hill, 2008

Anecdote 1

Hello Dr. Decker,

I'm remiss in not sending you this email earlier, but I wanted to recount an experience I had in the Emergency Room about three months ago with Dr. Luis Haro. I want to share firsthand with you what an extraordinary physician he is.

I live with my mother who is 91 and has fairly severe dementia. About three months ago, I came home to find her outside on the lawn. She had fallen, was unable to get up, and had a nasty bruise and scrape on her elbow. She is a tiny woman so I managed to get her up and we headed for the Emergency Room. Once there, we were seen quickly and everyone was very solicitous of her. She's also almost deaf so sometimes this is no easy task.

Dr. Haro introduced himself and was very patient and kind—and spoke with enough volume so she could hear him. As he examined her, he asked her to stand up and take a few steps. As she began to do so, she bumped into him. My mother in her day was quite a wit and some of that has remained. She looked up at him after bumping against him and said, "Well, I suppose we could waltz." And he replied, "Yes, we could." He then proceeded to take her in his arms and waltz a few steps around the cubicle. My mother was absolutely enchanted as she loves to dance and I started to cry. The sight of this tiny fragile old woman being waltzed around the room by this most handsome young man was just too much. I don't think I've ever been prouder to be a Mayo employee than that night. To witness that interaction and know this is the caliber of doctor we have here, someone whose medical expertise is a given but whose compassion and kindness—and humanness—are extraordinary was very moving.

I know in the grand scheme of Emergency Medicine this scenario has little significance. My mother had a bad bruise and a scrape but really was just fine. Her physical symptoms healed in a day or two but the "healing" that occurred that evening with his interaction with her is really what sets Mayo apart and will last in my memory forever.

Writing as a patient's family member, I want to tell you that your department and Mayo are very, very lucky to have Dr. Haro as a member of Staff (pp. 173–174). Quoted vignette reproduced with permission of McGraw-Hill Global Education Holdings, LLC. Copyright © 2008 by the McGraw-Hill Companies, Inc.

Anecdote 2

I was called to the transfusion lab in the middle of night to look at a cross match before we could go ahead with a kidney transplant. As I left the lab, I noticed one of the techs was working. As it was then about 2:00 a.m., I decided that I'd talk to her later. The following morning I brought her into my office and asked, "What were you doing in the lab at two in the morning? You weren't working on kidney. I know, because I was there." This young, blonde, blue-eyed, Minnesotan turned bright red, acutely embarrassed, and said to me, "Dr. Moore I was hoping you wouldn't see me." My heart sank when she said that. I thought, oh my God, what has she done? She continued, "I was doing the platelet antibody test during the day, and I accidentally used a solution of the wrong molarity and lost all the platelets. So by the end of the day when I read the tests on all the patients, it was a bust—and I knew it was a bust—I couldn't read it. So I was back doing the test again."

I replied, "That's really wonderful of you, but you probably could have done it today without having to come back last night in the middle of a January blizzard." She said, "Dr. Moore, I can't have the patients at Mayo Clinic waiting an extra day in the hospital because I fouled up a lab test."

My jaw hit the floor at this point, so I said, "Well, that is very laudable. Make sure you put in for your overtime." She looked at me as if I had told her to rob the poor box in the church. She replied with a certain outrage, "Dr. Moore, I can't have Mayo paying me for my mistakes!"

I sat there thinking I don't believe I'm hearing this. This particular technologist was a hard-working young woman, a wonderful technologist, but in a way that was ordinary in our lab. Her attitude, her work ethic, her sense of ethics was such that this is just how she behaved. She was appalled that I would suggest that she be paid for her overtime at two in the morning. Employees like this are what make Mayo great (pp. 185–186). Quoted vignette reproduced with permission

Anecdote 3

Working in critical care, we often deal with death and dying. It is how our team approached this particular death that represents the ultimate team effort. Mr. M had recently received a terminal diagnosis, and he and his wife of more than 50 years were struggling with the decision of further aggressive treatment versus palliative care. At Mayo, we function as a team with ease even in the most difficult situations. All the appropriate team members did their part to assist this couple during a very difficult time. Nursing continued to give excellent bedside care. The case manager and social worker spent time with Mr. and Mrs. M detailing options for both hospice and acute care while helping them attend to any personal matters and possible impending arrangements. A family conference was provided at the bedside to allow for Mr. M to participate in the decision making. Physicians, a social worker, a case manager, the chaplain, and nursing were present. Although Mr. M was ready to make the decision to end aggressive treatment, Mrs. M could not accept the end was near. Treatment continued and everything was done to prolong Mr. M's life. The chaplain prayed with the family and told Mr. and Mrs. M to call at any time if they needed him.

This is where the real teamwork begins. W, the young nurse caring for Mr. M, had never cared for a patient who was so close to death. I, being an experienced 20-year veteran, let her know I was there for her during this difficult time if she needed me. W was both thankful and relieved. Mr. M was becoming more critical as the day went by and Mrs. M was realizing how much he was suffering. At approximately 4:00 p.m. that afternoon, Mrs. M called W into the room and asked that her husband be made comfortable and be allowed to pass on in peace. W notified the physician and asked me if I could come into the room when Mr. M's passing was imminent.

An hour later, all the appropriate paperwork (do not resuscitate order) was signed allowing for comfort measures and for Mr. M to die peacefully when his time came. Mrs. M was at his side with both W and me nearby to offer support. The other nurse on our pod continued to care for my patients, so I could help W help this couple say goodbye. I consider myself quite skilled and compassionate when it comes to death, but on this day I became the student and watched and learned.

At 6:00 p.m., Mrs. M requested the chaplain be called to pray with her as her husband became less responsive and closer to his death. I instructed W on how to page the chaplain only to find out he was on another pod with another family who was in a similar situation. He said he would be with us in about 20 minutes. Mr. M did not have 20 minutes. Mrs. M was crying and requesting the chaplain so a prayer could be said while her husband passed on. It was very clear Mr. M would not live another 20 minutes. I grabbed the tissues and prepared to comfort

Mrs. M and show W the best compassion I had. When I entered the room, I saw W, who was of a different faith, take Mrs. M's hand in one hand and Mr. M's hand in the other and begin to pray. She asked the Lord to bless their 50-year marriage using their first names (I am not sure I would have been able to recall their first names that quickly). Her voice was strong, clear, and sweet and did not waver as she recited the Lord's Prayer while Mr. M took his last breath.

I stood by the entrance to the room and sobbed. My emotions were mixed. Both sadness for Mrs. M's loss and joy that we, the team, provided what the patient needed. W was the ultimate team player. She assumed another's role, making our system flawless when it mattered most (pp. 264–265). Quoted vignette reproduced with permission of McGraw-Hill Global Education Holdings, LLC. Copyright © 2008 by the McGraw-Hill Companies, Inc.

Notes

1 Berry, L. L., and Seltman, K. D. (2008). *Management lessons from Mayo Clinic: Inside one of the world's most admired service organizations.* New York, NY: McGraw-Hill, pp 7–8. The Mayo Clinic has also been described as "an American treasure." See "Winslow, R. Mayo's tricky task: Revamp what works." (June 3–4, 2017). *The Wall Street Journal*, pp. A1, A10.

2 The Mayo Clinic case, coauthored with Phoebe Massimino and Meg Joseph, was initially presented at an academic conference. The full citation is: Massimino, P. M., Joseph, M. L., and Kopelman, R. E., "Explaining hospital performance with the Cube One Framework: Is the Mayo Clinic reputation deserved?" Paper presented at the 2013 Meeting of the Southern Management Association and included in the Proceedings, 2013, pp. 120–138, (New Orleans). Subsequently, the work was published in a journal: Massimino, P. M., Joseph, M., L., and Kopelman, R. E. 2015. "Hospital performance and customer-, employee-, and enterprise-directed practices: Is the Mayo Clinic reputation deserved?" *International Journal of Management Cases*, 17(3), 28–48.

3 The survey research study was also coauthored with Phoebe Massimino and Meg Joseph. The full citation is as follows: Massimino, P. M., Kopelman, R, E., and Joseph, M. L. 2015. "Explaining hospital performance via the Cube One framework." *Journal of Organizational Effectiveness: People and Performance*, 2(1), 73–90.

4 Mayo Clinic History. (n.d.). Retrieved at http://www.mayoclinic.org/about-mayo-clinic/history. Accessed on August 7, 2014 (n.p.).

5 Berry, L. L., and Seltman, K. D. (2008). *Management lessons from Mayo Clinic: Inside one of the world's most admired service organizations.* New York, NY: McGraw-Hill, pp. 21–22.

6 Ibid., p. 5.

7 Barry and Seltman, op. cit., p. 97.

8 Op, cit., p. 194.

9 Ibid., p. 115.

10 Dulling, J. A., Swensen, S. J., Hoover, M. R., Dankbar, G. C., Donahoe-Anshus, A. L., Murad, M. H., and Mueller, J. T. (2013). "Accelerating the use of best practices: The Mayo Clinic model of diffusion." *The Joint Commission Journal on Quality and Patient Safety*, 39(4), 167.

11 Ibid., p. 21.

12 Ibid., p. 8.

13 Ibid., p. 27.

14 *Mayo Clinic Model of Care.* (2014), p. 9.

15 Ibid., p.10.

16 Fried, Jason. (March 2015). "Why you should make the little things count." *Inc.*, 37(4), 100. Retrieved at https://www.inc.com/magazine/201503/jason-fried/make-the-little-things-count.html

17 Beck, M. (May 27, 2015). "Making a cost case for proton-beam therapy." *The Wall Street Journal*, pp. B1, B4.

18 Rosenbluth, H. F., and Peters, D. M. (1992). *The customer comes second: And other secrets of exceptional service.* New York, NY: William Morris Publishing. Also, see Sharp, I. (2009). *Four Seasons: The story of a business philosophy.* New York, NY: Portfolio.

19 Barry and Seltman, op.cit.

20 Ibid., p. 252.

21 Viggiano, T. R., Pawlina, W., Lindor, K. D., Olsen, K. D., and Cortese, D. A. (2007). "Putting the needs of the patient first: Mayo Clinic's core value, institutional culture, and professionalism covenant." *Academic Medicine*, 82, 1089–1093.

22 Ibid., p. 27.

23 Mayo Clinic Model of Care. (2014), np.

24 Diversity Inc. (n.d.). "Mayo Clinic: No. 8 in The DiversityInc top 10 hospitals and health systems." Retrieved at http://www.diversityinc.com/mayo-clinic/. Accessed on August 8, 2014.

25 Barry and Seltman, op. cit., p. 33. Quotation reproduced with permission of McGraw-Hill Global Education Holdings, LLC. Copyright © 2008 by the McGraw-Hill Companies, Inc.

26 Ibid., p. 58.

27 Ibid., p. 52. Quotation reproduced with permission of McGraw-Hill Global Education Holdings, LLC. Copyright © 2008 by the McGraw-Hill Companies, Inc. Not surprisingly, not all employees find the Mayo patient/team culture congenial. It has been observed that people who are not comfortable with it "usually leave within a few years. Those who stay for five years usually stay for life." See Saito-Chung, D. (August 15, 2016). "The Mayos built clinic on dedication and trust." *Investor's Business Daily*, pp. A4, A6.

28 Universom. (2014). "Universum top 100 ideal employer rankings." pp. 3–8. It might be noted that among humanities majors, Mayo was ranked the 23rd best employer.

29 Ibid., p. 90.

30 Ibid., p. 224.

31 Ibid., p. 260.

32 *Mayo Clinic Model of Care.* (2014), p. 11. Quotation reproduced with permission by Mayo Clinic Health Systems.

33 Ibid., pp. 69–70. Quotation reproduced with permission by Mayo Clinic Health Systems.

34 Saver, C. (2013). "Best Practices lead to greater consistency in vendor credentialing." *OR Manager*, 29(11), 1–4. Retrieved at http://www.ormanager.com/wp-content/uploads/2013/11/ORM_1113_p.01_Vendor.pdf. Accessed on August 6, 2014.

35 Dilling, J. A., Swensen, S. J., Hoover, M. R., Dankbar, G. C., Donahoe-Anshus, A. L., Murad, M. H., and Mueller, J. T. (2013). "Accelerating the use of best practices: The Mayo Clinic Model of Diffusion." *The Joint Commission Journal on Quality and Patient Safety*, 39(4), 167.

36 Ibid., p. 169.

37 Ibid.

38 Ibid, p. 171.

39 Winslow, R. (June 3–4, 2017). "Mayo's tricky task: Revamp what works." *The Wall Street Journal*, pp. A1, A10. Pertinent to the need to improve efficiency, the CEO at Mayo noted the continuing pressure on reimbursement rates. Pertinent to the pressure to reduce costs, at Cleveland Clinic, for example, annual costs were cut by $800 million from 2013 to 2016. Yet operating income dropped 71% between 2015 and 2016.

40 Barry and Seltman, op. cit., p. 76. Quotation reproduced with permission of McGraw-Hill Global Education Holdings, LLC. Copyright © 2008 by the McGraw-Hill Companies, Inc.

41 Comarow, A. (July 16, 2012). "Inside the rankings." *U.S. News & World Report*, pp. 85, 98.

42 Reichheld, F.F. (2006). *The ultimate question: Driving good profits and true growth.* Cambridge, MA: Harvard Business School Press.

43 Rudawska, I. (2009). "Dilemmas in measuring the quality of professional services—example of health care." *International Journal of Management Cases*, Special Issue: New Trends in Management and Economics in Poland, p. 6. This article was part of a special issue with the link Retrieved at http://www.ijmc.org/ijmc/Vol_11.1_files/IJMC_11.1.pdf

44 Due to unavailable data, the sample was reduced from 136 to 127 hospitals.

45 Glassdoor.com data were only examined for hospitals with six or more reviews during the study period (September 2012–January 2013). This yielded a sample of 82 hospitals.

46 Ehreth, J. L. (1994). "The development and evaluation of hospital performance measures for policy analysis." *Medical Care*, 32(6), 568–587.

47 Lemieux-Charles, L., McGuire, W., Champagne, F., Barnsley, J., Cole, D., and Sicotte, C. (2003). "The use of multilevel performance indicators in managing performance in health care organizations." *Management Decision*, 41(8), 760–770. The quotation appears on p. 761.

48 Love, D., Revere, L. and Black, K. (2008). "A current look at the key performance measures considered critical by health care leaders." *Journal of Health Care Finance*, 34(3), 19–33.

49 Griffith, J. R. and Alexander, J. A. (2002). "Measuring comparative hospital performance." *Journal of Healthcare Management*, 47(1), 41–57.

50 Veillard, J., Champagne, F., Klazinga, N., Kazandjian, V., Arah, O. A. and Guisset, A.-L. (2005), "A performance assessment framework for hospitals: The WHO regional office for Europe PATH project." *International Journal for Quality in Health Care*, 17(6), 487–496.

51 Miller, M. R., Pronovost, P., Donithan, M., Zeger, S., Zhan, C., Morlock, L., and Meyer, G. S. (2005). "Relationship between performance measurement and accreditation: Implications for quality of care and patient safety." *American Journal of Medical Quality*, 20(5), 239–252. The quote appears on p. 239.

52 Brand, C. A., Barker, A. L., Morello, R. T., Vitale, M. R., Evans, S. M., Scott, I. A., Stoelwinder, J. U., and Cameron, P. A. (2012). "A review of hospital characteristics associated with improved performance." *International Journal for Quality in Health Care*, 24(5), 483–494.

53 Gerowitz, M. B., Lemieux-Charles, L., Heginbothan, C., and Johnson, B. (1996). "Top management culture and performance in Canadian, U.K., and U.S. hospitals." *Health Services Management Research*, 9(2), 69–78.

54 Shwartz, M., Cohen, A. B., Restuccia, J. D., Ren, Z. J., Labonte, A., Theokary, C., Kang, R., and Horwitt, J. (2011). "How well can we identify the high-performing hospital?" *Medical Care Research and Review*, 68(3), 290–310.

55 Unruh, L. (2008). "Nurse staffing, and patient, nurse, and financial outcomes." *American Journal of Nursing*, 108(1), 62–71. Also see, Harmon, J., Scotti, D.J., Behson, S., Farias, G., Petzel, R., Neuman, J. H., and Keashly, L. (2003). "Effects of high-involvement work systems on employee satisfaction and service costs in veteran health care." *Journal of Healthcare Management*, 48(6), 393–406.

56 Nayar, P., Ozcan, Y.A., Yu, F., and Nguyen, A. T. (2013). "Benchmarking urban acute care hospitals: Efficiency and quality perspectives." *Health Care Management Review*, 38(2), 137145. Also see, Schwartz et al. op. cit.

57 West, M. A., Borrill, C. S., Dawson, J. F., Scully, J., Carter, M., Anelay, S., Patterson, M. G., and Waring, J. (2002). "The link between the management of employees and patient

mortality in acute hospitals." *International Journal of Human Resource Management*, 13, 1299–1310. Also see West, M. A., Guthrie, J. P., Dawson, J. F., Borrill, C. S., and Carter, M. R. (2006). "Reducing patient mortality in hospitals: The role of human resource management." *Journal of Organizational Behavior*, 27, 983–1002.

58 Bojke, C., Castelli, A., Street, A., Ward, P., and Laudicella, M. (2013). "Regional variation in the productivity of English National Health Service." *Health Economics* 22(2), 194–211. Relatedly, studies have examined relationships among independent variables. For example, research has consistently found positive associations between measures of nurse satisfaction and patient satisfaction. See Atkins, P. M., Marshall, B. S., and Javalgi, R.G. (1996). "Happy employees lead to loyal patients." *Journal of Health Care Marketing*, 16(4), 14–23. Also see McHugh, M. D., and Sloane, D. M. (2011). "Nurses' widespread job dissatisfaction, burnout, and frustration with health benefits signal problems for patient care." *Health Affairs*, 30(2), 202–210. Still another demonstration is provided by Otani, K., Waterman, B., and Dunagan, W. C. (2012). "Patient satisfaction: How patient health conditions influence their satisfaction." *Journal of Healthcare Management*, 57(4), 276–292.

59 Sparrow, P., and Cooper, C. (2014). "Organizational effectiveness, people and performance: New challenges, new research agendas." *Journal of Organizational Effectiveness*, 1(1), 2–13. The quotation appears on p. 4.

60 West et al., op. cit.; also, West et al., op. cit.

61 Murphy and colleagues have specified the basis for the reputational rating. See Murphy, J., Geisen, E., Olmsted, M. G., Williams, J., Pitts, A., Bell, D., Morley, M., and Stanley, M. (June 22, 2012). *Methodology: U.S. News & World Report best hospitals 2012–13*. Retrieved at http://www.usnews.com/pubfiles/7-17AdultMethReport2012_Final. pdf. As they state, a hospital's reputational score is based on average responses from board-certified physicians who are asked to nominate those hospitals in their specific field of care, irrespective of expense or location. More specifically, they are required to consider the best hospitals for patients with serious or difficult conditions.

62 To circumvent the arbitrary weightings of the *U.S. News & World Report* ratings, e.g., awarding two extra points to hospitals in the top ten, and the one extra point for hospitals in the next ten, and zero points were added for the next 30 hospitals we averaged hospital scores across specialties. The ultimate source of the scores, however, reflects a relatively nontransparent ("proprietary") formulation which consists of the following major components and weights: reputation (32.5%), survival score (32.5%), patient safety (5%) and overall structure (30%). The overall structure score is comprised of 11 different sub-criteria across the 12 specialty areas. The same structure weights were applied to all 12 specialties, but items differed across specialties; the most common of which are whether the hospital is considered a nurse magnet hospital, nurse staffing scores, patient services, patient volume, and whether the hospital is using advanced technology. Component scores are not provided for the 11 structure factors, which add to the nontransparent nature of the composite hospital score. Nonetheless, the *U.S. News & World Report* measure is the most comprehensive multidimensional source of hospital performance data.

63 Comarow, A. (July 16, 2012). "Inside the rankings." *U.S. News & World Report*, pp. 85–98 describes the process by which the universe of approximately 5,000 U.S. hospitals was reduced to about 2,000. "To be considered for rankings in any of the 12 data-driven specialties, a hospital had to meet any of four criteria: be a teaching hospital, be affiliated with a medical school, have at least 200 beds, or have at least 100 beds plus four or more medical technologies. ... The hospitals next had to meet a volume requirement to be ranked in a particular specialty. Additionally, other criteria are examined that are unique to each specialty." p. 86. Quotation reproduced with permission of *U.S. News & World Report*.

64 We included data from all four Mayo hospitals, because CMS and AHD report separate data for each Mayo facility. In Rochester: Mayo Clinic/Saint Marys/Methodist,

and Rochester General. As per the Mayo Clinic website, "Mayo Clinic, Saint Marys Hospital and Rochester Methodist Hospital form an integrated medical center dedicated to providing comprehensive diagnosis and treatment in virtually every medical and surgical specialty," see www.mayoclinic.org. The Mayo Jacksonville (Fla.) and Phoenix (Ariz.) sites are the other two hospitals included in the Mayo vs. non-Mayo analyses. The weighted average of the four Mayo hospitals was compared to the other "best hospitals" in the study.

65 For comparisons of patient satisfaction, the patient is treated as the unit of analysis. Given the CMS methodology, this yielded a minimum of 300 patient surveys per hospital. The numbers of respondents were the scores for all four Mayo hospitals and the 134 non-Mayo hospitals. The scores and statistics were as follows for the three satisfaction measures: overall ten-item satisfaction scores for Mayo and the other 134 best were 77.3 versus 70.4 (after converting to proportions out of 100%, $Z = 5.12, p < 0.001$); would recommend the hospital, 83.5% versus 72.2% ($Z = 8.61; p < 0.001$); and patients rating the hospital a 9 or 10, 86.3% versus 78.2% ($Z = 7.12, p < 0.001$).

66 Patient satisfaction data were obtained from the U.S. CMS site, and the sample size was 2,482. Operational performance data were obtained from the American Hospital Directory, and for these measures the sample size was 3,841.

67 The larger difference between patient satisfaction scores at Mayo in comparison to the U.S. sample of approximately 3,000 hospitals—in comparison to the scores in the *U.S. News & World Report* list reflects the restriction of range associated with the latter sample. The *U.S. News & World Report* list is comprised of less than 3% of U.S. hospitals.

68 It is recognized that employee evaluations posted on Glassdoor.com are not a random sample and may unduly weight very high or very low scores. Yet this phenomenon would be equally applicable to non-Mayo hospitals. Further, due to the small number of respondents in many cases, there is a substantial threat of sampling error. The sample of employee satisfaction scores from Mayo totaled 72 responses. These were drawn from an organization with thousands of current employees—and many thousands of former employees who were eligible to respond. Unfortunately, Glassdoor.com sample sizes were small for most hospitals with only about one-half of the best non-Mayo hospitals meeting our requirement of a minimum of six ratings. Indeed, this requirement reduced the sample of hospitals in these analyses from 136 to 82. In addition, because employees self-select to contribute to Glassdoor.com, the sample may not be representative.

69 There were 132 non-Mayo hospitals in the USNWR listing.

70 In 2013 the Mayo Clinic subsumed Saint Marys and Methodist hospitals. The second Mayo hospital in Rochester is Rochester General.

71 In the article in *Journal of Organizational Effectiveness: People and Performance*, results were analyzed on a correlational basis, without the focus on the Mayo Clinic. Median correlations were $r = 0.26, 0.32$, and 0.14, for patient-, employee-, and enterprise-directed practices, respectively. On a correlational basis, efficiency-related measures were the least related predictors. However, incorporating all three sets of metrics, a multiple regression equation yielded a very high degree of association: $R = 0.62$.

72 Babic-Hodovic, V., Mehic, E., and Arslanagic, M. (2012). "The influence of quality practices on BH companies' business performance." *International Journal of Management Cases*, 14(1), 305–316.

73 Podsakoff, P. M., MacKenzie, S. B., Lee, J.-Y. and Podsakoff, N. P. (2003). "Common method biases in behavioral research: A critical review of the literature and recommended remedies." *Journal of Applied Psychology*, 88(5), 879–903.

74 However, it must be noted that there are inherent restrictions when using publicly reported data originally collected for other purposes, including that the data might not be available at the desired level of detail.

75 The distinction between two types of productivity improvement was discerned by Dr. Phoebe Massimino.

76 Lemieux-Charles, L., McGuire, W., Champagne, F., Barnsley, J., Cole, D., and Sicotte C. (2003). "The use of multilevel performance indicators in managing performance in health care organizations." *Management Decision*, 41(8), 760–770. The quote appears on p. 767.

77 Castelli, A., Dawson, D., Gravelle, H., Jacobs, R., Kind, P., Loveridge, P., and Weale, M. (2007). "A new approach to measuring health system output and productivity." *National Institute Economic Review*, 200(1), 105–117.

78 Medin, E., Hakkinen, U., Linna, M., Anthun, K. S., Kittelson, S. A. and Rehnberg, C. (2013). "International hospital productivity comparison: Experiences from the Nordic countries." *Health Policy*, 112(1), 80–87.

PART IV

11

TOWARD AN ORGANIZATIONAL DIAGNOSIS

Successful organizations are need-satisfying places. A satisfied and loyal customer base ensures a stream of "top line" revenue.[1] Employees, insofar as they are essential to converting inputs to outputs, should also be satisfied and loyal.[2] Practices that lead to productivity and cost-effectiveness contribute to a higher marginal revenue product, which, in turn, permits higher wages, lower prices, better quality, and a return to the providers of capital (investors, lenders, donors, tax payers, grant providers).

Fields such as management, organizational behavior, human resource management (HRM), production and operations/service management, marketing, economics, quality control, industrial and organizational (I/O) psychology, and information technology (IT) are all pertinent to implementing the Cube One framework, and domain-specific techniques (e.g., supply chain management, incentives, employee onboarding, customer surveys, analysis of large data) must be considered.[3]

The Cube One framework distinguishes between stated or printed policies/guidelines, and actual enacted practices. As Tsoukas and Chia put it, "organizations do not simply work, they are *made to work*."[4] (Emphasis is in the original article.) Thus, enacted practices make organizations work. Organizations commonly make various claims (e.g., regarding diversity, environmental sustainability, family-friendly work policies, and merit pay) that are sometimes inconsistent with enacted practices. A cross-section of employees provides the best source of data as to "what is really going on."[5]

The systematic measurement of actual practices is a fundamental feature of the Cube One framework. The frequency with which practices are enacted is crucial.[6] Such information, obtained in a quantitative fashion, enables an organization to compare itself to other organizations; to examine trends; and to ascertain possible areas for improvement—which may reside in some subunits or divisions, but not others.[7]

The Cube One framework also provides a standardized measure of organizational performance. This enables comparisons between organizational units and tracking the effects of changes in practices over time.

Chapter 5 presented survey evidence from two large samples, each comprised of approximately 600 organizations. The data indicate that the Cube One framework is valid. In one of the large samples, the difference in rated performance between organizations classified as in Cube 1 versus organizations in Cube 27—the best and worst categories of organizations—exceeds 14 standard errors (or 14 Sigma).[8] Supportive results also exist among nonprofit and governmental organizations as well as for-profit companies, and among small and large organizations. Empirical support was also found in data collected from three other countries (Brazil, Singapore, and South Korea). Aside from examining correlations, having data pertinent to the levels of practices enacted permits classifying organizations into a taxonomy comprised of 27 cubes.

The case studies of Google, Continental Airlines, Nordstrom, Four Seasons, Zappos, and the Mayo Clinic also provide strong (albeit less systematic) empirical support for the Cube One framework. For example, after the arrival of Gordon Bethune, Continental Airlines literally went from "worst to first." According to *Fortune*'s rating of America's Most Admired Companies, Continental Airlines was the most admired airline for five consecutive years.[9] Examined through the lens of the Cube One model, Continental implemented critically important customer-, employee-, and enterprise-directed practices. Continental's stock price rose from $3.25 (before Bethune) to more than $50.[10]

Before describing in detail how the Cube One framework can be used for diagnostic purposes, we consider other approaches to organizational diagnosis. We then compare these other methods of diagnosis to the Cube One framework.

Nine Approaches to Organizational Diagnosis

1. In his 1972 book, *Organizational Diagnosis*, Harry Levinson recommends collecting extensive data from multiple sources: historical data (including prior crises), structured interviews, financial records, various written documents, and direct observation of people at work. The structured interview questions alone comprise Chapter 4 of his book.[11]

   Levinson's appendix A provides an 80-item attitude survey that contains questions about biographic information and employees' feelings. These data have been used to ascertain the strength of endorsement of attitude-related statements (using a Likert-type scale with endpoints of strongly agree and strongly disagree). One item is "Feel a lot of self-respect at work." However, given that the data come from a single company (described in a 125-page case study), norms cannot be developed that permit comparisons among organizations.

Levinson asserts that, in concert, the abundant data he advocates collecting allow the observer to form a theory-based hypothesis (his term) whereby organizations can anticipate and/or ameliorate their adaptive problems. In broad terms, the fundamental theoretical approach adopted by Levinson is psychoanalytic psychology. Ultimately, the primary issues he identifies relate to the personality of the president and his or her conscious and unconscious psychological limitations.

2. Kim Cameron and Robert Quinn provide a systematic means of diagnosing an organization's culture. Based on a six-item survey, the Organizational Cultural Assessment Instrument (OCAI) locates organizations in a four-quadrant matrix of cultural types. The profile of an organization will typically overlap one (or two) of the four types of cultures: clan, adhocracy, hierarchy, and market. Their research, focusing on organizational culture, does not provide a measure of organizational performance. Cameron and Quinn note that the OCAI is probably the most frequently used instrument for assessing organizational culture.[12]

3. Marvin Weisbord has formulated a diagnostic method that consists of six key variables. His "Six Box Model" consists of broad categories of issues that should be addressed.[13] Specifically, the "Six Boxes" pertain to the following:

    1. Purposes (What business are we in?)
    2. Structure (How is work divided up?)
    3. Rewards (Are there incentives for doing all that needs doing?)
    4. Leadership (Is someone keeping the boxes in balance?)
    5. Relationships (How is conflict managed among people?)
    6. Helpful Mechanisms (Including, how is coordination achieved across technologies?)

Weisbord offers suggestions as to how a diagnostician might assess each of the boxes. For example, with regard to managing conflict, he advises addressing two key questions: "Who has formal responsibility for resolution?" and "Who has the required knowledge and skills to manage the situation?" If those are two different people, do they both participate in resolving conflict? "Does the informal system assist in managing conflict?"

Weisbord also provides 12 questions that the analyst should answer to form a diagnostic profile. These items largely overlap the conceptual domains of the Six Boxes and include "Do people feel *motivated* to perform?" (Response endpoints are "high motivation" and "low motivation."), and "Is conflict managed to optimize *relationships*?" (Here the anchors are "well managed and badly managed.")

While some consultants will find the "Six Boxes" approach congenial and suitable for diagnostic purposes, several limitations might be noted. First, data are not systematically measured; hence scores cannot be compared with norms for diagnostic purposes. Second, no measure of organizational performance is provided, so it may be unclear after an intervention whether organizational performance has improved.

4. Michael Harrison and Arie Shirom have formulated an approach they call "sharp image diagnosis." In their view, much of the prior work on organizational diagnosis has focused on broad sets of conceptual variables. In contrast, their process starts with a broad scan of the organization, and then zooms in to focus on the specific factors that produce symptoms of organizational ineffectiveness.

The four steps in sharp-image diagnosis are: (1) Gather data for a comprehensive overview, and then focus on core problems and challenges; (2) Use theories to frame core problems and challenges, and then link them to organization features; (3) Develop a diagnostic model that captures critical challenges and the roots of ineffective outcomes; (4) Provide feedback on the relevant data of the model to the focal organization.[14]

Harrison and Shirom's evaluative criteria correspond closely with the components of Organizational performance as assessed by the Cube One framework. They include efficiency and quality; comparison of the client's performance to that of competitors; and the organization's current state versus the ideal standard.[15]

Harrison and Shirom have conducted some seemingly successful interventions that they credit to their sharp-image diagnostic approach. However, they provide no standardized measures of organizational practices or performance.

5. Richard Swanson, in his book, *Analysis for Improving Performance*, asserts that a thorough analysis provides the critical information needed to accurately define, frame, and guide an effective performance improvement intervention.[16] Instead of "Six Boxes," Swanson focuses on five performance factors:
    1. Goal alignment—Are the goals of employees and those of the organization congruent?
    2. Systems—Do they enhance or create obstacles that impede job performance?
    3. Employee capacity—Do employees possess the mental, physical, and emotional capabilities to perform well?
    4. Employee motivation—Do reward systems support performance?
    5. Employee expertise—Are selection and training programs effective?

Diagnosticians assess the five performance factors by interviews and documented evidence. Note that the last two performance factors resemble two enterprise-directed practices. However, no systematic measurements of the five factors exist that would permit comparisons to normative data; nor is there a standardized measure of organizational performance.

6. Clayton Alderfer presents a sophisticated and complex approach to organizational diagnosis.[17] He focuses primarily on the importance of embedded intergroup relations, which include factors such as race and gender. In several respects Alderfer's approach is consistent with other diagnostic methods. He sees six steps (or activities) as essential to performing an organizational diagnosis:
   1. Unstructured observations
   2. Unstructured interviews
   3. Establishing a relationship with the focal organization
   4. Developing hypotheses
   5. Establishing a system of liaisons between groups
   6. Preparing a contract letter

Alderfer acknowledges the advantages of standardized questionnaires as they permit comparisons over time and across subgroups. Yet he notes that standardized questionnaires may produce varying response rates among groups of people based on race and gender. Therefore, Alderfer recommends that the consultant or consulting team collaborate with participants from different groups, yielding an "organic" or "empathic" questionnaire.[18]

According to Alderfer, developing an organic questionnaire item entails taking the exact words of organizational members from multiple groups, tweaking them, and emphasizing that the investigators have worked organically with the system to design the questionnaire. Although Alderfer recognizes that this approach takes more time and resources than the administration of a standardized questionnaire, he sees important compensatory gains associated with improved relationships and arguably more apt survey questions.

Alderfer provides a sample of an organic questionnaire that uses a Likert scale to assess the strength of agreement with statements. Three sample statements are: "The actions of department leadership reflect my values." "Promotions go to the person most qualified for the job." "I respect the senior leadership of the department."

Alderfer's approach lacks norms for organically developed, organizationally unique surveys, and for organizational performance metrics. The term "organizational performance" does not appear in the index of his 532-page book.

7. David Nadler and Michael Tushman have developed an analytical and diagnostic framework that is probably the most widely used approach to organizational diagnosis; the Congruence Model.[19] Reflective of the broad applicability of the Congruence Model, several prominent consulting firms rely on it to counsel clients in virtually all types of industries and settings.

An important feature of the Congruence Model is its adoption of an open-systems design. In broad terms, inputs lead to a transformation process which in turn influences outputs, which cycle back to influence inputs. Six variables constitute the Congruence Model:

1. Inputs
   a. The environment (external factors) that could affect the organization (including competition and regulations).
   b. Resources, including capital, technology, information, reputation, and brand recognition.
   c. The history of the organization, including patterns of past behavior that may affect current functioning.
   d. The organization's competitive approach. Crucially, what is the organization's strategy and distinctive competences?[20]
2. Tasks/Technology
   a. The work activities necessary to accomplish the organization's strategy
   b. The competency requirements
   c. Job design
3. Formal Organizational Arrangements
   a. Structure of the organization, i.e., how activities are grouped
   b. Systems for hiring and training employees
   c. Reward systems
   d. Performance evaluation system
4. People
   a. Knowledge and skills
   b. Motivation
   c. Needs and preferences
   d. Loyalty
5. The Informal organization consists of arrangements that develop over time. Some see the informal organization as to how the organization and its components *actually* do their work—not how they are *supposed* to do their work (per the formal organization). Examples of factors that comprise the informal organization include
   a. Patterns of interactions among individuals
   b. Groups (or cliques) that develop with their own norms, rewards, and sanctions
   c. The tasks that a person or sub-unit actually performs (or chooses not to perform), which may be inconsistent with job descriptions
   d. Influence patterns
6. Outputs can be examined at multiple levels including
   a. Productivity and profitability
   b. Service/product quality
   c. Adaptability
   d. Creativity

The next step is to examine degrees of congruence or incongruence among the four components of the transformation process. For instance, an assessment should be made of the fit (or congruence) between people and formal organizational arrangements e.g., rules, procedures). Are peoples' needs and goals met? A different comparison entails examining the congruence between People and Tasks/Technology: do employees possess the requisite skills, or, at the other end of the spectrum, are they underutilized?

Levels of congruence or incongruence are in part dependent on moderating factors. At a professional meeting, circa 1999, many participants viewed the new president of AT&T (C. Michael Armstrong) as the first CEO who "got it." Instead of focusing on manufacturing and selling various telephone systems, he concluded that AT&T should focus on solving the information needs of current and prospective customers, not just providing hardware. Consequently, salespeople could no longer merely walk around with a clipboard and take orders for different products. Rather, salespeople had to be capable of assisting customers (or potential customers) in addressing and resolving their information problems. Formal organizational arrangements needed to change; this meant changing the structure, methods of selection, staffing, training, and so forth.[21]

Clearly, the Congruence Model does not contain standardized questions about practices; nor is there a standardized measure of organizational performance.[22] But it does address important issues partly exogenous (or external to) the Cube One framework, such as strategy and environment. Note, however, that the formal organizational arrangements component includes enterprise-directed practices (e.g., selection, incentives, performance appraisal) and the informal organization component has bearing on leadership practices related to employee-directed practices.

8. W. Warner Burke and George Litwin have developed an open-systems model that elaborates on the Congruence model. The four components of the transformational model described above are supplemented by eight transactional variables, which include culture, climate, employee motivation, and systems.[23]

The Burke–Litwin approach not only expands upon the Congruence Model but also provides standardized questions for each of the 12 component variables. A total of 150 questions scored on a five-point scale (plus three open-ended questions.) comprise the heart of the survey. The survey asks at least four questions per variable. Sample questions include "To what extent do you feel encouraged to reach higher levels and standards of performance in your work?" and "To what extent are the following communication mechanisms in the organization effective (e.g., grapevine, company newsletter, staff meetings, bulletin boards, etc.)?"

In one setting, a newly formed government-sponsored enterprise, the Burke–Litwin questionnaire was distributed to a stratified random sample of nearly 5,000 employees drawn from a total organizational population of approximately 23,500. Critical recommendations (such as "more consistency in managerial decision-making") initially improved the organization's effectiveness. However, the organization was in the early stages of development and undergoing significant changes. It is unclear whether the recommendations were subsequently implemented and whether they improved organizational performance.

As Burke has noted, the Burke–Litwin model is intricate and complex with bi-directional causality among all of the 12 variables. It is unclear whether normative data exist on the 12 variables or whether there is a standardized measure of organizational performance.[24]

9. Rensis Likert begins his 1967 book, *The Human Organization: Its Measurement and Value*, with the claim that "The art of management can be based on verifiable information derived from rigorous quantitative research."[25] Likert developed a widely used scale comprised of 46 managerial practices that he classified into six categories of operating processes. These practices, in turn, related to his four Systems of Management: Authoritarian (Systems 1 and 2), Consultative (System 3), and Participative/Group (System 4).

Most of Likert's practices can be classified as employee-directed; a few as enterprise-directed; none as customer-directed. With regard to employee-directed practices, sample items relate to trust in employees, multi-directional information flows, and supportive leadership. Enterprise-directed practices include setting high levels of goals and devoting substantial resources toward training.

Likert obtained data on organizational performance from multiple sources, including productivity indices based on measured outputs per hour. His questionnaire includes employee ratings of productivity, scrap loss, quality, and absenteeism. Although Likert's survey includes no managerial statements related to customer-directed practices, he does include the concept of quality as a component of rated performance.

There are several similarities between Likert's approach toward diagnosing and improving organizational performance, and the Cube One framework. First, published and validated instruments are available in the public domain. Second, Likert's model, like the Cube One framework, is theory-based. Third, data indicate that the model is valid and that management practices are related to organizational performance. Fourth, Likert provides a measure of rated performance, although without normative data. Finally, Likert's model is parsimonious, with six categories of practices and four Systems of Management.

A Comparison of Nine Approaches to Organizational Diagnosis With the Cube One Framework[26]

The Cube One framework collects data on the frequency of the enactment of three sets of practices: enterprise-, customer-, and employee-directed. None of the nine other approaches to organizational diagnosis include customer-related practices.

The Likert survey approach focuses primarily on employee-directed practices. Because Alderfer proposes the development of an organic questionnaire that is customized to groups in each organization, it is difficult to discern the extent to which categories of practices are enacted. Levinson incorporates a survey that relates primarily to employee attitudes and feelings. The Burke–Litwin approach includes surveys, with some items pertaining to management practices (one of the 12 variables analyzed). Cameron and Quinn provide six items that are used to assess an organization's cultural profile—not the frequency of specific behaviors.

An important issue that relates to using survey instruments to conduct an organizational diagnosis is whether the survey is published and in the public domain. The work of Likert meets this standard, as does Cameron and Quinn's six-item survey (which is pertinent to organizational culture). The Levinson survey is also publicly available. None of the other six approaches provide publicly accessible survey statements.

The Cube One framework provides normative data for the three major categories of managerial practices, for specific practices, and for organizational performance. Normative data permit an organization to evaluate and track the effects of practices on organizational performance over time and across component units. Likert's survey indicates the extent to which an organization can be classified as Systems 1–4, but norms evidently do not exist. The same applies to the survey questions relating to organizational performance.

The Cube One framework is a parsimonious model, focusing on three sets of practices as determinants of organizational performance.[27] Weisbord's "Six Boxes" and the Nadler and Tushman Congruence model can also be viewed as parsimonious. At the other extreme, Ann Howard and Associates assert that: "A complete [organizational] diagnosis could involve collecting a staggering amount of information." Douglas Bray, who for 28 years was involved in human resource research at AT&T, similarly concluded that "the total diagnostic job in even a moderate-sized company would be immense even if only management-level employees were included."[28]

Unlike the massive amounts of data often seen as necessary for an organizational diagnosis, the Cube One framework offers a theory-based survey currently in the public domain and available essentially "off-the-shelf." As noted in Chapters 2, 3, and 4, it is advisable to incorporate a few additional and/or more up-to-date practices, even though normative data will not be available for the new items.

We must acknowledge the positive features of some diagnostic frameworks, particularly Nadler and Tushman's Congruence model and Levinson's extensive approach to data collection and psychoanalytic theory.

Using the Cube One Framework for Diagnostic Purposes

The distribution of a Cube One-based survey is essentially an intervention, albeit a modest one. However, it should only be undertaken after considerable thought and planning and with "buy-in." We recommend introducing the survey (which takes about 20 minutes to complete) in the context of statements that strive to mitigate perceived threats. Completion of the survey should be anonymous and should elicit minimal biographic information that could be used to identify respondents. The completed surveys must be physically or electronically returned directly to an outside party—with no possibility of interception by managers or executives.

With regard to a small organization, the survey should be distributed for voluntary completion by all employees and managers. If the focal organization consists of multiple divisions or departments, data should be sought from a stratified random selection of employees and managers. To preserve anonymity, the survey should (if distributed electronically) be forwarded by respondents to an outside party, an entity not part of the focal organization. If the survey is carried out by the old-fashioned paper-and-pencil method, respondents should drop the completed survey in a mailbox to be sent—postage paid, of course—to an outside party.)

The use of surveys is widespread at large companies. Studies of the proportion of companies using surveys ranged from 60 to 80%. The median proportion is 70%.[29]

The normative data (shown below) pertain to the original version of the survey, which is identical to 90% of the items that appear in each of the ten-item scales at the ends of Chapters 2–4.[30] (It would be possible to include a few new items along with the original items—presented below—as well as the slightly modified items that appear in Chapters 2–4.)

Table 11.1 provides the means of the ten separate Enterprise-Directed items using the original version of the survey. (The items in the original version appear in the table.)[31] The mean item score across all ten items appears in the bottom row of Table 11.1. To ascertain whether scores from a particular unit are significantly below the norm, cut points are provided for samples of 25, 50, and 100 respondents.

To illustrate the interpretation of the data in Table 11.1, the first Enterprise-Directed Practice reads as follows: "Individuals are held accountable for accomplishing specific (quantifiable) goals." The mean score for this item, based on a sample of 609 respondents, is 3.89. A sample with 100 respondents would have a significantly lower score if the mean item score was below 3.75. The cut points for samples of 50 and 25 respondents, respectively, are 3.65 and 3.55.

The mean is also provided for the sum of all ten Enterprise-Directed items. The mean item score for all ten Enterprise-Directed Practices is 3.11. The cut points for samples of 100, 50, and 25, respondents are 3.00, 2.94, and 2.87, respectively. The summated overall Enterprise-Directed score (EntSum) score for the ten items is 31.1 (which is 3.11 × 10). The use of summated scores enables each of the three sets of practices to be more easily compared to each other.

Table 11.2 provides the means of the ten separate Customer-Directed items using the original version of the survey. (The items in the original version appear in the table.)[32] The mean is also provided for the average of all ten Customer-Directed items. In order to ascertain whether scores from a particular unit are below the norm, cut points are provided for samples of 25, 50, and 100 employees.

TABLE 11.1 Means and Cut Points for Enterprise-Directed Behaviors

Managerial Behaviors (Practices)	M	SD	M n = 100	M n = 50	M n = 25
Individuals are held accountable for accomplishing specific (quantifiable) goals.	3.89	1.01	3.75	3.65	3.55
Individuals receive specific performance feedback that is useful for improving their performance.	3.34	1.12	3.18	3.07	2.96
Where possible, the performance of individuals and groups is quantifiably measured and monitored over time.	3.30	1.19	3.13	3.01	2.90
Salary increases (e.g., raises, bonuses) are proportionate to an individual's job performance.[33]	2.90	1.33	2.71	2.58	2.45
Promotions are based almost entirely on job performance.	3.14	1.21	2.96	2.85	2.73
Individuals are selected for employment based on objective criteria (e.g., written tests, performance tests, work samples, etc.).	2.65	1.28	2.47	2.34	2.22
Training is provided for employees who need to upgrade their knowledge and skills.	3.29	1.19	3.12	3.00	2.89
Organizational performance improvement is financially rewarded by a group incentive plan (e.g., gainsharing, profit-sharing, etc.)	2.24	1.58	2.01	1.86	1.71
Management encourages the delegation of decision-making authority to lower-level employees (i.e., real empowerment)	2.69	1.17	2.52	2.41	2.30
Individuals are encouraged to perform a wide variety of tasks whenever possible.	3.61	1.05	3.46	3.36	3.26
Analysis of means of 609 organizations for Enterprise-Directed Practices.	3.11	0.70	3.00	2.94	2.87

TABLE 11.2 Means and Cut Points for Customer-Directed Behaviors

Managerial Behaviors (Practices)	M	SD	M n = 100	M n = 50	M n = 25
Customers are regularly surveyed via questionnaire regarding their satisfaction with products and/ or services.	2.59	1.77	2.34	2.17	2.00
Focus groups (i.e., in-depth interviews) are regularly held with customers to gain a fuller understanding of wants and/or needs.	2.27	1.26	2.09	1.97	1.85
Products and/or services are continually upgraded as part of an ongoing program of quality improvement.	3.32	1.15	3.15	3.04	2.93
The best practices of competitors are studied and adopted, or improved upon, where possible (i.e., benchmarking).	3.01	1.22	2.83	2.72	2.60
The goal of customer satisfaction importantly influences operational decisions at all organization levels.	3.47	1.18	3.30	3.18	3.07
Prices of goods/services are continually reviewed to improve the organization's competitive position.	3.06	1.36	2.86	2.73	2.60
The quality of products/services is regularly assessed by an independent organization as part of a continuing audit.	2.64	1.58	2.41	2.26	2.11
Customer satisfaction is an important factor in determining pay increases of individuals or departments.	2.25	1.24	2.07	1.95	1.83
Employees are granted wide latitude to use their own judgment in order to satisfy customers.	3.00	1.20	2.82	2.71	2.59
Product or service innovations are regularly sought and budgeted for on a continuing basis.	2.91	1.15	2.74	2.63	2.52
Analysis of means of 609 organizations for Customer-Directed Practices.	2.90	0.80	2.73	2.66	2.58

The third Customer-Directed practice item reads as follows: "Products and/ or services are continually upgraded as part of an ongoing program of quality improvement." The mean score for this item based on a sample of 609 respondents is 3.32. A sample with 100 respondents would have a significantly lower score with a mean below 3.15. The cut points for samples of 50 and 25 respondents, respectively, are 3.04 and 2.93. The overall summated score of customer-directed practices (CSum) is 29.0 (which is 2.90 × 10).

Table 11.3 provides the means of the ten separate Employee-Directed items using the original version of the survey. (The items in the original version appear in the table.)[34] The mean is also provided for the average of all ten Employee-Directed items. In order to ascertain whether scores from a particular unit are below the norm, cut points are provided for samples of 25, 50, and 100 employees.

The eighth Employee-Directed Practice (Table 11.3) reads as follows: "Employees are treated with respect as mature adults. Communications are straight-forward, not condescending or patronizing." The mean score for this item based on a sample of 609 respondents is 3.41. A sample with 100 respondents would have a significantly lower score if the mean item score was below 3.24. The cut points for samples of 50 and 25 respondents, respectively, are 3.12 and 3.01. The summated score of the means of the ten-item scale of Employee-Directed Practices (ESum) is 32.0 (3.20 × 10).

Interpretation of Data

If feasible, data should be collected for the entire enterprise, division, or departments. The next step is to compare summated scores for Enterprise-, Customer-, and Employee-Directed Practices, using the cut points provided in Tables 11.1, 11.2, and 11.3. Data should also be compared to overall normative data with regard to Organizational performance, and if applicable, the norms for non-profit/government organizations, for-profit companies, and for small (under 500 employees) and large companies (more than 500 employees). Table 11.4 provides cut points for the entire sample and component types of organizations—by sector or size.[35]

Initial comparisons must be viewed as tentative assessments. To make valid inferences about the functioning of the entire enterprise, divisions, and departments, data should be analyzed to assess interrater agreement. Wide disparities among employee perceptions would raise the question as to whether there are adequate levels of agreement within divisions as well as within departments. The formulas to calculate the key metric pertinent to interrater agreement, i.e., shared perceptions ($r_{wg(j)}$) are provided in the end notes.[36]

A basic initial analysis—which can be performed after adequate levels of inter-rater agreement have been found, examining either $r_{wg}(j) \geq .90$ or $r^*_{wg(j)} \geq .80$ — would be an examination of the levels of summated (or composite) Enterprise-, Customer-, and Employee-Directed scores (i.e., EntSum, CSum, and ESum).

TABLE 11.3 Means and Cut Points for Employee-Directed Behaviors

Managerial Behaviors (Practices)	M	SD	M n = 100	M n = 50	M n = 25
Open, two-way communication is employed. All employees are informed about new developments and encouraged to express their ideas and complaints.	3.06	1.11	2.90	2.79	2.68
Distinctions between hierarchical ranks are minimized. Management downplays status symbols (e.g., executive dining rooms and other perks).	2.83	2.14	2.52	2.31	2.11
Employee layoffs are avoided where possible, by first attempting to place employees in other jobs within the organization.	3.26	2.45	2.91	2.67	2.44
Employee growth is encouraged by providing in-house training and/or reimbursements for outside training/educational programs.	3.46	2.42	3.11	2.88	2.65
Work-family conflicts are minimized by adopting such policies as flexible work hours, day care assistance, and encouraging managerial tolerance.	2.76	1.28	2.57	2.45	2.33
The organization responds to employee concerns by taking appropriate actions, not just by words.	2.82	1.06	2.67	2.56	2.46
Managerial integrity is demonstrated in dealing with employees. All employees are given the same information; promises are kept.	2.98	1.32	2.79	2.66	2.54
Employees are treated with respect and as mature adults. Communications are straight-forward, not condescending or patronizing.	3.41	1.18	3.24	3.12	3.01
Employees know they can make (a few) mistakes. Management attempts to minimize the role of punishment and fear.	3.43	1.09	3.27	3.17	3.06
Management encourages employees to feel that they are part of a team.	3.59	1.14	3.42	3.31	3.21
Analysis of means of 609 organizations for Employee-Directed Practices	3.20	0.86	3.03	2.95	2.87

TABLE 11.4 Means and Cut Points for Organizational Performance

	Mean	SD	M n = 100	M n = 50	M n = 25
All organizations	20.11	5.06	19.233	18.9	18.42
For-Profit	20.01	5.06	19.114	18.785	18.31
Nonprofit/Government	20.26	5.09	19.29	18.976	18.51
Large organizations	21.49	4.26	20.681	20.418	20.026
Small organizations	19.83	5.4	18.734	18.415	17.932

For illustrative purposes, assume a sample of $n = 40$ (respondents) drawn from an organization where the three summated scores of EntSum, CSum, and ESum are 40, 42, and 26, respectively. Evidently, the focal organization is low on Employee-Directed practices. Indeed, a simple t-test would reveal that the focal unit scored significantly lower on ESum practices compared to EntSum and CSum. A difference of eight points would be statistically significant, given the realistic assumptions provided in the end notes.[37] A logical next step would be to compare scores for each Employee-Directed practice item to ascertain if there are specific practices that should be enacted more frequently.

By analyzing three sets of practices, the Cube One framework provides a systematic approach to organizational diagnosis and improvement. In contrast, Edward Lawler, the founder and director of the USC Center for Effective Organizations, has observed that this is often not what goes on. In his words:

> Organizations have trouble putting all their pieces together so that they are moving in a consistent way. They tend to pick a practice here or there that they hear what somebody else is doing, instead of developing an overall integrated effective management strategy.[38]

McKinsey and Company have found that the enactment of multiple organizational dimensions ("outcomes," in their terminology), as opposed to just attending to one or two dimensions of the nine they identify, provides superior results. Dimensions include practices that primarily relate to enterprise- and employee-directed practices. Examples include establishing an open and trusting work environment; providing financial incentives along with rewards and recognition; and conducting employee performance reviews. Unfortunately, their instrument—McKinsey's Organizational Health Index (OHI)—is proprietary and available for use exclusively with consultation provided by McKinsey.[39]

The Cube One framework can be used to classify organizations in terms of 27 cubes.[40] In the large sample survey using the original statements, only 12% of organizations were categorized in Cube One; 14% were classified in Cubes 2–4 (representing two High scores and one Medium). In contrast, Cubes 18 to 26—representing organizations with two Low scores—accounted for 27% of organizations, and Cube 27 (Low, Low, Low) accounted for 11% of the sample. Twenty-six percent of organizations had at least two High scores, and 38% had at least two Low scores—revealing ample opportunities for organizational improvement.[41]

The dictum of the Cheshire Cat in *Alice and Wonderland* is arguably incomplete. To wit, the statement, "If you don't know where you are going, any road will take you there," is less constructive than "If you don't know where you are, it is impossible to know which road will take you where you want to go."[42] The Cube One framework enables an organization to know its location in terms of the 27 cube taxonomy, and provides a set of guidelines for determining the most appropriate road(s) to take to get to Cube One.

Notes

1 Arguably, competition enhances customer satisfaction.
2 Organizations must often compete for employees. As a four-page ad by IBM in the *New York Times* noted: "A company's constituents all have choices—the employees of where to work, the investors of where to put a dollar [and] customers choose which company wins their business." See *New York Times*, (June 16, 2011) p. A19.
3 Yet, as noted in detail below, many approaches to organizational diagnosis are grounded in a single disciplinary field, or set of techniques.
4 Tsoukas, H. and Chia, R. (2002). "On organizational becoming: Rethinking organizational change." *Organization Science*, 13(5), 577, italics in original.
5 A Dilbert cartoon makes this point. Dogbert, the consultant, reports that employees are making suggestions as to needed changes. The Pointy-Haired Boss (PHB) says that he's not going to pay for this kind of information. Dogbert then asks PHB if he would be interested in knowing what competitors are doing. PHB says, yes. Dogbert then notes that what competitors are doing is exactly what employees suggest.
6 In a sense, the items used to measure enterprise-, customer- and employee-directed practices can be seen as managerial behaviors, and loosely analogous to the approach used in behavioral analysis. The slogan of the Florida Association for Behavior Analysis is "Behavior Counts," which is a *double entendre*. Not only do behaviors matter, they can also be counted.
7 As noted in Chapter 1, In 1876, Lord Kelvin (née Sir William Thompson) advanced the following argument:

> When you can measure something about which you are speaking and express it in numbers, you know something about it; but when you cannot express it in numbers, your knowledge is of a meagre and unsatisfactory kind; it may be the beginning of knowledge, but you have scarcely in your thoughts, advanced to the stage of science, whatever the matter may be.[25]

8 A difference of 14 Sigma provides validity evidence that is not just statistically significant, but virtually incontrovertible.
9 Before Bethune implemented changes, he described Continental's performance as follows: "We weren't just the worst big airline. *We lapped the field.*" See Bethune (1980). *From worst to first*, p. 4. Italics in original.
10 As noted in Chapter 7, Continental merged with United Airlines in 2010.
11 Levinson, H. (with J. Molinari, and A, G. Spohn). (1972). *Organizational diagnosis*. Cambridge, MA: Harvard University Press. It might be noted that Levinson was keenly aware of employees' facial expressions. He sought to ascertain the proportion of people

who were smiling and those whose appearance was sullen, and saw this as an indicator of organizational health.

12 Cameron, K. S., and Quinn, R. E. (2011). *Diagnosing and changing organizational culture*, 3rd ed. San Francisco, CA: Jossey-Bass. The claim that the OCAI is probably the most widely used instrument to measure culture appears on p. 27. Managers are encouraged to use a 60-item Management Skills Assessment Instrument (MSAI)—provided in appendix B—to identify their personal areas of weakness. Examination of correlations between managerial skills within each of the four quadrants yielded a median correlation of $r = 0.155$ (see page 191).

13 Weisbord, M. S. (1978). *Organizational diagnosis*. Cambridge, MA: Perseus.

14 Harrison, M. I., and Shirom, A. (1999). *Organizational diagnosis and assessment*. Thousand Oaks, CA: Sage.

15 The three evaluative criteria overlap closely to the three items that constitute the measure of organizational performance in the Cube One framework.

16 Swanson, R. A. (1994). *Analysis for improving performance*. San Francisco, CA: Berrett-Koehler. Toward the conclusion of his book, Swanson offers the observation that good analyses make good solutions. Good solutions make heroes, p. 246.

17 Alderfer, C. P. (2011). *The practice of organizational diagnosis*. New York, NY, and Oxford, UK: Oxford University Press.

18 In fact, Alderfer claims that nothing is more important to the organizational diagnostic process than the relationships between the consultant or consulting team and the leadership of the client system.

19 Nadler, D, and Tushman, M. (1980, Summer). "A model for diagnosing organizational behavior: Applying a congruence perspective." *Organizational Dynamics*, 9(2), 35–51. Also see Walton, E., and Nadler, D. (1994). Chapter 4 in Howard, A. and Associates, *Diagnosis for organizational change*. New York, NY, and London: The Guilford Press. (pp. 85–105). (It might be noted, anecdotally, that at Harvard Business School the Congruence Model is referred to as "the magic diamond.")

20 If an organization lacks a distinctive competence, it is, by definition, dominated in all respects—e.g., quality, price, selection, delivery, etc.) Thus the claim is often made that an organization that lacks a distinctive competence lacks a future.

21 Presentation by Mirian Graddick-Weir at the Metropolitan Association for Applied Psychology (METRO), ca. 1999.

22 It is difficult to calibrate levels of incongruence, and to ascertain if a particular lack of fit is truly detrimental to organizational performance. See Harrison, M. D. (1987). *Diagnosing organizations: Methods, models and processes*. Newbury Park, CA: Sage. Still another "wrinkle" is that subsequent to their initial piece, Nadler & Tuschman note that a lack of fit may be a two-edged sword. In the short term, congruence relates positively to organizational performance. But a system with high congruence can be resistant to change and hence in the longer-term this could have a negative effect in the long run. See Nadler, D. A., and Tushman, M. L. (1989). "Organizational frame bending: Principles for managing reorientation." *Academy of Management Executive*, 3, 194–204.

23 Burke, W. W., and Litwin G. H. (1992). "A causal model of organizational performance and change." *Journal of Management*, 18(3), 523–525.

24 Burke, W. W. (1994). "Diagnostic models for organization development." Chapter 4 in Howard, A. and Associates, eds. *Diagnosis for Organizational Change*. New York, NY, and London: The Guilford Press. (pp. 53–84).

25 Likert, R. (1967). *The human organization: Its measurement and value*. New York, NY: McGraw-Hill, The quote appears on page 1.

26 Many other approaches to organizational diagnosis have been described in print. For example, Harold Leavitt conceived of organizations as multivariate systems—see Leavitt, H. J. (1965). "Applied organizational change in industry." In J. G. March, ed. *Handbook*

of organizations. (pp. 1144–1170). Pascale and Athos developed the 7S model that was commercialized by McKinsey and publicized by Peters and Waterman—see Pascale, R. T., and Athos, A. G. (1981). *The art of Japanese management.* New York, NY: Simon and Schuster; Peters., T. J., and Waterman. R. H. (1982). *In search of excellence.* New York, NY: Harper & Row. Noel Tichy developed the TPC framework—see Tichy, N. M. (1983). *Managing strategic change.* New York, NY: Wiley. More recent approaches include Behavioral Systems Analysis by Heather McGhee and Lori Diener-Ludwig.—see McGhee, H. M., and Diener-Ludwig. (2012). "An introduction to behavioral systems analysis for rehabilitation agencies." *Journal of Rehabilitation Administration,* 36(2), 59–71 and Carl Binder's integration of organizational culture with performance management—see Binder C., (2016). "Integrating organizational-culture values with performance management." *Journal of Organizational Behavior Management,* 36(2–3), 185–201. In brief, according to Warner Burke: "Pick 100 organizational consultants, and we would have 100 different diagnostic models." See Burke, W. W. (1994). "Organizational models for organization development." Chapter 3 in A. Howard & Associates, *Diagnosis for organizational change.* New York, NY, and London: The Guilford Press.

27 Some see a hallmark of good science as the use of a limited (parsimonious) number of variables to explain a phenomenon. Following the early formulation of Occam's Principle—that the simplest explanation is often the best—Karl Popper argued for parsimony for another reason. A preference for simple theories need not appeal to practical or aesthetic considerations. Rather, the preference for simplicity may be justified by its falsifiability criterion: simpler theories are preferred to more complex ones because their empirical content is greater; and because they are better testable. See Popper. K. R. (1992). Chapter 7 (on simplicity) in *The logic of scientific discovery,* 2nd ed. London: Routledge. (pp. 121–132). The idea here is that a simple theory applies to more cases than a more complex one, and is thus more easily falsifiable. In contrast, an in-depth analysis typically invokes more variables than there are cases. Hence, in statistical terms, there are no degrees of freedom. But some see parsimonious models as a form of reductionism, which oversimplifies the explanation of reality. See Robinson, D. N. (1995). "The logic of reductionist models." *New Ideas in Psychology,* 13, 1–8.

28 Howard & Associates, op cit., p. 277.

29 Kraut, A. I. (2006). "Moving the needle: Getting action after a survey." Chapter 1 in Allen Kraut, ed. *Getting action from organizational surveys.* San Francisco, CA: Jossey-Bass, (pp. 1–32).

30 In addition to two new items, five items were minimally tweaked.

31 Each of the ten Enterprise-Directed practice items was significantly correlated with organizational performance. One way to verify or "double-check" response scores with respect to pay increases being associated with job performance is to calculate the correlation between performance and the amount or percentage increase in pay. This calculation was conducted using data from a large department 500+ store chain. See Kopelman, R. E., Rovenpor, J. L., and Cayer, M. "Merit pay and organizational performance: Is there an effect on the bottom line?" *National Productivity Review,* 1991, 10, 299–307.

32 Each of the ten Customer-Directed practice items was significantly correlated with organizational performance.

33 Each of the ten Employee-Directed practice items was significantly correlated with organizational performance.

34 In Tables 11.1, 11.2, and 11.3, it has been assumed that the Standard Deviation within the focal organization is 85% of the Standard Deviation in the large sample comprised of approximately 600 organizations.

35 As noted by Darell Rigby, many techniques may be used, and the use of multiple practices [which is consistent with the Cube One framework] helps improve organizational performance. This approach can mitigate the impact of one-time tools, which may be

based on current fads. But, he laments: "There is no equivalent of the *Consumer Reports* for management to use in evaluating the tools available to them." See Rigby, C. (2001). "Management tools and techniques." *California Management Review*, 43(2), 139–160. (The quote appears on p. 139.)

36 Lindell, M. K. (2001). "Assessing and testing interrater agreement on a single target using multi-item rating scales." *Applied Psychological Measurement*, 25(1), 89–99. See Formula 8. It might be noted that Lindell's formula for $r^*_{wg(j)}$ is an update of the original formula $r_{wg(j)}$ developed by James, L. R., Demaree, R. G., and Wolfe, G. (1984). "Estimating within-group interrater reliability with and without response bias." *Journal of Applied Psychology*, 69, 85–98. The formulas are as follows:

$$r_{wg(j)} = \frac{j\left(1 - \frac{\overline{s_x^2}}{s_{EU}^2}\right)}{j\left(1 - \frac{\overline{s_x^2}}{s_{EU}^2}\right) + \frac{\overline{s_x^2}}{s_{EU}^2}} \quad \text{Formula (1) on Page 89 Lindell (2001).}$$

$$r^*_{wg(j)} = 1 - \frac{\overline{s_n^2}}{s_{EU}^2} \quad \text{Formula (2) on Page 90 Lindell (2001).}$$

$$s_{EU}^2 = \frac{c^2 - 1}{12}$$

Where $c = 1, 2, 3, 4, .5$, these are the possible ratings, i.e., categories in the response scale. Cut points have been based on examination of prior data for EntSum, CSum, and ESum, collected from one organization.

37 The significance levels are based on the assumption that the SD of each summated score is 10% of the mean score. The formula for the t – test is

$$\text{Test Statistic: } t = \frac{\overline{x_1} - \overline{x_2}}{\sqrt{\frac{s_p^2}{n_1} + \frac{s_p^2}{n_2}}} \quad \text{where t has } n_1 + n_2 - 2 \text{ d.f.}$$

$$s_p^2 = \frac{(n_1 - 1)s_1^2 + (n_2 - 1)s_2^2}{(n_1 + n_2 - 2)}$$

38 Interview with Edward Lawler published in *T & D* (July, 2008), 73–75. Quoted material reprinted with permission of the American Society for Training and Development. © 2008 T + D.

39 Gagnon, C., John, E., and Theunissed, R. (September 2017), *McKinsey Quarterly*. Retrieved at https://www.mckinsey.com/business-functions/organization/our-insights/organizational-health-a-fast-track-to-performance-improvement. For a more detailed description of the nine outcomes and associated actions see Retrieved at https://www.mckinsey.com/~/media/mckinsey/industries/public%20sector/how%20we%20help%20clients/organization/organizational%20health%20indexpsp.ashx

40 Cut points for the large U.S. sample were as follows. High is ≥ 35; Low is ≤ 26. This corresponds to approximately 0.8 SD for each dimension.

41 Kopelman, R. E., and Prottas, D. J. (2012). "Rationale and validity evidence for the Cube One framework." *Journal or Managerial Issues*, 24(1), 27–46.

42 This addendum to the wisdom of the Cheshire Cat has been attributed to Ron Holifield, the CEO of Strategic Government Resources. No date.

12

TOWARD IMPLEMENTATION

The Greek philosopher Heraclitus observed, in 513 B.C., "Nothing is constant except change."[1] But even change is changing. In today's world of accelerating technological and societal changes, framed by globally interconnected participants, the slope of change over time has become increasingly steep.

Consider the continuing relevance of the "big picture" provided by Alvin Toffler in *Future Shock* (1970). If the past 50,000 years of human existence were divided into lifetimes of approximately 62 years each, there would have been about 800 such lifetimes. Of these, 650 would have been spent in caves. If we update Toffler by 50 years, electricity would have been used in three lifetimes; petroleum in two; and computers, of course, in the most recent lifetime.[2] The past 30 years have witnessed cell phones, GPS systems, search engines, social media, big data analytics, internet-based surgical procedures, and so forth.

Changes can be small and incremental, and entail the tweaking of a process, or they can be large-scale and transformative, widely affecting work behaviors, technology, and strategy. Overall, evidence from the past two decades indicates that the failure rate for planned change has remained steady at about 70% (according to Kotter and Cohen in 2002, and more recently reported in the 2015 edition of McKinsey Digital.)[3] Notwithstanding the modest success rate, according to Kotter and Schlesinger writing in the *Harvard Business Review*, most companies or divisions undertake moderate changes at least once a year and initiate sizable changes every four or five years.[4]

An organization's members will often object to a proposed or enacted change. Employees may entirely refuse to cooperate or, more commonly, follow the letter but not the spirit of the change: just "going through the motions" while deliberately allowing mistakes to occur. They may express resentment and complaints to anyone who will listen, or they may comply with change without committing to its success. These reactions have been commonly labeled "resistance to change."

Reasons for resistance include fear of the unknown; threats to expertise and power; threats to pay and perquisites; an anticipated reduction in responsibilities; an anticipated increase in responsibilities; or a dislike of the way change was decided or implemented. Sometimes, though, resistance is not based on self-interest. Rather, it reflects a genuine belief that proposed or enacted changes will be detrimental to the functioning of the organization.

Self-interest does often impede change. As related by Renato Tagiuri, U.S. Admirals (circa 1900) opposed the introduction of continuous-aim gun mountings on naval ships. Although the change offered a 20-fold (2,000%) improvement in the accuracy of naval gun fire, the Ordnance Admirals saw the continuous-aim gun mounting not merely as a technical innovation, but as a threat to their careers and entire way of life.[5]

In 1848, Dr. Ignaz Semmelweis discovered that when physicians washed their hands with a chlorinated lime solution, the incidence of mortality after childbirth fell from 18% to 1%. (Note that this case also represented a nearly 20-fold improvement in outcomes.) But Dr. Semmelweis's colleagues not only rejected his suggestion: they rejected him. Within a year he was dismissed from the clinic where he had practiced medicine. In part, the resistance to change resulted from a threat to an important status symbol. A blood-smeared smock was a sign of a physician's experience and expertise.[6]

In 1513, Niccolò Machiavelli wrote, "It must be considered that there is nothing more difficult to carry out, nor more doubtful of success, nor more dangerous to handle, than to initiate a new order of things."[7] Fortunately, recent research has elucidated effective approaches to implementing change, including the work of the following theorists, researchers, and consultants.

Kurt Lewin

Perhaps Lewin's most notable contribution to understanding the process of planned change is his Psychological Force Field model, according to which a person's behavior depends upon properties of the individual, and the person's contextual environment.[8] A person's behavior (including attitudes) exists in a state of quasi-stationary equilibrium, the result of two opposing forces: pushing forces that encourage moving behavior/attitudes in one direction, and restraining forces that seek to restrain or move behavior/attitudes in the opposite direction.[9]

The notion of quasi-stationary equilibrium is consistent with the tendency toward homeostasis—i.e., the tendency for continuation of the stability associated with the status quo. A person who drives his/her car very fast, or very cautiously, is likely to drive the same way every day. Likewise, people hold consistent views of matters such as religion or reproductive rights. They may be pro-life or pro-choice, but do not vacillate on a daily basis.[10]

One way to create change, given the existence of quasi-stationary equilibrium, is to increase the pushing forces. Another is to reduce the restraining forces. Lewin, with a background in physical sciences, posited that for each increase in the pushing forces there will be an equal and opposite increase in the restraining forces (according to Newton's third law: for every action, there is an equal and opposite reaction). Suppose Person A suggests that Person B should swim for 30 minutes every morning and gives three reasons why A thinks this is a good idea. In all likelihood, even if B has asked for advice, the likely response will be, "Yes, but ..." B will then conceive of, and possibly vocalize, three or more reasons why daily swimming is not a good or feasible idea.[11]

According to Lewin, "there is nothing so practical as a good [i.e., valid] theory."[12] On the surface this assertion may appear self-contradictory (or oxymoronic), as the term "theory" is often equated with esoteric, academic issues; not really pertinent to practical matters.[13] To the contrary, a good theory can be useful in addressing all four levels of knowledge: description, explanation, prediction, and control.

With regard to the highest level of knowledge (control) Lewin accepted the challenge of attempting to address a practical matter by leading a team of researchers tasked with the daunting challenge of changing the eating habits of the U.S. population. During the early 1940s, the U.S. population rarely ingested what have been called "organ meats": brains, hearts, or kidneys. Because these foods were going to waste, Lewin conducted a field experiment to see if eating habits could be changed.[14]

Lewin compared the efficacy of two approaches to changing the behavior with regard to food habits. His sample population comprised the people who made food decisions for their families, i.e., gatekeepers. The first condition consisted of having a charming lecturer, Alex Bavelas, give a well-crafted speech in which he made four points.

- Organ meats possessed all the same nutrients as conventional meats.
- Organ meats could be purchased at as small fraction of the cost of traditional cuts of meat (i.e., they are economical).
- The purchase of organ meats could be interpreted as a patriotic act, enabling the preferred cuts to be sent abroad to assist the war effort.
- Recipes with favorable reviews demonstrated the possible preparation of tasteful meals using organ meats.

The second condition consisted of having a group discussion about the purchase of organ meats that sought to reach a consensus. A knowledge expert (a dietitian) was present during the discussions but instructed to provide information only if requested. The group discussion/consensus condition was designed to uncover the restraining forces to eating organ meats, and thereby possibly reduce them. So, if a participant expressed skepticism, saying, perhaps, "Gross, disgusting," and another participant asked, "How do you save money if you have to throw the food out?" a third participant might address these concerns by describing how she and her spouse enjoyed a delicious meal that included organ meats.

Clearly the two conditions paralleled (1) increasing the pushing forces and (2) identifying and potentially reducing the restraining forces. Unlike the lecture condition, participants in the group decision/consensus condition could express their concerns, and this process allowed for a possible mitigation of the restraining forces. An assessment of the effectiveness of the two conditions consisted of conducting in-person interviews seven days after the experiment. Participants in the group discussion/consensus condition were, on average, ten times more likely to consume organ meats compared to those who experienced a lecture.[15]

Granted, the experiment was rudimentary in terms of scope and controls, but the results were dramatic. Based in part on this research, Kurt Lewin has been called the "father of group dynamics." To this day, groups are widely used to achieve sizable changes with regard to such problems as alcoholism and obesity.

Gordon Lippitt

In their text, *Implementing Organizational Change*, Lippitt and colleagues offer several practical suggestions aimed at implementing change to improve organizational performance.[16] For starters, they assert that "the best people to solve complex organizational problems are those who face them every day."[17] (This claim is entirely consistent with the Cube One framework.)

At times, organizational problems will need to be addressed by modifying the formal hierarchy. According to Lippitt et al., a task force charged with overseeing change should accomplish the following:

1. Define the mission and composition of the task force (e.g., a "diagonal slice of employees").
2. Collect and analyze data to determine what needs to be changed.
3. Select among feasible courses of action, i.e., generating an appropriate way to achieve needed changes.
4. Plan and recommend changes in activities and processes—including their scheduling and implementation to produce the needed changes.
5. Review, evaluate, modify, and reevaluate the results obtained.[18]

Lippitt and colleagues are particularly attuned to the type of data collected at pre- and post-intervention phases. Ideally, data should provide "the hard kernels of quintessential data, those that ring true, those so self-evident that no [one] can deny their validity, and [these data] simply are not that easy to come by."[19] (The Cube One framework, while arguably not providing the "quintessential" form of data, does provide the "hard kernel" of objective metrics.)

The task force should include people who have the power to affect an organization's future, and these people should play a prominent role. Influential people can be found in managerial and non-managerial roles at all levels of the organization. Some managers and employees may feel threatened by the task force's recommendations. It will be necessary (to use Lippitt's metaphor) to navigate between the rocks of skepticism and the quicksand of apathy.[20]

Lippitt, a former research collaborator with Kurt Lewin,[21] recommended enthusiastic project leadership, ample and credible organization-wide communications, and an "indelible commitment on the part of members of the task force." Lippitt adds, "For the sake of argument, though, let us assume acceptance and commitment [by all organizational members]."[22] According to John Kotter, whose work is discussed in depth below, such an assumption is unrealistic.

Lippitt and colleagues describe in great detail their consulting work at a department within the World Bank. However, the effectiveness of their three-year consultation was unclear, in large part because there were no objective pre- and post-intervention indicators of success. Indeed, they noted that hard data would have been essential to evaluate the effectiveness of their intervention.[23] On the whole, they concluded that their intervention did increase participatory management at the World Bank, and therefore was modestly successful. They lamented the modest results, attributing them to the cautious Word Bank culture, i.e., due to the "bureaucrats who do not stick their necks out ... playing everything safe."[24]

Gina Abudi

In her text, *Implementing Positive Organizational Change*, Abudi provides several useful ideas and suggestions, based largely on her more than 25 years of consulting experience in change management. She begins by noting how the change context is critical.

Change happens for one of two reasons. Change can be reactive and happen because an organization is forced to change. This often yields negative emotions—especially from people who are forced to change their work behaviors or whose lives will change. As Peter Senge cogently put it: "People don't resist change: They resist being changed!"[25] But when an organization is proactive, initiating changes to capitalize on an opportunity, the changes are generally viewed favorably.

Abudi asserts that it is a good idea to inform employees about the possibility of change before a project is launched. Having conversations with employees at all levels may mitigate resistance. Further, employee participation may improve the effectiveness of the change process, as extensive evidence shows that participatory decisions are often of higher quality.[26]

Abudi acknowledges that notwithstanding attempts to increase participation and involvement, not every employee will be a champion of change. A survey completed by employees in organizations that had experienced failed change efforts yielded six common explanations.

1. The vision for the change was neither clearly communicated nor understood.
2. Employees did not know how the change would impact the organization and themselves, personally.
3. Employees felt they lacked a hand in shaping the change initiative.
4. Communications about the change were ineffective and insufficient.
5. Employees did not discover early on what they will need to learn and how the organization would support them.
6. Employees did not believe that that the important matters that needed to be considered early on had been considered.

In addition to providing a recipe for how to undertake a successful change initiative, Abudi urges consideration of the following questions:

1. Is the vision clear and understood?
2. Do employees understand why there is a need for change?
3. Does leadership understand the impact of change on employees?
4. Is the desired end-result defined?
5. Are there clear metrics to measure success?
6. Does senior leadership enthusiastically support the change initiative?
7. Are there sufficient resources available to implement the change?[27]

Abudi urges employers to address the following key question, "What will happen if the organization does not change?" The change might negatively affect some employees, but failure to act may entail even greater employee losses, if the organization closes. Employees should be assured that they will receive training if new tools or software are involved. Employees should also be told how they will benefit from the change. Finally, too many changes may cause employees to see the organization as chaotic, each change reflecting "the new flavor of the month."[28]

Bert Spector

Spector's *Implementing Organizational Change* adds a few additional insights to those mentioned above.[29] He asserts that one should not assume that poor organizational performance will create an urgent need to change. He cites the case of Nissan, which had lost money in seven out of the prior eight years before the arrival of Carlos Ghosen in 1999. The company had debt of almost $20 billion and was losing more than $20 million monthly, yet the top executives were seemingly accepting of and resigned to such outcomes.

Ghosen rapidly and substantially cut costs, saying, "I don't see how one can manage a business without keeping one eye glued to expenses. It's a fantasy to think otherwise."[30] Ghosen was also considerate of employees' lives. When it came to the "make" or "buy" decision, Ghosen had a marked preference for changing people within the organization. Ghosen thought it more beneficial—more powerful—to change people than to change persons.[31]

Spector identifies five criteria he sees as essential for improving organizational performance:

1. Explicit delineation of key components
2. Operational definition of the components
3. Empirical validation of the framework
4. Face validity, i.e., it makes sense to managers and employees
5. Generalizability to different organizations[32]

Spector considers the pros and cons of using questionnaires to guide organizational change. The advantages are: (1) scalability and the ability to collect abundant data; (2) the potential speed in introducing change; (3) anonymity is assured—making it more likely to get an accurate reading; (4) questionnaires enable the establishment of benchmarks, thereby permitting comparisons across units and over time. The main disadvantages are (1) surveys may not identify the root causes of problems; and (2) the resulting data may not create adequate commitment to motivate behavioral changes.[33]

John Kotter

In their 2002 book, *The Heart of Change*, Kotter and Cohen present a cohesive eight-step approach to implementing effective large-scale changes.[34] According to Kotter and Cohen, the central issue in all eight stages is changing people's behavior. Strategy, structure, culture, and systems are important. But "the core problem is behavior—what people do, and the need for significant shifts in what people do."[35]

Step 1. Increase Urgency

Successful change occurs because of a sense of urgency shared by a sizable group of relevant people: about 50 to 100 in small organizations and 500 to 1,000 in larger ones. Kotter and Cohen assert that although a careful analysis is important and may change peoples' thoughts, it will not typically suffice to change their behaviors. Gut-level feelings, often the result of a dramatic visual presentation, drive behavioral change. Perhaps the most dramatic presentation that Kotter and Cohen cite entailed a purchasing manager who put 424 different gloves on the large, expensive boardroom table. Attached to each glove was the price paid. Evidently, each plant purchased its own gloves, ranging in price from $5 at one plant to $17 at another. When the division presidents saw the 424 different gloves, they didn't say anything, but stood there stunned. This visual demonstration created the sense of urgency that resulted in a $200 million annual saving.[36] Another visual demonstration entailed a videotape of an extremely frustrated customer. This undoubtedly was more effective than receiving a quantitative report indicating that the average customer satisfaction score was merely 2.3 out of 5 points on a satisfaction survey.

Four sets of behaviors can stop the launch of needed changes:

1. Complacency, driven by false pride or arrogance
2. Immobilization resulting from self-preservation against fear or panic
3. Anger, reflected by "You can't make me change"
4. Attitudes that are pessimistic, skeptical, or cynical

Step 2. Build the Guiding Team

Kotter and Cohen state that two components are essential to creating an effective guiding team. The first is the team's composition. The "right people" include individuals with requisite knowledge and skills; individuals with credibility, connections, and stature; individuals with formal authority and managerial skills; and people with the leadership skills associated with creating a vision. The director of a division that will likely be affected by changes must be a member of the guiding team. The presence of too few key players suggests that the sense of urgency is low.[37] The second component is teamwork—which requires trust and goodwill.

Step 3. Get the Vision Right

Visions and strategies are the hard part, because they entail venturing into new territory. "And if they are not set correctly, you're dead," the authors say.[38] They recommend visions that are emotionally moving, and sufficiently bold to make an exciting vision a reality.

Step 4. Communicate for Buy-In

Keep communication simple and heartfelt; indicate an understanding of what people are feeling; speak to anxieties, confusion, anger, and distrust; and use new technologies to communicate the vision. Do not under-communicate; do not view the process as the mere transfer of information.

Question-and-answer sessions can be effective if management is suitably prepared. One company's guiding team identified more than 200 questions that employees might ask, and then prepared specific 30-second responses to address each potential question. Documenting and rehearsing the answers required a sizable commitment by the guiding team. In contrast, a ten-minute response that drones on will be far less persuasive.

Step 5. Empower Action

Remove barriers to change—such as a boss who resists. A resisting boss could be retrained, to possibly gain cooperation—but this is unlikely to work. A more feasible solution might be sending the resisting boss to spend six months with an external entity, such as a distant customer. A third "solution" is to ignore the strongly opposed person, but this will likely be counterproductive, as it will not prevent constant attempts to undermine the initiative. A fourth option, rarely chosen, is to confront and possibly demote or fire the person.

Additional barriers include systems that can be simplified along with a reduction of bureaucratic red tape (which should be cut vertically, not horizontally). Limit the number of planned changes to one or two, three at most: not the 15 items that desperately need immediate attention. Don't try to do everything at once.

Step 6. Create Short-Term Wins

In large organizations, a change effort may ultimately require hundreds of projects, and may take years.[39] The guiding team should publicize a few high-visibility changes that have achieved demonstrably positive results. These unambiguous wins will possibly gain the support of powerful players whose support is needed. Further, short-term wins help build a sense of momentum regarding the success of the change effort.

Step 7. Don't Let Up

Don't let up after a few wins. Many additional behavioral changes will usually be needed in a large-scale change effort. Reduce non-essential tasks that absorb time. One company that had previously required managers to complete a 25-page monthly report found a way to reduce it to two pages, providing data only on key metrics. Collectively, managers saved more than 1,000 hours a year by this modification.

In this regard, the dramatic turnaround at Nissan by Carlos Ghosen provides a vivid example. After Ghosen's first three-year turnaround plan was accomplished in two years, people began feeling that their mission was accomplished. But Ghosen then proposed a second three-year plan, considerably more challenging than the initial one. He didn't let up.[40]

Step 8. Make Changes Stick

To change the culture of an organization—the final step—individuals who are constructive, exhibit the new norms, and are in visible positions should be recognized and given opportunities for career enhancement. New employee orientations should show what the organization cares about. Tell vivid stories, over and over, about the new organization and why it succeeds. Repetition is helpful.

John Kotter's 2008 book, *A Sense of Urgency*, reiterates the same eight-step approach to implementing large-scale change, focusing almost exclusively on the first step, which he says is by far the biggest challenge to successful change. He distinguishes between a true sense of urgency—wanting to rapidly make changes and to win—versus a false sense of urgency, often manifested by frenetically engaging in numerous trivial activities, with the unstated intention of "eventually" making major changes.

One problem with generating a real sense of urgency is that it is not a natural state of affairs. It must be created. Not surprisingly, in organizations that have survived for many years, complacency is often the norm.

For instance, Kotter describes an interview he held with a CEO who stated that his company will soon have to lay off two to three thousand people. The CEO added that "if we had acted a year ago we probably wouldn't be in this mess." When asked why his company did not act a year ago, the CEO finally acknowledged "with 20/20 hindsight there was complacency and too much arrogance."[41]

Unfortunately, if you confront people with the observation that they are being complacent, almost assuredly they will dispute your claim and often be seriously offended. Even in cases where problems are hard to deny, people may shrug their shoulders and acknowledge "Of course we have challenges." They then will fault other departments for the problems. Kotter concludes: "Very, very smart people can be astonishingly complacent in the face of needed change."[42]

One member of a high-level task force disguised his objections by various subtle means. Eventually, the head of the task force recognized how relentlessly this member defended the status quo; disrupted tough conversations about the need for organizational change; and created within his division an astonishingly low sense of urgency. When confronted, the division manager chose to take early retirement.

A Disastrous Attempt at Change

Kotter describes in detail a complete failure to enact change. A high-tech company, formerly quite successful, experienced slippage in sales and loss of its industry-wide technological lead. Its executive committee, instead of addressing the matter promptly, solicited proposals from several consultants. After studying the consultants' 100-page reports for four months, the CEO then created a task force. Only two of the top ten executives were on the task force. The CEO was not.

The task force members had difficulty coordinating their calendars, so they first met a month later. Four members of the task force wanted to get moving immediately, but the other 11 wanted to discuss what exactly the proposed strategy was, and whether it was the right one. Between the first and second meetings the task force members privately started to discuss who was to blame for the company's eroding position.

At the second task force meeting, a sub-task force was created to communicate the new strategy. Choosing its members took up most of the second meeting. Problems were not addressed. Six months after the second task force meeting, margins and market share continued to slip.

The CEO was extremely frustrated with the lack of action. Ten more sub-task forces were formed with ambiguous charters; more meetings were held; papers were written and distributed; and the VP Sales delivered a 60-slide presentation. But nothing changed.

Due to a pervasive low sense of urgency, the company's fortunes further declined; careers were damaged; customers could not achieve their plans without the products they had been promised; the stock price tanked. Everybody lost— except for the firm's number-one competitor.[43]

Kotter goes on to emphasize that a true sense of urgency is based on *feelings*: a compulsive determination to *move, and win, now*. He notes the adage that great leaders win over the hearts and minds of others. The expression is not "Great leaders win over the minds of others."[44] Thoughtfully created emotional experiences (such as the 424 pairs of gloves or the videotape of the bitterly disappointed customer) can engender internalized reactions and raise sights.

David Cooperrider

Over the past 30 years, Cooperrider has been instrumental in formulating and popularizing an approach to organizational change called Appreciative Inquiry (AI). The basic premise of AI is that the questions asked shape the way things are seen (i.e., framed). If the focus is on what's wrong and who's to blame, people will become defensive, angry, and resistant. Instead, AI proposes that the focus should be on the best of "What has been;" "What did we do during the times when we were successful?" and envisioning "What might be." Ideally, the process should generate creative new ideas and a general feeling of positive affect, trust, and emotional bonding.[45]

Consider the situation that confronted a major airline a while ago. At one terminal, the airline encountered serious problems with lost baggage. Rather than focusing on why things were going wrong (to put it politely), and who was to blame, the AI consultant framed the matter in terms of how the company could create an "exceptional customer arrival experience." Employees were asked to recall prior periods when baggage loss was minimal, to recreate these past successes, and to incorporate creative new approaches.

Another case that can aptly be seen through the lens of AI entailed addressing the financial pressures that confronted Bain & Co. (the consulting firm) in the early 1990s. Orit Gadiesh, with 15 years' experience as a Bain consultant, was the newly appointed vice chair. She was tasked with giving the introductory speech at

Bain's annual meeting in 1992. The immediate problems were two-fold: first, the founders of Bain had sold their ownership interest for $300 million of interest-paying bonds—the annual interest being $25 million. Second, shortly after the bond sale, the economy went into a recession, and Bain had to go through two rounds of layoffs just to stay afloat. The firm's solvency was in doubt.[46]

Before addressing the entire company at the large annual meeting, Gadiesh had to decide what to say. On the one hand she could speak to the consultants in a language they clearly understood—free cash flow and financial metrics. In fact, Jon Marks, a director of the firm, emphasized how the corporate culture favored a rational analysis. In general, people were skeptical of talk that was "soft and squishy." On the other hand, she considered approaching the matter from a different, emotional perspective—the feelings associated with being a consultant at Bain & Co. She decided to give a "no numbers" talk and spoke "from the heart" about her feelings and pride in Bain's dedicated team and its numerous effective consulting initiatives. Her takeaway line: "*It's time to turn around our collective pride in what we do!*" When Gadiesh finished her talk, a moment of silence was followed by thunderous applause.[47]

An Expanded Normative Model of Planned Change

Gene Dalton initially developed key portions of the model described below.[48] A decade later, I elaborated on the model, expanding it from six to eight components, and empirically supported it with numerous case studies.[49] The present rendition incorporates examples that speak to the newly expanded 12-facet model.

1. Felt Need

The existence of tension or pain is a precondition for change in human behavior at multiple levels.[50] In the words of Harry Levinson, "Where there is no pain, there is no problem; where there is no problem, there is no action."[51]

The optimal time for an intervention in an organizational setting is when there is sufficient tension. An important—and arguably crucial—task of the CEO role is to create a palpable sense of need for change. However, as noted by both Spector and Kotter, poor organizational performance cannot be expected to create sufficient tension to enact changes. Executives and employees may have a sense of complacency, and a desire to perpetuate the *status quo*—notwithstanding declining performance.

Consider the case of Monolithic Memories, Inc. (MMI), where Irwin Federman, the CFO, was suddenly appointed president after the board of directors fired the company's founder. Operational results had become increasingly dismal. In the 12 months prior to Federman's appointment, MMI experienced professional turnover of 125%. It was virtually impossible to replace departing professionals. The company's products were of poor quality, and customers distrusted the company due to its consistent failure to meet promised commitments. The company's suppliers did not trust MMI either, many insisting on cash payment upon delivery.

MMI was running sizable deficits and had only enough cash on hand to last six to eight weeks. Federman was nervous and frightened as he had never before been president of anything. So, he called all employees together for a meeting. He told them, "We are a bunch of losers." As he put it, the multitudes denied it. Federman replied, "Ridiculous! Look at what we're doing. If this is not losing, I don't know what is. And if you are unsure now, all doubts will be dispelled in eight weeks when you're in the unemployment office."

Federman next gathered the managers together to reiterate his message providing a similarly blunt heads up. He said, "We have no margin for red ink anymore. None—not a little. Zero, *nada*. Either we fix it, or we say, 'what the hell' and go out looking for jobs full-time right now."

Evidently, Federman's comments (which portrayed a visually clear-cut consequence—the unemployment office) struck a responsive chord. Managers worked out plans with dramatic changes in priorities and tasks performed. Within four weeks the company was profitable—and remained so, every month for nine years, despite three industry recessions. During this period not one employee at MMI was laid off. Subsequently, MMI was acquired by Advanced Micro Devices (AMD) for an amount that increased MMI's net worth 50-fold from when Federman assumed the role of president.[52]

The approach adopted by Federman highlights Schein's second type of anxiety. Anxiety 1 pertains to the ability to adapt; Anxiety 2, to the consequences of not adapting.[53]

In a *Harvard Business Review* article entitled, "Why is it so hard to tackle the obvious?" C.K. Prahalad says that the answer revolves around inertia. If an organization has achieved some measure of success, it will develop a dominant logic—such as, for example, the Xerox Way. This tendency explains why organizations often fail to acknowledge the threats posed by new rivals—typically until it is too late to catch up.[54] Prior success diminishes the felt need for change.

With regard to the importance of felt need and the use of the Cube One framework for organizational improvement, even the initial intervention—the distribution of a short questionnaire to be completed on a voluntary and anonymous basis—could encounter resistance. Prahalad recommends providing at least a brief explanation as to why the survey is being expanded (or initially conducted).

Examination of the results of the survey will reveal the extent to which change is needed, if any is. If massive, large-scale changes are needed, it may make sense to follow Kotter and Cohen's entire eight-step regimen, leading up to a culture change. But if the needed changes are only modest to moderate, the normative model may be more appropriate. In either case, top management must experience and convey a real felt need (and sense of urgency).

2. Visible Top Management Support

Visible top-level support along with felt need constitute the two most essential ingredients to accomplishing effective planned change. It has been widely recognized that top management support is critical to successful efforts.[55] Visible support can raise confidence, because top management is showing that the change is doable and, further, that management is willing to provide needed resources. Expectations of success may represent a self-fulfilling prophecy.[56]

Visible top management support can help overcome inertia and cynicism. Many employees, including managers, may be disinclined to change their work behaviors—and will passively resist change for a variety of reasons including fear and skepticism. Many employees will not voice their concerns overtly. Rather, they may believe (or hope) that the proposed change will be just another monthly initiative that will soon fade away, to be replaced by yet another new idea ("gimmick of the month.") So, people may just "duck" until the proposed change works its way to organizational oblivion.

Senior managers, perhaps subtly, should convey the idea that there will be positive consequences associated with providing support for the planned change. To counteract skeptics, top management must not merely be supportive and fully behind the proposed change effort, but rather—*figuratively and literally*—out front leading the charge. Top management should make it clear that their support is unequivocal and the change inevitable, saying something like: "This train is going north; if you want to go south you should get off now."

One case study found that because top management lacked visible involvement, a $50 million investment designed to improve productivity achieved less than a 1% improvement over two years. Subsequently, top management played an active role in implementing the change by vigorous advocacy, and by providing training. Two years later productivity rose by 7.7%, and achieved a financial savings of $7 million.[57] The authors of the study stated, "Most important to the success of any organizational improvement effort is the support of the person at the top—not in word, but in deed."[58]

Another case study demonstrating the importance of visible top management support has been published with the title, "100 days to Better Service in Health Care."[59] The case describes two consultants who assisted in conducting a TQI (Total Quality Improvement) intervention in an inner-city hospital. At the outset approximately 12% of patients' charts (medical records) could not be found when patients showed up for their scheduled appointments, i.e., charts already existed. This led to patients having to wait at least two hours, often four—and sometimes, after waiting around all day, being informed that their appointments needed to be rescheduled.

A task force comprised of 14 employees was assembled, including people in almost all relevant roles: registrar, receptionist, physician, registered nurse, primary-care medical assistant, internal quality control specialist, and assistant clinic director. The names of the participants were shared with top management of the hospital. Participants knew that the project would be time-intensive and would add to their extensive regular work responsibilities. However, they were also promised that the project would be concluded in 14 weeks (100 days).

The hospital president and executive vice president presided at a kick-off meeting. The president thanked the participants for their willingness to improve organizational performance, a matter of considerable importance, further, the president because the hospital's catchment area contained six competitive health care providers, plus numerous physician-based groups. The president concluded that he was looking forward to reading about the task force's accomplishments in 100 days, the time period the consultants specified as necessary to complete the change effort.

The task force produced positive results. The incidence of missing charts dropped by 54%, which corresponded to a reduction of 3,500 fewer frustrating service incidents annually; and an ROI of approximately 430%. Before the intervention, employees at all levels merely shrugged off the missing charts problem as if it were an intractable condition endemic to an inner-city hospital.

Lacking a control condition, it is not possible to demonstrate unequivocally and indisputably that the following claim is correct. Specifically, the consultants believed that the presence and imprimatur of the hospital president was crucial to the success of the intervention. Had there been no kick-off meeting accompanied by the president's visible and passionate endorsement, it is quite likely that the number of participants would have dropped off to six at the second weekly meeting, and to three at the third (and final) meeting.

3. Gradual Clarification

To paraphrase Renato Tagiuri: Sudden change=>Massive anxiety=>Massive resistance.[60] It remains desirable, to the extent possible, to gradually clarify the ramifications of a change effort. To be sure, upon hearing about an impending change, employees will wonder how the change will affect their future work (and non-work) life situations—Schein's Anxiety 2. As one management consultant observed, the bottom line for everyone is "What will this mean for me?" "Will I be better off?"[61] "Will the change affect the career prospects of my department and/or my supervisor?" (Employees often advance in organizations in tandem with their supervisors.)

An almost limitless number of specific questions will likely come to peoples' minds reflective of Anxiety 1: Will new competencies be needed? How much time and energy will be entailed to acquire them? Will I be successful in acquiring them?

The four-year experience of change at AT&T provides a dramatic demonstration of the benefits of gradual clarification. In the 1950s, AT&T had approximately 350,000 employees who served as telephone (i.e., switchboard) operators.[62] In the early days of the telephone, they would melodically ask "Number, please," and the caller would speak a number where the first few digits quaintly related to a location, such as TRafalgar 4 or MUrray Hill 5.[63]

In the 1950s, the company announced that it was looking into the technical feasibility of direct dialing, and gave assurances that if direct dialing were adopted, no one would lose anything—employment, seniority, pay, retirement benefits, and so forth. Two years later, AT&T announced that direct was indeed feasible. Many telephone operators were switched to different functions such as connecting long-distance calls or providing information about telephone numbers—"Information, please."

Another illustration of the relevance of gradual clarification to achieving effective change is the case of a retail company that decided to introduce significant technological changes. One branch manager promptly informed all her direct reports about the impending changes, and even informed employees in other departments. Employees at her branch were not pleased about the impending changes, but at least they had time to contemplate how to handle them. As the change progressed, the manager kept her employees updated on operating details. At another branch, the store manager wanted to protect his employees from fretting about impending changes, and only notified them the week before the changes were introduced. He shielded his employees because he didn't want people to get upset. Instead, when they found out about the change, they were *more* than upset. They were shocked and furious. Three months after the changeover, an evaluation study found that change was going smoothly at the first branch, but the second was in turmoil. Many employees in the second branch resigned, and those who remained had difficulty adjusting. Cooperation and satisfaction were low; performance was poor.[64]

An additional problem associated with lack of information relates to the creation of an information vacuum. If management fails to share information about impending changes, rumors may circulate through informal (and probably less accurate) channels, such as the grapevine.[65]

4. Psychological Ownership

As noted in the classic article by Tannenbaum and Schmidt, employee participation in the decision-making process is likely to increase both decision acceptance and decision quality.[66] Per Kopelman's Dictum: "The hand that shapes the change changes its possessor."[67]

Even if an employee's ideas are not incorporated in the final decision, the person may reluctantly conclude, "I still do not agree with the change, but at least I've had a chance to express my concerns. And if the change fails, don't blame me!" Thus, by participation, opposition may be somewhat mitigated and perhaps converted to compliance—and maybe, down the road, to commitment.

According to Larry Greiner, the process utilized in "all successful changes is essentially the same—a large number of people collaborate to invent solutions that are of their own making and have their own endorsement."[68] Participation tends to produce a sense of psychological ownership. Participation in the early stages of a change process may also permit individuals to protect their own interests.[69]

Kotter and Schlesinger provide an illustration of the use of participation in a small financial services company. A president created a task force of eight second- and third-level managers to help design and implement changes in his company's reward system, giving them six months to complete the assignment, and requiring their filing a brief monthly progress report. The task force presented its recommendations, which the president largely accepted. He then assigned the force to help the human resources director implement the changes.[70]

Along these lines is the consensus-seeking protocol adopted by many Japanese companies (*nemawashi*). This process is subsequently followed by the formal documentation of agreed on decisions (*ringi*). This two-step process may delay implementation for months, but sabotage and oppositional behaviors are rare.

By contrast, U.S. firms often attempt to implement change rapidly—and end up taking longer to "iron out the wrinkles" and achieve cooperative behaviors. We have found this pattern in two similar healthcare settings in the U.S. One manager pushed a change through rapidly but wound up taking more time and effort to accomplish the change compared to the manager who patiently solicited participation and support.[71]

Mary Kay Ash, the legendary entrepreneur in cosmetics, recognized the importance of participation, noting that if you want the support of people, you need to get them involved. In her words: "People will support that which they help create and the more that people are permitted to participate in a new project, the more they'll support it."[72]

Management *must not* use employee participation as a ploy—e.g., giving people the impression they will be able to influence a change—when in fact employee participation is a bogus façade. This type of manipulation (sometimes called "psychological participation") is eventually seen through and resented. Professor Robert Sutton characterizes this ploy as the single biggest mistake bosses can make when making decisions.

> "A few years back," [Sutton] recalls, "a professor I know joined a committee formed by university administrators to provide input from faculty, students and staff on the design of their new building. It turned out to be sham participation: Nearly all design decisions were made before the committee ever met.
>
> My colleague says administrators and their architects had already decided that most people would sit in open offices—even though users interviewed listed privacy as their top priority, and the professor had reinforced these preferences with studies showing that open offices reduce productivity, satisfaction and social interaction.

My colleague resigned from the committee in frustration a few months later. He says he felt used because 'not one thing I said or argued for the whole time mattered.' And now, several years later, he is still angry about the time he wasted and, more so, about being misled."[73]

5. Increased Self-Esteem

The content of a change, as well as the process by which it is introduced, will likely affect employee reactions and, ultimately, the success of a change effort.[74] In broad terms, changes introduced with employee participation tend to increase participants' intrinsic satisfactions and self-esteem. Intrinsic satisfactions include feelings of competence; a sense of personal growth; the acquisition of new skills; an alignment with the goals of the organization; the view that the organization's mission is important (e.g., working at the Mayo Clinic); the experience of autonomy and being trusted. As noted in Chapter 9, the first rule in the Nordstrom corporate handbook is to use your best judgment at all times. The second rule is to go back to the first rule.

Several case studies illustrate the wrong way to introduce change. In the Hog-Noff Mortgage and Finance Company case, the newly appointed president, who happened to be the nephew of the largest shareholder, immediately set out to take total command. In his initial meeting with executives, he announced that individuals would soon achieve extreme levels of efficiency, and that they could show their loyalty to the company by following his directions. He went on to say that it was okay for managers to have ideas, but most of their thinking will be done by top-level executives He also indicated that the changes would take place promptly, indeed "effective immediately."[75]

In the classic Dashman Company case, the newly appointed vice president of purchasing (Mr. Post) sent out a form letter to the formerly autonomous purchasing directors at the company's 20 independently run plants.[76] The letter instructed the purchasing directors to submit all planned purchases to his office for prior review and approval—despite the fact that the company's busiest season was rapidly approaching. The vice president prefaced the changes with "hereafter." That meant no gradual clarification. Further, Mr. Post implied that he was their new "boss," when in fact he served in a staff position, since purchasing directors reported to their division directors. By complying with his orders, the purchasing directors would have experienced a massive loss of authority, autonomy, and self-esteem.

Students in my graduate healthcare administration courses provide examples of changes, some successful, others unsuccessful. One student's situation entailed the installation of time clocks in a hospital. The time clocks were not to be used by executives, physicians, or similarly situated high-level medical providers. When the hospital's social workers were told that they would have to clock in, they were furious and indignant.[77]

The venerable case of the Lamson Company describes two changes: one that worked out well and one destined to fail.[78] The Lamson Company was a small independent oil refinery company that decided to build a costly new refinery that used state-of-the-art technology. Twelve of its best workers from the two existing plants staffed the new distillation tower. It took nearly three years to get the new tower fully operational. The workers appreciated the increased complexity of their work, which they deemed to be akin to white-collar work. They also appreciated interacting with the engineers who were constructing the tower. The workers made many suggestions and when their ideas were adopted, they felt they were "even doing engineering work."

Thus, self-esteem increased and clarification took place gradually. The second planned change at the Lamson Company was the sudden announcement that the 12 workers were to be rotated back to the old towers about one-third of the time so that an additional six new workers could be trained to operate the new tower. The original workers wrote a thoughtfully crafted letter that they sent to six levels of management. Reflective of the intensity of their feelings, the letter was sent to the recipients' homes, and signed by all 12 workers. The letter claimed that they were unable to work in multiple facilities and still retain their knowledge about the new tower.

This claim is clearly spurious. If new workers were capable of rotating, surely those with 33 months' experience could as well. What the original workers meant is not what they wrote. It wasn't that they lacked the *ability* to rotate. Rather, they did not *want* to go back to their old locations, as this would result in reductions in social, extrinsic, and intrinsic satisfactions. Their elite status and cohesive identity would be greatly diminished. They would also experience less pleasant working environments; and perhaps most importantly, they would experience a loss of status. The original "elite" workers might be greeted by sarcastic comments such as, "So you're back here again, are you?" Given the strong feelings of the 12 workers, and their indispensable role—i.e., they were the only people capable of operating the new tower—the planned change almost assuredly was not going to be carried out.

These examples illustrate how managerial behaviors can diminish employee self-esteem and prompt resistance to change.

The next three cases entail raising self-esteem. First, we return to the case of Irwin Federman at MMI and the remarkable turnaround he achieved. In addition to dramatically raising felt need, Federman recognized that a person's expectations for achievement derive from his/her self-esteem. So, he gave all managers unlimited purchasing authority, signaling his trust in their judgment, and possibly raising their self-esteem. In Federman's words,

> If you keep your people waiting outside your office, if you don't return phone calls, if your agenda always takes precedence over theirs ... you are systematically robbing your people of their dignity, and precluding the

growth of self-esteem, which …is the key to grander expectations and ultimately nobler achievement.[79]

In the Relay Assembly Room experiment, described in the classic text *Management and the Worker*,[80] productivity consistently increased over a period of two years, notwithstanding the numerous changes that were introduced. Gene Dalton's interpretation:

The treatment the women were given seems almost perfectly

> designed to increase their sense of self-esteem. A new supervisor made every effort to obtain the women's whole-hearted cooperation for each change, consulting them about each change even canceling changes which did not meet with their approval. The women's … well-being and opinions were the subject of genuine concern … which gave the women a greater sense of importance and worth.[81]

Robert Guest's study of an automobile plant provides a third example of how self-esteem can facilitate the implementation of planned change. The plant was the company's least efficient one, prior to the arrival of a new production manager. The new manager acknowledged in his initial meeting with supervisors that the plant had a bad reputation. He said he had heard that many employees were incapable of doing their jobs. He stated: "I am willing to prove that this is not so, and until shown otherwise, I personally have confidence in the group." After three years the plant was the most efficient one in the division.[82]

6. Altering Component Subsystems

As Lewin noted, organizations tend toward equilibrium. Small changes tend to get ironed out (a process analogous to homeostasis). Inertia provides the backdrop that change efforts must address. Ironically, organizations often become increasingly locked into unsuccessful patterns of practices in times of adversity.[83]

Changes must encompass multiple subsystems. Consider, for example, the process by which a lay person becomes a monk or a nun. A correspondence course will not likely be effective. Rather, the person will likely move to a monastery or abbey; the stay will be long-term (perhaps for life); the person will experience vast changes in everyday life, such as time of awaking, dress, daily activities, patterns of interactions, etc. Only after the passage of years can the prospective monk (or prospective nun) expect to take vows. The monastery and nunnery are total organizations that alter virtually all aspects of a person's life.[84]

Organizational changes that affect only one characteristic, such as structure or technology, are generally less effective than programs that change multiple systems.[85] If managers merely direct supervisors to provide more training to their employees, there is unlikely to be much change. Desired changes are more likely to "take" if they entail changes in multiple organizational processes. Supervisory training of employees is more likely to occur if tied to formal goal setting and performance appraisal criteria, performance evaluations, and rewards. Absent the bundling of multiple systems, desired changes often fail to materialize.

7. Facilitation and Support

Implementing change often entails acquiring new skills. The Lamson Company case shows how patient training can result in effective change. The first change at Lamson occurred with the facilitation and support of management.[86]

Personalized one-on-one coaching often achieves results superior to in-class training. In a health agency, 31 managers received classroom training, resulting in a 22% increase in productivity. Subsequently, 23 of the 31 managers also received individual coaching. Among the managers whose training was augmented by personalized coaching, the improvement in productivity was 88%.[87]

A report, based on input from 650 managers, focused on identifying the best practices associated with successful change. Establishing change management coordinating teams was deemed the most effective managerial practice, according to 62% of the managerial respondents. Such teams engaged in creating, planning, and delivering the training. Trainees had the opportunity to receive ongoing consultation and support from the trainers. Hands-on training was overwhelmingly seen as the most effective training technique, and one-on-one coaching was also an important part of participants' training efforts.[88]

Another study focused on the problems encountered by a highly talented and accomplished leader who was hired to head a division in another company. Unfortunately, her "cavalier, abrasive style and lack of political savvy" resulted in her losing credibility with her management team. An organization called Wisdom Councils helped provide personalized coaching to rebuild trust and respect.[89]

A competition to recognize the best human resource management (HRM) projects in Israel (in 2018) included a description of facilitation and support at Meso (name disguised), a producer of food products. Meso encouraged employees to be in constant motion and to "enjoy in-house growth," according to the director of training at HR headquarters. Sixty% of the key management positions at Meso were staffed by teams of employees; 50% of managers were multi-trained to perform more than one job.

Meso promoted a culture in which managers coach their subordinates, helping them grow and succeed within the organization and "sketch their own career paths." One-on-one coaching addressed personal as well as professional matters. The coaching and training program promoted assessment and feedback on a regular basis, and entailed shared thinking to achieve organizational and personal goals. Meso experienced improvements in productivity, organizational performance, creativity, personal growth, and a heightened capacity to cope with change and emergencies.[90]

8. Preserving Exchange Favorability

In *The Functions of the Executive*, Chester Barnard conceptualized an exchange which occurs between the individual and the organization.[91] Individuals provide various forms of contributions (e.g., time, effort, knowledge, skills), and the organization either provides directly or indirectly facilitates various forms of inducements, e.g., extrinsic, intrinsic, and social rewards. Adopting an open-systems perspective, Barnard noted two prerequisites to organizational survival. The organization had to be effective in accomplishing its fundamental purpose (raison d'etre), and individual employees had to achieve some of their personal goals. Absent organizational effectiveness, capital would flee; absent personal goal satisfaction, individuals would.

Individual contributions and organizational inducements exist in a dynamic system of sustained interdependence. Increased contributions lead to increases in organizational effectiveness—which, in turn, provides the wherewithal for increased personal goal satisfaction, leading to further increases in contributions. The reverse also applies. Low effectiveness ultimately leads to even lower effectiveness.[92]

Employees may view a change that requires increased contributions as an unwelcome development: for example, when management in the Lamson Company announced that all 12 employees in the new tower would rotate among three towers instead of just working in the new one. Likewise, a change resulting in employees receiving reduced inducements will often meet resistance. The workers in the new tower at Lamson were a cohesive team; they saw themselves as high-status employees. Requiring them to rotate back to the old towers would reduce their sense of being an elite team. The intrinsic reward of regarding their work as "white collar" would diminish if not disappear. Moreover, the working conditions in the two old towers were less favorable, what with poor ventilation and less cleanliness.[93]

Furthermore, a change that simultaneously increases contributions and reduces inducements will be seen as a "really bad deal"—and this characterizes the proposed change at Lamson where there was abundant evidence of strenuous resistance.

Might there have been a way to reach agreement with the 12 workers in the new tower, whereby they would agree to rotate (on a part-time basis) back to the old towers? Preserving exchange favorability might have been achieved in several ways. First, the 12 workers would need assurance they would exclusively staff one of the old towers, three people to a shift. Second, an upgrade in their job title would be appropriate insofar as they were experienced in running both the old and new towers. Third, an increase in pay for working in multiple towers might relieve some of their discontent.

Of course, the conjectured attempt to preserve exchange favorability might still have been rejected. As noted above, reactions to change reflect both the substance of the change and the process by which it is decided. Top-level executives should have consulted the employees in the new tower about this rotation plan—but they didn't. They simply announced the plan.

In the Dashman Company case, purchasing directors who had previously operated with autonomy and authority (and reported to their division directors) clearly faced reductions in intrinsic rewards if they followed Mr. Post's dictum: viz., submitting planned purchases for prior approval by his office. Post's plan also increased required contributions. When coupled with decreased inducements, it was entirely rejected. Post did not receive a single request for purchasing approval six weeks into the busy purchasing season.

The New York City Department of Sanitation provides a successful illustration of the preservation of exchange favorability. The change entailed switching from back-loading (three-person) trucks to side-loading (two-person) trucks. Initially, the workers and their union (local 831, IBT), were vehemently opposed to the change, as it would result in a 33% reduction in staffing. Management might have asserted that they had the right to implement the change as it was not a negotiable issue. Instead, management addressed workers' primary concern by guaranteeing that there would be no layoffs or other adverse staffing changes. The decision ultimately went to an impasse panel, which noted eight advantages to sanitation workers associated with the use of the side-loading truck—most having to do with safety. (With back-loading trucks, not infrequently—especially on rainy, icy, or foggy days—cars would skid into the worker loading the truck.) The panel also noted that although workers would walk less, they would load more. To facilitate worker (i.e., union) agreement, the panel decided that workers on two-person trucks should receive a shift differential in pay. The combination of employment security, higher pay, and improved worker safety yielded what the impasse panel labeled "a quick and peaceful resolution."[94]

Reducing required contributions can also facilitate preservation of exchange favorability. In the case cited by Kotter, managers saw their monthly reporting requirement reduced from 25 pages to two pages, with the abbreviated report just focusing on key metrics.[95]

Another example of preserving exchange favorability involves an Israeli firm, MCTV (name disguised), which provided multi-channel satellite TV equipment and services. The company wanted to merge its five logistics centers into one, in order to economize on costs. However, employees who lived far away did not want a longer commute to the new logistics center. MCTV preserved exchange favorability in four ways. First, employees were taken to the new logistics center while it was under construction, and encouraged to help design their future work spaces. Second, employees were consulted about how to organize the transportation lines to the new center. Third, they were shown how the company's long-term success would be enhanced by the efficiencies obtained, which would make the added commutation time worthwhile. Finally, the company fully absorbed the added transportation costs and the added time spent commuting. The result was almost 0% departure of employees.[96]

Expanding the Normative Model from 8 to 12 Components

Based on the research and writing mentioned above, especially the work of Lewin, Lippitt, Abudi, Spector, Kotter, Cooperrider, and Schein, we can further expand the eight-item checklist comprising the revised Normative Model of Planned Change. Incorporating four more components, the resulting model might be labeled the Expanded Normative Model of Planned Change.

9.   Creating a Guiding Team

Visible top management support entails far more than the public endorsement (or imprimatur) of the CEO of an organization. As Lippitt et al. put it, "We have learned how true it is that people who possess the power to affect the organization's future must take leading roles ... in the change process.[97]"

The composition of the guiding team, therefore, is critical. As Kotter notes, the team should be comprised of people with pertinent skills and knowledge; who possess leadership skills (even if the leadership is informal); who have credibility and status; and who have connections with influential people. The team must also include people who will likely be affected by the change.[98] Moreover, sub-teams should be created so that all managers and employees get a brief overview of the project and become acquainted with its purpose and objectives.[99] Abudi recommends letting people know about the impending project before its official launch and encouraging them to express their thoughts regarding the purpose of the proposed project (psychological ownership and gradual clarification). Ultimately, the guiding team should oversee the entire change process. This would include tasks such as selecting members of the guiding team, analyzing data, choosing courses of action, reviewing results, and possibly making modifications.

With regard to implementing change via the Cube One framework, the guiding team will be integral in obtaining consent to distribute a short, voluntary, and anonymous questionnaire. This may merely amount to embedding a short questionnaire within a larger one if the organization regularly surveys employees.

10.   Achieving Short-Term Wins

A pilot study with modest and measurable aims, and, ideally, kernels of "hard data," could facilitate a short-term win. Along these lines a small pilot study by a chain of retail stores studied 15 stores where the goal was improved customer service. Salespeople received brief training to greet customers and to smile. The proportion of salespeople greeting customers rose from 33 to 58, an increase of 80. The proportion of salespeople smiling rose from 32 to 49%, an improvement slightly above 50%.[100]

Of course, absent the publicizing of short-term wins, the effects will be minimal. Wins should be celebrated and promoted, thereby acknowledging that a project is moving in the right direction. Initial positive results will likely allay fears about the viability of the change effort and may reduce the stated (or silent) objections of some skeptics, although probably not all doubters. Indicators of progress will provide a sense of momentum, and some influential people may lend their support.

In *The Power of Habit*, Charles Duhigg suggests that winning can become a habit: "Once a small win has been accomplished forces are set in motion that favor another small win." But the process is not linear and continuous.[101]

Let objectors voice their concerns. In terms of the Lewin model, this will help reveal, and possibly reduce, some restraining forces. Some commentators see the process of encouraging people to vocalize objections as akin to the martial arts of interpersonal relationships. The force of the opposing argument can be used in a jiu jitsu-like manner to gain advantage via leverage.[102]

11. Addressing Objections/Attacks

As Kotter and Whitehead have noted, four basic strategies exist for "shooting down" a proposal, regardless of its merits.[103] The first is to spread fear about possible negative outcomes, possibly invoking failed prior change efforts. Second, is sowing confusion by referencing (possibly obscure) alternative approaches that are allegedly superior, and likely unknown to either advocates or bystanders. Third, a proposal can encounter death by delay. The attacker may start by saying that this proposal may have merit, but some significant issues need to be addressed and resolved before adoption. Finally, the attacker may ridicule the project, thereby attempting to challenge the character or competence of the proposing team or spokesperson. These strategies may be combined. (Welcome to the world of hardball politics!)

With regard to improving organizational performance via the Cube One framework, at least two dozen specific attacks/criticisms are likely to emerge.[104] In all cases, the response to an attack must be respectful and polite, pertinent to the issue(s) raised, and brief. A lengthy discourse will likely leave most participants confused and bored. (If the reader views preparation of responses to a dozen possible attacks as daunting, consider the company cited by Kotter, which compiled a list of 200 specific questions/criticisms and prepared brief responses—all of which needed to be memorized!)[105]

Here are ten likely objections (or attacks) that will threaten to derail the implementation of the Cube One framework. Note that most of the responses are positive in tone and stated crisply.

Attack 1:	This whole approach is too simplistic. (If the attacker is particularly vicious, the comment might be followed by an insult such as "this looks like the kind of work done by a third grader.")
Response 1:	Yes, this approach is simple, but that's not the same as simplistic. As Leonardo da Vinci put it, simplicity is the ultimate form of sophistication. Our approach does not include all potentially relevant factors, but it does provide a clear-cut basis for beginning the analysis of a complex situation.
A2:	This approach abandons our traditional values and culture.
R2:	Yes, we propose to look at a new set of measures in order to improve organizational performance. The surest way to abandon our values and culture is to fail to make changes. In fact, the key question to ask is neither "What are we going to do?" nor "How we are going to do it?" Rather, the key question is "WHY are we going to do it?" And the answer is to preserve our culture and climate for the future.[106]
A3:	If this approach is so great, how come other organizations are not using it?
R3:	There is a first time for all new approaches. Going forward, this model will make our organization more successful, far more so than organizations that do not measure practices.
A4:	The plan is off to a reasonably good start, but there is a fatal flaw, and if you are unaware of it, one can only wonder what other key issues you have failed to address.
R4:	Yes, our approach may not include all potentially relevant variables or touch all of the bases. But it can be expanded. Please tell us after this meeting about the ingredients you think are missing so that we can possibly include them.
A5:	Improving customer satisfaction, increasing employee satisfaction, and reducing costs: all of this is obvious and, in fact, we are already doing it.
R5:	Your observation is correct. Although effective practices are often known, the question is how often are they actually enacted? This is the key issue. It may be found—as you suggest—that all that's needed are a few tweaks. But the bigger issue that you allude to is the "knowing-doing gap." We know, for example, that we should eat right, exercise, and get a good night's sleep.[107] But although almost everyone *knows* what to do, they often don't do what they should. For example, by the year 2020, notwithstanding the adoption of wearable fitness devices, it is estimated that 75% of all adults in the U.S. will be obese or overweight.[108] Our approach will help us

measure how well we are doing—providing, figuratively, a scale to monitor weight.

A6: Your proposal is on the right track, but it doesn't go far enough. (Or it goes too far.)

R6: Fortunately, our brief survey can be expanded to widen its scope, if need be. (Or it can be reduced in length and scope.)

A7: We have so many reporting requirements, and we're swamped with day-to-day work. We already have too much to do to spend time completing another survey.

R7: We are aware of everyone's work demands, but the 30-item survey will take at most 20 minutes to complete; more likely 15 minutes. The survey will enable us to use evidence-based management to improve organizational performance. As many of you know, evidence-based management is what achieved such remarkable results for the Oakland A's (as shown in the book *Moneyball*) and the Houston Astros (in *Astroball*).[109]

A8: We tried using surveys before and they did not work. Why repeat the same failed approach?

R8: What was done previously used surveys to assess attitudes [or morale or engagement]. What we seek to measure is different. We are measuring the frequency of managerial behaviors, not employee attitudes. It matters how an instrument is used. If someone writes with an eraser, it's a mistake to conclude that a pencil doesn't work.

A9: Perhaps this project may have merit, but this is the wrong time to undertake another project.

R9: Yes, sometimes it won't be possible to juggle another ball. But we are adding about 10 to 15 minutes of time to find out how we're doing as an organization. If a matter needs attention, we should not postpone assessment and constructive action.

A10: Before we undertake another project, we should study the details to be sure the specifics are appropriate for our organization before we roll it out.

R10: We can be pretty confident because this initiative is based on extensive research. In five studies conducted in four countries, results have consistently been positive. The findings have been published in several peer-reviewed journals, and peer reviewers are typically skeptical and critical. Results are equally strong in both the for-profit and nonprofit/government sectors, and among small and large organizations.

Note that the responses above tend to shift the conversation from the past tense to the future tense. As Heinrichs has argued, the past tense is often about blame and recrimination. The future is about fixing things. So, the template for a response might be framed as follows: "You have made a good point, but how are we going to …"[110]

Kotter and Whitehead note that it is important for managers (or members of the guiding team) to keep an eye on the reactions of participants (the audience) in the forum where objections are being voiced and addressed. Facial expressions and gestures provide an indication of support. Of course, it will be ideal to achieve 100% support. But this level is unrealistic. Rather, achieving support of about 70% would be acceptable and 80% would be excellent.[111]

12. Creating a Positive Halo

Great leaders win both the hearts and minds of followers. Change efforts should evoke feelings to win hearts. This is what Orit Gadiesh accomplished in her "no numbers" speech to Bain consultants.

The positive halo is what Jay Heinrich calls the "killer image."[112] The challenge in applying the Cube One framework lies in converting quantitative data into an image of a better future. A speaker who can tell a story about the way things were (in business school lingo this is the "A" case), describe the intervention undertaken (the "B" case), and report on improved results (the "C" case), provides the basis for an emotional connection.

The Cube One framework provides a model (theory) that describes the central ingredients associated with successful organizational performance. However, in the absence of a conceptually based approach, organizations may go from one fad to the next. Consider the case of a major utility that was suffering from low performance. As related by Harlow Cohen, an experienced consultant:

> The utility tried to implement a total quality management effort, benchmarked the best companies, created and distributed a mission and values statement, trained all employees in problem-solving techniques and facilitation skills, conducted team building sessions, formed steering committees, and scored itself against the categories of the Baldridge award. When all these efforts failed to produce the desired outcomes, it turned its attention toward still other programs. Program after program, and fad after fad, rolled across the organization with marginal success, until downsizing was the only option remaining. The paradox was that many of its managers [already] knew where the opportunities to improve performance were hidden.[113]

Lacking a theory-based diagnostic framework, and measures with normative data, the utility went from one pre-packaged program to another. In contrast, the Cube One framework provides a model that identifies sets of managerial practices to enact. The Cube One framework empirically (not just conceptually) incorporates a multidimensional perspective drawing from several fields of study, including management, marketing, human resource management, industrial and organizational psychology, operations management, and to a limited extent economics and information technology. Most management books, though, take the perspective of a single discipline or even a technique within a discipline (e.g., goal setting or reward systems).

The Cube One framework provides a method of measuring the three independent (i.e., causal) variables, and the end-result variable, organizational performance. Management books typically offer interesting suggestions but provide no way to measure the extent to which suggestions are enacted. A few widely read books assess organizational performance in terms of stock market valuations. Such a metric is pertinent to only a small subset of corporations and is essentially inapplicable to nonprofit or government organizations.

For the most part, management books do not provide systematic and replicated evidentiary support. In contrast, the Cube One framework has been equally successful in explaining organizational performance among nonprofit/governmental organizations as well as for-profit companies; and among large and small organizations. The Cube One framework has served as a useful lens for interpreting the successes of several prominent organizations, including Continental Airlines, Google, Zappos, Four Seasons, Nordstrom, and the Mayo Clinic.

The Cube One framework provides a method for measuring levels of enacted practices and organizational performance. Measurement is integral to conducting a systematic organizational diagnosis, which, in turn, provides the basis for an evidence-based approach to improving organizational performance. Levels and changes in causal (practice-based) variables can be tracked; and normative data are available for comparative purposes. The ability to perform a conceptually based organizational diagnosis can obviate the search for magic elixirs, or silver bullets, as exemplified by the large utility case.

In the opinion of Doug Lemov, an educational administrator, almost every major historical innovation has been preceded by an advance in measurement.[114] Perhaps this someday this will be applicable to the Cube One framework.

Using the Cube One framework, managers can measure enterprise-, employee-, and customer-directed practices, as well as organizational performance. The availability of a useful model provides no guarantee that appropriate changes will be implemented. The expanded normative model will be helpful in enacting changes.

Finally, as Tsoukas and Chia wisely observed, organizations do not simply work; they are *made to work*.[115] The Cube One framework provides a map that any organization can use to get to Cube One, or at least get close to it. Moreover, the model is not a zero-sum game; all organizations can potentially benefit from its use.

To the extent that organizations enact high levels of enterprise-, employee-, and customer-directed practices, they will become more need satisfying places for the key parties involved in making organizations work. That is the ultimate objective of this book.[116]

Notes

1 Cited in Kotter, J. P., and Schlesinger. (1979). "Choosing strategies for change."" *Harvard Business Review*, 57(2), 106–114. Also see, Abudi, G. (2017). *Implementing positive organizational change.* Plantation, FL: G. Ross Publishing.

2 Toffler, A. (1970). *Future shock.* New York, NY: Random House. See p. 15. Illustrative of accelerating change, it took 68 years for 50 million people to ride in an airplane. It took 19 days for 50 million people to use Pokemon GO. Jones, Del. (June 3, 2019). "Aflac's Dan Amos doesn't duck risk, he manages it." *Investor's Business Daily*, p. A4.

3 Kotter, J. P., and Cohen, D. A. 2002. *The heart of change.* Boston: Harvard Business School Press. The 2015 data were provided in Abudi, op. cit., pp. 5–6. On the "other side of the coin," it should be noted that Kotter, J. P. (2008). *A sense of urgency.* Boston: Harvard Business Press indicates that change efforts exceed initial goals in about 10% of interventions, and these successful changes in virtually all instances followed the eight-point framework presented in Kotter and Cohen (2002).

4 Kotter, J. P., and Schlesinger, L. A. (1979). "Choosing strategies for change." *Harvard Business Review*, 57(2), 106.

5 Tagiuri, R. (1973). "Notes on the management of change: Implications of postulating a need for competence." In J. D. Glover, R. M. Hower, and R. Tagiuri, eds. *The administrator: Cases on human aspects of management*, 5th ed. Homewood, IL: Irwin. See pp. 2101–203.

6 Hall, J. (Spring, 1983). "Dr. Semmelweis and the problem of learned ignorance." *Data Forum* 2, pp. 1, 8.

7 Kotter and Schlesinger, op. cit., p. 106.

8 More formally stated, $B = f(P, E)$

9 The psychological force field is described in Lewin, K. (1951). *Field theory in social science: Selected theoretical papers* (D. Cartwright, Ed.). New York, NY: Harper & Row.

10 The tendency toward homeostasis applies to the autonomic nervous system. If a person exerts considerable physical effort for an extended period of time, the person is likely to find that his/her body is cooled off by perspiration. At the other extreme, the person who, in very cold weather, is waiting outside for an extended period of time will ordinarily experience the shiver response—which adds about four to six degrees of body heat. With regard to day-in-and-day-out behaviors, a tendency toward stability has been noted in Duhigg, C. (2012). *The power of habit: Why we do what we do in Life and Business.* New York, NY: Random House.

11 Lewin, op. cit.

12 See Weick, K. E. (2003). "Theory and practice in the real world." In Tsoukas et al., eds. *The Oxford handbook of organization theory.* Oxford, U.K., and New York: Oxford University Press, p. 460.

13 Space does not permit a thorough explication as to how a good theory can be practical. In brief, a good theory helps at four levels of knowledge: description (by knowing what to look for); explanation (answering the "why?" question); prediction (what will happen in the absence of intervention); and control (making things turn out as desired).

14 As an aside, it might be noted that Lewin is credited with pioneering in the conduct of "action research" which attempts to change a given state of affairs.

15 Lewin, K. (October, 1943). "Forces behind food habits and methods of change." *The problem of food habits.* Washington DC: National Research Council, National Academy of Sciences, pp. 35–65. See especially pp. 61-63.

16 Lippitt, G. L., Langseth, P., and Mossop, J. (1986). *Implementing organizational change.* San Francisco: Jossey Bass.

17 Ibid., p. 53.

18 Ibid., p. 59.

19 Ibid., p. 16.
20 Ibid., p. 51.
21 Lewin, K., Lippitt G. R., and White, R. K. (1939). "Patterns of aggressive behavior in experimentally created social climates." *The Journal of Social Psychology*, 10(2), 271–299.
22 Ibid., p. 104. Not only does this assumption beg the question, it brings to mind a mildly amusing tale. Three scientists stranded on a small desert island, come across a cache of canned foods. The chemist starts to find a way to oxidize the lids off the cans; the physicist tries to amplify the sun's heat to burn the lids off; and the economist takes out his pad and writes: assume a can opener.
23 Ibid., pp. 121, 126, and 139.
24 Ibid., p. 167
25 Abudi, op. cit., p. 9.
26 In this regard see the essay by Bennis, W. (December 31, 1989). "Followers make good leaders good." *New York Times*, section 3, p. 3.
27 Abudi, op. cit., p. 29.
28 Abudi, op. cit., p. 264.
29 Spector, B. (2010). *Implementing organizational change: Theory into practice*, 2nd ed. Upper Saddle River, NJ: Prentice Hall.
30 Ghosen, C., and Ries, P. (2005). *Shift: Inside Nissan's historical revival.* New York, NY: Currency. See pp. 39–40.
31 Spector, op. cit., p. 110. (In late 2018, Ghosen was arrested in Japan due to alleged personal financial improprieties. His career at Nissan probably will not recover.)
32 Spector, op. cit., p. 62. Spector gives credit to David Nadler for these criteria. See Nadler, D. A. (1980). "Role of models in organizational assessment." In Nadler et al., eds. *Organizational assessment: Perspectives on the measurement of organizational behavior and the quality of work life.* New York, Wiley. (pp. 125–126). As an aside, the Cube One framework meets all these criteria.
33 Spector, op. cit., p. 69. Although anonymity does allow the passive non-vocal dissenter to express views, potential exists for entirely inaccurate responding, sometimes referred to as "straight lining." The Cube One framework's focus on the frequency of behavior, rather than attitudes, makes it easier to detect deliberate inaccurate responding.
34 Kotter, J. P. and Cohen, D. S. (2002). *The heart of change: Real-life stories of how people change their organizations.* Boston: Harvard Business School Press. The model was first presented in Kotter, J. P. (1996). *Leading change.* Boston: Harvard Business School Press. With regard to the focus on large-scale change, the term comes up at least two dozen times in *The heart of change.* The summary of Kotter and Cohen's eight-step approach toward implementing change is reproduced with the permission of Harvard Business Publishing.
35 Ibid., p. 2.
36 Ibid., pp. 29–31.
37 Ibid., p. 59.
38 Ibid., p. 68.
39 Ibid., p. 127.
40 Magee, D. (2003). *Turnaround: How Carlos Ghosen rescued Nissan.* New York, NY: Harper Business.
41 Ibid., p. 4.
42 Ibid., p. 22.
43 Ibid., pp. 26–35.
44 Ibid., p. 45.
45 Cooperrider D. L., and Srivastva, S. (1987). "Appreciative inquiry in organizational life." chapter in Woodman, R. W., and Passmore, W. A., eds. *Research in organizational change and development*, Volume 1. Stamford, CT: JAI Press. V(pp. 129–169). A more

recent text is Cooperrider, D. L., Whitney, D., and Stavros, J. M. (2008). *Appreciative inquiry handbook: For leaders of change*, 2nd ed. Brunswick, OH: Crown Custom Publishing Inc., and Oakland, CA: Berrett-Koehler Publishers, Inc.

46 Rothbard, N., and Conger, J. (1993; revised January 5, 1995). Orit Gadiesh: Pride at Bain & Co. (A). Case 9-493-031. Boston, MA: Harvard Business School.

47 Rothbard, N., and Conger, J. (1993. revised January 14, 1994). Orit Gadiesh: Pride at Bain & Co. (B). Case 9-494-047. Boston, MA: Harvard Business School. It should be noted that the year before her speech, business had started to improve at Bain & Co.

48 Dalton, G. W. (1976). "Influence and organizational change." In J. B. Ritchie and P. Thompson, eds. *Organizations and people: Readings, cases, and exercises*. St. Paul, Minn.: West Publishing. (pp. 363–387). (Gene Dalton was my first doctoral dissertation adviser.)

49 Kopelman, R. E. (1986). *Managing productivity in organizations: A practical, people-oriented perspective*. New York, NY: McGraw-Hill. The number of supportive case studies cited was based on data from approximately 400 organizations. See pp. 284–285.

50 The multiple levels are intrapersonal, interpersonal, organizational, and societal. For the present undertaking, the emphasis is, of course, on changes at the organizational level.

51 Levinson, H. (February 15, 1979). Invited address before the New York Association of Applied Psychology (METRO).

52 Federman, I. (March, 1992). "Can turnarounds be this simple?" *Journal of Management Inquiry*, 1(1), 57–60. Quotations reproduced with permission of SAGE Publishing.

53 Schein, E. H. (Winter, 1993). "How can organizations learn faster? The challenge of entering the green room." *Sloan Management Review*, 34(2), 85–92. Along these lines, in my graduate courses I typically assign a 30–40 page term paper to teams of students. As time goes by the teams seemingly conclude that the pain of writing the paper is less than the pain of getting an F.

54 Prahalad, C. K. (June, 2010). "Why is it so hard to tackle the obvious?" *Harvard Business Review*, 88(6), 36.

55 Researchers and writers such as Chris Argyris, Richard Beckhard, Robert Blake and Jane Mouton, Gene Dalton, Larry Greiner, and as noted above, Gordon Lippitt, and John Kotter, have advanced this view.

56 See Stotland, E. (1969). *The psychology of hope*. San Francisco, CA: Jossey-Bass.

57 Tubbs, S. L., and Widgery, R. N. (1978). "When productivity lags, check at the top: Are key managers really communicating?" *Management Review*, 67(11), 20–25.

58 Ibid.

59 Kopelman, R. E., Olivero, G., and Hannon, N. (November, 1997). "100 days to better service in health care." *Training & Development*, 51(11), 84–85. Another article describing the intervention is Kopelman, R. E. (2003). "GMFAC: How a simply successful approach to organizational excellence worked at a large city hospital." *Journal of Organizational Excellence*, 23, 37–42.

60 Tagiuri, op. cit., p. 207.

61 Cook, D. D. (March 9, 1981). "Labor faces the productivity challenge." *Industry Week*, 208(5), 64.

62 Information on the history of telephone operators is available at https://ethw.org/Telephone_Operators

63 Information about the conversion of telephone numbers from names to purely numbers is provided in Ferretti, F. (July 24, 1978). "PHone EXchanges LOse THeir LEtters." *The New York Times*. Retrieved at https://www.nytimes.com/1978/07/24/archives/new-jersey-pages-phone-exchanges-lose-their-letters-imagine-an.html

64 Davis, K. (1981). *Human behavior at work: Organizational behavior*, 6th ed. New York, NY: McGraw-Hill, pp. 214–215

65 Sigband, N. (1982). "Proaction…Not reaction for effective employee communication." *Personnel Journal*, 61(3), 190.

66 Tannenbaum, R., and Schmidt, W. H. (May–June, 1973). "How to choose a leadership pattern." *Harvard Business Review*, 51(3), 162–180. Bennis, op. cit., cites evidence that participatory group decisions are usually superior to those made by an individual.

67 One of my students thought the dictum was "the hand that shapes the change shapes the professor."

68 Greiner, L. E. (1967). "Patterns of organizational change." *Harvard Business Review*, 45(3), 119–130. Greiner also states that failure tends to result when there is no sharing of influence via joint participation of managers and employees. See p. 125.

69 Kopelman, op. cit., p. 280.

70 Kotter and Schlesinger, op. cit., p. 109.

71 Lambert, C. A., and Kopelman, R. E. (1981). *An instance of planned change (A)*. Boston: HBS Case Services, case 9-481-714. Also the companion case by Lambert, C. A. and Kopelman, R. E. (1981). *An instance of planned change (B)*. Boston: HBS Case Services, case 9-481-715.

72 Ash, M. K. (September, 2000). "Time for a change." *Workforce*, 79(9), 109–111; the quote is on p. 111.

73 Sutton, R. I. (October 30, 2018). "The biggest mistakes bosses make when making decisions: No 1: Telling people they have a voice when they really don't." *Wall Street Journal*, pp. R1–2. Quotation reproduced with permission of Dow Jones and Company, Inc. © 2018 Dow Jones and Company, Inc.

74 Dalton, op. cit., pp. 376–379.

75 Stoner, J. A. F. (1982). *Management*, 2nd ed. Englewood Cliffs, NJ: Prentice-Hall, p. 491. This case was developed for instructional purposes. It is hard to imagine a more insulting and threatening way to begin a relationship and make changes. Originally in Bridges, F. J., and Chapman, J. E. (1977). *Critical incidents in organizational behavior and administration*. Englewood Cliffs, NJ: Prentice-Hall, p. 157.

76 Lombard, G. F. F. (1942). "Dashman Company." In Glover, J. D., Hower, R. M., and Tagiuri, R., eds. *The Administrator: Cases on human aspects of management*, 5th ed. Homewood, IL: Richard D. Irwin, Inc. (pp. 499–500). The case was originally designated as 642-001.

77 My recollection is that the outcome of this case entailed the hospital no longer requiring social workers to clock in.

78 Anonymous. (1948). Boston: HBS Case Services, cases 9-449-003 to 9-449-007. The case was also published in Glover, op. cit, pp. 5–7.

79 Federman, op. cit., p. 60. Quotation reproduced with permission of SAGE Publishing.

80 Roethlisberger, F. J., and Dickson, W. J. (1966). *Management and the worker*. Cambridge, MA: Harvard University Press. The 1966 book is the 14th printing of a book originally published in 1939.

81 Dalton, op cit., p. 379. (The term "women" is substituted for the term "girls," which appeared in the original.) Quotation reproduced with permission of Cengage Learning.

82 Ibid., pp. 367, 377. Quotation reproduced with permission of Cengage Learning.

83 Kopelman, R. E. (1986). *Managing productivity in organizations: A practical, people-oriented perspective*. New York, NY: McGraw-Hill, p. 277. The tendency to cling to unsuccessful practices was described in terms of organizations behaving neurotically.

84 The importance of a total organization is also pertinent to addressing serious issues such as drug addiction. An hour a week with a counselor is unlikely to prove effective in changing behaviors insofar as the person's life remains unaltered during the remaining 167 hours a week.

85 Friedlander, F. (1980). "The facilitation of change in organizations." *Professional Psychology*, 11(3), 520–530. Also see Dunn, W. N. and Swierczek, F. W. (1977). "Planned

organizational change: Toward grounded theory." *The Journal of Applied Behavioral Science*, 13(2), 135–157. Dunn and Swierczek cite evidence from 67 cases.

86 Dashman Company, op. cit.

87 Olivero, G., Bane, K. D., and Kopelman, R. E. (1997). "Executive Coaching as a transfer of training tool: Effects on productivity a public agency." *Public Personnel Management*, 26(4), 461–469.

88 Prosci, Inc. (2012). *Best practices in change management.* (the Prosci benchmarking report), p. 89.

89 Case accessed on September 6, 2018. Retrieved at http://wisdomcouncils.com/case-studies/leading-change-case-study1.htm

90 This case was provided by Aharon Tziner based on his and Edna Rabenu's work judging the best HRM projects in Israel. Correspondence occurred in September, 2018. It might be noted that Meso's program, which paralleled Nestlé's belief in people, led to the development of PDP (People, Development, and Performance)—an employee development process that routinely includes coaching. By "Own your growth," Nestlé (and Meso) have established coaching skills among all managers, using dedicated workshops, tools, and skill training.

91 Barnard, C. I. (1938/1966). *The functions of the executive.* Cambridge, MA: Harvard University Press.

92 According to Barnard, effectiveness and personal goal satisfaction were essential to countering the tendency toward entropy. Cube One framework adds a third necessary condition for organizational survival: customer satisfaction and loyalty.

93 The idea of viewing resistance to change in terms of Barnard's model was originally introduced in Kopelman, R. E. (1986). *Managing productivity in organizations: A practical, people-oriented perspective.* New York, NY: McGraw-Hill. See p. 273.

94 Kelly, M. A. (December 10, 1980). *Opinion and recommendations in the matter of the impasse between the city of New York department of sanitation and the uniformed sanitationmen's association, local 831, I. B. T.* See especially pp. 5–6. That the change was successful was reported by Haberman, C. (March 21, 1980). "Regan sees 'major' advance in two-man garbage trucks." *The New York Times*, p. 48. The first-year savings to the city was $7.2 million, and that was after only one-quarter of the back-loading trucks were replaced. This savings led to an increase in the shift differential of 44%.

95 Kotter and Cohen, *The heart of change*, pp. 152–154. [93]

96 This case was provided by Aharon Tziner based on his and Edna Rabenu's work with judging the best HRM projects. Correspondence occurred in September, 2018.

97 This is what Kotter did when he followed up his eight-step change protocol—*The heart of change*—with another book—*A sense of urgency*—that essentially reiterated the crucial importance of the first step. As a "human interest" note, John Kotter and I were the only two graduates of the Harvard Business School's doctoral program in spring, 1974.

98 Kotter and Cohen, *The heart of change*, p. 58.

99 Ibid., p. 127. Small organizations may find it useful to get 50 to 100 people involved; in large organizations the number of participants may range from 500 to 1,000 (see p. 183). In fact, Kotter suggests that large-scale change in sizable organizations may entail "hundreds of projects," p. 127.

100 Pfeffer, J., and Sutton, R. I. (Spring, 2006). "Management half-truths and nonsense: How to practice evidence-based management." *California Management Review*, 48(3), see 85–86.

101 Duhigg, C. (2012). *The power of habit: Why we do what we do in life and business.* New York, NY: Random House; the quote appears on p. 112. The original source for the quote is Weick, K. E. (1984). "Small wins: Redefining the scale of social problems." *American Psychologist*, 39(1), 40–49.

102 Hornsey, M. J., and Fielding, K. S. (2017). "Attitude roots and jiu jitsu *persuasion*: Understanding and overcoming the motivated rejection of science." *American Psychologist*, 72(5), 459–473.

103 Kotter, J. P., and Whitehead, L. A. (2010). *Buy-In: Saving your good idea from being shot down*. Boston: Harvard Business Review Press.

104 Kotter and Whitehead provide in their book 24 criticisms and possible responses. The present discussion includes six of their attacks, and all ten attacks and responses have been set in the context of the Cube One framework.

105 Kotter and Cohen. *The heart of change*, pp. 85–86.

106 Note the widely bought book by Simon Sinek (2009). *Start with why: How great leaders inspire action*. New York, NY: Portfolio Penguin.

107 In fact, about 90 years ago (in 1928) a popular song advised as follows: Eat an apple every day; get to bed by three; don't eat meat ooh, ooh; cut out sweets, ooh; or you'll get a pain and ruin your tum-tum … (Granted, advice about exercising was missing from these lyrics; but the importance of physical fitness has been known for millennia.)

108 See https://en.m.wikipedia.org/wiki/Obesity_in_the_United_States. Accessed on July 7, 2018. According to the piece, in 2007 according to the World Health Organization (WHO), the U.S. had the highest prevalence of overweight or obese adults in the English-speaking world. The finding was 74.1%. According to the Organization for Economic Co-operation and Development (OECD), the proportion is expected to reach 75% by 2020.

109 Lewis, M. (2004). *Moneyball*. New York, NY: W. W. Norton & Company; Reiter: B. (2018). *Astroball*. New York, NY: Crown Archetype.

110 Heller, P. (March 19, 2012). Jay Heinrichs can persuade you to do just about ANYTHING (and he'll show you how). *Bloomberg Businessweek*. Retrieved at http://magsreview.com/bloomberg-businessweek/bloomberg-businessweek-march-19-2012/3378-jay-heinrichs-can-persuade-you-to-do-just-about.html

111 Kotter and Whitehead, op. cit., p. 68.

112 Heller, op. cit.

113 Cohen, H. B. (August, 1998). "The performance paradox." *Academy of Management Executive*, 12(3), 32–33.

114 Lemov, D. (June 1, 2013). "A toolkit for teachers." *HBS Alumni Bulletin*, p. 31.

115 Tsoukas, H. and Chia, R. (2002). "On organizational becoming: Rethinking organizational change." *Organization Science*, 13(5), 577, italics in original.

116 This endeavor was partly inspired by the book by Lawler, E. E. III, Mohrman, A. M. Jr., Mohrman, S. A., Ledford, G. E. Jr., Cummings, T. G., and Associates (1985). *Doing research that is useful for theory and practice*. San Francisco, CA: Jossey-Bass. (Lawler et al.'s book is cited near the beginning of Chapter 1 and is also the last one cited. Perhaps this symmetry might be seen as Victorian.)

AUTHOR INDEX

SUBJECT INDEX